Families of Handicapped Children

Families of Handicapped Children

Needs and Supports Across the Life Span

Edited by
Rebecca R. Fewell
and
Patricia F. Vadasy

5341 Industrial Oaks Boulevard
Austin, Texas 78735

Library of Congress Cataloging-in-Publication Data

Main entry under title:

Families of handicapped children.

    Bibliography: p.
    Includes index.
    1. Handicapped children—Family relationships—
Addresses, essays, lectures. 2. Handicapped children—Home
care—Addresses, essays lectures.
I. Fewell, Rebecca R. II. Vadasy, Patricia F.
HV888.F36 1986   362.4'088054   85-12167
ISBN 0-936104-84-8

5341 Industrial Oaks Boulevard
Austin, Texas 78735

10 9 8 7 6 5 4 3 2 1   86 87 88 89 90

To the parents and family members who gave their time to share with the authors their personal experiences and insights. This book would not have been possible without their trust and their strong spirit of cooperation. We hope that their children will benefit from the perspective on families' needs that these families have helped to define.

Contributors

Thomas F. Catron, Vanderbilt University, Nashville, Tennessee.

Keith A. Crnic, Psychiatry and Behavioral Sciences, University of Washington, Seattle, Washington.

Arthur H. Cross, Human Developmental Psychology and Counseling, Appalachian State University, Boone, North Carolina.

Carl J. Dunst, Family, Infant and Preschool Program, Western Carolina Center, Morganton, North Carolina.

Linda Marie Espinosa, Dr. Charles R. Drew Early Childhood Development Center, San Francisco, California.

Rebecca R. Fewell, College of Education, University of Washington, Seattle, Washington.

Judith M. Leconte, Child Development and Mental Retardation Center and School of Social Work, University of Washington, Seattle, Washington.

Bruce L. Mallory, Education Department, University of New Hampshire, Durham, New Hampshire.

Donald Joseph Meyer, Experimental Education Unit, Child Development and Mental Retardation Center, University of Washington, Seattle, Washington.

Cathleen M. Tooley Moeller, Experimental Education Unit, Child Development and Mental Retardation Center, University of Washington, Seattle, Washington.

Margaret Roberts, Merrywood School, Bellevue, Washington.

Marsha S. Shearer, Education Service District 121, Seattle, Washington.

Ida Mae Sonnek, Minnesota Department of Education, St. Paul, Minnesota.

Vaughan Stagg, Department of Psychology, Louisiana State University, Shreveport, Louisiana.

Carol Marie Trivette, Family, Infant and Preschool Program, Western Carolina Center, Morganton, North Carolina.

Patricia F. Vadasy, Experimental Education Unit, Child Development and Mental Retardation Center, University of Washington, Seattle, Washington.

Contents

Contributors . . . . *vi*

Preface . . . . *ix*

Part I Intrafamilial Supports

1 *A Handicapped Child in the Family* 3
Rebecca R. Fewell

2 *Fathers of Handicapped Children* 35
Donald J. Meyer

3 *Understanding Sibling Needs and Influences* 75
Keith A. Crnic and Judith M. Leconte

4 *Grandparents and the Extended Family of Handicapped Children* 99
Ida Mae Sonnek

5 *Mothers of Deaf-Blind Children* 121
Patricia F. Vadasy and Rebecca R. Fewell

6 *The Effect of Professionals on the Family of a Handicapped Child* 149
Cathleen M. Tooley Moeller

7 *Roles and Support Networks of Mothers of Handicapped Children* 167
Carl J. Dunst, Carol M. Trivette, and Arthur H. Cross

8 *Three Mothers: Life-span Experiences* 193
Margaret Roberts

9 *Single Mothers: A Social Phenomenon and Population in Need* 221
Patricia F. Vadasy

Contents/II

Part II Extrafamilial Supports

10 *Family Support in Public School Programs* **253**
Linda M. Espinosa and Marsha S. Shearer

11 *Networks of Social Supports for Parents of
Handicapped Children* **279**
Vaughan Stagg and Thomas Catron

12 *Supports from Religious Organizations and
Personal Beliefs* **297**
Rebecca R. Fewell

13 *Interactions Between Community Agencies
and Families Over the Life Cycle* **317**
Bruce L. Mallory

Appendix **357**
Author Index **371**
Subject Index **379**

Preface

As the title of this book suggests, a theme which unites the following chapters is the developmental nature of families' experiences in caring for a handicapped child. Mothers, fathers, siblings, and other relatives all play a variety of roles within the family, and the presence of a handicapped child will have an impact on those roles that will change over time. The birth of a handicapped child will present opportunities for some family members to fill roles and develop skills they would otherwise not find necessary. The child benefits from what these family members learn to contribute to the child's development, and further, the child contributes to each member's development. Influences are reciprocal, and each family system is dynamic and unique. The individual role strains that family members often experience are a function of the family members' needs, the handicapped child's needs, and the supports available to the family—dynamic variables that are in flux over the course of the child's development.

These family experiences are presented in the two parts of this book that together reflect the life-span development of the family. The focus in Part I is on the experiences of family members in their roles within the family system. The family is the context for much of the young child's development, and the family system generates its individual pattern of adapting to the needs of the young child and defining new roles which members must assume. A theme in these chapters is the reciprocal influences which individual family members have on the handicapped child and which the child has upon the family. This reciprocal perspective reflects the framework of life-span development that has influenced psychologists, sociologists, and others who are interested in social interactions and human relationships (Baltes & Brim, 1979; Baltes & Schaie, 1973; Lerner, 1976; Riegel, 1976).

For example, this life-span view has been applied to a study of the reciprocal nature of child-family interactions and development (Lerner & Spanier, 1978), and the chapters in Part I of this volume extend that study to families in which there is a handicapped child. The life-span orientation acknowledges the potential for all family members to affect each other's development, as well as for the family to be influenced by the environments in which members interact.

As the child develops, influences from outside the family become more numerous and important, and Part II is concerned with many of these extrafamilial supports. These include school-based services and supports, related services and therapies, and community and medical services. As the child develops, not only does the family come into contact with a wider variety of service providers, but members also derive strength and assistance from informal and personal sources, including their friends, their faith, and their church affiliation. These are themes that the authors explore in Part II.

Whenever possible, we have let individual family members speak for themselves in this book. This approach, in part, is made necessary by the lack of empirical data on extended family members, and by the limitations of the available findings on members of the child's immediate family. The approach also represents a concession that our measures of family members at any single point in time offer limited insights into what it means to learn of, accept, and respond to a child's special needs. In support of this subjective approach, we refer to Bogdan and Taylor's (1975) defense of qualitative social science research methods. The authors contrast the positivistic theoretical perspective, which searches for facts and causes, to the phenomenological perspective, which attempts to understand behavior. Qualitative methods help us understand what others are experiencing, and to see the individual in a context, rather than as an isolated variable.

This book represents an effort to combine these two research perspectives to study the family of the handicapped child. A group of chapters highlight the experiences and feelings of individual family members — mothers, fathers, siblings, and grandparents. Other chapters examine the influence of specific supports in these individuals' lives. Some of the authors present empirical data on family characteristics, their common stresses, their most valuable supports, their changing needs. These data, however, are often supplemented with anecdotal evidence, so as not to "lose sight of the subjective nature of human behavior. . .to allow us to know people personally and to see them as they are developing their own definitions of the world" (Bogdan & Taylor, 1975, p. 4).

The excerpts from interviews and the statements by family members we present offer insight into family experiences that outsiders—professionals, researchers, service providers—often lack. Only recently have researchers who study the handicapped child begun to focus upon family as well as child outcomes of programs and services. This change accompanies an increased appreciation of the ecological nature of the family system in which the child is embedded. Longitudinal data on families' experiences have also been scarce. Even when these data become available, however, direct observations and first-person accounts by family members themselves will always add detail to quantitative data, as well as suggest family concerns that warrant closer study.

We wanted the parents, siblings, and grandparents to speak for themselves in this book, because all too often, practitioners lack opportunities to meet these relatives and understand their experiences. Teachers and therapists may get to know the handicapped child's mother and her concerns through parent conferences or the mother's participation in a home-based program or therapy. But they may rarely hear the father's perspective, or be aware of the sibling's experiences. Professionals may learn of the needs of parents of young children, but may not ever find out what those parents experience as their child grows older. Yet those future needs have implications for the services families are currently receiving, and when professionals have a life-span perspective, they can help families prepare for and cope with what are often stressful transitions.

The perspectives of these "other" family members—fathers and siblings particularly—are becoming better understood, thanks to the work of individuals like Michael Lamb, Brian Sutton-Smith, James Levine and the Fatherhood Project, Tom Powell and the Sibling Information Network, and popular writers and journalists like Bob Greene and Glen Collins. We hope that the chapters we have gathered together here will add to this general literature on families, and help students, professionals, and parents better understand each family member's contribution to caring for and educating a child with special needs.

In Chapter 1 Fewell introduces the reader to the perspective that is reflected in the collected chapters of this volume: that a host of intra- and extrafamilial variables influence family interactions, and that the handicapped child will have an impact on the entire family ecosystem. Fewell outlines the important supports to which families have access—spousal, sibling, kinship, friendship, and community supports—which significantly affect the family's ability to meet a handicapped child's multiple and changing needs. She also describes child characteristics that influence family coping and family interactions, both within the family system, and in family members' roles in their community.

Several authors examine the special experiences and roles of the immediate members of the handicapped child's family. In Chapter 7, Dunst, Trivette, and Cross describe the impact of employment and marital status on mothers' roles and social supports. The authors present the results of a study of 96 mothers of handicapped and at-risk infants and preschoolers which revealed the influence of social support on a wide range of family outcomes, including mother-child interactions and child functioning. Specific types of social supports are identified which had differential effects on family outcomes, and the authors draw implications from these findings for early interventions that would enhance family as well as child functioning.

The experiences of mothers of severely handicapped adolescents are examined in Chapter 5 by Vadasy and Fewell. The authors report on a follow-up study of mothers of children born during the rubella epidemic. They review the policies developed to serve this cohort of children, and present their findings of mothers' experiences against the background of the special services and programs that have been organized for the deaf-blind. Individuals within these families prove to be important supports to the mothers during the child's younger years, whereas extrafamilial supports become more important across the family's development. The mothers' needs for supports and training for their child after age 21 are examined in light of currently available services. The authors' findings emphasize the need to develop policies that help families of severely handicapped children make the transition from school-based to community-based services as the child approaches adulthood.

In Chapter 8 Margaret Roberts offers readers a very personal glimpse into the lives of three mothers as they attempt to cope with their child's special needs. The accounts offer insights into how parents face crises, such as the diagnosis of their child's handicap, how they derive strength from available supports, how they cope with recurring grief and unanswered questions, and how they face questions about the future, which are often made to seem manageable only by attending to the child's myriad daily needs.

Roberts' chapter is complemented by Cathleen Tooley Moeller's first-hand account in Chapter 6 of her experiences as the mother of a young child with Down syndrome. Moeller describes the important roles that several professionals played in her family's life as she and her husband learned to adjust to their son's handicap. Drawing on her own experiences and those of other parents of handicapped children whom she has come to know, Moeller comments on professional qualities and skills that provide parents with the strength and confidence to fill their demanding roles. Moeller's chapter describes both the vulnerability that parents experience in their interactions with the professionals who serve their child, as well as the intensity of bonds that often develop between these individuals who share the child's best interests.

Finally, the needs of a special group of mothers who are increasing in numbers are Vadasy's focus in Chapter 9, which offers readers an overview of the demographics and characteristics of families headed by females. Vadasy reviews the impact of single-parent status on the family's economic well-being and on the mother's physical and emotional needs. Findings are included on single mothers of handicapped children with implications for policies that would support these parents in their multiple and demanding roles.

Fathers are no longer the forgotten parents, and in Chapter 2 Donald Meyer shares his understanding of how the father experiences his child's handicap over the course of development. Meyer examines how fathers of handicapped children experience typical stages in the family's life cycle, from anticipating the child's birth, to launching the adult child into an independent life and preparing for the parents' retirement and old age. Many factors will mediate the father's experience of these events, and Meyer makes note of these, including child and family characteristics. In light of fathers' unique experiences, Meyer suggests interventions and services that match the changing needs of these often underserved parents.

In Chapter 3, Crnic and Leconte review the research on the relationships between handicapped and nonhandicapped siblings, keeping in mind the limitations of the small body of findings to date. They examine the nonhandicapped child's experiences, including benefits the sibling experiences, such as increased maturity and tolerance, as well as the contributions the sibling makes to the handicapped child's care and training. Crnic and Leconte describe an adaptational model for sibling coping which is mediated by variables such as sex, age, birth order, socioeconomic status, developmental changes, and parental attitudes. Their review of sibling concerns will be of special interest to parents, and to professionals who wish to provide family supports which address sibling as well as parent needs.

Another group of often overlooked family members is Sonnek's subject in Chapter 4. Sonnek reminds readers of trends in the aging of the U.S. population and the significant role of grandparents in family networks. She reviews the literature on grandparent roles and findings on the impact of a handicapped child on these roles and family relationships, and describes several models for meeting grandparents' needs. Sonnek's findings on the complexity of the maternal grandmother's role suggest that it is influenced by many factors in addition to the child's handicap. Like the child's parents, the grandparent's ability to cope with the child's handicap will be influenced by the broader social context in which the grandparent functions.

As the child develops, influences from outside the family become more important, both for the child's education as well as for the parents' coping. Espinosa and Shearer, in Chapter 10, review the supports families access through their child's education program. The authors note regional variations in those services, with urban/rural differences and local funding priorities influencing the family's available resources. Variations also exist in the level of parent involvement in the child's school, as well as in the ability of school personnel to interact effectively with parents, and these differences will affect how well families can utilize school-based resources.

Stagg and Catron (Chapter 11) examine aspects of social support networks that influence family members, and the impact of a handicapped child on these networks. They compare the support networks of mothers of mentally retarded children and mothers of nonhandicapped children, and find they are quite similar. The mothers of young retarded children report less satisfaction with their supports than the mothers of nonhandicapped children, and the mothers of teenage retarded children report high levels of satisfaction, suggesting changes in family stress related to the handicapped child's age, as well as possible cohort effects.

Often overlooked in our secular society is the strength many families of handicapped children find in their religion. In Chapter 12, Fewell distinguishes two types of support parents derive from their personal belief systems and from their formal church organization. She provides data on the religious supports experienced by mothers of handicapped children that show the value of personal belief systems for mothers with difficult roles to fill. Fewell examines the specific kinds of instrumental, emotional, educational, and structural assistance religious groups provide their members, and the religious resources that enable parents to face the difficult questions that arise when a child with special needs is born.

Educational organizations address the primary needs of preschool and school-age disabled children and their families. Other community agencies supplement school-based supports in providing medical treatment, information, and parent support. In Chapter 13, Mallory examines assumptions underlying a theoretical model of how families interact with community agencies, a longitudinal model which allows for personalized relationships between families and professionals. Mallory offers criteria with which to evaluate these programs to insure that they enhance the family system and provide families with options that personalize rather than stigmatize, and suggests program models which are most likely to accomplish those goals.

Families, especially in times of stress, look both within and outside their family systems for help in meeting the extra demands they face. The chapters in this book may serve to introduce some readers to these resources, and help them appreciate the ecology of support systems and the adaptiveness of human systems in times of crisis. Other readers may take away a more personal insight into the experiences of individual family members, and may better appreciate how a handicap can affect the roles of parents as well as other relatives. Yet other readers may learn of the educational and community supports which address the special needs of the child and family. Regardless of whether the reader is a student who is relatively new to the field or a practicing professional, we hope that the chapters will stimulate an ecological perspective to identifying and providing supports, as well as a basis for developing policies that address the needs which the family members have shared and expressed so clearly in these pages.

References

Baltes, P.B., & Brim, O.G., Jr. (Eds.). (1979). *Life-span development and behavior* (Vol. 2). New York: Academic Press.

Baltes, P.B., & Schaie, K.W. (Eds.). (1973). *Life-span developmental psychology: Personality and socialization.* New York: Academic Press.

Bogdan, R., & Taylor, S. J. (1975). *Introduction to qualitative research methods: A phenomenological approach to the social sciences.* New York: Wiley.

Brim, O.G., Jr., & Kagan, J. (Eds.). (1980). *Constancy and change in human development.* Cambridge, MA: Harvard University Press.

Lerner, R. (1976). *Concepts and theories of human development.* Reading, MA: Addison-Wesley.

Lerner, R.M., & Spanier, G.B. (Eds.). (1978). *Child influences on marital and family interaction: A life-span perspective.* New York: Academic Press.

Riegel, K.F. (1976). The dialectics of human development. *American Psychologist, 31,* 689-700.

REFERENCES

PART I

Intrafamilial Supports

1

A Handicapped Child in the Family

Rebecca R. Fewell

The basic premise underlying this book is that families are the most appropriate agents for transmitting basic human competencies to their children. The authors in this volume attest to the important role played by extended family members and community agencies to support the primary or nuclear family in carrying out their caregiving tasks. The assumption is valid regardless of family members' economic status, cultural preferences, political leanings, or their physical, mental, or emotional states. When families have members with very special needs, all family members and community agencies will be affected. There is no fail-safe plan which a family should follow. Each situation is unique. Nevertheless, much information exists on common concerns and problems and on the processes and solutions that have enabled families and agencies to support the handicapped person in reaching his or her fullest potential.

Theoretical Perspectives on the Family's Ecosystem

Throughout history and across cultures, the family has been the primary agency for survival. Although the forms of families vary, the tasks are universal. Parents or parent surrogates across all cultures assume the responsibility for transmitting to their offspring the competencies required by the social, economic, and political forces of their society or social group.

Family members do not operate in vacuums. Members are influenced and changed by other members, and by the circumstances in which they exist. If society's goal is to help families carry out their caregiving tasks, then it is necessary that we understand the influences that family members and their environments have on one another. To do this, it is helpful to examine theories of family interactions that include an ecological perspective. The ecosystem approach is broad-based and includes family, peers, and all persons having a significant effect on a child's behavior (Salzinger, Antrobus, & Glick, 1980).

A number of theorists (Belsky & Tolan, 1981; Bronfenbrenner, 1977, 1979; Sameroff & Chandler, 1975; Thomas & Chess, 1977) have described models to convey how family interactions evolve, and have included their perceptions of the impact of a family member with special needs. Sameroff and Chandler (1975) and Sameroff (1980) describe the transactional model that reflects a link between risk factors and developmental outcome, resulting "from a continual interplay between a changing child and a changing environment as the child entered higher levels of cognitive and social functioning" (Sameroff, 1980, p. 345). In this model, the environment is the only accountable reason for deviance in the more mature levels of functioning. Sameroff (1980) noted a caution concerning the limitations of the transactional model for studying certain situations such as those in which a major restriction or physical deviancy exists. Such aberrations are unusually strong factors that produce impacts greater than many environmental variables, and as a result, justify the use of a single factor or interactional model. Examples of such powerful single factors are deafness, blindness, and other handicapping conditions. He summarizes:

> A transactional model is needed to explain development in environments that are sensitive to and can compensate for early deviances so that they are not transformed into later deficits. However, when the range of environments is restricted, either through ignorance or choice, outcomes can be found which appear to be additive or produced by single risk factors taken alone. (p. 346)

If we use this model to examine dyadic transactions involving parents and a child with an impairment, a parent's actions are seen to influence the child's behavior, and the child's actions the parent's behavior; however, the contribution of the impairment to the transactions between parent and child may be so strongly influenced by the impairment that this single factor accounts for the quality of the transactions between the parent and child. The conclusion drawn by Korn, Chess, and Fernandez (1978) from their in-depth study of 243 children with rubella syndrome and their families supports this assumption: "The impact of the child on the family appears to be more related to the characteristics of the rubella children, with their wide variety and number of handicaps, than to the attributes of the parents" (p. 324).

A similar paradigm has been described by Thomas and Chess (1977) as the "goodness-of-fit" model for adaptive development. This relational, person-context match model permits the examiner to predict outcomes. If a child's individual characteristics match the demands of a particular setting, adaptive outcomes accrue. In contrast, mismatched children, whose characteristics are incongruent with the setting, can be expected to develop alternative outcomes. This model helps explain why children with very similar conditions have extremely different outcomes.

Likewise, Belsky and Tolan (1981) subscribe to the principle that, under most circumstances, development is the product of the complex and continuous interaction between an ever-changing organism and his or her environment. However, like Sameroff and Chandler (1975), Belsky and Tolan feel under certain conditions such as severe anoxia in the post partum period, "it is likely that some developmental possibilities (e.g., normal intellectual functioning) will be foreclosed" (p. 110). In such cases, subsequent behavior is a reflection of these earlier experiences.

The concerns of Sameroff and Chandler and of Belsky and Tolan about the impact of certain conditions are reflected by Wohlwill (1979), who describes developmental continuities and discontinuities as dependent upon the continuity and discontinuity of the environment. These concerns have been clearly demonstrated in the studies of Waters (1978) and Vaughn, Waters, Egeland, and Sroufe (1979). Waters observed marked stability in the attachment (to mother) ratings of 50 middle-class infants between 12 and 18 months of age. However, when Vaughn et al. examined a larger sample of lower class infants, the results were not replicated. Internal analyses revealed that the infants who showed unstable attachment classifications across the six-month period were likely to have undergone several major environmental disruptions.

From these perspectives, development, both biological and social, is seen as a process of continual adaptation due to the constant states of change in the individuals and the environment. The accommodations of individuals are always short-lived because of the progressive and transactional nature of the process itself. While changes and accommodations are inevitable and indeed essential, extreme situations and events can create a discontinuity that affects the entire ecosystem, requiring a closer examination of transactions in order to support families in their predestined roles. Fortunately, many ecosystems are inhabited by persons with remarkable plasticity, from whom far more is possible than can be dreamed, particularly when they face the challenge of caring for a vulnerable child.

The Nurturing Mission

A universal role of families is to nurture the young child. The family provides for the child's physical needs and fosters the development of an integrated person capable of living in society and transmitting culture (David, 1979; Lidz, 1963). Parents foster the child's competence, defined by Ogbu (1981) as "a set of functional or instrumental skills" (p. 414), derived from culturally defined adult tasks. Connally and Bruner (1974) distinguish between specific and general competency skills but stress the latter. General skills reflect operative intelligence, the "knowing how" rather than simply "knowing that," while other general skills are related to emotional, linguistic, and practical considerations. These skills make up what the authors have described as the "hidden curriculum in the home" (p. 5) and are those skills essential for coping with existing realities. A person's ability to function is related to how well he or she masters these competencies.

These theoretical perspectives suggest that some children fail to develop appropriate competencies for later success in society because they have impaired systems and their learning abilities are not sufficient to enable them to achieve the societal expectations. Other children fail because the parents failed in their child-rearing tasks. At times, parents' failures can be traced to the lack of support available to the parents from their extended families or their community agencies. Success or failure does not have to be limited to one cause, but can be due to a combination of factors transacting at a given point in time, a testimony to the complexity of the human situation.

The nurturing mission of adult family members for their young is difficult yet joyous. The presence in the family of a child with special needs requires more effort from the other family members; yet in giving more, family members develop the capacity to face more intense experiences — of pleasure as well as pain.

Family Supports

To simplify our writings throughout this book we will assume that a family is a group of two or more people that, in our case, includes at least one parent or parent substitute, and one handicapped child related by blood, marriage, or adoption. These persons constitute a family system by virtue of the fact that they bear a definable relationship to one another (Geismar, 1971). The family is greatly influenced by persons outside the immediate nuclear group. Extended family members and other kin, neighbors, and co-workers are supportive agents. Additionally, support is also rendered through less personal connections such as institutions, agencies, and governmental policies. Unger and Powell (1980) described three types of support provided by social networks: (a) instrumental support, (b) emotional or social support, and (c) referral and information. Networks provide different types of support. In this section we describe three social support systems and examine the types of support each provides when a nuclear family has a handicapped child.

Spousal support. In a recent survey of 80 mothers of children with Down syndrome, mothers indicated spouses to be the most important of 19 possible support persons (Fewell, Belmonte, & Ahlersmeyer, 1983). Similar findings on the same scale were reported by Dunst, Trivette, and Cross (in press) in a study of Appalachian parents. Vadasy and Fewell (Chapter 5) report similar findings when mothers of deaf-blind children were surveyed. Crnic, Greenberg, Ragozin, Robinson, and Basham (1983) in their study of mothers of premature infants found that intimate support had the most positive effects on mothers' attitudes and behaviors. Spouses share in the emotions, the physical care, the nurturance, and the concerns about the future. They can listen to one another, cry, laugh, and play together. The mutual support that parents provide each other is important, since there is evidence that the presence of a handicapped child affects marriages one way or another. Gath (1977) studied marital stress by comparing 30 parents of children with Down syndrome to 30 matched parents of normal children. While a number of differences were noted in the 5-year study, marked differences were present in the quality of the parents' marital relationship. Marital breakdown or severe disharmony was found in nine of the families with children having Down syndrome, but in none of the controls. Yet on the other hand, positive measures were also higher in families that had children with Down syndrome. These parents felt drawn closer together and strengthened in their marriages by their shared tragedy, a view also reported by Burton (1975). On the other hand, in D'Arcy's (1968) study, 73 of 90 mothers of children with Down syndrome claimed their marriages remained happy or unchanged after the child's birth. Friedrich's (1979) finding that marital satisfaction was the single best predictor of a family's positive coping behavior when rearing a handicapped child indicates the importance of the spousal relationship to total family adjustment.

Support from other children. Families report their other children are very important to them in the care of their handicapped child. Older daughters are apparently given more responsibilities in caretaking roles. Like Gath (1973, 1974), Fowle (1968) found the oldest female to be more adversely affected by the presence of a retarded child in the home than was the oldest male sibling. In their study of mothers of deaf-blind children (Vadasy & Fewell, Chapter 5), mothers most often indicated that their daughters were the second-most important source of support, while sons were listed as the third-most important source of support by 10% of the respondents.

Kinship networks. Grandparents play very important roles in the lives of grandchildren, both in terms of their personal interactions with the handicapped child and in their support to the child's parents. Grandparents are available to help with child care, and provide material, psychological, and emotional support. Uzoka (1979) and Sussman (1959) have presented evidence that kinship networks are active despite geographical separations. Extensive intergenerational relationships abound across class and cultural lines. Caplan (1976) described nine supportive tasks of family and kin systems: (a) collecting and disseminating information; (b) providing feedback and guidance; (c) acting as sources of ideology; (d) acting as guides and mediators in problem-solving; (e) acting as sources of practical service and concrete aid; (f) providing a haven for rest and recuperation; (g) acting as a reference and control group; (h) acting as a source and validator of identity; and (i) contributing to emotional mastery.

The kind of support an individual derives from family may be related to physical proximity, although face-to-face contact is not required to sustain the relationship (Litwak, 1960; Troll, 1971). Relatives who live close to each other aid in the care and supervision of children (Caplan, 1976; Sussman, 1959) and house maintenance tasks (Sussman & Burchinal, 1962). Resource exchanges (e.g., gifts, clothes, household items, and money), shared social and recreational activities, and psychological and emotional supports commonly strengthen bonds between kinship network members (Sussman & Burchinal, 1962). Cohler and Grunebaum (1981) found the telephone to be an important link between family members. Given the importance of kinship support, it is logical that a nuclear family will reach out to members of this network when faced with a situation that is stressful or requires more resources than they have at hand. Schell (1981) eloquently describes the family support that enabled him and his wife to get a more stable perspective on their emotions, integrate their feelings about their infant daughter who had Down syndrome, and begin a plan of action to optimize her development. Schell points out that often one member of the family offers special support, and in his case it was a sister-in-law, "Aunt Cindy." Schell's worries and fears about the future were significantly allayed by family support: "Cindy's remaining an energetic force in our lives, as she was before Christina's birth, has helped us to feel like any family with caring and sharing relatives" (p. 25).

Friends, Neighbors and Co-workers

McAdoo (1978) examined family support systems and found friends ranked second in importance behind kin. Friends and neighbors provide a important source of support with short-term assistance such as babysitting, meals during an illness, and care of property in one's absence. Gabel and Kotsch (1981) found that family friends and babysitters frequently attended the bimonthly evening clinics the Family, Infant, and Toddler Project held for families of handicapped children. Turnbull (1978) tells of a surrogate grandmother relationship that developed between her handicapped son and a neighbor, yet she also laments broken friendships with others due to her son's handicap. The personality and sensitivity of the individual appear to be the critical variables in determining who will be supportive.

Community Agencies and Governmental Policies

A number of agencies offer informational support for families with handicapped children. Most notable of these are advocacy groups such as associations for retarded citizens, Easter Seal societies, parent-to-parent groups, and coalitions for citizens with disabilities. These organizations often offer emotional or material support as well. As Fewell describes in Chapter 12, churches and other religious organizations are also important sources of support for families with handicapped children.

Schools, educational agencies, day care centers, and health agencies also provide support that is informational. Public laws such as P.L. 94-142 and numerous court cases (e.g., *Armstrong v. Kline*, 1979; *Pennsylvania Association for Retarded Children v. Commonwealth of Pennsylvania*, 1972) have played critical roles in supporting families with handicapped members. Legislation and litigation have opened school doors to all handicapped children, lowered ages for entrance, and provided for parent participation in educational decisions about their child. This kind of support is widespread and long-lasting, enabling parents to plan for the future with a greater degree of certainty.

Characteristics of the Handicap

A child's particular needs at a given point in the child's life will have an impact on family and community responses. In this section we will consider three major variables that influence the family's ability to adapt: the type of impairment; the severity of the impairment; and the age of the child which is associated with characteristic critical periods of family adjustment.

Types of Impairments

Handicaps can be described as conditions that cause persons to be perceived as different from what others think to be appropriate. According to this view, what is a handicap or who is handicapped is in the eyes of the viewer, and is in reality a value judgment made from the viewer's perspective. Persons will differ in their judgments based on their cultural heritage (Edgerton, 1970), their experiences with similar conditions, and their personal value systems (Pickarts & Fargo, 1971).

Mental retardation. When parents first learn that their child is mentally retarded, they are usually devastated. This is normal, expected, and appropriate. Long-nurtured hopes and dreams vanish and are replaced by fuzzy and distasteful images based on often negative past encounters with retarded persons. Mental retardation, probably the most dreaded diagnosis a parent can receive, carries the stigma of a static condition resulting in a social destiny of isolation, dependency, and institutionalization.

Mental retardation is also a historical and a social concept that sets individuals apart from others. By performance standards, the mentally retarded person is judged inadequate and, according to Sarason and Doris (1979),

> This inadequacy is sufficiently troublesome to those in that context to warrant actions to achieve three purposes: to keep performance standards intact, to reduce or eliminate the discomfort of those who are troubled by the individual's inadequacy, and to be helpful to the individual as help is defined by the moral-ethical values of that social context. (p. 38)

In describing society's perspective, these authors indicate "the retarded child has always been a second-class human being for whom one should have pity, and toward whom one should be human, but for whom society has no use" (p. 77). The societal definition of mental retardation has changed dramatically over the past 15 years. Through scientific research, we have new evidence that refutes past assumptions about limitations. Through political advocacy, we have legislative and litigative reforms, and a new social awareness of the meaning of human behavior is emerging.

Behavior that is viewed by some to be different at a point in time in a given situation may not be viewed as different by others. While the discriminatory nature of the label is now deplored, society has yet to agree on what constitutes mental retardation. It is defined by the arbitrary criteria of a given individual's behavior at a point in time, and is reflected in the viewer's actions. It is viewed only in the context of a transaction between an individual and his or her ecological milieu. Fortunately, the concept of mental retardation is elusive in time and space, and in the view of some (Gliedman & Roth, 1980; Sameroff &

Chandler, 1975; Sarason & Doris, 1979), it must be discarded entirely. Braginsky and Braginsky (1971) are adamant in their position: the concept "has no scientific value whatever, merely serving to obfuscate and distort the meaning of the behavior of the rejected child" (p. 176). The label is particularly tragic for families who subscribe to cultural definitions of success which include high expectations for intellectual performance.

Hearing impairments. About 0.075% of all school-age children are deaf, and another 0.5% are considered hard of hearing. Among the leading causes of severe hearing impairments are heredity, maternal rubella, prematurity, meningitis, and blood incompatability (Moores, 1978). Only between 16 and 30% of deaf children have deaf relatives (Reis, 1973). This has implications for the efforts family members must make to learn to communicate with the deaf child.

Hearing impairments alone will not delay a child's motor or cognitive development. However, reduced language experiences affect performances on achievement tests and on some cognitive measures. Deaf children are often socially less mature than their hearing peers, and they are more than twice as likely to have emotional problems as hearing children (Graham & Rutter, 1968; Levine, 1960). Family members are especially likely to experience the effects of these associated delays and problems as the child grows older. In many cases families with deaf members develop strong social ties with other such families, forming what is often referred to as a deaf community.

Visual impairments. Blindness or severely limited vision can be caused by genetic conditions, infections, diseases, or traumatic events. A visual impairment of genetic origin may result in blame or guilt on the part of a parent, or it may result in a parent's understanding and acceptance because of the parent's previous experience with the condition. Adventitious blindness permits natural family bonds to develop, yet places stress on families to adjust to a permanent change that has far-reaching consequences.

Visual impairments are usually measured by the degree of acuity. Legal definitions are based on these measures, and services are often based on these classifications. However, the most important factor in determining the effects the vision loss will have on the individual is the individual's functional use of sight. The presence of some useful vision makes a big difference in the impact the impairment has on the child and the family.

Blindness from birth results in delays in the development of certain sensorimotor schemes, and in the acquisition of abstract concepts (Fewell, 1983; Fraiberg, 1977; Stephens, 1972). However, Higgins (1973) examined the performance of blind children 5-11 years of age and found no evidence of a general developmental lag. Developmental lags and less efficient movement characterize the motor development of blind children from birth through adulthood (Adelson & Fraiberg, 1974; Norris, Spaulding, & Brodie, 1957). Blindness does not lead to language deficits; however, the blind child's language may be characteristically different in the early years (Landau, 1983; Mills, 1983; Urwin, 1983; Warren, 1977). There is evidence of delayed and aberrant social skills among the blind (Fewell, 1983). However, the way family members relate to the young blind child will have an important impact on the child's social skills and self-concept.

Blind persons are described in literature, seen on television, and are encountered in our communities. Blindness may conjure images and memories of talented musicians or begging street vendors. Stereotypes of certain handicaps influence how families experience their child's handicap. However, far more formidable in influencing the family's reaction is personal knowledge of a blind person. Knowing that a blind person can think, communicate, and carry on the process of daily living independent of others makes blindness appear less devastating than some of the other handicaps.

Physical impairments. One major physical handicap is cerebral palsy, a disorder of muscle control resulting from brain injury during the early stages of development. The injury is likely to affect several areas of the brain, resulting in multiple handicaps. Between 60 and 70% of children with cerebral palsy are mentally retarded; 70 to 80% have impaired speech, 50% have visual problems, and 35 to 45% have seizures (Healy, 1983). Although cerebral palsy may not be detectable in the first few months of life, most cases are diagnosed by 18 months of age.

It is the motility of physically impaired children that is most obviously affected by their disabilities. Limited movement is likely to affect the acquisition of self-care and social skills. The child's inability to move causes others to lower their social expectations for the child, making the physical disability a handicap.

It should be noted that many children with cerebral palsy have normal mental abilities, as do children with some of the other handicaps we have reviewed, and they can progress well in regular classrooms if accommodations are made to enable them to participate in the curriculum and activities. When environmental adaptations are made, these children are among the easiest to integrate into regular classrooms.

Other physical impairments such as spina bifida, hydrocephalus, and muscular dystrophy occur less frequently, and present entirely different problems. For example, in muscular dystrophy the child, the family, and friends often face the child's gradual degeneration. Occupational therapy and counseling are important services to help the child remain independent for as long as possible, and to adjust to the condition as abilities fade.

Severity of Impairments

The less serious an impairment, the easier it is for an individual to participate in everyday activities with his or her peers. More serious impairments often demand specialized medical, educational, physical, and emotional assistance. The involvement and concern of families follow a similar course. Because the severity of an impairment affects the family's reactions and ability to nurture the child, it is appropriate to examine the impact of the severity of the handicap on the child and the family.

Mild impairments. The mild handicaps are often not detected as early in life as more severe and obvious impairments. This fact has several implications for the handicapped child and his or her family. First, because the impairment may not be recognized until the child enters school, the family will have proceeded in their nurturing mission as though their child did not have special needs. If questions do arise, relatives and professionals alike are quick to reinforce hypotheses that involve comparisons to "Uncle Harry" or "all three-year-olds" (Fewell & Gelb, 1983).

Second, mild handicaps are more prevalent and consequently, there are more services available to respond to them. For example, speech clinicians and reading teachers are common in most elementary schools. With the thrust of P.L. 94-142, mildly handicapped children are served in the least restrictive environment possible, and for many of them, this is the regular classroom with services from a resource room, itinerant teacher, or clinician. The presence of the mild problem may be known to those children in the child's immediate education environment, but seldom known to others in the school or neighborhood setting.

Third, parent reactions to a diagnosis of a mild handicap such as a learning disability are varied. Osman (1979) reported parents of children seen in her diagnostic clinic for learning-disabled children go through emotional stages similar to those experienced after a severe loss or death in a family. The invariable set of first questions can be expected. Osman refers to a learning disability as "a family affair," suggesting its widespread effect on all family members. The effects of such impairments are often limited to situations in which the child must respond to predetermined stimuli in set ways. When learning-disabled children are able to adapt solutions to their own learning style, they are often able to compensate for their problems, and others may be completely unaware a problem exists. In the postschool years, mildly handicapped persons are candidates for jobs that are not stressful, given their limitations, and that match the expectations of their age group. Once this occurs, parents and family members are often relieved of the stresses they experienced while the child was in the learning environment.

Moderate impairments. Persons with moderate handicaps are sometimes perceived as "normal," and at other times viewed as "abnormal." The situational context determines both the performance of the handicapped individual as well as the perceptions of those surrounding the person. As Fewell and Gelb (1983) have indicated, the ambiguity of this situation has implications for both the handicapped person and for the family. According to Stonequist (1937), the marginal person is one who may claim membership in two worlds, but who is not completely at home in either world. At times the person seems to belong to the nonhandicapped world, while at other times the person is grouped with the severely impaired. This dilemma creates continual psychological stress, as both the handicapped person and his or her family must determine how the persons in the particular environment are perceiving them, and then choose how to adapt to the situation. Gliedman and Roth (1980) illustrate the curse of marginality poignantly in their classic book, *The Unexpected Minority.* In presenting the stress this duality places on the handicapped person, they write:

> Lurking behind the decision to 'pass' [to participate in the non-handicapped world without acknowledging one's disability] are its potential costs—costs that sometimes include the possibility of bad faith. Passing requires time and energy. It requires ingenuity and usually subjects the individual to considerable emotional strain. Most of those who pass successfully live in constant fear of being found out—e.g., the child with a reading disability, the adult who has spent time in a residential institution for the mildly retarded, the child with a chronic illness such as epilepsy which many consider to be shameful, the adult with a concealable defect or disease that exerts an influence upon his fears that is out of all proportion to able-bodied society's attitudes toward the disability. Most crucially of all, passing undermines the self's sense of authenticity and genuine worth. I seem to be a regular guy or a normal kid. But is this able-bodied person, this careful fabrication, the real me? And if I must always dissemble to hide my handicap, who is the real me? Am I leveling with myself, or am I acting in bad faith? Passing is a kind of social 'white lie'—perfectly understandable yet unpredictable in the devastation it may wreak on an individual's ability to know where the mask leaves off and the true person begins. Insecurity, rigidity, extreme conformity, and overdramatization of the role one assumes are among the occupational hazards of the individual who successfully passes. (p. 85)

Parents of moderately impaired children are likewise faced with stress resulting from society's view of their child. Parents will strive to help their handicapped child adapt to the impairment and to society's expectations of nonhandicapped persons, yet at the same time, they are members of the society that accepts the handicapped person's need for additional support services. In recognizing and openly supporting their child, family members are frequently viewed as if they too are handicapped, a concept described by Goffman (1963) as a "courtesy stigma." Turnbull and Turnbull (1978), Darling (1983), and Paul and Beckman-Bell (1981) cite many examples of situations in which parents are made to feel as though they have the same problem their child has.

Severe impairments. Severe handicaps are usually identified much earlier in life than are mild or moderate handicaps. Many are recognizable at birth. The diagnosis is always a source of great sadness, and the hurt is felt by all the family, friends, neighbors, indeed, by everyone who knows the family. Rosen (1955) has noted that parents react to the birth of a handicapped child in a fairly predictable manner, and move through the following stages of adaptation: awareness of a problem, recognition of the problem; search for a cause; search for a cure; and acceptance of the problem. Roos (1963), the father of a handicapped child, relates the more individual and intimate emotions parents experience, noting a loss of self-esteem, shame, ambivalence, depression, self-sacrifice, and defensiveness. While such negative reactions characterize many of the earlier studies, it is indeed encouraging to see more recent studies examining families' positive coping strategies and reporting the effectiveness of intervention in significantly reducing stress, feelings of inadequacy, guilt, and in increasing self-esteem (Vadasy, Fewell, Meyer, Schell, & Greenberg, 1984).

While severe handicaps are initially shocking and a source of on-going stress, parents can benefit from factual information which helps them understand from the beginning what the family and the child will face. Accurate information reduces ambiguity and enables parents to begin as early as possible to plan for their child's future, as Schell (1981) described. Parents who are thus prepared are less likely to experience the confusion created by the ambiguity of many mild and moderate handicaps. It is clear that the severely handicapped child will need services, and will need them throughout his or her life. Parents who accept this fact can prepare themselves to assume an advocacy role. Parents of severely handicapped children will need to plan more extensively for their child's future, as it may be clear that independence is simply not possible for the child.

Predictable Crises Over the Child's Life Span

In general, most families share certain critical experiences as their child grows up. Satir (1972) refers to these as major, natural, and common steps that create at least temporary anxiety before readjustment takes place. When the child grows and develops and matches the cultural expectations associated with these periods, family members experience satisfaction and associated feelings of accomplishment.

Children with handicaps will be slower accomplishing these

milestones, however, and some may never achieve them. As the handicapped child approaches these critical periods, the parents may experience renewed sorrow and apprehension as they compare what is with what might have been. Six events or periods that are often stressful for the family with a handicapped child are briefly described, as well as some of the expectations that handicapped children fail to meet during these crises periods, and how the child's development contributes to family life and health.

Encountering the handicap. How early parents learn about their child's handicap largely depends on the nature of the handicap. When a handicap, such as Down syndrome or Tay-Sachs disease, has a genetic origin, parents are usually informed within a few days of the child's birth. Deafness, physical impairments, and language and learning disabilities are examples of handicaps that may not be discovered until the child is older. The confirmation that there is a serious and enduring problem is always a crisis and affects all family members. The immediate reactions of sadness, grief, and disappointment are normal and expected. Although as time passes, parents begin to understand the meaning and implications of the child's handicap, pain lingers, and feelings of confusion, anxiety, anger, avoidance, denial, and rejection often recur. For some families, this initial crisis may be experienced as a time of sharing, support, and commitment from family members and others.

All human infants enter the world in a totally dependent state. While physically impaired infants may require some additional care, their needs are still virtually the same as those of nonhandicapped infants. In many ways, this is the period when the family's care and treatment of their handicapped child is most normalized, and when society is least likely to stigmatize or call attention to the child's differences. Mothers of handicapped infants as well as mothers of nonhandicapped infants share basic caretaking concerns like how to prevent diaper rash, what kind of pacifier to provide, or what kinds of foods to introduce. These common concerns can help the mother of the handicapped child feel less isolated and appreciate the many ways in which her child is like its agemates.

Early childhood. Once children can walk, can feed themselves, are toilet trained, can verbally express their needs and feelings, and can entertain themselves for brief periods of time, parents experience relief and a sense of satisfaction at having helped their child achieve these important steps towards independence. If a child's impairments are such that these milestones are considerably delayed, it is quite obvious that the caregiving responsibilities of the family members will be extended in time, and that increased physical and emotional effort will be required to continue the caregiving routines. The task of diapering a three-year-old is simply not as easy as it was when the child was one year old. The larger and heavier child requires more energy to lift and carry. The emotional burden is also great: parents anticipate the end of diapers and two o'clock bottles, and when these things don't end, it can shatter dreams and invite questions about the future. Featherstone (1980) described this fear:

> I remember, during the early months of Jody's life, the anguish with which I contemplated the distant future. Jody cried constantly, not irritable, hungry cries, but heartrending shrieks of pain. Vain efforts to comfort him filled my nights and days. One evening when nothing seemed to help, I went outside, intending to escape his misery for a moment, hoping that without me he might finally fall asleep. Walking in summer darkness, I imagined myself at seventy, bent and wrinkled, hobbling up the stairs to minister to Jody, now over forty, but still crying and helpless. (p. 19)

For many families, a crisis occurs when they seek, then find an agency that can provide their child with early intervention services. A crisis may ensue for a number of reasons: (a) parents see older children with the same impairment and get a glimpse of what their child may be like in a few years; (b) parents become aware that the services their child needs may present a financial drain, or may require time commitments or conditions they had not anticipated; (c) parents who begin to share their experiences with other parents may realize they may need to advocate to get the services their child needs; and (d) parents learn they are expected to be their child's primary teachers as well as caregivers and nurturers. Parents may find that professionals treat them as patients who need treatment (Seligman, 1979; Turnbull & Turnbull, 1978) rather than as experts in their own roles as careproviders. As parents begin to realize what education and therapy services mean, and what a major focus these services will be for their family for the next 21 years, they may feel helpless and overwhelmed.

School entry. When the handicapped child fails to fit into the mainstream of the traditional educational system and requires special schools or classes, a separate transportation system, and a very special curriculum, parents are again confronted with their child's differences and can be very sad. By the time the child is school age, more persons are likely to be aware that the child is different. Siblings may find this to be a very difficult time. As more of their schoolmates learn that they have a brother or sister who is disabled, siblings may acquire a courtesy stigma. They may be treated as if they, too, are different, especially if both children attend the same school. Parents who are themselves high achievers and who have high expectations for their children have to significantly modify their goals for their handicapped child.

Adolescence. All families experience the series of adjustments parents and children must make as children leave childhood and enter adulthood. As children grow and become more capable, parents must continue the letting-go process and begin to appreciate their child's growth, separateness, and independence. For the handicapped child, the body may mature while the the mental, emotional, and social state of the child may lag behind. For parents, this time may be difficult as they realize their child's long term and more acute dependency.

Adolescence is a time when peers have a major influence on one another, and hours are spent in the company of one's agemates. Peer acceptance is extremely important, as one's self-acceptance is shaped by how peers, as well as parents, respond. The visible handicaps can have an important effect on peer acceptance. Other factors that may influence peer acceptance are peers' previous experience with persons with similar handicaps, and their knowledge or perceptions of the impact of the impairment on the individual. First-hand experience with a handicapped child is a major factor in nonhandicapped children's positive responses to the handicapped child. Peer and group acceptance is important in this critical stage for learning appropriate social skills, which in turn will influence societal acceptance in the years to come. As parents observe their child during this period, their anxiety about the future may increase if their child is isolated and spends more time with the family than with friends.

Beginning adult life. Public education services, often taken for granted, provide extremely valuable benefits for the family of the handicapped child. The system helps the child acquire independence and life skills. It also offers respite for the parents during the years when their handicapped child receives services for 5 to 6 hours a day. As the end of the child's public education experience approaches, families face the crisis of the future. In Chapter 5, Vadasy and Fewell describe the anxieties and concerns reported by mothers of deaf-blind children as their children neared the end of eligibility for the services they had been receiving since shortly after birth. It is a time for facing hard questions and making difficult decisions, and it is usually stressful. In some areas, and for some children, the choices may be extremely limited. The child may be unable to participate in the decision-making process, again reminding parents that they must continue to play a major role in the life of their child with special needs.

Maintaining adult life. When a handicapped child becomes an adult, decisions must be made as to where the person will live, and the level of care he or she will need. These decisions will often determine how the child will spend his or her adult life, and changes will be relatively few during the ensuing years. The parents may continue to make decisions for their child, or to support the child although the child may not live with them. When the parents can no longer perform these roles, another crisis occurs: they seek ways to make sure their child is cared for when they have died. The advice and assistance of social workers and other family members are extremely important in enabling parents to finally turn over all responsibility for the child to others. This culminating crisis, when it is resolved effectively, can result in the parents' feeling of satisfaction and joy, feelings similiar to those they experience when their other children marry or become independent.

Although family structure changes, families continue to be the major support units in the lives of human beings. Older members nuture younger members, and as the young mature, the process reverses. Beyond immediate family units are a host of significant others who also support families. When a family has a handicapped child, all the actors in this support network must adapt to the extended needs of the handicapped member. The adaptations family members make are often significant, and individual destinies may be determined by the experience. Family adaptations change as the child matures; the stress at various periods may affect family members differently, for much depends on the familial and environmental contributions to the dynamic interactions of adaptation at a given point in time.

Impact of the Child on the Family

A child with special needs imposes demands which stress the family's ability to function effectively. The entire family becomes more vulnerable to the influences, situations, and transactions of the environment. The child with special needs can no longer be viewed or served in isolation; the myriad persons, agencies, and institutions that touch the child must be included in a service plan. Hobbs (1980) described the unit of service as "not the child but the child-in-setting," then referred to the system of service as ". . .ecological to take into account the situational, developmental, the transactional character of the demands on a service delivery system" (p. 275). To be proactive participants in the ecosystem of a child with special needs requires an understanding of the complex and dynamic interactions within the system that influence one another. Before describing the variables that are within a family's structure, it is wise to be cognizant of McEwan's (1975) appreciation of family differences, and Speer's (1970) reminder of the capacity of our knowledge. David (1979) summarized McEwan's concerns:

> Each family has its own dynamics of formation, growth, maturation, and dissolution, affected by numerous biological, psychological, sociocultural, economic, and educational variables. . .not all families have functions in every area and. . .not all areas appertain to each family for the whole of its natural history. (p. 305)

Speer addresses our very limited knowledge of what constitutes healthy family functioning, a warning also warranted by the professional tendency to focus almost entirely on family dysfunction, when in truth, many families with handicapped children cope effectively, and some consider themselves fortunate in their experience. Speer asserts:

> We know almost nothing about the satisfaction, closeness, meaning-achieving, autonomy, problem-solving, communication, change, and basic relationship-organizing processes of exceptionally well-functioning, broadly and deeply satisfied, fulfilled families. (pp. 273-274)

These admonitions should encourage us to view families in the context of their immediate ecosystem, to appreciate the role of each person's history, and to anticipate the impact that present interactions among family members will have on the future well-being of all.

Described in the sections that follow are family variables that are influenced by a child with special needs. In the remaining chapters of Part I, authors convey, in some detail, the impact of the handicapped child on immediate and extended family members, the persons included in what Bronfenbrenner (1977; 1979) has described as the child's "microsystem." Authors in the second part of this book address the impact and service transactions of persons, agencies, and institutions within what Bronfenbrenner views as the three remaining levels for analysis of human development, the "mesosystem," the "exosystem," and the "macrosystem." These enmeshed systems are comprised in the complex ecosystem that must be considered to plan successful interventions.

Interactions Between Parents and Children

The interactions between a parent and a child are always unique. Each child's birth is anticipated and dreamed about. The bond between parent and child that begins before birth strengthens after birth as the dyad members come to know one another in new ways. Klaus and Kennell (1978) describe the early engaging interactions between parent and child, during which behaviors such as fondling, kissing, cuddling, and prolonged gazing signal an emerging attachment. The birth of an infant with impairments has an immediate effect on these early interactions. The family's dreams and expectations are threatened by the initial diagnosis. The information is shocking and is never forgotten. Feelings of intense emotional upset are described by parents (Allen & Allen, 1979; Featherstone, 1980; Murphy, 1981; Turnbull & Turnbull, 1978). With time, equilibrium returns, and the parent and child begin to know one another.

All infants contribute to their own development. The parent, in responding to the infant, is changed by the infant, and reciprocally, the infant responds to the parent and is changed by the parent. Infants with impaired systems have a more difficult time communicating their needs, feelings, and states. This communication process can be frustrating for parents and can result in inappropriate responses to the child. Learning to communicate effectively with the handicapped child will take longer. Parent and child may develop a private system of communication that is not readily understood by others but that meets their own special needs.

Impact on Siblings

Each member of the family will have to make special adjustments to the handicapped child's special needs. Grossman (1972) conducted the most extensive study of siblings, studying 83 college students who had a retarded brother or sister, and a matched control sample with normal brothers and sisters. Grossman's data revealed the following findings: (a) A number of subjects benefitted from the experience, in that they seemed to be more tolerant, more goal-oriented; (b) some subjects were bitter and felt guilty about their feelings toward their parents, and many feared that they too were defective; (c) parental attitudes and reactions to the retarded brother or sister were the strongest single influence on the normal sibling's acceptance; (d) siblings from upper-income families experienced fewer burdens than siblings from lower-income families as their families did not require as much help from them in the caregiving role. Graliker, Fishler, and Koch (1962) reported very positive effects after interviewing adolescents ages 13-18. Breslau, Weitzman, and Messenger (1981) also reported positive reactions, although their findings were mixed; they found that older female siblings may be more at risk for negative consequences than younger siblings. Featherstone (1980) reports many examples of mixed reactions. Clearly, many factors interact to determine siblings' reactions, with their responsibilities for the child being a pervasive element in their immediate and long-term reactions. For more information on sibling interactions and reactions to handicapped brothers and sisters, see Chapter 3 of this volume.

Impact on Grandparents and Other Relatives

It is often not appreciated how strongly the birth of a handicapped child affects grandparents and other family members. Grandparents often experience a dual grief—a mourning for the loss of an expected grandchild who would carry on the family tradition, and a sorrow for the lifelong burden and reduced opportunities their own child faces in raising the grandchild. Fortunately, professionals are beginning to realize that grandparents are a potential source of support for families. Gabel and Kotsch (1981) describe a program designed to help grandparents and other extended family members express their support in productive ways. In their studies of family supports, German and Maisto (1982), Sonnek (Chapter 4), and Vadasy and Fewell (Chapter 5) found that grandparents were very important sources of support for parents.

The support of an aunt, uncle, or another relative can also be extremely important to the handicapped child and the parents (Schell, 1981). When these relatives don't seem to understand or enter into a supportive role, their reactions to the child can be extremely painful for parents (Ferris, 1980).

Members of the extended family, although at greater remove from the child, are also affected. Kinship bonds transcend space and generations, and these relationships can be the source of important social support for child-rearing tasks; when these family members do not respond for one reason or another, there is a void and the immediate family's tasks are more difficult.

Family Roles

Individuals fill a variety of roles, both inside and outside the family, and these roles vary across time and conditions. Shakespeare described it thus:

All the world's a stage,
And all the men and women merely players:
They have their exits and their entrances;
And one man in his time plays many parts,
His acts being seven ages. (Shakespeare, *As You Like It,* II,7)

In an interview with a father in the SEFAM Project at the University of Washington, the following question was asked exploring the issue of role changes for a parent of a handicapped child:

Interviewer: When you come to the class, you have to assume a lot of the caretaking jobs that traditionally have been left to the mother, such as feeding and changing diapers. Did you change a lot of diapers with your (nonhandicapped) older daughter?

Father: No way. I think it's more the mom's role, but it shouldn't be, it's just the way society thinks. But when you have a handicapped child, it can change your whole outlook on life. It's like someone dropped a curtain in front of you—you gotta change. If you had a normal kid, things would have been tromping along, mom would have continued changing the diapers. When you have a handicapped kid, you gotta start thinking about new ways to do things—that means changing diapers and stuff.

This father's reaction was instant and to the point, a clear indicator that family members need to provide more support for one another when a handicapped child is born and, indeed, take on roles that they had not anticipated. Often, the new roles are added to the traditional roles which family members are expected to continue as they maintain their self-esteem, their integrity as a family, and their place in the community (Turnbull & Turnbull, 1978).

Vadasy et al. (1984) investigated the roles of mothers and fathers of 23 young handicapped children in the SEFAM program and found evidence of the demands experienced by the parents, particularly the mothers. The majority of the mothers (65%) reported they spent over five hours daily with their special needs child, while only 27% of mothers said they spent over five hours daily with the other children in the family. While there was disagreement between parents as to who was responsible for most of the child care, 61% of the fathers and 57% of the mothers agreed that the mothers were responsible for most of the child care. Thirty-five percent of the fathers, but only 4% of the mothers felt child care was shared equally. When these parents were queried about housework, 39% of the fathers, but only 13% of the mothers said the housework was shared equally. These findings suggest parents who agree on many things can disagree about who has the responsibility for daily activities around the home. These findings can also be compared to national data on role sharing which indicates that married men average under 3 hours of housework per week, which is about one sixth the time spent on housework by working wives (Hofferth & Moore, 1979; Stafford, 1980).

Gallagher, Cross, and Scharfman (1981) also investigated parent role responsibilities in families with a young handicapped child. The researchers compared responses from mothers and fathers on the *Gallagher-Cross Parent Role Scale.* For each of the scale's 20 role dimensions, parents indicate who plays the role in their family by scoring items along a 5-point continuum, ranging from "father alone" to "mother alone." The researchers found remarkable agreement between mothers and fathers as to who performs what roles. The data provide a portrait of traditional family role responsibilities, with the six roles directly related to child care being carried out predominantly by the mother. Further analysis revealed fathers felt they should participate more in family activities involving the handicapped child, and the mothers' responses concurred.

Role demands, particularly those experienced by mothers, were poignantly conveyed by a mother interviewed by Winton and Turnbull (1981). Commenting on her desire for a break from the responsibilities of child care during school hours, she said: "A lot of times I get tired of having a role—God, I don't want to solve that—I am paying you to take him for 3 hours and lady make it work" (p. 15).

Farber and Lewis (1975) are particularly sensitive to the tendency of educators to lose sight of the role of the parent as family member, and to regard the parent as a teacher, failing to appreciate, in their

opinion, what is unique about parents' roles: "The parents are then sym-
bolically rather than functionally used." The authors provide an
excellent example, so common in many programs: "The parent may be
required to imitate the classroom teacher in his or her orientation to
the child" or "act as a paraprofessional" (p. 40). Parents who are used
in such a manner are not permitted to fulfill their primary and unique
roles:

> The parent role has meaning only as a component in a complex of
> family roles. In effect, by undermining the special qualities of the
> parent-child relationship, which is a highly personal experience
> involving parents and sometimes grandparents, as well as siblings
> as significant persons, these programs turn the parents into just
> another group of school personnel, another group of adults trying to
> be helpful. (p. 40)

As we noted earlier, siblings can also be asked to take on more of
a careproviding role than they would have ordinarily. Older sisters
appear most likely to be asked to assume a greater role in caretaking,
a finding in studies by Farber (1959) and Grossman (1972), and discussed
by Seligman (1983). For many, these extra roles have had a direct and
positive influence on their futures, as in the case of this sister of a
severely handicapped sibling: "The choice of a career then became
obvious to me. What better way was there to serve others than to enter
the field of special education where I could help people like my brother
lead more fulfilling lives" (Helsel and Helsel, 1978, p. 112). For some,
the added responsibilities mean that the sibling must sacrifice other
social, athletic, or school activities in which the sibling would otherwise
participate.

Family Time

The time demanded to provide help, support, and care for a child with
severe impairments can amount to an intensive, exhausting, never-
ending 24-hour care routine (Lyon & Preis, 1983). Parents may feel they
must give all their time to their handicapped child, and may fail to take
time for themselves. Klein (1977) reported that several sets of parents
of deaf-blind children said they had never been on a vacation alone, and
seldom went out on weekends because of the difficulty in finding a
babysitter.

While many of the time demands originate with the child (e.g., the
extra time it can take to help the child eat, drink, toilet; travel time
to school and community services), community agencies can also demand
a parent's time. Parents who have the responsibility for 24-hour care
of a child with special needs sometimes need a break; they may not want
to have to work in the child's classroom once a week, or more often in

some cases. Parents may not feel comfortable admitting these feelings, particularly when they are first searching for services. At this time, the parent is particularly vulnerable, and often feels unprepared for the task of parenting the child. Parents often feel great relief and gratitude when they first locate services or a program for their child. Contrary to what they might have expected, once the parents locate professionals who apparently have the skills to help the child, the parents may find that the agency professionals also want some of the parents' time. Caught between their child's needs and their own desire and need for relief and respite, the parents often succumb to the professional's demands for fear of being perceived as "bad" parents if they are not willing to give the extra time to the class. The demands that parent participation programs often make of parents are viewed by Farber and Lewis (1975) as "representative of the kind of innovation which is characteristic of the enterprise model of educational organization and function," and Horejsi (1979) has commented on the higher social and psychological price that parents of handicapped children must pay for six hours of relief during the school day. The benefits of parent participation are often clearer to professionals than to parents. The practice is cost-effective, and if the children do not show the heralded benefits, "the managers have a built-in scapegoat for explaining failure—the inability or low motivation of parents to act as teachers or tutors to their own children" (p. 39). Thus the parents who go along with an agency's demands against their own instincts, and who fail to ask what alternatives are available may find themselves both used and abused in far-reaching ways. While parents' experiences will vary (e.g., Jablow, 1982), it behooves agency personnel to be sensitive to parents and their needs at a given point in time; circumstances will change, and needs will also. Maybe later a parent will want to be in the classroom almost daily, but perhaps not for now.

Family Finances

Responding to a child's special needs will be costly. Added expenses are simply a fact of life, be it a relatively minor expense like eye glasses, special shoes, or a hearing aid, or major expenses that will be experienced across a life-span, such as special living arrangements, special services, or adaptive equipment for mobility in the community. It will cost more for families and for community agencies to provide for individuals with special needs. Community agencies are accustomed to providing special services, and are thus aware of the costs of adding a new person to their rolls. Their budgets are designed to absorb the expenses. Families seldom anticipate these expenses, and they may be overwhelmed by the costs. The financial difficulties of providing for the child's special needs are reported often (Blackard & Barsh, 1982; Christ-Sullivan, 1976; Dunlap & Hollinsworth, 1977; Moroney, 1981). Yet families manage to find ways to continue the caring function. Moroney reminds us that "large numbers of handicapped children are living with and being cared for by their relatives—far more than are in institutions" (p. 194). Yet Moroney continues, "we have not developed a network of supportive services for these families" (p. 194). Moroney (1979) has pointed out that our knowledge of how to substitute and take over for families is much more developed than our knowledge of how to support families as primary caregivers. He suggests that professionals view families as needing resources to carry out their responsibilities rather than viewing family members primarily as resources themselves.

Family Relations with Society

Throughout this book, the overriding concern of the authors is to faciliate understanding and support for families of children with special needs. In their chapters, the authors share their insights and the insights of others, and they suggest strategies to help families respond to exceptional needs. It is one thing to work with the persons within a handicapped child's immediate and extended family to plan and provide services and respond to needs; it is more difficult to identify and to rally support for these human needs from society at large. It isn't that "society" doesn't care. The issue is far more complex. It involves social policy for the handicapped, underlying attitudes about the role of the handicapped in society, and assumptions about family responsibility. Families with special needs face a number of obstacles in their efforts to help their handicapped members fit into society and to obtain needed resources. Family and social values are discussed briefly in this section.

Past and Present Attitudes Towards the Handicapped

Many attitudes towards handicapped persons are derived from historical references that assign handicapped persons to the roles of beggars, freaks who were placed on public display, or court jesters whose uncontrollable movements were regarded as entertainment for others. Always, handicapped persons were considered liabilities to their families and society (Lowenfeld, 1981). Even the word "handicapped," derived from "cap in hand," conveys a negative image.

More recently, society has come to define an impairment as a medical condition to be "treated." Society provided what became known to many as "state hospitals" or places where persons with mental or emotional problems were supposedly "treated," but were more often "warehoused" for the remainder of their lives. Recalcitrant children were often threatened with banishment to such places, or accused of causing their parents to succumb to dreadful destinies such as their death. The stigma of the handicapped person is one of shame and inferiority (Wright, 1960), which marks the person as tainted and discounted (Goffman, 1963). Such views are not consistent with normal societal roles of friend, lover, co-worker, or autonomous adult (Gliedman & Roth, 1980), and society is reluctant to change its views. While attitudes have changed and the handicapped are no longer ostracized or warehoused, the current use of the medical model in planning services often means that we lose sight of the person behind the handicap. For many handicapped individuals and their families, the most devastating consequences of being handicapped are often not the direct physical or mental results of impairment itself, but rather the attitudes and reactions of those who are not handicapped. Georgie Miller (1981) conveys convincingly her feelings about society's attitude:

> I detest the thought of anyone saying, "She's blind." It makes me madder than anything, because I am not blind. I'm visually impaired, or visually handicapped ... A lot of people automatically start treating me like a piece of china, and I detest that. I am a person, and I don't need to be handled like I'm going to break. I've always felt that way. (p. 152)

The value society places on persons with impairments is also reflected in whether persons with impairments are given entry to everyday roles and activities, or are kept at a distance. This tendency to distance ourselves from the handicapped is illustrated in our answers to questions such as "Would you rather be deaf, or blind, etc.?" The less obvious an impairment, the more socially acceptable it is. Moderately handicapped persons can often fit into both the nondisabled world, and the world of the handicapped. Yet, the ambiguity of moderate conditions is itself a paradox: it permits one to participate in society at certain times and under some conditions; at other times and under different conditions, the person is clearly excluded. So that, while the label may be a useful tool to obtain services, it may also be a stigma that will do far greater damage to the person's self-concept.

Emotional Support for Families

Finally, another problem with relying upon a diagnostic label to provide services for the handicapped person is that it fails to consider services the family needs in order to function. Fortunately, professionals are beginning to recognize the irony of this situation in light of social policies which stress deinstitutionalization and community placement. If families are to provide care, they must be supported in their efforts.

The family's role is made easier when members receive appropriate economic supports and services, as well as emotional and social support for their efforts. These latter intangible supports, which provide important psychological benefits to families, depend upon social attitudes towards the handicapped. Martha Jablow (1982), a mother of a handicapped daughter, understands why persons "squirm, fidgit and change the subject" (p. 172) when retardation is mentioned. She pinpoints the fear that prevents many from seeing the person behind the handicap. In her enlightening and moving book, *Cara,* she also expresses hope for change with future generations:

> I understand this discomfort. I have felt it myself. While waiting for a train, I was approached by a young man who sat down next to me and began a conversation about his friend who worked in a pet store. The young man was clearly retarded, his speech understandable but repetitious. I would just as soon have been somewhere else. But I thought of Cara and hoped that a stranger at a train station would be a patient, cordial listener if she initiated a chat. I recognized in my first reaction to this young man the unease that causes many people to fear the retarded. And I wondered how much of that fear is at the root of many people's reticence to integrate the retarded into their communities and schools. Until future generations become more accepting of their brothers and sisters with handicaps, uneasiness about the subject will continue. (p. 172)

References

Adelson, E., & Fraiberg, S. (1974). Gross motor development in infants blind from birth. *Child Development, 45,* 114-126.

Allen, J.C., & Allen, N.L. (1979). Discovering and accepting hearing impairment: Initial reaction of parents. *Volta Review, 81,* 279-285.

Armstrong v. Kline, 476 F. Supp. 583 (E.D. Pa. 1979).

Belsky, J., & Tolan, W.J. (1981). Infants as producers of their own development: An ecological analysis. In R.M. Lerner & N.A. Busch-Rossnagel (Eds.), *Individuals as producers of their development* (pp. 87-115). New York: Academic Press.

Blackard, M.K., & Barsh, E.T. (1982). Parents' and professionals' perceptions of the handicapped child's impact on the family. *Journal of the Association for Severely Handicapped, 7,* 62-69.

Braginsky, D., & Braginsky, B. (1971). *Hansels and Gretels?* New York: Holt, Rinehart & Winston.

Breslau, N., Weitzman, M., & Messenger, K. (1981). Psychologic functioning of siblings of disabled children. *Pediatrics, 67,* 344-353.

Bronfenbrenner, U. (1977). Toward an experimental ecology of human development. *American Psychologist, 32,* 513-531.

Bronfenbrenner, U. (1979). *The ecology of human development: Experiments.* Boston: Harvard University Press.

Burton, L. (1975). *The family life of sick children.* London: Routlege & Kegan Paul.

Caplan, G. (1976). The family as a support system. In G. Caplan & M. Killilea (Eds.), *Support systems and mutual help* (pp. 19-36). New York: Grune & Stratton.

Christ-Sullivan, R. (1976). The role of the parent. In A. Thomas (Ed.), *Hey, don't forget about me: Education's investment in the severely, profoundly, and multiply handicapped* (pp. 36-45). Reston, VA: Council for Exceptional Children.

Cohler, B.J., & Grunebaum, H.U. (1981). *Mothers, grandmothers, and daughters: Personality and child care in three-generation families.* New York: Wiley.

Connally, K.J., & Bruner, J.S. (1974). *The growth of competence.* New York: Academic Press.

Crnic, K. A., Greenberg, M. T., Ragozin, A. S., Robinson, N. M., & Basham, R. B. (1983). Effects of stress and social support on mothers and premature and full-term infants. *Child Development, 54,* 209-217.

D'Arcy, E. (1968). Congenital defects: Mother's reaction to first information. *British Medical Journal, 118,* 18-29.

Darling, R.B. (1983). Parent-professional interaction: The roots of misunderstanding. In M. Seligman (Ed.), *The family with a handicapped child* (pp. 95-121). New York: Grune & Stratton.

David, H.P. (1979). Healthy family functioning: Cross-cultural perspectives. In P.I. Ahmed & G.V. Coelho (Eds.), *Toward a new definition of health* (pp. 281-319). New York: Plenum.

Dunlap, W.R., & Hollinsworth, J.S. (1977). How does a handicapped child affect the family? Implications for practitioners. *The Family Coordinator, 26,* 286-293.

Dunst, C.J., Trivette, C.M., & Cross, A. (in press). Social support networks of Appalachian families with handicapped children: Relationship to personal and family well-being. In S. Keefe (Ed.), *Mental health in Appalachia.* Lexington, KY: University of Kentucky Press.

Edgerton, R.B. (1970). Mental retardation in non-Western societies: Towards a cross-cultural perspective on incompetence. In H.C. Haywood (Ed.), *Sociocultural aspects of mental retardation* (pp. 523-559). New York: Appleton-Century-Crofts.

Farber, B., (1959). Effects of a severely mentally retarded child on family integration. *Monographs of the Society for Research in Child Development, 24.* Chicago: University of Chicago Press.

Farber, B., & Lewis, M. (1975). The symbolic use of parents: A sociological critique of educational practice. *Journal of Research and Development in Education, 8,* 34-43.

Featherstone, H. (1980). *A difference in the family.* New York: Basic Books.

Ferris, C. (1980). *A hug just isn't enough.* Washington, DC: Gallaudet College Press.

Fewell, R.R. (1983). Working with sensorily impaired children. In S.G. Garwood (Ed.), *Educating young handicapped children* (pp. 235-280). Rockville, MD: Aspen.

Fewell, R.R., Belmonte, J., & Ahlersmeyer, D. (1983). *Questionnaire on family support systems.* Unpublished manuscript, Experimental Education Unit, University of Washington, Seattle.

Fewell, R.R., & Gelb, S.A. (1983). Parenting moderately handicapped persons. In M. Seligman (Ed.), *The family with a handicapped child* (pp. 175-202). New York: Grune & Stratton.

Fowle, C. (1968). The effect of the severely mentally retarded child in his family. *American Journal of Mental Deficiency, 73,* 468-473.

Fraiberg, S. (1977). *Insights from the blind.* New York: Basic Books

Friedrich, W.N. (1979). Predictors of the coping behavior of mothers of handicapped children. *Journal of Consulting and Clinical Psychology, 47,* 1140-1141.

Gabel, H., & Kotsch, L.S. (1981). Extended families and young handicapped children. *Topics in Early Childhood Special Education, 1,* 29-35.

Gallagher, J.J., Cross, A., & Scharfman, W. (1981). Parental adaptation to a young handicapped child: The father's role. *Journal of the Division for Early Childhood, 3,* 3-14.

Gath, A. (1973). The school-age siblings of mongol children. *British Journal of Psychiatry, 123,* 161-167.

Gath, A. (1974). Sibling reactions to mental handicap: A comparison of the brothers and sisters of mongol children. *Journal of Child Psychology and Psychiatry, 15,* 187-198.

Gath, A. (1977). The impact of an abnormal child upon the parents. *British Journal of Psychiatry, 130,* 405-410.

Geismar, L. (1971). *Family and community functioning: A manual of measurement for social work practice and policy.* Metuchen, NJ: Scarecrow Press.

German, M. L., & Maisto, A. A. (1982, February). The relationship of a perceived family support system to the institutional placement of mentally retarded children. *Education and Training of the Mentally Retarded*, pp. 17-23.

Gliedman, J., & Roth, W. (1980). *The unexpected minority: Handicapped children in America*. New York: Harcourt Brace Jovanovich.

Goffman, E. (1963). *Stigma: Notes on the management of spoiled identity*. New York: Jasson Aranson.

Graham, P., & Rutter, M. (1968). Organic brain dysfunction and child psychiatric disorder. *British Medical Journal, 3*, 695-700.

Graliker, B.V., Fishler, K., & Koch, R. (1962). Teenage reactions to a mentally retarded sibling. *American Journal of Mental Deficiency, 66*, 838-843.

Grossman, F.K. (1972). *Brothers and sisters of retarded children: An exploratory study*. Syracuse, NY: Syracuse University Press.

Healy, A. (1983). Cerebral palsy. In J. A. Blackman (Ed.), *Medical aspects of developmental disabilities in children birth to three* (pp. 31-37). Iowa City: University of Iowa.

Helsel, E., & Helsel, B. (1978). The Helsels' story of Robin. In A.P. Turnbull & H.R. Turnbull (Eds.), *Parents speak out: Views from the other side of the two-way mirror* (pp. 94-115). Columbus, OH: Charles E. Merrill.

Higgins, L.C. (1973). *Classification in congenitally blind children*. New York: American Foundation for the Blind.

Hobbs, N. (1980). An ecologically oriented, service-based system for the classification of handicapped children. In S. Salzinger, J. Antrobus, & J. Glick (Eds.), *The ecosystem of the "sick" child* (pp. 271-290). New York: Academic Press.

Hofferth, S.L., & Moore, K.A. (1979). Women's employment and marriage. In R.E. Smith (Ed.), *The subtle revolution*. Washington, DC: Urban Institute.

Horejsi, C. R. (1979). Social and psychological factors in family care. In R. H. Bruininks & G. C. Krantz (Eds.), *Family care of developmentally disabled members: Conference proceedings* (pp. 13-24). Minneapolis: University of Minnesota.

Jablow, M.M. (1982). *Cara: Growing with a retarded child*. Philadelphia: Temple University Press.

Klaus, M.H., & Kennell, J.H. (1978). Parent-to-infant attachment. In J.H. Stevens & M. Mathews (Eds.), *Mother/child, father/child relationships* (pp. 5-29). Washington, DC: National Association for the Education of Young Children.

Klein, C. (1977). Coping patterns of parents of deaf-blind children. *American Annals of the Deaf, 122*, 310-312.

Korn, S., Chess, S., & Fernandez, P. (1978). The impact of children's physical handicaps on marital quality and family interaction. In R.M. Lerner & G. B. Spanier (Eds.), *Child influences on marital and family interaction: A life-span perspective* (pp. 299-326). New York: Academic Press.

Landau, B. (1983). Blind children's language is not "meaningless." In A.E. Mills (Ed.), *Language acquisition in the blind child* (pp. 62-76). San Diego: College-Hill Press.

Levine, E.S. (1960). *Psychology of deafness*. New York: Columbia University Press.

Lidz, T. (1963). *The family and human adaptation*. New York: International Universities Press.

Litwak, E. (1960). Occupational mobility and extended family cohesion. *American*

Sociological Review, 25, 9-21.

Lowenfeld, B. (1981). *Berthold Lowenfeld on blindness and blind people.* New York: American Foundation for the Blind.

Lyon, S., & Preis, A. (1983). Working with families of severely handicapped persons. In M. Seligman (Ed.), *The family with a handicapped child* (pp. 203-232). New York: Grune & Stratton.

McAdoo, H.P. (1978). Factors related to stability in upwardly mobile black families. *Journal of Marriage and the Family, 40,* 761-778.

McEwan, P.J.M. (1975). *Psycho-social aspects of the family and health care* (Document MCH/WP/73.11). Geneva: World Health Organization.

Miller, G. (1981). Georgie Miller. In M.D. Orlansky & W.L. Heward (Eds.), *Voices: Interviews with handicapped people* (pp. 151-155). Columbus: Charles E. Merrill.

Mills, A.E. (1983). Acquisition of speech sounds in the visually-handicapped child. In A.E. Mills (Ed.), *Language acquisition in the blind child* (pp. 46-56). San Diego: College-Hill Press.

Moores, D.F. (1978). *Educating the deaf: Psychology, principles, and practices.* Boston: Houghton Mifflin.

Moroney, R.M. (1979). Allocation of resources for family care. In R. H. Bruininks & G. C. Krantz (Eds.), *Family care of developmentally disabled members: Conference proceedings* (pp. 63-76). Minneapolis: University of Minnesota.

Moroney, R.M. (1981). Public social policy: Impact on families with handicapped children. In J.L. Paul (Ed.), *Understanding and working with parents of children with special needs* (pp. 180-204). New York: Holt, Rinehart & Winston.

Murphy, A.T. (1981). *Special children, special parents.* Englewood Cliffs, NJ: Prentice-Hall.

Norris, M., Spaulding, P.J., & Brodie, F.H. (1957). *Blindness in children.* Chicago: University of Chicago Press.

Ogbu, J.U. (1981). Origins of human competence: A cultural-ecological perspective. *Child Development, 52,* 413-429.

Osman, B.B. (1979). *Learning disabilities: A family affair.* New York: Warner Books.

Paul, J.L., & Beckman-Bell, P. (1981). Parent perspectives. In J.L. Paul (Ed.), *Understanding and working with parents of children with special needs* (pp. 119-153). New York: Holt, Rinehart & Winston.

Pennsylvania Association for Retarded Children v. Commonwealth of Pennsylvania, 343 F. Supp. 279 (E.D. Pa. 1972).

Pickarts, E., & Fargo, J. (1971). *Parent education.* New York: Appleton-Century-Crofts.

Reis, R. (1973). What is a resource room program? *Journal of Learning Disabilities, 6,* 609-614.

Roos, P. (1963). Psychological counseling with parents of retarded children. *Mental Retardation, 1,* 345-350.

Rosen, L. (1955). Selected aspects in the development of the mother's understanding of her mentally retarded child. *American Journal of Mental Deficiency, 59,* 522-528.

Salzinger, S., Antrobus, J., & Glick, J. (1980). *The ecosystem of the "sick" child.* New York: Academic Press.

Sameroff, A.J. (1980). Issues in early reproductive and caretaking risk: Review and current status. In D.B. Sawin, R.C. Hawkins, L.O. Walker, & J.H. Penticuff (Eds.), *Exceptional infant* (vol. 4, pp. 343-359). New York: Brunner/Mazel.

Sameroff, A.J., & Chandler, M.J. (1975). Reproductive risk and the continuum of caretaking casualty. In F. Horowitz (Ed.), *Review of child development research* (pp. 187-243). Chicago: University of Chicago Press.

Sarason, S.B., & Doris, J. (1979). *Educational handicap, public policy, and social history: A broadened perspective on mental retardation.* New York: Free Press.

Satir, V. (1972). *Peoplemaking.* Palo Alto, CA: Science and Behavior Books.

Schell, G.C. (1981). The young handicapped child: A family perspective. *Topics in Early Childhood Special Education, 1,* 21-27.

Seligman, M. (1979). *Strategies for helping parents of exceptional children.* New York: Free Press.

Seligman, M. (1983). Siblings of handicapped persons. In M. Seligman (Ed.), *The family with a handicapped child* (pp. 147-174). New York: Grune & Stratton.

Shakespeare, W. *As You Like It.* Act II, Scene 7.

Speer, D.C. (1970). Family systems: Morphostasis and morphogenesis, or "Is homeostasis enough?" *Family Process, 9,* 259-278.

Stafford, F.P. (1980, December). Women's use of time converging with men's. *Monthly Labor Review, 103,* 57-62.

Stephens, B. (1972). Cognitive processes in the visually impaired. *Education of the Visually Handicapped, 4,* 106-111.

Stonequist, E.V. (1937). *The marginal man: A study in personality and culture conflict.* New York: Scribner's.

Sussman, M.B. (1959). The isolated nuclear family: Fact or fiction. *Social Problems, 6,* 333-340.

Sussman, M.B., & Burchinal, L. (1962). Kin family network: Unheralded structure in current conceptualizations of family functioning. *Marriage and Family Living, 24,* 231-240.

Thomas, A., & Chess, S. (1977). *Temperament and development.* New York: Brunner/Mazel.

Troll, L.E. (1971). The family of later life: A decade review. *Journal of Marriage and the Family, 33,* 263-290.

Turnbull, A.P. (1978). Moving from being a professional to being a parent: A startling experience. In A.P. Turnbull & H.R. Turnbull (Eds.), *Parents speak out: Views from the other side of the two-way mirror* (pp. 131-140). Columbus, OH: Charles E. Merrill.

Turnbull, A.P., & Turnbull, R.R. (1978). *Parents speak out: Views from the other side of the two-way mirror.* Columbus, OH: Charles E. Merrill.

Unger, D.G., & Powell, D.R. (1980). Supporting families under stress: The role of social networks. *Family Relations, 24,* 134-142.

Urwin, C. (1983). Dialogue and cognitive functioning in the early language development of three blind children. In A.E. Mills (Ed.), *Language acquisition in the blind child* (pp. 142-161). San Diego: College-Hill Press.

Uzoka, A.F. (1979). The myth of the nuclear family. *American Psychologist, 34,* 1095-1106.

Vadasy, P.F., Fewell, R.R., Meyer, D.J., Schell, G., & Greenberg, M.T. (1984).

Involved parents: Characteristics and resource of fathers and mothers of young handicapped children. *Journal of the Division for Early Childhood, 8,* 13-25.

Vaughn, B., Waters, E., Egeland, B., & Sroufe, L. (1979). *Individual differences in infant-mother attachment at 12 and 18 months: Stability and change in families under stress.* Unpublished manuscript, University of Minnesota, Minneapolis.

Warren, D. (1977). *Blindness and early childhood development.* New York: American Foundation for the Blind.

Waters, E. (1978). The reliabilty and stability of individual differences in infant-mother attachment. *Child Development, 49,* 489-494.

Winton, P.J., & Turnbull, A.P. (1981). Parent involvement as viewed by parents of preschool handicapped children. *Topics in Early Childhood Special Education, 1,* 11-19.

Wohlwill, J. (1979). Cognitive development in childhood. In O. Brim & J. Kagan (Eds.), *Constancy and change in human development* (pp. 359-444). Cambridge, MA: Harvard University Press.

Wright, B.A. (1960). *Physical disability: A psychological approach.* New York: Harper & Row.

2

Fathers of Handicapped Children

Donald J. Meyer

While an increasing amount of information is available about the father's reaction and initial adaptation to the diagnosis of his child's disability, less is known about the effects of the child's handicap on the father as the child grows into adulthood. This chapter will attempt to explore the changing effects of the child's handicap on the father over the child's lifespan. After reviewing the research literature and personal accounts by fathers, implications for providing services and supports to meet fathers' changing needs will be discussed.

Parental Stress Over the Life Cycle

> I thought about Noah and how he would never recover and how we would never get over him. He's an affliction here to stay, one that continually unfolds. (Greenfeld, 1979b, p. 52)

In his sensitive and often painfully honest books about his severely handicapped son, Josh Greenfeld allows the reader to witness the impact of his son's handicap from the time it was first suspected, through the initial frustrations of obtaining an accurate diagnosis and adequate educational programs, to the sorrow of Noah's still slow, still erratic behavior in his tenth year. What Greenfeld describes in his often angry books runs counter to what family theorists have thought about parents of children with handicaps.

The early literature on parent reactions (American Medical Association, 1964; Menolascino, 1977) suggested that parents, confronted by the "novelty shock" of the diagnosis, proceeded through predictable stages leading to a final resolution. Miller (1968) suggested that parents go through stages of disintegration, characterized by shock, denial, and disorganization; adjustment, when parents alternately accept and deny the existence of the handicap; and reintegration, when parents pull themselves back together and begin to function more effectively and realistically. While these stages are not totally inaccurate, they are based on the assumption that following reintegration, parents resume a life that, while it is not entirely normal, is not unduly stressful.

Greenfeld's experiences more closely resemble the emerging view of parents' adaptation to a child's disability. This view holds that although parents regain equilibrium following the initial shock, their adjustment may be temporary: Parents will be subject to chronic, stressful reminders of the tragedy of the child's disability throughout the child's lifespan (Olshansky, 1962; Wikler, 1981). Wikler, Wasow, and Hatfield (1981) interviewed parents and social workers and found that 67% believed that parents experience chronic sorrow across developmental stages. Further, the social workers tended to overestimate the impact of the disability in the early years and underestimate the stress parents experience later in the life cycle.

Wikler (1981) contends that these stresses occur "when a discrepancy emerges between what parents expect of a child's development and of parenting as opposed to what actually takes place when rearing a mentally retarded child" (pp. 283-284). She notes that some of these stresses are related to hardships unique to mental disability, such as stigmatized social interactions and a prolonged burden of care. Others are typical parental responses to retardation such as grief and a need for specific information. Wikler's concept of reoccurring crises and stress will be further discussed in context in the remainder of the chapter.

Some family theorists, such as Duvall (1962) have observed that families, like individuals, proceed through a life cycle consisting of overlapping stages. Just as an individual grows, develops, matures, and ages, undergoing continual change and readjustment throughout his or her life, families also have a life cycle. They are "born"; they grow, change, and age. Events, such as divorce, desertion, or death will profoundly affect the family life cycle. However, few changes in the family will have a greater effect on the life cycle than the birth of a disabled child. The remainder of this chapter will explore the impact of the child's disability on the family's life cycle, especially as it pertains to the father.

The Father's Experience

While there has been an explosion of research on fathers in the past few years, still relatively little is known about fathers of handicapped children. Mothers of handicapped children have been the traditional focus of research. Most studies of fathers focus on the father's reaction to the diagnosis or his initial adaptation. Much less is known about the effects of the child's handicap on the father as the child grows into adulthood. In the sections that follow, chapters, articles, and books written by fathers themselves will be reviewed to fill in the void in the research literature. Caution is advised when making inferences from the research and accounts presented: Intervening variables such as disability type and support measures will allow for a wide range of experiences among fathers. This chapter will focus primarily on fathers of children with mental retardation. However, other factors in addition to the type of handicap will influence a father's experiences. For example, the experience of a father with a passive child with Down syndrome may be quite different from the experience of a father whose child is also physically disabled or has aggressive or autistic behaviors. Similarly, the experience of a father whose marriage is sound and whose employment is secure prior to the diagnosis of the child's handicap may differ greatly from the experience of a father whose marriage is unstable and who is unemployed at the time of diagnosis. Intervening variables and mediating factors will be discussed later in the chapter.

The stages in the family life cycle referred to in this chapter are those described by Duvall (1962). As we shall see, the stages in the family life cycle will be markedly different for fathers and families with handicapped children. In some cases, these stages may be nonexistent.

Stage One: The Beginning Family

The initial stage in the family life cycle typically begins when the couple marries, and it continues until the woman becomes pregnant. Like all stages, this stage is subject to variation and exception. For instance, if the woman is pregnant at the time of the marriage, the "developmental tasks" of this stage will include those of the following stage, the expectant couple.

According to Duvall (1962) the primary developmental tasks for the new couple are to adjust to one another and the new aspects of their relationship. These primary adjustments will likely involve many secondary adjustments in order to fulfill basic requirements for housing;

finances; sexual, emotional, and intellectual communication; division of domestic responsibilities; establishing relationships both as individuals and as a couple; and developing a compatible philosophy of life.

Obviously, the experiences of couples who later have a handicapped child will be much the same in this stage as the experiences of other couples. It is during this time, however, that a couple will either succeed or fail at developing a relationship that can withstand the test of a child's handicap.

Gath (1977) suggested that the stability of the marital relationship prior to birth of the special child may mediate the effects of the child's handicap on the family. She studied 30 families with children who have Down syndrome and an equal number of matched controls. Negative findings, such as marital breakdown or severe marital disharmony, were found in 30% of the index families and in none of the control families. Severe tension, high hostility, or marked lack of warmth between husband and wife were noted in several of the families with handicapped children. It is interesting to note that although negative measures were higher in the parents of children with Down syndrome, the positive measure were also higher for this group. Gath observes that, despite their grief, the parents of almost half of the children with Down syndrome involved in the study felt that their marriage was strengthened after the birth of the handicapped child.

Studies by Gath and others (Farber, 1972) suggest that the presence of a handicapped child can be a critical factor in dissolving a marriage in which there are problems or instability prior to the child's birth and, conversely, can be a unifying factor for parents who enjoyed a strong, close marriage prior to the birth of the handicapped child.

Stage Two: The Expectant Couple

Barring amniocentesis, the expectant couple will be unaware of their future child's handicap. Duvall (1962) notes that it is during this time that the expectant father will address the developmental tasks of planning for the child's arrival, learning what it means to become a father, and supporting his wife through pregnancy and childbirth.

Preparing for a Handicapped Child

Brazelton (1979) suggests that expectant parents also engage in another less obvious, yet important task: preparation for the possibility of a handicapped child. Brazelton's colleagues conducted psychoanalytic interviews weekly with expectant mothers and monthly with fathers during the last trimester of pregnancy. The purpose of the interviews was to ascertain "what kind of people they were" in hopes of predicting "what kinds of parents" they would become. When parents were given a chance to share their innermost thoughts during the interviews, Brazelton's colleagues discovered the expectant parents to be filled with inner turmoil. Many doubted their abilities to be an effective parent, and expressed ambivalence about wanting the child, and fears about bearing a damaged child. The expectant parents' fears and concerns were so pronounced that Brazelton's colleagues predicted that all the fathers would become paranoid schizophrenics and all the mothers would be severely depressed!

Of course, follow-up visits showed both fathers and mothers to be healthy parents. While the interviews clearly failed to show predictive validity, Brazelton suggests they point out an important function of the expectant parents' thinking: The couple's anxiety, ambivalence, and fears prepare them to cope with *any* child they may bear—active, passive, or handicapped. By anticipating the possibility of a handicapped child, parents rehearse some coping strategies and are somewhat better prepared for the shock that accompanies the birth of a handicapped child.

Couples who receive the results of amniocentesis may need to make their initial adjustment to their child's confirmed handicap during this stage. Improved medical technology has made amniocentesis a relatively safe and accepted means of diagnosing over 100 diseases. For many at-risk expectant parents, amniocentesis can assure them that their child does not have a genetic defect.

The Impact of Therapeutic Abortion

If the fetus is genetically defective, according to researchers, families may pay a psychiatric price when they elect a therapeutic abortion upon being told their child is "genetically defective." While women who undergo an elective abortion often experience emotional and psychological effects, undergoing a therapeutic abortion for genetic defects is more traumatic for several reasons. Women who choose elective abortions for psychosocial or socioeconomic reasons during the first trimester of pregnancy appear to be at minimal risk for negative long-term psychological sequelae (Blumberg & Golbus, 1975). These pregnancies are usually unplanned and the abortions are performed early in the pregnancy, before the onset of quickening.

Therapeutic abortions, on the other hand, are usually performed on mothers who had welcomed the pregnancy. Compounding the trauma of terminating a desired pregnancy is the fact that having anmiocentesis makes a second-trimester abortion necessary. Amniocentesis to detect hereditary disease or congenital defects is performed at 14 or 16 weeks of fetal gestation (U.S. Department of Health, Education, and Welfare, 1979), and after the procedure, four weeks are needed for cell culture and analysis. By this time the fetus has begun to quicken, or move, which causes parents to begin to perceive it as a potential "future child" with all the corresponding fantasies and hopes (Blumberg, Golbus, & Hanson, 1975). Because the resulting therapeutic abortion takes place during the fourth month of pregnancy, it cannot be performed by aspiration as is the case during the first weeks of pregnancy. Couples who elect abortion following an unfavorable diagnosis experience physical and emotional effects that are not unlike those experienced by parents of a stillborn child (Silvestre & Fresco, 1980).

According to the study by Blumberg et al. (1975), the decision to terminate a pregnancy because of a genetic defect is one of the more shocking and traumatic experiences that a married couple endure. The majority of couples studied by Adler and Kushnick (1982) reported that the termination of pregnancy was a tragic event. The termination was preceded by a 24- to 36-hour waiting period. They reported that for the women, this period of waiting to terminate the life of a moving fetus was agonizing. Blumberg et al.'s (1975) study of 13 families that had undergone amniocentesis and elective abortion revealed that 12 of 13 (92%) of the women and 9 of 11 (82%) of the men were seriously depressed.

Couples in Adler and Kushnick's (1982) study of 15 families revealed that most mothers experienced a brief period of denial followed by a combination of feelings: sadness over losing the baby, relief that it was over, guilt, bitterness as to why it happened to them and not to others, and doubts about their ability to reproduce satisfactorily. For the majority of mothers, this phase lasted two to three months, and in some cases persisted more than one year. Husbands in this study saw themselves as the family "realists." According to the authors, their decisions seemed to require less soul-searching as compared with their wives.

Despite the emotional trauma of the procedure, most couples in both studies reported they would repeat the course of action, and consider a therapeutic abortion preferable to the alternative birth of a genetically defective child.

Because families who abort a genetically defective fetus are at risk for psychological sequelae, Blumberg et al. (1975) strongly recommend that physicians inform the couple of the experiences of others, and discuss the method of abortion in order to promote a well-considered decision. Following the abortion, they strongly recommend that couples receive supportive counseling or psychotherapy.

Improved technology may lessen the trauma of abortion following amniocentesis. A relatively new procedure, chorionic villi sampling (CVS) may be performed at 8 to 10 weeks gestation. It is a painless procedure that does not involve the insertion of a needle into the amniotic cavity. Instead, it samples the tissue outside of the developing embryo by means of a plastic catheter that is introduced into the vagina and through the cervical opening. The results of the genetic analyses, either chromosomal or biochemical, can be completed in 25 hours. If a genetic defect is detected, elective abortion is possible in the first trimester of pregnancy (Pergament, Ginsberg, Verlinsky, & Halperin, 1984).

Carrying a Defective Fetus to Term

Unfortunately, little research is available on parents who, following the diagnosis of a genetically defective fetus, elect to carry the fetus to term. It is reasonable to presume, however, that these parents will spend the rest of the pregnancy in shock and grieving, anticipating the birth of the defective child. For fathers, the developmental tasks noted by Duvall (1962) will take on new, ironic meanings. Not only must the father plan for the child's arrival, but now he must anticipate an impending tragedy requiring skills, resources, and services with which he may be unfamiliar. The developmental task of supporting his wife will also take on a new meaning. Instead of joining his wife in hopeful anticipation, he may have to comfort his wife in their mutual sorrow. They may regret having had the amniocentesis. Said one expectant father after learning that his yet-to-be born son had Down syndrome:

> I don't know why we even had the amniocentesis. They recommended it because my wife is 36 years old. But we're not the type to have an abortion. It really hasn't helped knowing — my wife just cries all of the time.

While amniocentesis and CVS can help predict if a child will be born with a handicap, such knowledge will not be without costs to the parents. Parents who receive a positive diagnosis for a genetic defect will not only be forced to consider or reconsider moral questions regarding abortion and quality-of-life issues, but they will also face a profound loss as well. The feared tragedy is now confirmed, and the time of pregnancy, once filled with hope and anticipation, now becomes a time for resolving painfully difficult moral dilemmas.

Stage Three: The Child Bearing Years

The birth of a child, especially a first child, signals many changes for the family: not only does a new dependent individual enter the family's social equation, but new roles and redefinitions of old roles are required of family members. As the first child is born, so are new family roles "born." Wives become mothers; husbands become fathers; parents become grandparents; only children become siblings.

Fathers' Developmental Tasks

Below are developmental tasks, adapted from Duvall (1962), that fathers will face during the childbearing years:

1. *Reconciling conflicting conceptions of his role as a father.* While many men grew up with a narrow definition of the role of the father, many are eager to actively participate in the daily routines of child-rearing (Young & Hamilton, 1979). Consequently, many men will need to resolve the discrepancies between the fathering role they grew up with and the role they would like to assume.

2. *Accepting his share of responsibilities for the child.* As the father's role changes, so will the nature of his involvement with his child. One of the most noteworthy changes is fathers' participation in caregiving responsibilities. The level of a father's involvement in caregiving activities will be reflected in the strength of the child's attachment to the father, according to a study by Kotelchuck (1976). He observed that children who did not relate to their fathers (as indicated by children who spent less than 15 seconds with fathers upon their arrival) were primarily from families where the father was seldom the caregiver. Ross, Kagan, Zelazo, and Kotelchuck (1975) found a significant relationship between the child's attachment behaviors and the number of diapers changed by the father in a week! Kotelchuck (1976) suggested that there seems to be a minimum level of paternal caregiving necessary for a relationship to exist. Lewis and Weinraub (1974) suggest that fathers need to be encouraged to assume more caregiving responsibilities to strengthen father-infant attachment.

3. *Maintaining breadwinner status.* Despite fathers' increasing interest in being more involved in the daily lives of their young children, and despite the increase in working mothers (45% of all mothers of preschool age children work, according to the U.S. Department of Labor, 1980 statistics), most fathers are still accorded the breadwinner's role in the family. Because employers rarely promote people who work less than full time, and because job sharing remains more of an ideal than a reality, many fathers face the same dilemma as single parents or so-called "super-moms." That is, how can a father provide for his family's economic well-being, remain involved and available to his children, and still have time and energy for his wife and himself?

4. *Conforming to new regimens that incorporate the child's needs.* First-time fathers will experience, first-hand, the effects of an infant whose needs will take priority over those of other family members. The infant's sleep and feeding schedules will require major adjustments in the father's life.

5. *Encouraging the child's full development.* The growing research on fathers and their young children strongly suggests that fathers affect their children's development in significant ways. A father's greatest contribution to his child's early development appears to be his role as the child's play partner. While researchers found that mothers were more likely to pick up their babies for caregiving purposes, fathers most often held their children to play with them (Lamb, 1976). Moreover, fathers' play is clearly different than mothers' play. Power and Parke (in press) found that fathers of 8-month-old infants engaged in significantly more physical games, such as bouncing or lifting, than mothers. Regarding the fathers' style, Brazelton states: "The father adds a different dimension (than the mother), a sort of play dimension, teaching the baby about some of the ups and downs — and also teaching the baby another important thing: how to get back in control" (Collins, 1979, p. 50). Fathers' play may also have an important impact on the child's later social and cognitive development (Clarke-Stewart, 1980; Pedersen & Robson, 1969). In a summary of studies on paternal characteristics, Weinraub (1979) concluded that the characteristics of the father that are most clearly related to optimal child development, particularly in boys, include paternal warmth, acceptance, and involvement.

6. *Redefining himself as a father.* For many men, becoming a father will profoundly change their lives. Many men regard fatherhood as a rewarding time of personal redefinition. Parke (1981) noted: "Fathering often helps men clarify their values and set priorities. It may enhance their self-esteem if they manage its demands and responsibilities well" (p. 11).

Adjusting to the Father's Role

The husband's adjustment to fatherhood can be profound. If he is becoming a parent for the first time, he experiences a major developmental milestone in his own life that makes him take stock of his accomplishments and his satisfaction with his career, family, and marriage. A new baby may stimulate him to reexamine his life goals.

Numerous researchers have found that both mothers and fathers often experience depression and mild stress after the birth of a new child. These feelings may result from fatigue, economic worries, changes in routine, and role adjustments. Becoming a father is a happy, but at times difficult experience.

Greenberg and Morris (1974) studied fathers' reactions to their newborn infants and used the term engrossment to describe the bond that develops between father and infant. More than mere involvement of a father and his infant, engrossment refers to that point in the father-infant relationship when the infant assumes an integral role in the father's life, and the father, in turn, feels an increased sense of self-esteem and worth. The authors note seven characteristics of engrossment:

1. *Visual awareness of the newborn.* The father perceives his newborn to be attractive or beautiful.
2. *Tactile awareness of newborn.* The father desires and derives pleasure from contact with his newborn child.
3. *Awareness of distinct characteristics of the newborn.* The father becomes aware of and can describe the unique characteristics of his child.
4. *Perception of the infant as perfect.*
5. *Feelings of strong attachment to the newborn.* The father forms a strong attachment to his child, and consequently he focuses much of his attention on the newborn.
6. *Feelings of extreme elation.*
7. *Feelings of increased self-worth.* For many men, becoming a father for the first time provides opportunities for personal reflection and redefinition.

A father's joy and the child's appeal, as demonstrated by these characteristics of engrossment, will help a father compensate for many of the adjustments he will have to make in his life.

The Initial Crisis of the Child's Diagnosis

Given the anticipation the father experiences prior to the child's birth and the father's readiness to attach to his child, it is not difficult to understand the impact that a child who is diagnosed as handicapped will have on the father.

A crisis for a family has been defined as an event that creates unusual difficulties for the family (Kirkpatrick, 1955). An event that is permanent and involuntary (such as a child's handicap) will create a greater crisis (Price-Bonham & Addison, 1978) than an event that is discrete or short term. According to Wikler (1981), the impact of the child's diagnosis will be the most disturbing crisis parents will face during the handicapped child's life. However, as we shall see, it will not be the last crisis.

Wikler contends that parents of handicapped children will be subject to periodic, stressful crises throughout their children's lives. These crises fall into two categories: those crises that occur when there is a discrepancy between their expectations for the child's development and their child's actual progress; and those experienced only by families with handicapped children.

When parents receive their child's diagnosis, parents' dreams for their fantasized ideal child are often abruptly crushed. Parental grief is often exacerbated by professionals' insensitivity at the time of diagnosis. Price-Bonham and Addison (1978) note seven major errors professionals make relative to informing parents of a child's disability: delay in defining the problem, false encouragement of parents, too much advice on matters such as institutionalization, abruptness, being hurried, a lack of interest, and a hesitancy to communicate.

Roos (1978), a father of a mentally retarded child as well as a professional in the field of special education, bitterly recalls the insensitivity he and his wife experienced at the time of his son's diagnosis. He writes of the doctor's reluctance and delays in sharing the diagnosis, and the "parent as patient" attitude reflected by the physician who offered Roos and his wife tranquilizers when they expressed anxiety over their child's condition. Roos claims that many doctors regard mental retardation with "professional hopelessness" because they are impotent to cure it. This negative attitude and subsequent mistreatment of parents occurs at such a vulnerable time that it can increase parents' grief and jeopardize their future relationships with doctors and other professionals.

None of the fathers of children with Down syndrome that Erickson (1974) met with knew anything about the disability at the time of their child's diagnosis. Some fathers reported difficulty obtaining information from the doctors, and others only learned about the disability after their wives had been informed. The fathers recommended that professionals wait to inform the parents of the diagnosis until both parents are together, and provide parents with a supportive and knowledgeable person to talk to during this time. As one father said: "There is no optimal time to be told your child has Down syndrome but there is an optimal way in which parents can be informed" (Erickson, 1974, p. 23).

Adaptation after the Initial Diagnosis

Following the diagnosis, the parents may grieve the loss of the hoped-for child. It is during this time that parents may, in their anger and frustration, seek to hold someone — themselves, their spouse, their doctors, or God — responsible for their child's handicap. When the evidence of the handicap is not clear, as it is with Down syndrome, but slow to emerge, parents may alternately accept and deny the existence of the handicap. The following three excerpts from Josh Greenfeld's *A Child Called Noah* (1979a) illustrate one family's denial, realization, and blame:

> Noah still strikes me as sluggish, apathetic, not very alert. But Foumi's convinced he's all right. I worry about him in a deep way. (p. 39)

> Let's face it: Noah has temper tantrums, he does not walk by himself, he is unable to talk coherently. We live in a shadow of a doubt and worry about him constantly. (p. 48)

When I stay home all day and observe Noah constantly it becomes apparent to me that he is a disturbed child. I cannot get angry with him. I cannot get angry with myself. I cannot get angry with Foumi. But she can get angry at me and America. Wanting children in general was always a vanity of mine; she did not want children at all. She particularly did not want to have a child when she was pregnant with Noah. But being broke and in America, an abortion could not be seriously considered at the time. . . .Also we wonder about the obstetrician now, did she induce Noah's birth too early? Did she deprive Noah of proper nourishment by insisting that the eighty-eight-pound Foumi diet? (p. 53)

Shit! I wish we had not induced him. . . .I thought by marrying outside of my race that bad genes — the diabetes on my father's side, the mental illness of cousins on my mother's side — could be eliminated. Instead, I have further scattered bad genes. (p. 61)

Josh Greenfeld's concern about his son's delay and his wife's denial of the problem is an example of how husbands and wives may adapt in different styles and at different paces to their child's handicap. Differences in adaptation can place added stress on marriages (Price-Bonham & Addison, 1978). Opportunities to effectively support one another may be diminished if, for instance, one parent is grieving and the other is worried about the burden of care presented by the child's special needs (Wikler, 1981).

The impact that the child's handicap will have on the father has been investigated by several authors and researchers. Cummings (1976) noted that because fathers are playing a larger role with their children, "there is increasing likelihood of fathers experiencing the handicaps more immediately and sentiently than did fathers only two generations ago" (p. 247).

His survey of fathers with mentally retarded children revealed that fathers were often depressed and preoccupied with their children's special needs, many felt inferior as fathers, and many were dissatisfied with their children and spouses.

Fathers have also been found to perceive their handicapped child as a threat to their self-concept. Fathers who view their handicapped child as an extension of their egos are apt to become more isolated and to reduce or withdraw from social interactions (Call, 1958; Illingworth, 1967).

The sex of the handicapped child appears to have an effect on the father. Tallman (1965), Farber (1972), and Farber, Jenne and Toigo (1960) found that the child's handicap had a greater initial impact on the father if the retarded child was a boy. Fathers may also be especially vulnerable to extrafamilial influences and social stigma caused by the child's handicap (Tallman, 1965).

The difficulties experienced by fathers may have second-order effects on other family members. Several authors have suggested that the father's attitude may set the pattern for the attitudes that other family members in the home form about the handicap (Peck & Stephens, 1960; Price-Bonham & Addison, 1978). Farber's (1972) finding that parents of a retarded boy show a lower degree of marital integration than parents of a retarded girl supports this notion (Peck & Stephens, 1960; Turnbull, Brotherson, Summers, & Turnbull, in press). The greater impact on the father by the retarded son will affect the couple's marital integration.

The father's reaction to the diagnosis will influence the impact of the child on the marriage. Tavormina, Ball, Dunn, Luscomb, and Taylor (1977), in an unpublished manuscript as noted by Gallagher, Cross, and Scharfman (1981), suggest that there are four major parental styles in adapting to the crisis of having a handicapped child:

1. The father divorces himself from the child, absorbing himself in work or outside activities, leaving the mother entirely responsible for the child.
2. Both parents reject the child, who is often institutionalized as a result.
3. The child becomes the center of the family's universe, and all family members subordinate their needs to accommodate the handicapped child.
4. Both parents jointly support the child and each other while maintaining their individual identities and an approximation of normal family life.

Disproportionately high desertion rates by fathers of handicapped children have been reported (Reed & Reed, 1965) as well as high divorce rates in families with handicapped children (Tew, Lawrence, Payne, & Rawnsley, 1977). Some researchers (Schufeit & Wurster, 1976) claim that, when matched for social class, the divorce rate for families with mentally retarded children does *not* differ significantly from the rate for families with nonhandicapped children. Turnbull et al. (in press) attempt to resolve the mixed research results by suggesting that for many marriages, the impact of a child's handicap can be the "straw that breaks the camel's back."

Conversely, many families claim that a child's handicap has strengthened their marriage and brought the family closer together. Gath's (1977) study showed that while negative measures were higher for families of children with Down syndrome, this group also had higher positive measures when compared to families with nonhandicapped children. Almost half of the couples surveyed felt that their marriage was strengthened after the birth of the handicapped child.

It is important to note that each parent's reaction to the diagnosis will be unique and will depend, in addition to other factors, upon the supports available, the severity of the infant's handicaps, and the child's prognosis. These intervening variables will be discussed later in the chapter.

Stage Four: Families with Preschool Children

A family with a preschooler will devote considerable time and energy to encouraging their child's development. Duvall (1962) outlines many of the developmental tasks required of a preschooler:

1. Settling into healthful daily routines of rest and activity.
2. Mastering good eating habits.
3. Developing physical skills appropriate to the child's stage of motor development.
4. Mastering the basics of toilet training.
5. Becoming a participating member of the family.
6. Beginning to master his or her impulses and to conform to others' expectations.
7. Developing healthy emotional expressions for a wide variety of experiences.
8. Learning to communicate effectively with an increasing number of others.
9. Developing an ability to handle potentially dangerous situations.
10. Learning to be an autonomous person with initiative and a conscience.

Although these significant developmental tasks always require some parental guidance and encouragement, the nonhandicapped child's acquisition of these skills is much more independent than that of the handicapped child. A developmental disability will often have significant effects on all of the child's developmental tasks. Consequently, some developmental tasks will not be accomplished during the child's preschool years, and others may never be accomplished. Normally trying periods, such as the so-called "terrible twos" may extend for several years. Developmental milestones that nonhandicapped children achieve with relative ease will require extraordinary encouragement from the handicapped child's parents and teachers.

The child's delayed development will have an impact on the parents during this stage of the family's life cycle. Because the period of intense nurturing which occurs during the child's infancy and preschool years must be sustained for a family with a developmentally disabled child, the need for one parent — usually the mother — to be home and available will also be extended (Wikler, 1981). The father's usual roles of playmate or model for his children will be diminished or nonexistent with a child who is moderately-to-severely handicapped (Gallagher, Cross, & Scharfman, 1981).

It is during this stage that the child's disabilities will become more obvious. When the child does not attain normal developmental milestones, parents are at risk for increased stress. Two of Wikler's (1981) five predictable crises resulting from a discrepancy in expectations of the child's development occur during this stage — when the child should have begun walking (12-15 months) and talking (24-30 months). These poignant reminders of their child's disability may reawaken the parents' grief for the loss of their fantasized normal child. Further, Wikler contends that as the disability becomes more apparent, parents will experience stressful stigmatized social interactions.

The Child's Impact on Parent Roles and Concerns

Because of the stigma, or physical evidence of the child's handicap, fathers and mothers may face "hostile stares, judgemental comments, murmurs of pity, and intrusive requests for personal information whenever they accompany their child to the store, on the bus, or at the park" (Wikler, 1981, p. 282). Fathers, more so than mothers, are affected by the physical aspects of a child's disability and are more sensitive to how the child may affect the family's social and community image (Price-Bonham & Addison, 1978). Fathers of handicapped preschoolers will need information on how to answer questions from relatives and strangers, encourage their child's development, and obtain additional information on the disability itself (Meyer, Vadasy, Fewell, & Schell, 1982).

Several authors have noted that fathers express more concern than mothers over future problems, such as economic and social dependency, and legal and educational matters (Hersh, 1970; Love, 1973; Meyer et al., 1982). Liversidge and Grana (1973) report that at a meeting, fathers of deaf preschoolers wondered aloud "Will she be happy?" "Will he have normal children of his own?" and "Will he be able to earn a living?"

Fathers' orientation towards the child's future is a function of traditional parental roles that may be intensified when a handicapped child is present. Fathers, according to Gumz and Gubrium (1972), have a tendency to perceive their child's mental retardation as an instrumental crisis, meaning they are especially concerned about the cost of providing for the child, the child's future success, and the child's ability to be self-supporting in the future. Mothers, conversely, have a tendency to experience the birth of a handicapped child as an expressive crisis. This means that mothers will be especially concerned with the emotional strain of caring for the retarded child, and the desire that he get along well with others, and be happy regardless of academic achievement or job success.

Although each parent's roles and concerns appear to be somewhat more defined in families with handicapped children, they are by no means exclusive. Gumz and Gubrium (1972) found that a high percentage of mothers were concerned about the high cost of raising a retarded child, and fathers of handicapped children were also concerned with the day-to-day concerns of raising a child with special needs.

Fathers at the SEFAM (Supporting Extended Family Members) Fathers Program at the University of Washington frequently discuss the emotional impact of the child's handicap on the family and other typically expressive concerns, such as feeding and toilet-training. Said one father when asked if he had changed as many diapers for his older, nonhandicapped daughter as he now does for his handicapped daughter:

> No way. I think it's more the mom's role, but it shouldn't be. It's just the way society thinks. But when you have a handicapped child, it can change your whole outlook on life. It's like someone dropped a curtain in front of you — you have to change. If you had a normal kid, things would have been trompin' along, and mom would have continued changing the diapers. But when you have a handicapped kid, you have to start thinking about new ways to do things — that means changing diapers and stuff. (Meyer, 1982)

Like mothers, fathers desire to do something that will ameliorate their child's disability. However, many fathers — as well as mothers — are uncertain of what their role should be. Gallagher et al. (1981) studied parents of young handicapped children and found that:

> Across all groups there was general agreement that there should be more father involvement with the handicapped child. The fact that this does *not* happen or *has not* happened is an area in need of investigation, but there is no doubt that it *should* happen (p. 12).

Fathers Program Needs and Benefits

Parent involvement components of early intervention programs have the potential to facilitate fathers' involvement with their handicapped children. However, many so-called parent programs are functionally "mother programs" because they are often held at times inconvenient for fathers, and tend to reflect mothers' concerns (Meyer et al., 1982). Markowitz's (1983) exploratory study reported several factors determining fathers' participation in preschool programs. Interviewing directors of preschool programs for young handicapped children, Markowitz found that:

- Almost 50% of the directors reported that fathers who had a traditional concept of parents' roles were less likely to become involved in their child's education.
- Forty percent mentioned that fathers are more likely to become involved if the child has a special meaning to the father (namesake, first born, first son).
- Two thirds of the directors noted that the fathers' work schedule will influence fathers' level of involvement. They reported that fathers who do shiftwork, are unemployed, or have flexible schedules are

often more involved than fathers who have traditional work schedules.

- Over 50% of the directors also noted that fathers will be more likely to be involved if the child has a severe or specific handicap (such as Down syndrome or cerebral palsy) than if the child has a mild or unspecified developmental delay. This suggests to Markowitz that fathers may need or want more evidence of the child's disability than mothers to convince them that their participation is important.

Markowitz also concluded that fathers who do participate are in their mid-20s to early 30s in age, and are more educated than those who do not participate. However, Crowley, Keane, and Needham (1982) reported active involvement in a group of lower- to middle-class fathers of deaf children in the economically depressed South Bronx.

Programs especially designed for fathers, reflective of their often instrumental concerns, and held at times convenient to fathers may be helpful. SEFAM's Fathers Program has reported that fathers who had participated in the program reported significantly less stress, guilt, and depression than newly enrolled fathers. Fathers in the program also reported more satisfaction on several measures. Wives of men who had participated in the program also reported less stress, pessimism, and depression, as well as greater satisfaction than wives of newly enrolled fathers (Vadasy, Fewell, Meyer, & Greenberg, in press). This suggests that programs for fathers of handicapped preschoolers may be valuable for fathers and provide second-order benefits for mothers as well.

These benefits to both parents can be especially helpful for parents of handicapped children in the preschool stage of the family life cycle. It is during this stage that the child's disability can permanently affect the parents' relationship. Mothers may expend prolonged periods of time attending to the child's needs, and fathers may "view the retarded child as interfering with his previously companionate relationship with his wife" (Farber & Ryckman, 1965, p. 1). Couples may go years without socializing outside of the home (Illingworth, 1967). Many may give up activities they previously enjoyed together, according to Schonnell and Watts (1956), who also found that more fathers (26%) than mothers (18%) report having to alter their social life.

Stage Five: Families With School Age Children

Families with nonhandicapped children use this stage to encourage the child's continuing independence and growth. According to Duvall (1962), children in this stage will accomplish the following developmental tasks: (a) learning the basic academic, emotional, and life skills required by school children; (b) mastering the appropriate physical skills; (c) developing meaningful understanding for the use of money; (d) becoming an active, cooperative family member; (e) increasing abilities to relate effectively to others, both peers and adults; and (f) continuing to learn to handle feelings and impulses.

As with the previous stage, a child's handicap will deeply affect the goals that are expected of and attained by a child at this stage.

Parents will be at-risk for stress at the very beginning of this stage. Wikler (1981) contends that the beginning of public school — when the child enters a special education program instead of kindergarten or first grade — is a stressful period for parents of handicapped children. They are reminded of the child's delay in a new way, and experience a social stigma. By being placed in a special education classroom, the child, and therefore the family, is publicly labeled as different.

Even parents who desire to have their children "mainstreamed" with nonhandicapped children may experience stress when they are reminded frequently of the discrepancy between their child and the nonhandicapped peers (Gallagher, Beckman, & Cross, 1983). According to a review by Turnbull and Blacher-Dixon (1980), other aspects of mainstreaming that may be stressful for parents are: sharing the handicapped child's stigma, feeling a lack of common interests with the other parents, worrying about their child's social adjustment, or providing support services necessary for the handicapped child in the nonhandicapped school setting.

As the discrepancy grows between the child's size and developmental capabilities, Wikler says, parents will experience increased stressful public encounters. Chronic problems, such as a lack of feeding or ambulatory skills, will be more burdensome as the child grows older and larger. The behavior, health, or seizure problems that handicapped children often have can be stressful, and they are exacerbated as the child grows older.

> We thought we were, for the most part through with the toilet cleanup details that no matter how much we rationalize and intellectualize are utterly demoralizing. But last night Noah let loose again in his training pants — his second accident of the day. (Greenfeld, 1979b, p. 5)

Because of the difficulty parents often face obtaining qualified baby sitters, respite-care opportunities for family members may be decreased as the child grows. Another problem parents of schoolage handicapped children often face is obtaining adequate information about coping and managing daily living tasks for handicapped children of this age. When available, management programs and books often address the problems of younger children instead of the chronic problems parents of older children may face.

Fathers' Negative Perceptions of Child and Self

As mentioned earlier, a father's expectations and acceptance of the handicapped child often play a large role in determining the family's attitudes toward the child. Fathers' perceptions of the handicapped child may, however, be influenced by external sources, such as the child's school placement. Meyerowitz (1967) compared three groups of children: moderately retarded children in a special class, moderately retarded children in a regular class, and nonhandicapped children in a regular class. Meyerowitz reported that fathers favored the retarded children placed in the regular class. The fathers of the moderately retarded children in the special class had a poorer estimation of their children's abilities and lower occupational expectations than did fathers of moderately retarded children placed in the regular class.

Wikler (1981) has noted other characteristics of a developmentally disabled child that may also contribute to fathers' negative perceptions. These include an increased visibility of the deviance, decreased I.Q. levels, increased age of a male disabled child (especially if over 9 years), and first-born status.

Cummings (1976) studied 60 fathers of school age children with mental retardation. Using four self-administered tests, Cummings sought to assess the fathers' prevailing mood (especially as it was influenced by the mentally retarded child), their self-esteem (both generally and in terms of the fathers' evaluations of their worth as fathers), their interpersonal satisfactions with family members and others, and their attitudes towards child-rearing.

When compared to an equal number of fathers of nonhandicapped children, Cummings found that fathers of mentally retarded children showed significant differences on three of the four variables. On the variable of prevailing mood, fathers of mentally retarded children were depressed and preoccupied with their children's special needs. The interpersonal satisfaction variables revealed significant decreases in the fathers' enjoyment of index children, and in their evaluation of their wives and other children. Self-esteem variables revealed that these fathers scored lower on expressed self-acceptance and a sense of paternal competence. According to Cummings, this suggests that these fathers may feel relatively inferior in their roles as fathers, and in their male roles.

When clustered by age, Cummings found that fathers of older handicapped children (9-13 years) showed slightly lower psychological stress levels than did fathers of younger (4-8 years) handicapped children. Older fathers also showed slightly lower ratings on depression, and higher ratings on both enjoyment of child and evaluation of wife.

These data, however, are inconsistent with studies reviewed by Gallagher, Beckman, and Cross (1983), which suggest that the child's increasing age is related to increased stress, due to the increasing difficulty of managing the older handicapped child and the greater visibility of the handicap.

Stage Six: Families With Teenagers

Teenage years are a period usually characterized by the adolescents' attempts to establish their own identity and differentiate themselves from their parents. Again, the experiences for families with handicapped children will be considerably different.

Duvall (1962) contends that nonhandicapped teenagers will need to confront the following developmental tasks:

1. Accepting one's changing body and learning to use it effectively.
2. Achieving a satisfying and socially accepted sex role.
3. Achieving more mature relations with agemates.
4. Achieving emotional independence from parents and other adults.
5. Preparing for an occupation and economic independence.
6. Preparing for marriage and family life.
7. Developing a workable philosophy of life that makes sense in today's world.

In every instance, the handicapped adolescent's experiences will be often disturbingly different from the experiences of a nonhandicapped teenager, causing special concern for the handicapped adolescent's parents. While the handicapped adolescent's body may change, the individual's cognitive handicap may limit his or her appreciation of the changes. Instead of achieving more mature relations with agemates, the adolescent's developmental delay may become increasingly apparent as his body approximates an adult's while his abilities remain those of a much younger child, thus making it increasingly difficult for peers to accept the adolescent.

Although a handicapped adolescent may be preparing for a future occupation, the prospects for economic independence are usually dim. A mentally retarded son's lack of vocational opportunity can be very troubling for fathers. Not only do fathers fear the long-term financial support that might be necessary (Hersh, 1970), but because a mentally retarded son will not achieve his father's aspirations, the father may feel deprived of the satisfaction of a son's achievements. The handicapped adolescent's emerging sexuality may be especially troubling when he or she lacks the cognitive skills to be a capable, nurturing parent.

The onset of puberty, the beginning of menstruation in a girl, and parental concerns over the child's sexuality will cause stress for parents of handicapped adolescents (Wikler, 1981). This stress is stimulated by the discrepancy between the adolescent's physical appearance and his or her mental and social abilities. Compounding this stress is parents' fears that their child will be sexually exploited.

Although this stage poses troubling problems for handicapped teenagers and their families, the picture is not totally bleak. Parents of handicapped children who successfully weather these crises often experience great personal growth. Rud Turnbull, a father of a teenage, moderately retarded son and a lawyer specializing in disability law, demonstrates a father's potential for personal growth in this period:

> Jay forces me to deal with paradoxes: about how the exceptional in life (mental retardation) becomes unexceptional by reason of its familiarity, about how a person's disability (Jay's) contributes to another's ability (mine) by stimulating growth, and about how the mysteries of life (why me?) are answered, bit by bit, ever so certainly. (Turnbull et al., in press, p. 3)

Stage Seven: Families as Launching Centers

This stage typically begins when a family's first child leaves home as a young adult, and ends when the last child leaves home, leaving the parents with an "empty nest." Young adults, during this stage, may engage in the following developmental tasks: (a) pursuing advanced education, (b) beginning a career, (c) learning to appraise and express feelings of love in an adult manner, and (d) choosing a marriage partner (Duvall, 1962).

For families with a handicapped child, this "launching" stage may occur earlier or much later than usual. It may take place much earlier than usual for families who institutionalize their handicapped child, and may extend for the life of the child if the child lives with the parents as an adult.

Fathers of children with handicaps may anticipate this stage for years before it actually occurs. Vadasy, Fewell, Meyer, Schell, and Greenberg (1984) found that fathers of very young handicapped children are already concerned about the child's future well-being as an adult. While fathers of nonhandicapped children can look forward to a time when their children are independent and their expenses are reduced, fathers with handicapped children may be required to support the more dependent adult handicapped son or daughter emotionally and financially (Price-Bonham & Addison, 1978). This support throughout the adulthood of the handicapped individual will crystallize the relationship at a parent-child status (Birenbaum, 1971) rather than allowing the relationship to develop into a more mature form.

Wikler (1981) notes that at this stage, parents may face three significant crises: the child's 21st birthday, the question of placement of the handicapped child outside of the home, and the question of guardianship and care for the handicapped adult.

The handicapped young adult's 21st birthday can be an especially troubling milestone for families. For the families Wikler studied, the handicapped child's 21st birthday was the second most stressful crisis for parents, following the initial diagnosis. The 21st birthday is a double crisis: while it normally symbolizes the young adult's independence, parents of a handicapped child will be reminded of the child's many needs before he or she can achieve independence. Further, the 21st birthday will signal a transitional crisis: schools will cease to provide services after this age, and adult services are often inadequate. Even when services such as group homes and sheltered workshops are available, parents will need to reassume many of the responsibilities that school staff had assumed to assure the child's well-being once he or she becomes ineligible for educational services.

De Boor's (1975) study of a father with a mildly retarded 21-year-old daughter finds him facing situations that other fathers may never face: bills from various agencies and doctors; his daughter's promiscuity, immaturity, and her inabilty to hold a job; and bureaucracies that are now seen as adversaries rather than allies. The father is no more certain of what will become of his daughter at age 21 than he was when she was seven. De Boor's study supports Wikler's (1981) contention that for many parents, the responsibilities for their handicapped child will increase instead of decrease with the child's age, as will the burden of care.

The Decision to Institutionalize

For parents who decide to place their child outside of the home, this stage may come unusually early. Deciding to place a child outside of the home is never an easy decision. Twenty-five years ago, parents were often urged to institutionalize their retarded children (Caldwell & Guze, 1960). More recently, in a spirit of deinstitutionalization, more parents are encouraged to keep their retarded children at home. For many parents, especially those who have children with handicaps that demand almost constant supervision, the decision to institutionalize or not becomes a Hobson's choice. Keeping the child at home can become an unbearable burden for a family; yet they cannot face the prospect of placing the child in what is usually an inadequate institution. Two excerpts from Josh Greenfeld's *A Place for Noah* (1979b) illustrate this:

> . . .I watch Noah guardedly. It is only a question of time before we will have to put him away. He is simply too retarded, too unable to take care of himself on an elementary level. The decision will somehow make itself. . . .(p. 28)

> Today we saw the future, Noah's future. We went to Letchworth Village, a fifty-year-old New York State institution in Rockland County. . .When I came home I looked at Noah. I had seen his fate—

sooner or later he will have to go to one of these places. I thought about it and shuddered. My impression of Letchworth was worse than my memory of a visit to Dachau. I vowed I would have to send Noah to a better place, one where he would not be irrevocably and irretrievably lost. (p. 28-29)

As Greenfeld discovers, adequate residential facilities are few and far between. However, even placing a child in an apparently adequate facility appears to have a psychic cost for parents. Hersh's (1970) study of families who placed their mildly mentally retarded children (age range 6-19 years) in a private facility with an excellent reputation revealed that:

Certain parental responses. . .were so repetitive as to suggest a near universality of response in the group studied. The central themes were identified as loss, relief, guilt and ambivalence, and fulfillment and a sense of well-being. (p. 99)

The sense of loss and relief, the author explains, often promoted guilt or ambivalence. If the parent was unable to prove that the institutionalized child was receiving services the family and community could not provide, the parental adjustment and the child's placement were both in jeopardy. This study also noted that when parents lose the option of maintaining an active parental role, it can cause them great anxiety.

The inverse, deinstitutionalization, is not without its costs to parents. According to Gallagher, Beckman, and Cross (1983), deinstitutionalization is often associated with increased stress to parents. They cite research (Fotheringham, Skelton, & Hoddinot, 1972) that showed "declines in family functioning were associated with declines in the child's intellectual development for children who remained at home but not for children who were institutionalized" (p. 14).

Stage Eight: Families in the Middle Years

The eighth stage in the life cycle, according to Duvall (1962), begins when the last child leaves home, and continues until the retirement of the principal breadwinner or the death of one of the spouses. Typically, this is one of the longest stages (Duvall estimates an average of 14 years). This stage may end abruptly at a spouse's premature death. Conversely, it may be delayed indefinitely by the presence of a dependent child who continues to live with the parents.

Parents of handicapped children often fall into the latter category, especially if their child is living at home with them. Parents of older handicapped children cannot anticipate enjoying many of the activities available to parents of nonhandicapped children of adult age (Birenbaum, 1971). Unless they have other children, they cannot look forward to the special joys of becoming grandparents. Parents of handicapped children will not be able to enjoy the freedom normally associated when children reach adulthood. Bob Helsel (Helsel & Helsel, 1978), a father of a 30-year-old man with cerebral palsy and mental retardation, states:

> . . .It seems to me as I approach retirement age and would like lots of personal freedom, [my son] will present a problem in limiting my ability to go where I want when I want. I don't know whether a solution will be found to give me the freedom that I would like to have or whether we'll just continue to be somewhat limited because of Robin. . . .(p. 107)

As the handicapped child and his parents grow older, the handicapped child — now an adult — may be even more difficult to manage emotionally as well as physically. Bob Helsel conveys his inability to make his son happier.

> . . .I feel frustration in that I can't relieve his frustration, so my feelings about Robin and my attitudes toward him are certainly different than they were when he was young. Simply, as he has changed, I have changed; not in a way that makes me less accepting. As I just mentioned, I feel more frustrated with Robin now than I ever did before. . . .I wish I could help him recapture the kind of attitudes he displayed as a youngster. I wish I could relieve his frustration. I wish I could make him a happier person. But I don't know how to do this and I don't know whether anyone can do it. It just bugs me; it is a constant thing. (pp. 105-106)

Stage Nine: Aging Families

The final stage of the family life cycle begins with retirement, continues through the death of one spouse, and ends with the death of the second spouse. The challenge of this stage, Duvall (1962) contends, is maintaining ego integrity and avoiding the despair which may darken the final years. The goal for this stage of the cycle is successful aging through continued activity and comfortable disengagement.

The developmental tasks an aging father may confront are:

1. Finding life meaningful after retirement.
2. Adjusting to the income of a retired worker.
3. Making satisfactory living arrangements with his wife.
4. Keeping well and maintaining physical health.
5. Maintaining social contacts and responsibilities.
6. Finding emotional satisfaction in intimate contacts with his loved ones.
7. Facing the possibility of death in constructive ways.

During these years, a handicapped adult child may pose special problems for aging parents that their peers will not have to face. Now, with the prospect of death looming larger in their lives than ever before, parents will worry about their child's care after they die. Bob Helsel (1978) notes:

> I suppose this is the biggest worry that a parent of a severely handicapped child has—what happens when I die? And there is no answer to that. As far as I know, there is no way to provide properly for him in the eventuality—at least I don't know of any. . .You can't amass enough capital to set up a private home for such a person. There just isn't an answer or a way to provide properly for such a child after your death. (p. 106)

During this stage, parents not only usually expect to provide less and less care to their children, but aging parents often rely on their adult children to care for them when they become too old or too sick to care for themselves. Unless there are also nonhandicapped children in the family, parents will not be able to rely on the possibility of care or support for their later years.

However, the presence of a handicapped child in the family can actually benefit some aging families by continuing to provide parents with meaningful roles. Bob Helsel's wife Elsie, offers this perspective:

> My husband and I will not have a footloose, carefree, romantic retirement lifestyle, but we will have something else—we will have the opportunity to feel needed as long as Robin needs us. (Helsel & Helsel, 1978, p. 100)

When older parents who have cared for their adult handicapped child at home are denied this sense of purpose, either through illness, a spouse's death, or infirmity, it can be especially hard on them. Josh Greenfeld noted in his journal:

> Last night I went to a meeting of the board at Noah's school. At the end of the meeting I was talking to the board president when an elderly man approached. "How's it going, Jim?" the president asked. Jim replied: "I miss him something awful." The president explained to me: "Jim's wife died during the winter. And Jim soon found he couldn't take care of his twenty-three-year-old son anymore and had to put him away!" "The house," Jim went on saying "feels awful empty". (Greenfeld, 1979a, p. 173)

A similar situation occurs in the cinema verite' documentary *Best Boy*. The film chronicles the experiences of a mentally retarded adult (the director's cousin) and his aging parents. At the director's insistence, the parents enrolled the son in a day activity center for the first time and placed him in a group home, all in preparation for the parents' eventual deaths. Surprisingly, the son makes the transitions quite easily. They are far less difficult for him than they are for his parents, especially his mother who during the course of the film loses the two men in her life—her husband to death, and her son to a group home. In the end it is the mother, not the son, for whom the viewer feels the most compassion. At the end of the film, the viewer learns that the mother died a year after the film was made. Given the ease of the son's transition to a life apart from his parents, one questions, in retrospect, the timing of the son's placement. The film suggests that professionals, when recommending placement of a handicapped adult outside of the home, not only consider the child's dependence on the parents, but also the aging parents' dependence on the handicapped child as a reason for living.

Implications for Supporting Fathers of Children with Special Needs

The impact of a child's disability and the experiences the father has will depend on a complex interplay of intervening variables and mediating factors that often transcend the family life cycle. Child characteristics are examples of intervening variables that will account for a range of experiences and levels of stress felt by fathers.

As a review of the life cycle literature suggests, the age of the child can be a variable in determining the amount of stress a father will experience. As the handicapped child grows, he may become more difficult to manage and his differences will become more apparent, increasing stressful situations for his parents (Farber, 1959; Price-Bonham & Addison, 1978). In addition, parents of older children with mental retardation often feel more isolated, less supported, and more in need of services than parents of young children who are retarded (Suelzle & Keenan, 1981).

The sex of the child also influences many fathers. Grossman (1972) reported that fathers are more accepting of daughters who are mentally retarded than they are of sons who are mentally retarded. A son who is mentally retarded appears to have a greater emotional impact on fathers than does a daughter who is mentally retarded (Farber, 1972).

Type and severity of handicap appears to account for differential paternal experiences. Cummings (1976) noted that fathers of mentally retarded children, when compared to fathers of chronically ill children, experience a greater negative impact. Parents of children with autism reported more overall stress, when compared to parents of children with Down syndrome and children who were served by an outpatient psychiatric clinic (Holroyd & McArthur, 1976). As children with autism grow older, they have a more stressful impact on the family and are less likely to find adequate services and community acceptance (Bristol & Schopler, 1983).

The extreme stress felt by fathers of autistic children is evident in the writings of Frank Warren (1978) and Josh Greenfeld (1979a, 1979b).

A father of a teenage son with autism, Warren's frustration with in-adequate social responses to his child's needs leads him to believe that social systems are subtly, but very effectively, killing his child. Greenfeld, who comes to refer to his older son Noah as brain damaged rather than autistic, expresses similar frustrations in finding adequate educational, medical, and residential care for his demanding son. In order to dramatize the plight of children like his son, Greenfeld (1979b) made national television appearances "advocating" mercy-killing of children like his son, contending "that if a society does not care it might as well kill, directly and swiftly and kindly, rather than indirectly and slowly and cruelly" (p. 159). While it is uncertain how many other fathers of children who are autistic or otherwise handicapped agree with Warren and Greenfeld that society is methodically killing their children, the two fathers speak strongly and clearly about the stress, frustration, and rage felt by many fathers of severely handicapped children towards society and a social service system ostensibly designed to help their children.

Mediating Factors

Throughout the family's life cycle, the family's reaction to reoccurring crises will be mediated by the family's interpretation of the stressful events, and their resources to manage those crises.

In order to cope successfully with stressful events, fathers may reinterpret or reframe the event. Turnbull et al. (in press) explain:

> Reframing involves both the ability to identify conditions that can be successfully altered and to initiate problem solving; and the ability to identify conditions beyond one's control and make attitude adjustments to live with them constructively. It is based on a positive perspective rather than a negative one. (p. 7)

As the name implies, reframing requires adjustments in a father's personal philosophy.

> It's ironical: If Noah has proven debilitating to our dreams, he has also provided the material for a kind of realization of ourselves. It's not the realization either of us anticipated or wanted, but then one cannot predetermine the scenario one is destined—or doomed— to act out, either. (Greenfeld, 1979b, p. 286)

Other fathers speak of new values and personal growth as a result of successfully coping with stresses associated with handicapped children. Said one father: "Before Eric came along I was on what you might call the corporate fast track. That's not so important to me any more. My family is more important to me now."

Given that fathers may set the pattern for a child's acceptance or rejection in the home (Peck & Stephens, 1960), a father's ability or in-ability to reframe stressful events can influence the family's emotional climate and the role the child will play in the family.

Still other fathers reframe their situation by providing support to other parents of handicapped children, often parents of newly diagnosed children. This reframing not only provides needed support, it also fosters a father's own personal growth. Being available to fathers and sharing experiences and information allows a father to transform a negative experience into a positive contribution.

Personal characteristics and access to resources can help fathers manage stressful events relating to their child's handicap. Farber (1960); Grossman (1972); Moore, Hamerlynck, Barsh, Spieker, and Jones (1982); and Rosenberg (1977) have found that class, education, and income are inversely related to stress in parents of special children.

Interpersonal supportive resources have been explored by Gallagher, Cross, and Scharfman (1981). Their data suggest that a major source of strength was the quality of the husband-wife relationship. Fathers of moderately to severely handicapped preschoolers reported that support from their wives and friends is very important, while support from neighbors is less important. In the chapter by Vadasy and Fewell (Chapter 5), the authors note that mothers of severely handicapped children also rank spousal support as most important, both when the child is young and when the child attains adolescence.

Implications for Intervention

There is a growing realization among parents and professionals in special education of the need to address the concerns of fathers of handicapped children. Cummings (1976) observed that fathers have "fewer opportunities to do something directly helpful for their handicapped child, something which provides concrete evidence of their loving, caring, and benevolent concern" (p. 253). He added that because organizations for parents and handicapped children offer fewer services for fathers, and request and obtain less participation from them, fathers have fewer opportunities to share their concerns and reduce their stress than mothers do.

One approach to correcting this neglect of fathers is to try to increase their involvement in existing programs developed with mothers' needs in mind. However, encouraging increased father attendance at meetings primarily attended by mothers may not be beneficial for either parent. When Markowitz (1983) asked representatives of early childhood special education programs how mothers behave around fathers when they both participate in programs, almost half described mothers as quieter, "taking a back seat," intimidated, or self-conscious compared to their behaviors when fathers do not participate. Only 13% of interviewees reported a positive reaction, such as increased maternal comfort, to the fathers' presence. According to almost half of the program representatives, fathers who *do* attend activities or meetings are quieter and do not share feelings, information, or experiences as readily as mothers. It appears that in the interest of providing an opportunity for parents to express their feelings openly and obtain information reflective of their often different concerns, fathers and mothers may be served better in separate programs.

A few programs specifically designed for fathers of handicapped children now exist and, according to preliminary reports, appear to benefit the participants and their families.

Crowley, Keane, and Needham (1982) reported on a program for fathers of profoundly deaf children in the South Bronx. The overall goal of the program was to improve the quality of each father's involvement in his deaf child's school and home life. Secondary goals included helping fathers learn more about deafness and cope with their feelings and attitudes. These goals were achieved through topical discussions, and informal discussions of attitudes and feelings.

While no data were presented, the authors reported that fathers found the information presented to be helpful in understanding and dealing with their deaf children. They found that fathers after one year of involvement in the program were more objective in observing their children's behavior, were more willing to participate fully in all aspects of their children's development, solicited advice from group leaders and other fathers for ways of dealing with behavior problems, and were less apt to compare their deaf children negatively to siblings or hearing peers than the year before.

A program for fathers and their handicapped preschoolers that is examining the benefits of participation upon parents is Supporting Extended Family Members (SEFAM) at the University of Washington. SEFAM, a Handicapped Children's Early Education Program (funded by the Department of Education) is an outgrowth of a pilot Father, Infant, and Toddler Program, which has been offered at the University's Experimental Education Unit since 1978 (Delaney, Meyer, & Ward, 1980). Based on the pilot effort and a review of the research, SEFAM staff developed program activities that encourage a father to:

- learn to read his child's cues and interpret his child's behavior;
- develop an awareness of activities, materials, and experiences suitable to the child's current stage of development;
- practice his skill as the child's primary caregiver;
- learn more about the nature of the child's handicap;
- discuss his concerns with other fathers in a similar situation;
- develop an awareness that he, as a parent, will be his child's primary educator and advocate;
- explore the changing role of the father in today's society; and
- examine the impact of the child's handicap on the entire family structure. (Meyer et al., 1982)

SEFAM activities are built around three major components: support (father to father), involvement (father and child), and education (the father learning more about his child's disability). At biweekly meetings cofacilitated by a father of a handicapped child and a special education teacher, fathers share concerns, joys, and information during a "fathers' forum"; learn and enjoy activities with their children; and obtain information from guest speakers that reflect the participants' concerns.

Delaney (1979) studied the pilot Fathers and Infants Program (later called simply the Fathers Program as the children grew older). His research revealed that during free play sessions participants showed a significant decline in ignoring behaviors (both in terms of frequency and duration) across seven sessions. He concluded that by increasing the father's awareness of his child's development it was possible to significantly reduce the amount of the father's ignoring behavior.

Vadasy, Fewell, Meyer, and Greenberg (1985) compared fathers who were newly enrolled in SEFAM's Fathers Program to fathers who had participated in the program for at least one year in order to determine whether a father's social supports, stress level, or self-esteem might change over the course of his involvement. In addition to this treatment-no-treatment comparison, they also retested eleven participants one year later to obtain a pretest-posttest measure. It was further hypothesized that fathers' participation in the program might have second-order effects upon their wives, who would experience increased support in their role. Both mothers and fathers were therefore asked to participate in the evaluation.

When controlled for child's age and parent's education and occupation, parents who had participated in the program, when compared to newly enrolled fathers and mothers, reported several benefits.

General stress. Fathers who had participated in the program reported significantly less sadness than did newly enrolled fathers ($p < .001$). Fathers also reported they experienced significantly less stress due to their child's limited capabilities than did newly enrolled fathers ($p = .05$). The wives of the men who had been enrolled in the program experienced less stress ($p = .08$) resulting from their child's personality characteristics, such as acting out, than wives of new enrollees. After fathers had been enrolled in the program for one year, their wives reported lower feelings of failure ($p = .05$) than wives of new enrollees.

Self-esteem. Participation in the program appeared to have a positive effect upon both mothers' and fathers' perceptions about themselves. Fathers who had participated in the program rated themselves as successful significantly more often ($p < .05$) then did newly enrolled fathers, and perceived their families as having significantly fewer problems ($p = .01$) than newly enrolled fathers.

Social supports. Participation in the program appeared to have a positive effect upon fathers' satisfaction with other extrafamilial supports. Fathers in the program reported significantly more satisfaction ($p < .05$) with organized religion. Veteran fathers were significantly more satisfied ($p < .05$) with the type of persons with whom they shared their problems.

While Vadasy et al.'s (1985) findings should still be regarded as preliminary, they support parents' and professionals' opinion that more needs to be done to address fathers' concerns.

Markowitz's (1983) interviews with early childhood special education program representatives revealed that, when asked how a father's involvement affects family functioning, two thirds observed one or several of the following positive trends: improved family communication, reduced stress and tension, more sharing of burdens and responsibilities, enhanced family support system, increased acceptance of the child, more consistent discipline, and more harmonious family functioning.

Markowitz (1983), Meyer et al. (1982), and Turnbull et al. (in press) have made recommendations for programs which involve fathers. The following points, made by these authors are worthy of review.

Staff attitude towards fathers. Special education, like psychology, has for too long ignored the "other parent." Of the lack of attention that psychologists have shown toward fathers, Parke (1981) has written: "We didn't just forget fathers by accident; we ignored them because of our assumption that they were less important than mothers in influencing the developing child" (p. 4). Programs will not be successful in increasing father participation unless staff believe that fathers are important, expect them to be involved, and treat them as equal parents (Markowitz, 1983). This will mean addressing correspondence to both parents, not just mothers; adapting program advertisements, brochures, and newsletters to appeal to fathers as well as mothers; and providing male staff members in order to facilitate fathers' comfort (Markowitz, 1983).

Flexible scheduling. Evidence of a program's attitude towards fathers will be reflected in its staff's willingness to maintain a flexible schedule in order to accommodate fathers. E. Mavis Hetherington made a telling remark about psychology that is applicable to special education: "A major reason fathers were ignored (by psychologists) was that fathers were inaccessible. To observe fathers you have to work at night and on weekends, and not many researchers like to do that" (Collins, 1979, p. 49). As Hetherington suggests, a father's work schedule may interfere with his involvement in a program, and increasing father involvement may require flexible program scheduling. Two programs that have reported success in attracting fathers have either met on Saturdays (Meyer et al., 1982) or during evenings (Crowley et al., 1982).

Programs for fathers. As previously mentioned, fathers wish to be involved with their special child yet are often unsure how to show their love and concern for their child (Cummings, 1976; Gallagher et al., 1981). Fathers also have fewer opportunities than mothers to share their experiences and special problems related to the special child (Cummings, 1976). However, as Markowitz's (1983) data suggest, increasing fathers' attendance at so-called parents' meetings (which are, in effect, mothers' meetings) may not benefit either fathers or mothers.

This suggests a need for programs that are designed for and reflect the interests of fathers. These programs should complement programs for mothers and the child's educational program. Due to the novelty of this concept, the ideal model for involving fathers has yet to be determined. SEFAM's Fathers Program shows promise, especially in urban communities. It has yet to be adapted for rural areas or for low income or minority populations.

Regardless of the model developed, programs that wish to address fathers' needs will help fathers if they provide fathers with the opportunity for:

Support. By providing fathers an opportunity to discuss their concerns with other fathers in a similar situation, programs can help decrease their sense of isolation and increase the social supports available to them. Through discussion, a father can examine the impact the handicapped child has had on himself, his wife, and his entire family. Fathers who share their family's experiences with other fathers can increase each other's understanding of relatives' needs and how to help their family members cope with their individualized stresses. Fathers of handicapped children, like many fathers, are exploring the new roles and options available to men. Because most men lack models for the role of male caregiver, fathers interested in being nurturing parents need a supportive environment in which to gather information, ask questions, and share their thoughts about child development, discipline, eating habits, and other typical child-related concerns. In this respect a fathers' program is a men's group—supporting its members in roles that differ from traditional sex roles—as well as being a parent's group. In order to provide fathers with a positive model, as well as to insure fathers' comfort, these programs should be led by a male staff member, a "model" father, or preferably be cofacilitated by both.

Involvement. Programs that actively involve the father with the handicapped child can expand a father's knowledge of suitable activities and experiences that will be enjoyable for both father and child. Involvement in activities at the program can foster increased father-child involvement outside of the program. Given the father's importance as a child's play partner (Clarke-Stewart, 1980), increased father-child involvement may contribute to the child's cognitive and social development, as well as fostering attachment.

Programs for fathers and children provide fathers with an opportunity to practice caregiving skills. As research suggests (Kotelchuck, 1976; Ross, Kagan, Zelazo, & Kotelchuck, 1975), increasing caregiving has implications for increasing father-child attachment, as well as increasing the respite care that is available to mothers. When programs involve fathers and children, mothers have respite during the hours that the father and child are in the program and, as the fathers become increasingly comfortable with providing care for the special child, mothers' chances for additional respite increase.

Education. Studies by Hersh (1970), and Love (1973) have shown that fathers—more so than mothers—are concerned with their handicapped children's future problems, such as educational, vocational, legal, and economic matters. Programs for fathers can provide information that will address these and other paternal concerns. Information may be written, presented by staff or guest speakers, or shared by father participants.

An educational component complements staff efforts to provide fathers with support and involvement. Studies comparing the relative superiority of parent groups that are primarily supportive with those that are primarily educational are inconclusive. However, it is believed that a program that combines educational and supportive approaches has the most to offer parents of handicapped children (Seligman & Meyerson, 1982; Tavormina, Hampson, & Luscomb, 1976).

Services for Fathers Across the Family's Life Cycle

The research that has been reviewed makes clear that fathers of children with handicaps have needs that change over the family's life cycle. While programs for new fathers of handicapped children can provide much-needed services to traditionally underserved family members, programs that address fathers' needs and concerns are needed throughout the family life cycle. Parents of older children with mental retardation report feeling less supported, more isolated, and more in need of expanded services than fathers and mothers of young mentally retarded children (Suelzle & Keenan, 1981).

Knowledge of predictable crises across the family life cycle allows interventionists to be proactive rather than reactive in alleviating family stress due to these crises (Wikler, 1981). Knowledge of fathers' needs allows interventionists to develop programs that reflect fathers' unique concerns. By expanding on these two bases of knowledge, programs can be developed for fathers that parallel programs for mothers and that are available across the child's life span. By providing programs for fathers over the child's life span, interventionists can insure not only that fathers have access to support and information; they can also make it possible for fathers, in turn, to better support their wives' efforts. As fathers become more informed and supported, more available to their wives and their handicapped child, the entire family's functioning is enhanced, enabling them to adapt to changing needs they will experience across the family's life span.

References

Adler, B., & Kushnick, T. (1982). Genetic counseling in prenatally diagnosed trisomy 18 and 21: Psychological aspects. *Pediatrics, 69,* 94-99.

American Medical Association. (1964). *Mental retardation: A handbook for the primary physician.* New York: Author.

Birenbaum, A. (1971). The mentally retarded child in the home and family cycle. *Journal of Health and Social Behavior, 12,* 55-65.

Blumberg, B., & Golbus, M. (1975). Psychological sequelae of elective abortion. *Journal of Western Medicine, 123,* 188-193.

Blumberg, B., Golbus, M., & Hanson, K. (1975). The psychological sequelae of abortion performed for a genetic indication. *American Journal of Obstetrics and Gynecology, 122,* 799-808.

Brazelton, T.B. (1979). Four stages of neonatal affective development (Lecture at the University of Washington, Seattle).

Bristol, M.M., & Schopler, E. (1983). Stress and coping in families of autistic adolescents. In E. Schopler & G.B. Mesibov (Eds.), *Autism in adolescents and adults* (pp. 251-278). New York: Plenum.

Caldwell, B., & Guze, S. (1960). A study of the adjustment of parents and siblings of institutionalized and non-institutionalized retarded children. *American Journal of Mental Deficiency, 64,* 839-844.

Call, J. (1958. September-October). Psychological problems of the cerebral palsied child, his parents and siblings as revealed by dynamically oriented small group discussion with parents. *Cerebral Palsy Review,* 3-15.

Clarke-Stewart, K.A. (1980). The father's contribution to children's cognitive and social development in early childhood. In F.A. Pederson (Ed.), *The father-infant relationship: Observational studies in the family setting* (pp. 111-146). New York: Praeger.

Collins, G. (1979). A new look at life with father. *New York Times Magazine,* pp. 31, 49-52, 65-66.

Crowley, M., Keane, K., & Needham, C. (1982). Fathers: The forgotten parents. *American Annals of the Deaf, 127,* 38-40.

Cummings, S.T. (1976). The impact of the child's deficiency on the father: A study of mentally retarded and chronically ill children. *American Journal of Orthopsychiatry, 46,* 246-255.

DeBoor, M. (1975). What is to become of Katherine? *Exceptional Children, 41,* 517-518.

Delaney, S.W. (1979). *Facilitating attachment between fathers and their handicapped infants.* Unpublished doctoral dissertation, University of Washington, Seattle.

Delaney, S.W., Meyer, D.J., & Ward, M.J. (1980). *Fathers and infants class: A model for facilitating attachment between fathers and infants.* Unpublished manuscript, University of Washington, Experimental Education Unit, Seattle.

Duvall, E.M. (1962). *Family development.* Philadelphia: Lippincott.

Erickson, M. (1974). Talking with fathers of young children with Down syndrome. *Children Today, 3,* 22-25.

Farber, B. (1959). Effects of a severely mentally retarded child on family integration. *Monographs of the Society for Research in Child Development,* 24 (Serial No. 71).

Farber, B. (1960). Family organization and crisis: Maintenance of integration in families with a severely mentally retarded child. *Monographs of the Society for Research in Child Development,* 25 (Serial No. 75).

Farber, B. (1972). Effects of a severely retarded child on the family. In E.P. Trapp & P. Himelstein (Eds.), *Readings on the exceptional child* (pp. 225-245). New York: Appleton-Century- Crofts.

Farber, B., Jenne, W., & Toigo, R. (1960). *Family crisis and the decision to institutionalize the retarded child,* (NEA Research Monograph Series, No. A-1). Washington, DC: Council for Exceptional Children.

Farber, B., & Ryckman, D.B. (1965). Effects of severely mentally retarded children on family relationships. *Mental Retardation Abstracts, 11,* 1-17.

Fotheringham, J.B., Skelton, M., & Hoddinot, B.A. (1972). The effects on the family of the presence of a mentally retarded child. *Canadian Psychiatric Association Journal, 17,* 283-290.

Gallagher, J.J., Beckman, P., & Cross, A.H. (1983). Families of handicapped children: Sources of stress and its amelioration. *Exceptional Child, 50,* 10-19.

Gallagher, J., Cross, A., & Scharfman, W. (1981). Parental adaptation to a young handicapped child: The father's role. *Journal of the Division for Early Childhood, 3,* 3-14.

Gath, A. (1977). The impact of an abnormal child upon the parents. *British Journal of Psychiatry, 130,* 405-410.

Greenberg, M., & Morris, N. (1974). Engrossment: The newborn's impact upon the father. *American Journal of Orthopsychiatry, 44,* 520-531.

Greenfeld, J. (1979a). *A child called Noah.* New York: Pocket Books.

Greenfeld, J. (1979b). *A place for Noah.* New York: Pocket Books.

Grossman, F.K. (1972). *Brothers and sisters of retarded children: An exploratory study.* Syracuse, NY: Syracuse University Press.

Gumz, E.J., & Gubrium, J.F. (1972). Comparative parental perceptions of a mentally retarded child. *American Journal of Mental Deficiency, 77,* 175-180.

Helsel, E., & Helsel, B. (1978). The Helsels' story of Robin. In A. Turnbull & R. Turnbull (Eds.), *Parents speak out: Views from the other side of the two-way mirror* (pp. 94-115). Columbus, OH: Charles E. Merrill.

Hersch, A. (1970). Changes in family functioning following placement of a retarded child. *Social Work, 15,* 93-102.

Holroyd, J., & McArthur, D. (1976). Mental retardation and stress on parents: A contrast between Down's syndrome and childhood autism. *American Journal of Mental Deficiency, 80,* 431-436.

Illingworth, R.S. (1967). Counseling the parents of the mentally handicapped child. *Clinical Pediatrics, 6,* 340-348.

Kirkpatrick, C. (1955). *The family as process and institution.* New York: Ronald Press.

Kotelchuck, M. (1976). The infant's relationship to the father: Experimental evidence. In M.E. Lamb (Ed.), *The role of the father in child development* (pp. 329-344). New York: Wiley.

Lamb, M.E. (1976). Interactions between eight-month-old children and their fathers and mothers. In M.E. Lamb (Ed.), *The role of the father in child development* (pp. 307-327). New York: Wiley.

Lewis, M., & Weinraub, M. (1974). Sex of parent x sex of child: Socioemotional development. In R.C. Friedman, R.M. Richart, & R.L. Vande Wiele (Eds.), *Sex differences in behavior* (pp. 165-189). New York: Wiley.

Liversidge, E., & Grana, G. (1973). A hearing impaired child in the family: The parent's perspective. *Volta Review, 75,* 174-184.

Love, H. (1973). *The mentally retarded child and his family.* Springfield, IL: Charles C Thomas.

Markowitz, J. (1983). *Participation of fathers in early childhood special education programs: An exploratory study of factors and issues.* Unpublished manuscript, George Washington University, Washington, DC.

Menolascino, F.J. (1977). *Challenges in mental retardation: Progressive ideology and services.* New York: Human Sciences Press.

Meyer, D. (1982). The fathers program [Slide/tape program]. Seattle: Experimental Education Unit, University of Washington.

Meyer, D., Vadasy, P., Fewell, R., & Schell, G. (1982). Involving fathers of handicapped infants: Translating research into program goals. *Journal of the Division for Early Childhood, 5,* 64-72.

Meyerowitz, H.D. (1967). Parental awareness of retardation. *American Journal of Mental Deficiency, 71,* 637-643.

Miller, L.G. (1968). Toward a greater understanding of the parents of the mentally retarded. *Journal of Pediatrics, 73,* 699-705.

Moore, J.A., Hamerlynck, L.A., Barsh, E.T., Spieker, S., & Jones, R.R. (1982). *Extending family resources.* Seattle, WA: Children's Clinic and Preschool.

Olshansky, S. (1962). Chronic sorrow: A response to having a mentally defective child. *Social Casework, 43,* 190-193.

Parke, R.D. (1981). *Fathers.* Cambridge, MA: Harvard University Press.

Peck, J.R., & Stephens, W.B. (1960). A study of the relationship between the attitudes and behavior of parents and that of their mentally defective child. *American Journal of Mental Deficiency, 64,* 839-844.

Pedersen, F.A., & Robson, K.S. (1969). Father participation in infancy. *American Journal of Orthopsychiatry, 39,* 466-472.

Pergament, E., Ginsberg, N., Verlinsky, Y., & Halperin, D. (1984). *First trimester prenatal diagnosis: An overview of chorionic villi sampling (CVS).* Chicago: Michael Reese Hospital and Medical Center.

Power, T.G., & Parke, R.D. (in press). Play as a context for early learning: Lab and home analyses. In I.E. Sigel & L.M. Laosa (Eds.), *The family as a learning environment.* New York: Plenum.

Price-Bonham, S., & Addison, S. (1978). Families and mentally retarded children: Emphasis on the father. *The Family Coordinator, 3,* 221-230.

Reed, E.W., & Reed, S.C. (1965). *Mental retardation: A family study.* Philadelphia: Saunders.

Roos, P. (1978). Parents of mentally retarded children - misunderstood and mistreated. In A.P. Turnbull & H.R. Turnbull (Eds.), *Parents speak out: Views from the other side of the two-way mirror* (pp. 12-27). Columbus, OH: Charles E. Merrill.

Rosenberg, S.A. (1977). *Family and parent variables affecting outcomes of a parent-mediated intervention.* Unpublished doctoral dissertation, George Peabody College for Teachers, Nashville, TN.

Ross, G., Kagan, J., Zelazo, P., & Kotelchuck, M. (1975). Separation protests in infants in home and laboratory. *Developmental Psychology, 11,* 265-257.

Schonnell, F.J., & Watts, B.H. (1956). A first survey of the effects of a subnormal child on the family unit. *American Journal of Mental Deficiency, 61,* 210-219.

Schufeit, L.J., & Wurster, S.R. (1976). Frequency of divorce among parents of handicapped children. *Resources in Education, 11,* 71-78.

Seligman, M., & Meyerson, R. (1982). Group approaches for parents of exceptional children. In M. Seligman (Ed.), *Group psychotherapy and counseling with special populations* (pp. 99-116). Austin, TX: PRO-ED.

Silvestre, D., & Fresco, N. (1980). Reactions to prenatal diagnosis: An analysis of 87 interviews. *American Journal of Orthopsychiatry, 50,* 610-617.

Suelzle, M., & Keenan, V. (1981). Changes in family support networks over the lifecycle of mentally retarded persons. *American Journal of Mental Deficiency, 86,* 267-274.

Tallman, I. (1965). Spousal role differentiation and the socialization of severely retarded children. *Journal of Marriage and the Family, 27,* 37-42.

Tavormina, J.B., Ball, N.J., Dunn, R.C., Luscomb, B., & Taylor, J.R. (1977). *Psychosocial effects of raising a physically handicapped child on parents.* Unpublished manuscript, University of Virginia, Charlottesville, VA.

Tavormina, J., Hampson, R., & Luscomb, R. (1976). Participant evaluations of the effectiveness of their parent counseling groups. *Mental Retardation, 14,* 8-9.

Tew, B.J., Lawrence, K.M., Payne, H., & Rawnsley, K. (1977). Marital stability following the birth of a child with spina bifida. *British Journal of Psychiatry, 131,* 79-82.

Turnbull, A.P., & Blacher-Dixon, J. (1980). Preschool mainstreaming: Impact on parents. In J. Gallagher (Ed)., *New directions for exceptional children* (Vol. 1, pp. 25-46). San Francisco: Jossey-Bass.

Turnbull, A.P., Brotherson, M.J., Summers, J.A., & Turnbull, H.R. (in press). Fathers of disabled children. In B. Robinson & R. Baret (Eds.), *Fatherhood.* Baltimore: University Park Press.

U.S. Department of Health, Education, and Welfare. (1979). *Antenatal diagnosis* (Report of a Consensus Development Conference. NIH Publication No. 80-1973). Washington, DC: Author.

U.S. Department of Labor. (1980). *Facts on women workers.* Washington, DC: Author.

Vadasy, P.F., Fewell, R.R., Meyer, D.J., & Greenberg, M.T. (1985). Supporting fathers of handicapped young children: Preliminary findings of program effects. *Analysis and Intervention in Developmental Disabilities, 5,* 125-137.

Vadasy, P., Fewell, R., Meyer, D., Schell, G., & Greenberg, M. (1984). Involved parents: Characteristics and resources of fathers and mothers of young handicapped children. *Journal of the Division for Early Childhood, 8,* 13-25.

Warren, F. (1978). A society that is going to kill your children. In A. Turnbull & R. Turnbull (Eds.), *Parents speak out: Views from the other side of the two-way mirror* (pp. 176-196). Columbus, OH: Charles E. Merrill.

Weinraub, M. (1979). Fatherhood: The myth of the second class parent. In J.H. Stevens & M. Mathews (Eds.), *Mother/child, father/child relationships* (pp. 109-134). Washington, DC: National Association for the Education of Young Children.

Wikler, L. (1981). Chronic stresses of families of mentally retarded children. *Family Relations, 30,* 281-288.

Wikler, L., Wasow, M., & Hatfield, E. (1981). Chronic sorrow revisited: Attitudes of parents and professionals about adjustment to mental retardation. *American Journal of Orthopsychiatry, 51,* 63-70.

Young, J.C., & Hamilton, M.E. (1979). Paternal Behavior: Implications for child rearing practice. In J. Stevens & M. Matthews (Eds.), *Mother/child, father/child relationships* (pp. 135-146). Washington, DC: National Association for the Education of Young Children.

3

Understanding Sibling Needs and Influences

Keith A. Crnic and Judith M. Leconte

It's hard to sum the feelings I had as a sibling of a handicapped child. A year ago, I would have said I felt mainly pride and resentment. I am proud of Jill's accomplishments, for she has done what too few profoundly deaf children will ever do. . . .I also mentioned resentment. I'll always remember striving for the attention that was often focused on Jill. . . .Now I have moved to the point where I also feel sadness. I sympathize with my sister, who will always have to struggle to maintain her place in the world . . . . Why didn't I help make it easier along the way?. . . .I don't know why. (Sibling of a deaf child).

It has been noted that our knowledge about children's development is much greater than our knowledge about the contexts in which they grow, and the processes by which these contexts affect development (Bronfenbrenner, 1979). There is consensus that the family provides the primary developmental context, but our understanding of the complexities of the family system as they affect a child's development is limited. This is especially true when the family includes a handicapped child.

Although the literature has focused upon increased difficulties in families with a handicapped child, there are certainly a wide range of potentially adaptive responses (Crnic, Friedrich, & Greenberg, 1983).

In much of the research to date, the model of a family with a handicapped child has included the mother, the father, and the affected child. Only recently have siblings begun to become a focus of increased concern and attention. This focus is indeed long overdue, as most families with a handicapped child also include children without handicapping conditions, and the family as a system can only be understood in the context of all its members. Conversely, the behavior and development of the siblings of a handicapped child can only be understood in the context of the entire family system.

The impact of a handicap on the sibling relationship is of significance because of the nature of this relationship. As Cicirelli (1982) has pointed out, there is evidence that the sibling relationship is of extremely long duration— that most people have a living sibling available to them until they are into their eighties or older. He has noted the intimacy of the relationship, and its frequent growth in intensity over time. Siblings play various roles throughout their lives, serving as role models both early in their lives as well as in their adult years. Cicirelli suggests that attachment theory be extended to siblings as well as parents, and that early sibling experiences contribute to feelings of family unity. When this relationship is affected by a sibling's handicap, both the handicapped and nonhandicapped sibling may lose out on long-term benefits that many siblings enjoy. These benefits include sharing a world beyond adult reach, for young siblings (Featherstone, 1980), as well as providing mutual support into old age after the death of parents and spouses.

As the quote at the beginning of this chapter suggests, being the sibling of a handicapped child evokes a range of emotional responses, from pride and enjoyment to irritation and resentment. At times, it's just plain confusing. While these emotions may seem little different from those characterizing all sibling relationships, the potential for more extreme responses exists, given the ongoing stress related to the presence of a handicapped child. Sibling attachments can be significantly disrupted, and this can have detrimental effects both on attachments within and outside the family, as sibling relationships often provide the model for later peer relationships. The quote also reflects the changing nature of the sibling relationship, which is not a still life but a constantly evolving interaction colored by changes within the entire family system.

Research on siblings of handicapped children has focused primarily on the relationship between the handicapped child and the normal sibling, or on the impact of the handicapped child on the normal sibling. Most often these studies have attempted to examine the impact of the handicapped child's characteristics (type of handicap, age, sex, birth order) on the child's siblings, although our understanding of these influences is still limited, particularly in terms of the way they interact with other family variables. The impact of the normal sibling on the handicapped child is rarely addressed. Each of these areas of study has important developmental implications, as characteristics of the normal sibling (age, sex, birth order) appear to have differential effects on both the sibling's relationship with the handicapped child, and the impact of the handicapped child on the normal sibling. The sibling relationship is imbedded in a family system which, in turn, influences and is influenced by the stresses that a handicap creates. Siblings, much the same as the family as a whole, are likely to demonstrate a range of adaptive responses to these stresses, mediated by familial, psychological, and personality influences on their coping styles. It is important to keep in mind the actual variety of factors which influence sibling and family interactions, particularly as we review studies that often capture only a thin slice of family data. As the body of research including siblings grows, and as these family members are included in interventions, permitting more professionals to appreciate their perspectives, we will obtain a more accurate picture of their experiences and needs.

Research on Handicapped and Nonhandicapped Siblings

The Nature of the Sibling Relationship

Only a few researchers have investigated the relationship between handicapped and nonhandicapped siblings, and, as is common to much of the research with families of handicapped children, the methodological adequacy of much of the existing research is questionable. These research difficulties (particularly the lack of control groups), as well as the fluid and complex nature of sibling relationships, limit the generalizations which can be made from the studies to date. Indeed, there appear to be conflicting indications regarding the nature of these sibling relationships.

Robinson and Robinson (1976) have noted that the handicapped child can have an integrative effect on the family, and anecdotal accounts from affected families give credence to such a notion (Canning & Canning, 1975). Several research studies would also appear to support this notion. In a series of sibling interviews, Miller (1974) found that nonhandicapped siblings primarily engaged in instrumental activity with their retarded brother or sister, and displayed more positive and less negative affect toward retarded siblings than nonretarded siblings. Likewise, McHale, Sloan, and Simeonsson (1982) reported that children with handicapped siblings were perceived as more supportive and accepting of the handicapped sibling than siblings of nonhandicapped children, and the children's self-reports of their feelings reflected similar supportive orientations.

There are indications, however, that the above noted positive findings are not universal. In the Miller (1974) study, the nonhandicapped siblings also indicated that their parents did not tolerate the expression of negative affect toward the retarded child, which casts some doubt on the siblings' reports. In a study of brother dyads using projective techniques (Pfouts, 1976), nonhandicapped brothers were noted to be ambivalent towards the retarded brother, while the retarded child was noted to be hostile toward his nonhandicapped sibling. Meuwissen (1971) has previously suggested that the nonhandicapped sibling's feelings of guilt may also inhibit expressions of negative feelings toward the retarded sibling.

Beyond the more subjective aspects of sibling relationships, it also seems that sibling status and roles vary in relation to the presence of a handicapped child. In his studies of family integration, Farber (1960) interviewed the siblings of severely retarded children living at home. From these interviews, two significant and consistent relationships emerged. First, siblings younger than the retarded child eventually assume a superordinate role in relationship to the retarded child; and second, female siblings were frequently encouraged to function as surrogate mothers for the retarded child. This latter finding has also been noted by other researchers, most notably Gath (1973) and Cleveland and Miller (1977). The role confusion that results is expressed by a young sibling with an older handicapped sister:

> I'm kind of like my sister's boss. I babysit *her,* and I tell *her* what to do, though sometimes I think how she's a lot older than me. Yet it does seem like I'm older. It's funny too, I'm 5'6", and she's really short, she's only about 4'11", and she looks up to me. Really. It's just always been that I could do so many more things than her. Like, she'd sit home, and I always had friends to talk to and go out with. She was like the little baby who had to stay behind.

The conflicting nature of the research on the sibling relationship reflects, in part, the difficulties apparent in research design, as well as the dynamic nature of these relationships. The roles, responses, and feelings of the nonhandicapped sibling toward the handicapped child are not likely to be static, but rather change as the sibling adapts to the handicapped child, and copes with the day-to-day process of interacting with the handicapped sibling in the various ecological contexts of which they are a part. For example, a sibling relationship is likely to be less stressful when both the handicapped and nonhandicapped child are younger, whereas stresses may increase as the handicapped child grows and falls farther behind peers, and when the nonhandicapped child grows and begins to substitute some peer values for family values.

Impact of the Handicapped Sibling

As there is variability in the relationships between handicapped and nonhandicapped siblings, so too is there variability in the impact of the handicapped child on the nonhandicapped sibling. Crocker (1981) has noted six dynamic factors that may vary across families and may affect the way a sibling experiences having a handicapped brother or sister:

1. Normal family patterns are altered. The household may be organized differently to adapt to the handicapped child's special needs, and family activities, like vacations, may have to be carefully planned to accommodate to the handicapped child's needs.
2. There is greater competition for parental attention and resources. Parents may need to devote more energy to the care of the handicapped child at certain times, as well as devote time to advocacy activities. More of the family's financial resources may need to be spent on the handicapped child than on the other children.
3. Siblings may have misconceptions about the sibling's handicap. While young siblings may worry that they may have been responsible, in some way, for their brother's or sister's handicap, older siblings may worry about whether their own children might be affected.
4. Siblings may have to act as a surrogate parent. Young siblings may have to assume more than the usual level of responsibility for the care of a handicapped brother or sister. These responsibilities may affect the nonhandicapped sibling's social life, and may cause older siblings to question their lifelong responsibility for the handicapped family member.
5. Siblings may feel obliged to compensate for the handicapped child. Even when parents do not explicitly state that the sibling must do better in order to make up for the handicapped child's limitations, siblings may feel an indirect pressure to succeed because their handicapped brother or sister cannot.
6. Siblings may experience confusion regarding parents' changing reactions to the handicapped child. Parents continue to experience cycles of grief and changing conflicts over the course of the handicapped child's life. These parental stresses have an impact on siblings as well as on the family's overall functioning.

Detrimental Effects. A number of studies have found detrimental effects on the psychological functioning of siblings of retarded children. These effects generally involve greater anxiety, more conflicts with parents, and lower sociability or emphasis on interpersonal relationships than in families without a handicapped child (Farber, 1960, 1963; Fowle, 1968; Grossman, 1972). Siblings, like parents, may experience guilt (San Martino & Newman, 1974) as well as anger (Breslau, Weitzman, & Messenger, 1981) towards the sibling. Gath (1973) also reported a greater incidence of behavior problems (as measured by parent and teacher ratings) in a group of 174 siblings of children with Down syndrome compared with 143 age-matched controls. Problems in the psychological adjustment of normal siblings have similarly been noted in multiple studies of children with chronic illnesses (Apley, Barbour, & Westmacott, 1967; Binger, Albin, & Feuerstein, 1969; Tew & Lawrence, 1973). Little is known, however, about the differential effects of intellectual, physical, sensory, or behavioral handicaps upon the nonhandicapped sibling, or about the impact of the severity of the handicap. As Skrtic, Summers, Brotherson, and Turnbull (1983) caution, the assumption is unwarranted that the impact increases with the severity of the handicap. A sibling may be more likely to identify with a mildly handicapped brother or sister, who may also be involved in more social and peer situations with the nonhandicapped sibling, than with a severely handicapped child. In one of the few studies of families of children with physical handicaps, Travis (1976) found that siblings who have excessive caretaking responsibilities for the physical care of a chronically, physically ill child leave home by age 16 or 17. Travis also notes the risks both children may be subject to in this type of relationship.

In normal sibling relationships, there is a certain balance between the instrumental and expressive activities siblings engage in together. A sibling's handicap may disrupt this balance. For example, in their home pilot observations of five older nonhandicapped siblings (median age 10 years) and their retarded brothers and sisters (median age 6.8 years), Stoneman and Brody (in press) found that there were clear role asymmetries; the nonhandicapped siblings most frequently assumed the roles of teacher and manager. When siblings who participated in workshops conducted by the Supporting Extended Family Members (SEFAM) Program in Seattle were interviewed about their experiences, many reported that the activities they least enjoyed with their handicapped brother or sister were babysitting and caretaking (feeding or dressing the child). The siblings said they most enjoyed playing with the handicapped child. The siblings also noted that they did not have enough time to do the things they wanted to do, as well as time to spend with their parents.

When the short form (54-item) version of Holroyd's (1973) *Questionnaire on Resources and Stress* (QRS) was adapted for administration to young children by SEFAM staff, it was administered to a group of 14 young siblings (mean age 10.6 years) of handicapped children (mean age 9.2 years). Seventy-one percent of the children ($n=10$) responded that they worried about what would happen to their sibling if something happened to their parents. Half of the siblings said they sometimes felt very embarrassed because of the handicapped child. Sixty-four percent ($n=9$) said they worried about what would happen to their sibling when the sibling gets older, and seventy-one percent ($n=10$) worried about what would happen to their sibling when the parents could no longer provide care. The concerns of this small group of siblings reflect many of the concerns reported elsewhere in the literature.

Positive Effects. While the majority of evidence suggests that siblings of handicapped children are prone to various behavioral and emotional difficulties, there are studies which suggest that these children do not have greater difficulties than children without a handicapped sibling (Gath, 1972; Gayton, Friedman, Tavormina, & Tucker, 1977; McHale et al., 1982). Of particular note is a subsequent study by Gath (1978) in which she found that disturbances seen in the normal siblings of children with Down syndrome were not causally related to the presence of the handicapped child, but rather were in evidence prior to the birth of the handicapped sibling. Other first-hand accounts of siblings attest to the often positive ways in which siblings adjust to a handicapped brother or sister.

> She's taught me to be really open to people. At my school there is a program for mentally retarded children now, but the teachers don't know how to handle them. They knew that I have a mentally retarded sister, and so when I would be out on recess, they would keep calling me in to help them take care of the kids. The kids would be jumping up and down and I would come in and hug them or something, and they would calm down. And the teachers would be amazed, and ask me "How did you do that?"

Siblings may develop an insight into human differences and a maturity that exceeds their age. Ann Turnbull (Turnbull, Summers, & Brotherson, 1983) has shared her 5-year-old daughter's natural acceptance and understanding of her 13-year-old mentally retarded brother. After Turnbull had used the analogy of the speeds on a record player to explain how her daughter Amy's mental abilities differed from her son Jay's mental abilities, her daughter added:

> She (Amy) thought for a minute and then said that I was failing to tell her one very important thing: "It (the brain) plays music on both speeds. Jay might be slow and Kate and I might be fast; but, Mommy, all three of us still play music". (p.9)

It should be noted here that Amy Turnbull (1985), now age 10, has gone on to share her understanding of individual differences with her peers as part of a research study she conducted with two groups of second graders. Amy undertook to find out whether children who received information about mental retardation improved their attitudes about people with mental retardation. Amy pre- and posttested two groups of children on the *Student Attitude and Perspective Scale* (Rude, 1982) and taught the experimental group a lesson about mental retardation which included a story, a film, and a discussion. She found that the attitudes of the children in the experimental group were significantly more positive as reflected in posttest scores than in pretest scores. There were no pre to post differences in the attitudes of the control group.

Another 10-year-old sibling reflected the acceptance of differences that siblings learn when she was asked if she ever worried whether her own children might be handicapped like her sister:

They might be, I'm not sure, but if they are, it won't really matter.

Grossman (1972) also found that some of the college-age siblings she interviewed seemed to have more tolerance and be more aware of the effects of prejudice than other young adults without similar experiences. A more personal benefit reported by Miller (1974) was a sense of pride expressed by siblings who had been involved in the growth and development of their retarded sibling. Others have reported positive ways in which siblings are affected by their brother's or sister's handicap (Cleveland & Miller, 1977; Farber, 1963; Holt, 1958; O'Neill, 1965).

Impact of the Normal Sibling

It is interesting that most of the sibling research has focused on the effect of the handicapped sibling on the nonhandicapped child, and no research has specifically attempted to assess the converse process. How does a normal sibling affect the handicapped child, and what are the parameters of these effects? Given the consistent finding that non-handicapped siblings do act as caretakers and parental surrogates (Cleveland & Miller, 1977; Farber, 1960; Gath, 1972), attention should be given to the notion of reciprocity within these sibling relationships. While no data exist which specifically address this issue, Schreibman, O'Neil, and Koegel (1983) have reported that siblings of autistic children can be trained in and successfully employ behavior management skills during interactions with their autistic siblings. This study suggests that normal children can assist their handicapped sibling in developing more positive behavior, but raises a question of whether siblings should be encouraged to perform as parental surrogates or be responsible for the management of their siblings' behavior. This will be further discussed in a later section.

When the nonhandicapped sibling assumes significant caregiving or teaching responsibilities, there are several possible outcomes. As noted, the nonhandicapped siblings may be resentful and stressed. They may, however, make important contributions to the handicapped sibling's development. They may contribute significantly to the social development of the handicapped child; indeed, they may play a major role in the child's socialization when a handicap isolates the child from his or her peers. Siblings may indirectly benefit the handicapped child by providing parents with instrumental assistance they could otherwise not afford. And conversely, nonhandicapped siblings who develop emotional or behavior problems as a result of family stress may require that parents give them more of their already limited time and attention, in effect, taking these family resources away from their handicapped brother or sister.

The nonhandicapped sibling's impact may vary across the family's life-span. The impact may be great when the handicapped child is young if the sibling assumes significant caregiving and teaching roles and is a key member in the handicapped child's limited social network. The impact may be great again when the children in the family are adults and the issue of the handicapped sibling's future care must be decided. These future concerns, however, must be anticipated when siblings are still young and begin to worry about what their role will be when they and their handicapped brother or sister are older. Powell and Ogle (1985) suggest strategies for addressing future concerns, among other special sibling needs for information, in their valuable resource on special sibling relationships.

Factors Which Mediate Sibling Functioning

As noted above, there is a rather striking lack of uniformity in the results of studies which have assessed both the relationship between handicapped and nonhandicapped siblings, and the effect of the handicapped sibling on the nonhandicapped child. Perhaps the most logical explanation for this, beyond methodological constraints of the research, involves the influence of various factors which seem to mediate sibling response. There are clear indications from the available research that factors such as sibling age and sex, as well as family socioeconomic status mediate child outcome.

Responsibility for caretaking. Among the most consistent findings in the existent sibling studies is the indication that female siblings are more likely than are males to be affected by having a handicapped sibling. (It may be, however, that the proper questions have not yet been asked to delineate male sibling outcomes.) Female children are more often given caretaking responsibilities for their handicapped sibling (Cleveland & Miller, 1977; Farber, 1960; Gath, 1972), and girls tend to show greater behavior problems than do boys with handicapped siblings. In fact, in the Gath (1973) study which noted greater behavior problems in siblings of handicapped children, this significant effect was entirely accounted for by girls, as when groups were divided by sex of child, boys with and without a handicapped sibling did not differ in parent and/or teacher report of behavior problems. Both Farber and Gath suggest that the greater difficulty for female siblings is related to the greater child care responsibility they have for their handicapped brother or sister. Further, Cleveland and Miller (1977) found that female adult siblings reported having had greater responsibilities for their handicapped sibling when young, and more frequently sought professional counselling as adults than did male siblings. These findings have implications for studies such as Schreibman et al.'s (1983) which recommend involving siblings in greater responsibility for their handicapped sibling. If previous research has correctly delineated a relationship between greater caretaking responsibility and the presence of behavioral or emotional problems, then training and expecting normal siblings to effectively use behavioral management techniques with their handicapped brother or sister may add to the caretaking burden, thereby increasing the potentials for behavioral or emotional difficulties in the normal sibling. This is an empirical question deserving of future study. Michaelis (1980) has also cautioned that nonhandicapped siblings not jeopardize their own social and academic learning by undertaking extensive responsibilities for teaching their handicapped sibling. On the other hand, siblings who derive positive benefits from their responsibilities for their handicapped sibling may be motivated to pursue a career in one of the helping professions (Cleveland & Miller, 1977), and may learn tolerance and sympathy for those less fortunate than themselves.

Age and birth order. The age and birth order of the normal sibling also appear to serve a mediating function for sibling outcome, although both these factors interact with the sex and age of the handicapped sibling, as noted above. First-born and older siblings appear generally less affected by the later presence of a handicapped sibling (Graliker, Fishler, & Koch, 1962; Grossman, 1972), while younger male siblings have been found to demonstrate greater adjustment difficulties (Breslau, 1982). Also, young handicapped children may present fewer adjustment problems to the nonhandicapped sibling than an older handicapped child, whose behavior may be more discrepant from that of peers. It seems apparent that these relationships may reflect the number of years or amount of time the siblings are together. Further, nonhandicapped siblings who are younger than the handicapped child are not likely to receive the amount of attention that their older siblings received, as parental energies are necessarily more directed to the handicapped child, and time becomes a more precious commodity than it was before the index child's birth. Nonhandicapped siblings who are older than the handicapped child may continue to benefit from the time and attention parents were able to provide them prior to the birth of the handicapped child.

Individual temperament. Finally, sibling adjustment may be a very individual process that is related to the sibling's temperamental characteristics. A study of nonhandicapped first-born siblings' adjustment to the birth of a second child in the family provides some clues to the range of quite dramatic responses children demonstrate to a new sibling, let alone a sibling with special and greater-than-usual needs. Dunn and Kendrick (1982) found in their study of 40 first-born children that there were strong associations between assessments of the children's temperaments made before their sibling's birth and the incidence of later problems observed in the first-borns, including feeding and sleeping problems and tantrums. This study suggests that temperamental differences may figure in children's responses to other stressful events, and temperament is an individual difference that has not been examined in siblings of handicapped children.

Relative to age and birth order are the reciprocal developmental contributions siblings typically experience over the course of their lives. Older siblings are typically role models for the peer relationships younger siblings will later enjoy. Siblings, at various times, function as models, confidants, protectors, companions, teachers, partners, and subjects for testing new ideas and relationships. A handicap often prevents siblings from sharing certain of these experiences.

> I've always wanted another brother or sister who I could confide in, someone my own age, like me.

Socioeconomic status. The family's socioeconomic status (SES) is also relevant to determining sibling impact, as nonhandicapped siblings' experiences appear to vary as a function of class. Siblings within lower class families tend to assume more caretaking responsibilities (Farber, 1960; Gath, 1974), whereas middle-class children are more affected by issues involving stigma and acceptance (Grossman, 1972). Lower class families are less likely to be able to afford help from outside the family than middle-class families. On the other hand, as Seligman (1983) notes, a marginally handicapped child with mild retardation may be more readily accepted by the lower class family, whereas the same child might fail to meet the higher intellectual and social goals that are set in a middle-class family. Also, siblings in families where parents set high goals for the children's educational attainment may face the pressure to compensate for the handicapped child's deficits.

> That's what they tell me, why can't you try harder. They want us to make up for our brothers and sisters, and they want us to be an example. But I'm the youngest, and I'm tired of picking up the slack for my sister.

> All their expectations are on me, because of my brother. If he brings home a D in a subject, they say, "Oh, well." But if I bring home a D, I get grounded for weeks.

Parental attitudes. Mediators of sibling adjustment, however, do not appear to be limited to factors which primarily involve stable family demographic characteristics. Indeed, some evidence indicates that the adjustment of normal siblings to the presence of a handicapped child is related to parental reactions and ability to cope with having a handicapped child (Graliker et al., 1962; Grossman, 1972). Indeed, parental openness and positive attitudes about the handicapped child have been found to be related to more positive sibling adjustment (O'Connor & Stachowiak, 1971). It is in this area that the father's example may be particularly influential to the family's adjustment (Meyer, Chapter 2; Peck & Stephens, 1960; Price-Bonham & Addison, 1978).

Sibling Perspectives

From the above review of research findings and first-hand accounts by siblings themselves, a somewhat confusing picture emerges regarding the siblings of handicapped children. Some data indicate that relationships between handicapped and nonhandicapped siblings are problematic, and that the normal sibling is prone to emotional and behavioral difficulties. Other data suggest that neither the relationship nor the psychological functioning of the normal sibling is impaired by the presence of a handicapped sibling. Just as families differ, so too do sibling responses to a handicapped child, and generalizations cannot be made for the population as a whole. Nevertheless, the presence of a handicapped child in the family is a significant and ongoing stressor (Crnic et al., 1983; Friedrich & Friedrich, 1981; Holroyd, Brown, Wikler, & Simmons, 1975) which presents special difficulties for the family in general, and for nonhandicapped siblings particularly.

Common Sibling Concerns

Information needs. Broad interpretations of the research findings, as well as clinical case reports, indicate that siblings of handicapped children have a number of concerns in relation to their brother or sister and their own status within the family. One recurrent theme appears to be the sibling's need for information about the handicapped child, particularly facts about the handicap. Sibling concerns typically include: the nature and extent of the handicap ("What is the matter with my brother or sister and what does that mean"); some notion of the etiology ("How did it happen?"); and some explanation for its occurrence ("Why did it happen?"). Siblings also wonder whether they too share the handicap. Even when the handicap is not hereditary, the stigma of the handicap will affect the sibling, for example, in peer relationships when the sibling is young, and even in the sibling's adult life. The authors (Meyer, Vadasy, & Fewell, 1985a) of a handbook for young siblings illustrate these worries in vignettes which introduce a discussion of common sibling concerns about the future.

Last month, Allen's parents sat the whole family down and told them the bad news: their new little brother has Down syndrome. "He'll be just like us in almost every way," his mother told them, "except it will take him longer to learn. The doctor said that he'll probably be mentally retarded."

This year Allen is having a terrible time in math. He has almost flunked his last two tests. Today when he had a hard time again on his math test, Allen wondered: Maybe I'm retarded too.

Generally, these are concerns that parents will help their children cope with, although the ability of parents to handle these concerns openly and effectively depends upon their own ability to cope with the same issues. The family's access to resources (doctors, teachers) who can address these concerns and questions may be an important factor in each member's adaptation.

Expectations. Another major concern for siblings of handicapped children is related to the expected degree of their involvement with their handicapped sibling, both within the family and in other social settings (peers, neighborhood, school, etc.). Already noted was the fact that siblings of handicapped children, especially sisters, often have greater caretaking responsibilities. Also, in order to care for and interact effectively with the handicapped child, some siblings may need special training in behavioral techniques, particularly when the handicapped child has behavior problems (e.g., Schreibman et al., 1983). Siblings are apt to perceive that parents use a double standard to judge their behavior and the behavior of a handicapped brother or sister who is difficult to discipline:

> I read in this one book that the parents never taught the retarded son what "no" meant, and his sister finally taught him. Like my brother will sometimes just watch cartoons for hours, and my parents will say, "Well, we'll try to make him cut down on that." But they don't, because he'd make a huge fuss and throw a tantrum if they did.

Siblings do have questions regarding their responsibilities toward their handicapped brother or sister, and family members need to clearly define their expectations. Is the normal child expected to manage or discipline the handicapped child; are special allowances made for the handicapped child's behavior; is the normal sibling expected to help integrate the sibling within neighborhood peer groups? These may be demands that unfairly burden a sibling who has developmental needs of his or her own.

Parents often assume that their nonhandicapped children share their perspectives and motivation to further the handicapped child's development. However, as Crocker (1983) points out, siblings are often quite involved in their own developmental fulfillment, and do not or cannot share the parental perspective. At times, these differences may mean that siblings are less involved than parents, while at other times they may be more involved. Featherstone (1980) has also commented on the nature of parent and sibling experiences, how they influence each other, and how they differ.

> So it is with children (siblings). Their needs resemble ours; their resilience mirrors our own....We need to balance this insight by standing it on its head: our children differ from us in important ways. Their understanding is limited by their circumscribed experience and by their developmental needs. They stand in a different relationship to the disabled child, being brothers and sisters, not mothers and fathers. Their fears and feelings, though they parallel ours, are not the same. They may identify far more closely with their handicapped sibling than we do, because he or she resembles them more closely, because the wider world sees them through one lens. They vacillate more often between conflicting loyalties to friends and family. (pp. 173-174)

When families understand and address these sibling concerns directly, there is less likely to be confusion and resentment about the sibling's role and responsibilities. Further, these are life span issues. Adult siblings of handicapped persons may be expected or feel responsible to become their siblings' caretakers when parents die or are no longer capable of caring for the handicapped person. First-hand experience with groups of young siblings suggests that they begin to anticipate these future concerns long before they are actually faced with their sibling's total care. Life planning for the handicapped child should also be a matter which all family members begin to discuss years before decisions must be made.

Featherstone (1980) notes how siblings' evolving adjustment to their brother's or sister's handicap is often a source of strength to parents. What she describes is the ecological fluidity of family adaptation, the manner in which individual family members continue to adapt and to influence the entire family unit.

> Fortunately, the confusions of a 5-year-old (sibling) often give way before a 6-year-old's more persistent questioning. Adolescence may bring, along with a passion for being regular and an exaggerated sensitivity to family difference, a capacity to perform genuinely useful services. Perhaps it is this almost irrepressible capacity for change that enables the children in the family to cope as well as they do— and the parents to regain the hope and vitality that the original diagnosis threatened. (p. 174)

Peer interactions. The nonhandicapped sibling functions in an ecological context that is more typical of peers rather than the service-oriented context of the handicapped child. This normal context includes peer groups, neighborhood, schools, and related community activities. Although the nonhandicapped sibling remains a member of these groups, his or her sibling's handicap may have an impact on these environments. For example, siblings often must cope with teasing, embarrassment, isolation, less time with parents, and less time to take part in social activities.

Sometimes when other kids find out about my sister, they say "Oh, I'm so sorry, oh, I'm sorry for you." But I don't want their sympathy. All I want is to be friends with them. And my sister wouldn't want their sympathy either.

Sometimes kids will ask lots of questions, like "Why is he that way?" or "What do all those technical terms mean?" They'll ask you stupid questions, like can she comb her hair, or can she dress herself, or can she do buttons. So I just tell them to bug off. That it's none of their business.

I used to have a really big problem with friends. We would go bike riding and they'd tease my sister because she couldn't ride a bike. I always kept quiet, and then I always felt kind of depressed afterwards, because I never said anything. But since I was about 8 or 9, I stopped doing things with people like that.

I've dropped a lot of friends because of the way they acted. I've dropped about 10 people because of that, such stupid things they do.

The nonhandicapped sibling often feels ignored, with unmet needs. And even though the normal siblings operate primarily within normal settings, having a handicapped brother or sister makes the normal sibling a "special child" as well, as traditional family routines may need to be significantly altered to accommodate the handicapped sibling (e.g., family vacation plans, going out to dinner), and peer groups may not be accepting.

I think that one of the things my parents did especially well was to include my brother and me in making decisions about our family. My sister has a heart condition too (in addition to Down syndrome) and so there were things we couldn't do because of her. Like if we wanted to go camping in the mountains, they would tell us, well, we really can't keep her warm enough if we went camping, but we could possibly do one of several other things in places that are warmer. And those kinds of things made our family really close.

Like when I switched schools in fifth grade, I asked a couple of kids over, and they met my brother. When I asked them over again, they didn't come.

These are feelings and experiences that siblings may not share with parents. As all parents know, young children are often remarkably silent about things that affect them in large ways. For a child who is at the age where he or she is attempting to establish some distance from parents, there is a strong possibility that the parents may not learn of the child's experiences with unkind peers or strangers. As the research and these interviews with siblings indicate, however, siblings face a variety of problems related to their handicapped sibling, and these stresses may in turn affect the family as a whole.

Sibling Coping and Adaptation

Having a handicapped sibling is a significant source of stress across the age span; however, the variability reported in the studies of siblings clearly suggests differences in sibling responses to a handicapped child, and different levels of adaptation. Less clear than the variability itself are the factors which might account for each variation in adaptation, and particularly for more positive adaptations. Previous research suggests a number of factors which appear to mediate sibling response, such as age, sex, and family SES (Simeonsson & McHale, 1981), supporting the notion that sibling adaptation is a transactional rather than a fixed process.

Positive Coping: An Ecological Perspective

Demographic factors alone, however, are insufficient to explain the range and complexity of sibling adaptational response. It is likely that sibling response to the stress of having a handicapped brother or sister will depend upon the specific coping resources available to the sibling. The coping resources available, as well as how and when they are used, are then mediated by the various ecological settings in which the sibling interacts. This adaptational model has been previously proposed to explain familial adaptations to retarded children (Crnic et al., 1983), and is equally relevant to sibling considerations. The model attempts to explain the range of sibling adaptations as a response to stress moderated by the interaction of available coping resources and ecological contexts. And yet, specific to sibling considerations, the developmental context of age must also be accounted for, as the degree of perceived stress and the coping resources available will vary as a function of sibling age.

Previous concepts of sibling adaptation have been pathology based; that is, deleterious outcomes have been expected. A competence or coping-based framework, however, should be considered as an alternative to the pathology model (Drotar, 1981). This alternative model would emphasize the tasks and strategies involved in living with a handicapped person. The model of coping resources presented by Folkman, Schaefer, and Lazarus (1979) provides a useful basis for understanding the coping process that siblings might utilize. Folkman et al. delineate five types of coping resources, each of which is assumed to moderate the adverse effects of stress as appraised by an individual: health-energy-morale, problem-solving skills, social-network supports, utilitarian resources, and general and specific beliefs.

While no specific studies of sibling coping are available which test this model empirically, several previous studies suggest the utility of several of these resources. Family SES, which can be assumed to reflect the family's utilitarian resources, does affect adaptation, as siblings from middle and higher SES families appear to fare somewhat better than siblings from lower SES homes (Farber, 1960; Grossman, 1972). The study by Graliker et al. (1962) suggests that general and specific beliefs are likewise influential, as teenage siblings' adjustment was positively related to parental attitudes and ability to cope. O'Connor and Stachowiak (1971) reported similar findings. One sibling's observations illustrate how sensitive even young children are to parental attitudes and feelings about the handicapped child:

> You know, sometimes I look at my brother's baby book, and my mother all of a sudden stopped writing about him when he was about a year old. And I think that's when she found out how he was—that he was retarded. Because, you know, some mothers keep up a baby book until their child is 3 years old.

Siblings are influenced by parents' spoken and unspoken feelings of acceptance, disappointment, denial, or grief. Seligman (1983) has pointed out how parents' attitudes are influenced in turn by their religion, demonstrating the intricate web of influences upon family adaptation. Finally, Gath (1978) found that normal siblings who were reported as having behavior problems also had similar difficulties prior to the birth of the handicapped child. This finding supports the importance of health and morale. To date, studies of sibling problem-solving or social networks have not been done, although it seems reasonable to assume that children with good problem-solving skills and with strong social supports would be less vulnerable to stresses related to their handicapped sibling than children without these resources.

While perceived stress is moderated by coping resources, further consideration must be given to the various ecological contexts of the siblings' family, peer groups, and societal institutions (e.g., schools), as well as the interactions within and between these contexts. Presently, no systematic descriptive base exists detailing the environments in which siblings with a handicapped brother or sister function, and by which they are influenced. It is intuitively apparent that the ecologies of families with a handicapped child will differ markedly from those of nonhandicapped children, thereby directly and indirectly influencing the ecology of the normal sibling. At a minimum, siblings of handicapped children may have less opportunity for social contact with peers and larger social groups, and increased contacts with medical and educational service providers than their peers. In addition, special siblings must certainly cope with a set of cultural attitudes regarding the stigma of the handicap (Goffman, 1963). The behavior and attitudes of others in these various settings seem likely to influence such factors as the siblings' beliefs, problem-solving skills, social contacts, morale, and other resources which will in turn affect the siblings' response to the handicapped child. These are relationships which must be assessed if sibling adaptations are to be both understood and facilitated. For example, the presence of a handicapped sibling can be hypothesized to affect the self-concept of the nonhandicapped sibling. As one sibling confided: "All of my life I've kind of grown up thinking that, well, maybe there is something wrong with me." When a sibling overidentifies with the handicapped child, it may result in unexpressed fears about catching the disability or being somehow different than peers.

The teasing and embarrassment that siblings sometimes experience may also result in a lower sense of self-esteem than that of nonhandicapped peers. Dyson, Fewell, and Meyer (1985) administered the *Piers-Harris Children's Self-Concept Scale* (Piers, 1969) to two groups of siblings to test this hypothesis. The group of 26 siblings of handicapped children (ages 9-11 years) demonstrated a significantly higher self-concept than a normal control group. Further, the female siblings had higher self-concept scores than the male siblings. These rather surprising results may be due to treatment effects, because the siblings of the handicapped children were participating in a special program that was specially designed with their needs in mind. If this was the case, however, the findings support the benefits of providing similar programs which address sibling needs.

Three Perspectives on Family Functioning

Family function. Turnbull, Summers, and Brotherson (1983) and Skrtic et al. (1983) have also recommended a framework for understanding how families as a whole function. The framework can be applied to various family subsystems, like the sibling subsystem, and includes three perspectives: family function, family structure, and family life cycle. For example, families function as a socializing agent, and as Skrtic et al. point out, a handicapped child may have differential effects upon a sibling's socializing experiences. One sibling may experience reduced social interactions because of caretaking responsibilities for a handicapped sibling or because of peer rejection, whereas another sibling may benefit from the teaching skills and positive attitudes learned as part of growing up with a handicapped family member.

Family structure. Family structure describes the various relationships that exist between members of the immediate and extended family. Certain rules define these relationships, which may be affected by a child's handicap. For example, in most families, grandparents play a nurturing and supportive role in the lives of their grandchildren. Many grandparents enjoy this role by spoiling and generously giving their grandchildren love and attention. When a grandparent is not able to fill this role because of a grandchild's handicap, it affects both the handicapped child as well as the nonhandicapped sibling. The indirect effects a sibling experiences are sensitively described by a 10-year-old sibling.

> We go to visit my grandparents, and they don't talk to my sister. They'll talk to the rest of us, but they don't talk to her. We'll get in the car to go home, and she'll cry and ask "Why don't they ever talk to me?"

Family life cycle. Finally, the family life cycle is affected by a handicapped child. Skrtic et al. (1983) trace the impact of a handicapped child upon siblings of different ages, and note the increasingly direct effects nonhandicapped siblings often experience as they mature. For example, preschool-age siblings may experience the handicapped brother or sister primarily in terms of the family's disruption, as members adjust to the handicap. Older siblings, on the other hand, may need to confront their responsibility for their handicapped brother or sister directly and independently in the event of the parents' death. This conceptual model of family systems provides a means of focusing on siblings as part of a complex network that has a life cycle of its own, a perspective that might result in more naturalistic research studies as well as more ecologically valid interventions for siblings.

Conclusions and Future Directions

In this chapter, we have attempted to address issues surrounding the relationship between the nonhandicapped and the handicapped sibling, the impact that each can have on the other, and the perspectives and needs of the normal sibling. Although it seems clear from both research and clinical reports that the effects of having a handicapped sibling vary greatly from individual to individual, and we cannot automatically assume that the effects will be deleterious, normal siblings are at risk for any number of social, behavioral, or emotional difficulties. This at-risk status is a function of the ongoing stress associated with the presence of a handicapped sibling, and it is likely that the nature of these risks and stress vary across the sibling's life-span.

How siblings adapt to these circumstances is related to the coping resources that are available, both within the context of the family and in the various other ecological settings in which they interact. Certainly, we need more descriptive research on siblings and families of handicapped children which will strengthen our understanding of the coping and adaptation process. Yet while such research is being conducted, we can no longer afford to exclude siblings when services are provided to families of handicapped children. Siblings must be recognized as part of the family system, and parents made aware of their roles as mediators of the normal sibling's response (e.g., Graliker et al., 1962). Further, sibling coping and adaptation should be a concern in its own right, and individual attention given to these family members which will enhance their effective use of available coping resources and facilitate positive adaptations, both for themselves and the rest of their family. In this regard, the long-term effects of behavioral training techniques upon both the nonhandicapped and handicapped child need to be evaluated. Care should be taken not to increase the burden of responsibility siblings often appear to experience already by expecting them to assume the role of teacher/manager for the handicapped child. Rather, supports should be provided which strengthen siblings' unique coping resources.

Several programs (Cerreto, in press; Hodges, Mott, & Jenkins, 1982) have taken this more positive competence-based approach to meeting siblings' unique needs and facilitating their contributions to the family's coping. Moses (1982) has described well the range of complex questions, worries, and feelings that young siblings can benefit from sharing. In his edited transcript of a two-day session with siblings, he provides an effective model for professionals to use to facilitate siblings' discussion of common concerns, not judging them, but respecting their perspectives. Powell and Ogle (1985) describe a variety of strategies to support siblings, including workshops, counseling, and training programs. The Supporting Extended Family Members (SEFAM) program in Seattle, which has provided a regular program for fathers of handicapped children, has also offered workshops for siblings. These workshops give siblings opportunities to obtain answers to questions they are often reluctant to ask about their sibling's handicap, and to form peer support systems with other siblings. The program's staff have written a handbook which discusses common sibling concerns and serves as a reference for information about specific handicaps (Meyer, Vadasy, & Fewell, 1985a). Formats for these SEFAM sibling workshops have included half-day Saturday meetings with small group discussions, and large group social activities, like cooking projects or musical entertainment (Meyer, Vadasy, & Fewell, 1985b). An extended three-day program has been offered during summer vacation, which allows staff (some of whom were themselves siblings) and siblings opportunities to discuss topics in more depth than in a short meeting. An overnight camping trip to a converted army fort not only offered the siblings an activity that made them feel special (an important consideration when the handicapped child is most often the focus of the family's attention and energies), but it also gave the staff and siblings the time to feel comfortable enough to share their personal experiences and concerns.

Because the nature of the nonhandicapped sibling's stress is likely to change over the course of the family's life-span, it would appear prudent to take a preventive approach and provide the young sibling with enhanced problem-solving skills and a network of social supports. Siblings may then utilize these positive resources to cope with a variety of special circumstances, and can adapt them to meet their changing needs in the future. More descriptive and naturalistic studies of siblings, studies which employ a control group and which examine reciprocal effects of siblings upon each other, will provide the professionals who work with these siblings with the information needed to guide siblings through predictable crises and stresses. Parents, too, will benefit from information on siblings' developmental concerns, and can help prevent many of the difficulties siblings experience due to the impact of the handicapped child on the family system.

References

Apley, J., Barbour, R. F., & Westmacott, I. (1967). Impact of congenital heart disease on the family: Preliminary report. *British Medical Journal, 1,* 103-127.

Binger, C. M., Albin, A. R., & Feuerstein, R. (1969). Childhood leukemia: Emotional impact on patient and family. *New England Journal of Medicine, 280,* 414-418.

Breslau, N. (1982). Siblings of disabled children: Birth order and age spacing effects. *Journal of Abnormal Child Psychology, 10,* 85-96.

Breslau, N., Weitzman, M., & Messenger K. (1981). Psychologic functioning of siblings of disabled children. *Pediatrics, 67,* 344-353.

Bronfenbrenner, U. (1979). Contexts of child-rearing: Problems and prospects. *American Psychologist, 34,* 844-850.

Canning, C. D., & Canning, J. P. (1975). *The gift of Martha.* Boston: Children's Hospital Medical Center.

Cerreto, M. C. In press. Siblings of children with chronic conditions: In N. Paul (Ed.), *Birth Defects Original Article Series.*

Cicirelli, V. C. (1982). Sibling influence throughout the lifespan. In M. E. Lamb & B. Sutton-Smith (Eds.), *Sibling relationships: Their nature and significance across the lifespan* (pp. 267-284). Hillsdale, NJ: Erlbaum.

Cleveland, D. W., & Miller, N. B. (1977). Attitudes and life commitments of older siblings of mentally retarded adults: An exploratory study. *Mental Retardation, 15,* 38-41.

Crnic, K. A., Friedrich, W. N., & Greenberg, M. T. (1983). Adaptation of families with mentally retarded children: A model of stress, coping, and family ecology. *American Journal of Mental Deficiency, 88,* 125-138.

Crocker, A. C. (1981). The involvement of siblings of children with handicaps. In A. Milunsky (Ed.), *Coping with crisis and handicap.* New York: Plenum.

Crocker, A. C. (1983). Sisters and brothers. In J. A. Mulick & S. M. Pueschel (Eds.), *Parent-professional partnerships in developmental disability services* (pp. 139-148). Cambridge, MA: The Ware Press.

Drotar, D. (1981). Psychological perspectives in chronic childhood illness. *Journal of Pediatric Psychology, 6,* 211-228.

Dunn, J., & Kendrick, C. (1982). *Siblings: Love, envy, and understanding.* Cambridge, MA: Harvard University Press.

Dyson, L., Fewell, R., & Meyer, D. (1985). *The self-concept of siblings of handicapped children.* Manuscript submitted for publication.

Farber, B. (1960). Family organization and crisis: Maintenance and integration in families with a severely retarded child. *Monographs of the Society for Research in Child Development, 25,* 1-95.

Farber, B. (1963). Interaction with retarded siblings and life goals of children. *Marriage and Family Living, 25,* 96-98.

Featherstone, H. (1980). *A difference in the family: Life with a disabled child.* New York: Basic Books.

Folkman, S., Schaefer, C., & Lazarus, R. S. (1979). Cognitive processes as mediators of stress and coping. In V. Hamilton & D. W. Warburton (Eds.), *Human stress and cognition.* New York: Wiley.

Fowle, C. M. (1968). The effect of a severely mentally retarded child on his family.

American Journal of Mental Deficiency, 73, 468-473.

Friedrich, W. N., & Friedrich, W. L. (1981). Comparison of psychosocial assets of parents with a handicapped child and their normal controls. *American Journal of Mental Deficiency, 85,* 551-553.

Gath, A. (1972). The mental health of siblings of congenitally abnormal children. *Journal of Child Psychology and Psychiatry, 13,* 211-218.

Gath, A. (1973). The school age siblings of mongol children. *British Journal of Psychiatry, 123,* 161-167.

Gath, A. (1974). Sibling reactions to mental handicap: A comparison of the brothers and sisters of mongol children. *Journal of Child Psychology and Psychiatry, 15,* 187-198.

Gath, A. (1978). *Downs syndrome and the family: The early years.* New York: Academic Press.

Gayton, W., Friedman, S., Tavormina, J., & Tucker, F. (1977). Children with cystic fibrosis: I. Psychological test findings on patients, siblings, and parents. *Pediatrics, 59,* 888-894.

Goffman, E. (1963). *Stigma.* Englewood Cliffs, NJ: Prentice-Hall.

Graliker, B. V., Fishler, K., & Koch, R. (1962). Teenage reactions to a mentally retarded sibling. *American Journal of Mental Deficiency, 66,* 838-843.

Grossman, F. K. (1972). *Brothers and sisters of retarded children: An exploratory study.* Syracuse, NY: Syracuse University Press.

Hodges, B., Mott, D. W., & Jenkins, V. (1982, November). *Let's grow together: Workshops for siblings of handicapped persons.* Paper presented at the annual meeting of the Southeastern American Association on Mental Deficiency, Louisville, KY.

Holroyd, J., Brown, N., Wikler, L., & Simmons, H. (1975). Stress in families of institutionalized and non-institutionalized autistic children. *Journal of Community Psychology, 3,* 26-31.

Holt, K. (1958). The home care of retarded children. *Pediatrics 22,* 744-755

McHale, S. M., Sloan, J., & Simeonsson, R. J. (1982, July 6-10). *Sibling relationships of children with autistic, mentally retarded, and non-handicapped children: A comparative study.* Paper presented at the annual meeting of the National Society for Autistic Children, Omaha, NB.

Meyer, D. J., Vadasy, P. F., & Fewell, R. R. (1985a). *Living with a brother or sister with special needs: A book for sibs.* Seattle: University of Washington Press.

Meyer, D. J., Vadasy, P. F., & Fewell, R. R. (1985b). *Sibshops: A handbook for implementing workshops for siblings of children with special needs.* Seattle: University of Washington Press.

Meuwissen, H. J. (1971). Family adaptation to a child with cystic fibrosis. *Journal of Pediatrics, 78,* 543-549.

Michaelis, C. T. (1980). *Home and school partnerships in exceptional children.* Rockville, MD: Aspen Systems.

Miller, S. G. (1974). An exploratory study of sibling relationships in families with retarded children. *Dissertation Abstracts International, 35,* 2994B-2995B.

Moses, K. (1982). *Brothers and sisters of special children. Interactions.* Madison, WI: Harry A. Waisman Center on Mental Retardation and Human Development.

O'Connor, W., & Stachowiak, J. (1971). Patterns of interaction in families with low adjusted, high adjusted, and mentally retarded family members. *Family Process, 10,* 229-241.

O'Neill, J. (1965). Siblings of the retarded: Individual counseling. *Children, 12,* 226-229.

Peck, J. R., & Stephens, W. B. (1960). A study of the relationship between the attitudes and behaviors of parents and that of their mentally defective child. *American Journal of Mental Deficiency, 64,* 839-844.

Pfouts, J. H. (1976). The sibling relationship: A forgotten dimension. *Social Work, 21,* 200-204.

Piers, E. P. (1969). *The Piers-Harris Children's Self-Concept Scale.* Nashville, TN: Counselor Recordings and Tests.

Powell, T. H., & Ogle, P. A. (1985). *Brothers and sisters— A special part of exceptional families.* Baltimore: Paul H. Brookes.

Price-Bonham, S., & Addison, S. (1978). Families and mentally retarded children: Emphasis on the father. *The Family Coordinator, 3,* 221-230.

Robinson, N. M., & Robinson, H. B. (1976). *The mentally retarded child.* New York: McGraw-Hill.

Rude, H. A. (1982). The student attitude and perspective scale. Greeley, CO: University of Northern Colorado.

San Martino, M., & Newman, M. B. (1974). Siblings of retarded children: A population at risk. *Child Psychiatry and Human Development, 4,* 168-177.

Schreibman, L., O'Neill, R. E., & Koegel, R. L. (1983). Behavioral training for siblings of autistic children. *Journal of Applied Behavior Analysis, 16,* 129-138.

Seligman, M. (1983). Understanding and communicating with families of handicapped children. In S. G. Garwood (Ed.), *Educating young handicapped children: A developmental approach* (pp. 435-474). Rockville, MD: Aspen Systems.

Simeonsson, R. J., & McHale, S. M. (1981). Review: Research on handicapped children: Sibling Relationships. *Child: Care Health and Development, 7,* 153-171.

Skrtic, T. M., Summers, J. A., Brotherson, M. J., & Turnbull, A. P. (1983). Severely handicapped children and their brothers and sisters. In J. Blacher (Ed.), *Severely handicapped young children and their families: Research in review* (pp. 215-246). New York: Academic Press.

Stoneman, Z., & Brody, G. H. (In press). Observational research on retarded children, their parents, and their siblings. In S. Landesman-Dwyer & P. Vietze (Eds.), *Living with retarded people.* Washington, DC: American Association on Mental Deficiency.

Tew, B., & Lawrence, K. M. (1973). Mothers, brothers and sisters of patients with spina bifida. *Developmental Medicine and Child Neurology, 15,* 69-76.

Travis, G. (1976). *Chronic illness in children: Its impact on child and family.* Stanford, CA: Stanford University Press.

Turnbull, A. P., Summers, J. A., & Brotherson, M. J. (1983). *Working with families with disabled members: A family systems approach.* Unpublished manuscript.

Turnbull, A. (with G.J. Bronicki & A. P. Turnbull). (1985). Changing second graders' attitudes toward people with mental retardation: Using kid power. Poster session presented at the Annual Meeting of the American Association on Mental Deficiency, Philadelphia, May 27-31.

4

Grandparents and the Extended Family of Handicapped Children

Ida Mae Sonnek

The increasing number of adults in the United States living beyond 65 years of age has resulted in a rapidly growing interest in the area of gerontology. In recent years, the importance of intergenerational relationships across the life-span has been recognized as an integral aspect of how families function. Further, the changing lifestyles of young adults have created new roles for some grandparents. In some cases, grandparents must take steps to safeguard their traditional role, for example, when they risk losing contact with grandchildren through the parents' divorce. In families with a handicapped child, the grandparents may need to make even more significant adjustments in their grandparenting roles. This chapter will examine the factors that influence grandparenting roles, including the effects of a handicapped grandchild as one of the factors affecting extended family interactions.

Accessibility of Grandparents and the Extended Family

Demographers have called our attention to the aging of the United States population. This trend has direct implications concerning the character of families in the United States as well as the roles the older family members may play. Approximately 70% of older persons in the United States have living grandchildren (Subcommittee on Human Services, 1982). The role of grandparent often extends over a large part of a person's life; women typically become grandmothers at 50 years of age, while men typically become grandfathers at 52 years of age (Subcommittee on Human Services, 1982). These trends, coupled with longer life expectancy, mean that grandparenthood may be a role that spans 20-30 years. Yet little is known about the role of grandparents. The lack of knowledge may be attributable, in part, to the independence and isolation that characterize the nuclear family, especially in carrying out its child-rearing function (Troll, 1971). Changes in the living arrangements of older Americans contribute to families' independence and isolation:

1. Census data from 1960 and 1970 indicate that the number of three- and four-generation households decreased by 10% during the 1960s (U.S. Bureau of the Census, 1976).
2. Multigenerational households represented only 4% of all households in 1976 (Harris, 1978).
3. The majority of older Americans live in a house they own (Gabe, 1981).
4. An increasing number of older Americans are maintaining their own household in geographic areas dissimilar from their younger counterparts (e.g., small towns versus metropolitan area; center city versus suburban areas) (Gabe, 1981).

Despite these trends, there is evidence that the nuclear family may not be as isolated as originally thought. It has been reported that:

1. Based on a probability sample, nearly 8 out of 10 older persons in the United States with children had seen at least one child during the week preceding the survey (Shanas, 1979).
2. Approximately 75% of grandparents see their grandchildren at least once every week (Harris & Associates, 1975).
3. Nearly half of all grandparents see their grandchildren every day (Atcheley, 1977).

A body of literature regarding family life in the United States has characterized it as a "modified extended family system" rather than as an isolated nuclear unit (Litwak, 1960; Sussman, 1959; Uzoka, 1979). The modified extended family is distinguished by a network of mutual aid and support between generations in spite of geographic distances separating them (Litwak, 1960). The availability of transportation

(Sussman, 1959) and the telephone (Cohler & Grunebaum, 1981; Leichter & Mitchell, 1968) are factors by which this network is fostered and maintained. This network of mutual aid and communication has been found to be operative not only in times of crisis (Hill, 1949; Shanas, 1967; Young, 1954), but on an ongoing basis as well (Shanas, 1960, 1962; Sussman, 1960).

Demographics of an Aging America

The percentage of older Americans has increased at a faster rate than the total population has increased. Between 1900 and 1970, the total population of the United States grew to almost three times its 1900 size, while the over-65 segment grew by seven times its 1900 size (Brotman, 1977). The over-65 population now comprises 10.5% of the total population (U.S. Bureau of the Census, 1976). Harris (1978) attributed this increase to three factors: (a) the high birth rate of the late 19th and early 20th century, (b) the high immigration rate prior to World War I, and (c) the dramatic increase in life expectancy during the 20th century.

The number of older persons is expected to increase steadily in the future. Assuming a stable fertility and mortality rate, the over-65 population will increase to 11.7% by 1990; 15% in 2020; and by 2030, to 17% of the total United States population (Gabe, 1981; Harris, 1978).

Changing Lifestyles of Adult Children

Because of the increase in divorce, female employment, and teenage pregnancy, adult children are more likely to ask extended family members to assume part or total responsibility for their young children. Only 63% of all children under 18 live with both biological parents; 22% live with either parent; 10% live with one biological and one stepparent; and 2% (1.6 million children) live with grandparents or other relatives (Select Committee on Children, Youth and Families, 1983). It is estimated that nearly one half of all children born in the 1970s will, by the time they are 18 years of age, have spent some portion of their lives in a single-parent situation (Hetherington, 1979) generally with a mother who is divorced (U.S. Bureau of the Census, 1979a). In addition, 65.7% of all married women living with their husbands, 78.6% of all women separated from their husbands, and 85.5% of all divorced women are in the labor force and have children under the age of six (U.S. Bureau of the Census, 1979b). Child care is a pressing need for these families. The United States Census Bureau (1979b) reported that 33.8% of 3- to 6-year-old children who had mothers working outside the home were cared for by relatives other than a parent. Lastly, since one birth in five in the United States is to a teenage mother (Zero Population Growth, 1976), 85% of whom keep their children (Alan Guttmacher

Institute, 1976), grandparents are particularly likely to assume some childrearing responsibility for the children of these young mothers.

Roles of Grandparents in Relation to the Nuclear Family

The literature describing the "modified extended family" as characteristic of family life in the United States is the rationale generally used for studying the nuclear family-extended family relationship. The definition of "modified extended family" is not always clear. Does it describe only the grandparent-nuclear family relationship, or does it include the relationships with siblings, aunts, and uncles of the nuclear family? Since discussions about the extended family tend to focus on the role of grandparents with few references to the roles of other extended family members, the following section will focus only on the role of grandparents. Society promulgates various assumptions about the importance of grandparents in the lives of its citizens. The second Sunday in September has been designated as Grandparent's Day, a day to specifically remember one's grandparents with cards or flowers. Advertisers constantly suggest ways of keeping in touch with grandparents—by sharing a set of prints when film is processed, or by using the telephone. The media and advertisers often reinforce stereotypes of typical "grandparenting" activities—telling tall tales, sharing information from times past, or describing how to survive in the woods.

The effect of these superficial attempts to acknowledge the role of the grandparent is questionable. There is an appreciation, however, of the importance of the grandparent-grandchild relationship that is reflected in popular programs. The best known of these programs is the Foster Grandparent Program, in which low-income retired persons serve as surrogate grandparents in programs for young children and handicapped individuals. These activities mark the emergence of a new area of knowledge referred to as "intergenerational education."

Despite a growing appreciation of the importance of grandparents, there is a paucity of theoretical and empirical knowledge to verify the appropriateness of these media and program efforts. The existing information about grandparenting comes from three sources in the literature: psychoanalytic studies on grandparenting, studies describing the "modified extended family system" and older persons' perceptions of old age, and research with grandparenting as a primary focus.

Psychoanalytic literature. Until the 1960s, studies of grandparenting were found primarily in the psychoanalytic literature. These studies focused almost exclusively on grandparents' influence, particularly that of the grandmother, on their grandchildren who were receiving psychiatric treatment for emotional or behavioral problems. LaBarre, Jessner, and Ussery (1960) examined case studies of 41 children undergoing psychiatric treatment who had a grandmother as a significant adult (e.g., living in the same household, a primary caregiver) to determine the direct influence the grandmother played in the child's life. Borden (1946) provided examples of case studies in which grandparents had played a decisive role in their grandchildren's problems. Articles such as "Grandma Made Johnny Delinquent" (Strauss, 1943) and "The Grandmother: A Problem in Child Rearing" (Vollmer, 1937) related the role of grandmother to a grandchild's deviant behavior. These researchers also concluded that grandparents, especially the grandmother, had a particularly powerful but negative impact on families, resulting in the grandchildren experiencing emotional or behavioral problems.

"Modified extended family system" literature. This area of research attempted to identify the type of activities, the participants in the activities, and the conditions under which these activities occurred in order to determine the existence of intergenerational relationships. As has been stated earlier, these studies indicated a network of mutual aid and support across generations. Many of the roles frequently associated with grandparenting have been drawn from the activities of grandparents described in this body of research.

The literature describes various instrumental supports grandparents provide. Babysitting is one of the most frequently cited ways grandparents help their adult children (Shanas, 1967; Sussman, 1953, 1962; Townsend, 1957). In addition, grandparents provide direct financial aid to their children (Sussman, 1953), or indirect aid by buying gifts for their grandchildren (Boyd, 1969a) and helping defray the grandchildrens' educational expenses (Bell, 1968). Grandparents have also been identified as family historians (Boyd, 1969a; Nimkoff, 1961) and as storytellers (Boyd, 1969a). Grandparents have been found to serve as mediators in conflicts between parents and their children (Schorr, 1960), as well as acting as a friend to their grandchildren (Radcliffe-Brown, 1952).

Grandparenting as a focus of study. Using data obtained from grandparents themselves about their grandparenting experiences, Albrecht (1954), Neugarten and Weinstein (1964), and Robertson (1977) were able to describe activities or roles associated with grandparenthood.

Examining the responsibilities that average elderly grandparents assume for their grandchildren, Albrecht (1954) found that purely social visits were the most common activity, with occasional babysitting, writing letters, caring for children while parents work, and providing a place for brief vacations for the children as other common activities. These results were obtained from a sample of 630 grandparents over 65 years of age.

Robertson (1977) compiled a list of behaviors associated with grand-parenting as described in the literature. This list included such behaviors as providing gifts, babysitting, providing home recreation, taking grandchildren on zoo and shopping trips, dropping in for visits, relating family history, teaching sewing or native language, taking grandchildren on vacations, taking children to church, providing advice on personal problems, work or religion. From a sample of 125 grandmothers, of which 38% were 70 years of age and 9% in their 40s, grandmothers tended to babysit, take part in home recreational activities, and drop in to visit more frequently than the other types of activities.

Neugarten and Weinstein (1964) used the responses of 46 maternal and 24 paternal sets of grandparents to open-ended questions (such as how often and on what occasions they saw their grandchildren), and determined that certain types of activities represented particular styles of grandparenting. The data enabled them to describe five styles of grandparenting:

1. Formal—provides special treats and indulgences for grandchildren; occasionally babysits.
2. Fun Seeker—joins the grandchild in specific activities for the purpose of having fun.
3. Surrogate Parent—assumes caretaking responsibility in such situations as mother working.
4. Reservoir of Family Wisdom—shares special skills or resources with grandchildren.
5. Distant Figure—brings gifts or visits only on holidays, other special occasions or birthdays.

Factors Affecting Roles of Grandparents

In the discussions of their findings, researchers occasionally noted differences in styles of grandparenting. This section will summarize the factors that these researchers have cited as possibly contributing to these differences.

Circumstances within the nuclear family. Researchers have found that grandparents, especially grandmothers, assume babysitting responsibilities in the following situations: during an adult child's illness (Sussman, 1962); at the birth of a child or employment of the mother (Albrecht, 1954; Neugarten & Weinstein, 1964; Sussman, 1953; Townsend, 1957); when grandparent is living with adult children (Shanas, 1967); and in nonemergency circumstances (Albrecht, 1954: Boyd, 1969a; Robertson, 1977; Townsend, 1957; Young & Wilmott, 1957). In addition, the nuclear family's financial status (Bell, 1968; Boyd, 1969a; Sussman, 1953; Young 1954) and interpersonal problems (Schorr, 1960) have been cited as reasons for grandparents' involvement in their children's lives.

Significance of grandparent role. Kivnick (1982) and Robertson (1977) contended that the personal significance that being a grandparent has for the grandparent affects the grandparenting activities engaged in by the grandparent. Each researcher has developed a framework by which the grandparent's understanding of grandparenthood may be determined. The Kivnick paradigm includes the following five components:

1. Centrality—the degree to which being a grandparent and engaging in grandparenting activities is the focal point of the grandparent's life.
2. Valued Elder—the degree to which grandparenthood is associated with being a wise and respected member of the family.
3. Immortality through Clan—the perception of achieving immortality by having grandchildren.
4. Reinvolvement with Personal Past—grandparenthood perceived as an opportunity to relive times past.
5. License to be Lenient—grandparenthood perceived as a license to be indulgent with grandchildren.

A composite of how grandparents perceive themselves in relation to each of these components would indicate the significance the role of grandparent has for them. Robertson (1977) described the meaning of grandmothering in terms of types of grandmothering. The four types of grandmothering are:

1. Apportioned—is concerned with grandchildren's welfare as well as aware of a need to receive some personal pleasure from doing things for grandchildren.
2. Symbolic—is primarily concerned with the welfare of grandchildren with little or no attention given to any personal satisfaction that might be achieved because of a relationship with grandchildren.
3. Individualized—puts a heavy emphasis on how grandchildren complement or enhance grandmother's life.
4. Remote—shows little or no involvement or concern about grandchildren.

Age of grandparent. According to Neugarten and Weinstein's (1964) findings, the formal grandparenting style is most common for grand-parents over 65 years of age, whereas the "fun seeker" or "distant figure" predominates for the under-65 grandparent. The younger widows studied by Lopata (1973), and the younger grandmothers in the Robertson (1977) study placed less emphasis on engaging in grand-mothering activities. In the Albrecht (1954) study, 30% of the sample were great-grandparents, and the type of activities in which these individuals engaged with their great-grandchildren and grandchildren varied from those activities engaged in by grandparents. For example, only 4% of the great-grandparents reported babysitting, whereas 19% of the grandparents reported doing this. Letters were reported as the only means of communication between generations for 48% of the great-grandparents and for 10% of the grandparents.

Sex of grandparent. Neugarten and Weinstein (1964) noted sex differences in styles of grandparenting. The "surrogate parent" style was more commonly associated with grandmothers, and the "reservoir of family wisdom" style was identified with grandfathers.

Bloodline of grandparent. Adams (1968), Stryker (1955), and Troll, Miller, and Atcheley (1979) have observed that closer ties exist along maternal bloodlines than along paternal bloodlines. Cohler and Grunebaum (1981) explain the importance of the maternal bloodline by pointing out that a woman's identification with her mother is one of the most important influences on the woman's maternal role.

In addition, maternal grandmothers and paternal grandfathers appear to be most supportive of the child-rearing techniques practiced within the nuclear family (Kahana & Kahana, 1971).

Parent-adult child relationship. In both the Lopata (1973) and the Neugarten and Weinstein (1964) studies, grandparents said that disagreements with their adult children negatively affected their role as a grandparent. Studying adult children's perspectives, Johnson and Bursk (1977) found that adult children perceived a higher quality of relationship with their parents when: (a) both shared similar values, (b) the relationship was based on mutual respect and trust, and (c) the relationship was based on realistic mutual perceptions. In the same study, adult children tended to rate the quality of the parent-adult child relationship as better when their parents were fairly active, busy in a variety of activities, and in good health. Boyd (1969b) concurred with Johnson and Bursk and added that the grandparenting role was further enhanced if the grandparents maintained their own home and made it an attractive place for family gatherings and for grandchildren's vacations.

Geographic proximity of grandparents to nuclear family. Lopata (1973), in a study of Chicago widows, found that those women who reported seeing their grandchildren frequently also described being able to develop a significant relationship with their grandchildren. Further, Boyd (1969a) indicated that, according to their adult children, parents' ability to maintain their own homes and live nearby strengthened the parent-adult child relationship.

Grandparents' desire not to interfere in the nuclear family. Albrecht (1954) and Robertson (1975) described grandparents' fears of being perceived as intruding in their children's families as a factor affecting grandparenting. Robertson (1975) cited this as an explanation of the discrepancies between what grandmothers wish to do with or for their grandchildren, and what they actually do.

Role of grandparents within nuclear family. In a cross-cultural study, Apple (1954) found that the power and authority of grandparents within the family influences the style of grandparenting. Grandparents who do not retain authority tend to be warm and indulgent toward their grandchildren, whereas grandparents with power and prestige are more formal and authoritarian.

Age of grandchildren. There is some evidence that grandparents' roles may need to change as their grandchildren grow older. Kahana and Kahana (1970) reported that 4- and 5-year-old children want grandparents who are indulgent, 8- and and 9-year-old children want active and fun-sharing grandparents; and 11- and 12-year-olds appear to be growing distant from their grandparents. Robertson (1976) found that adult children most often wanted a relationship with their grandparents that was based on emotional gratification.

In addition, Komarovsky (1962) reported the frequency of contact between children's mothers and their grandmothers was greatest during the first seven years of their mothers' marriages, and declined somewhat in succeeding years. The presence of young children and the role of grandmothers as an important source of child-rearing information were identified as significant factors fostering this contact between the mother and grandmothers.

Critique of Current Knowledge about Grandparenting

The evidence suggests that grandparenting has not been the subject of systematic investigation. Much of what is known about grandparenting, particularly about the roles grandparents play, has been extrapolated from the results of the "modified extended family" research. When grandparenting has been the focus of study, the research has taken a single generational perspective—primarily that of the grandparents. The results of such efforts have been generally limited to hypotheses about grandparenting. The findings of both the "modified extended family" research and the studies of grandparenting rarely include data on factors (e.g., age, sex, bloodline of grandparents, parent-adult child relationship) which appear to affect the type or frequency of grandparenting activities. There have been no known systematic research efforts to identify all the variables affecting grandparenting, to verify the effect of the variables on grandparenting, or to verify the significance of these variables across generations.

This review indicates that the role of grandparents is to provide support to the nuclear family. Given the tentative nature surrounding the knowledge about grandparenting, it appears that grandparents, to date, have been an unrecognized and possibly an underutilized resource in the study of the nuclear family.

Families of Handicapped Children and the Extended Family

The literature abounds with research findings that underscore the impact of a handicapped child on mothers (Dunst, Trivette, & Cross, Chapter 7; Vadasy & Fewell, Chapter 5). It is only more recently that attention has focused on the effects of such a child on fathers (Meyer, Chapter 2) and siblings (Crnic & Leconte, Chapter 3). There is a lack of empirical evidence describing the effect of a handicapped child on extended family members.

Effects of the Handicapped Child on Extended Family Relationships

Relationships with extended family members have been discussed in studies of families with handicapped children (Davis, 1967; Ehlers, 1966; Farber, 1959; McAndrew, 1976). McAndrew (1976) reported that one third of the 116 parents interviewed said that there had been negative changes in their relationships with their parents and friends as a result of the birth of their physically handicapped child. Similarly, strained family relationships in families with a mentally retarded child was the explanation given for the lack of "effective" support from maternal grandmothers (Davis, 1967). "Effective" support was defined as maternal grandmother being available to the family upon the family's request. Davis also reported that 75% of families with nonhandicapped children received this type of support, while less than 50% of families with a mentally retarded child received "effective" support.

Investigating the effect of a severely handicapped child on family integration, Farber (1959) found that frequent contact between the child's mother and her mother was conducive to high marital integration, whereas frequent contact with her mother-in-law tended to be a disruptive influence. Maternal grandmothers were perceived as providing help to their daughters; paternal grandmothers were perceived as being unsympathetic to their daughters-in-law and were frequently thought to blame the daughters-in-law for the child's handicapping condition or for placing an excessive burden on their sons. In contrast, Ehlers (1966) found that mothers describe having parents, in-laws, or other relatives living in the same house or nearby as being helpful. In Chapter 5, Vadasy and Fewell report that mothers of deaf-blind children rank grandmothers high on their list of supports.

Although family crises are most often defined as illness, natural disaster, or economic need (Hill, 1949; Shanas, 1967; Young, 1954), the birth of a handicapped child may be another form of crisis for the family. In times of crisis, children turn toward parents, and adult children turn to their parents. Yet families with a handicapped child who turn to their parents frequently report a lack of social support (Birenbaum, 1970; McDowell & Gabel, 1981). Parents of handicapped children appear to have smaller social networks than families with nonhandicapped children, due in part to reduced family networks (McDowell & Gabel, 1981).

Factors Contributing to Decrease in Support

The "modified extended family" concept, with its network of mutual aid and support operating both on a continuous basis and during times of crisis, has generated an appreciation that the extended family, as well as the child's family, may be affected by a handicapped child (Gabel & Kotsch, 1981; Schell, 1981). Gabel and Kotsch (1981) suggest that how the extended family member is affected by the handicapped child may affect intergenerational relationships in the family. First, because extended family members often experience strong emotional reactions to the child's handicap, they may not have sufficient emotional energy to cope with their own feelings of anger, guilt, or grief, as well as to provide support to the nuclear family. Secondly, because meeting the day-to-day needs of the handicapped child may require such specialized arrangements and techniques, extended family members may feel inadequate in offering assistance or providing advice. Both Pieper (1976) and Susser (1974) have also referred to these problems although there are no known empirical data to validate these assertions.

This review indicates that very little is known about the relationship between the extended family and the handicapped child. Because there appear to be differences between the type and amount of support extended family members provide families with a nonhandicapped child and those with a handicapped child, this would appear to be an area in need of empirical study.

Programs Serving the Extended Family of the Handicapped Child

An awareness of the significance of intergenerational relationships for the nuclear family, as well as the effect of the presence of a handicapped child on that relationship, has stimulated a general interest in the extended family by professionals working with handicapped individuals and their families. What has emerged are programs and research efforts focusing solely on the extended family of a handicapped child.

Programs that serve handicapped children often develop programs for extended family members. The Handicapped Children's Early Education Program (HCEEP) in the Department of Education, Office of Special Education has provided seed money for many of these efforts. Prototypes of these programs are the Family, Infant and Toddler Project at George Peabody College of Vanderbilt University (Gabel & Kotsch, 1981); the Family Intervention Project at Georgia State University (Berger & Fowlkes, 1980); the Grandparents' Workshop at the Atlanta Speech School (Rhoades, 1975); and the Training Grandparents of Children with Special Needs Project at the Advocates for Retarded Citizens, Seattle, Washington.

Family, Infant and Toddler Project. The extended family component of this project consists of bimonthly evening meetings to which parents of the children invite whomever they wish to attend. The meetings include: discussions of the child's educational program, demonstrations of educational activities accompanied by explanations of why they are being done, question-and-answer sessions regarding the child's current status or future prognosis, as well as opportunities for discussion of personal feelings and concerns.

Family Intervention Project. The focus of this program is the entire family system. Through the use of an Individualized Family Treatment Plan, family members engage in specified activities that help them utilize existing resources within the family system to meet the needs of the handicapped child. Activities focus upon educational and behavioral programs for the handicapped child, as well as strategies for dealing with community service systems. The project's goal is the development of a self-sufficient, ongoing support system for the handicapped child and the family.

Grandparents' Workshop. The family involvement program at the Atlanta Speech School includes a Saturday morning workshop specifically for grandparents of the infants and preschoolers enrolled in the school. The workshop includes a tour of the facility and presentations on the anatomy of hearing, hearing tests, the causes of hearing impairment, degrees of hearing impairment, distinctions between speech and language, and remediation techniques.

Participants in these extended family activities report an improved understanding of the handicapped child, as well as increased ability to offer support to the children and their families (Gabel & Kotsch, 1981). Unfortunately, none of the three projects described above provides empirical evidence regarding their effectiveness in creating and maintaining support of the family with a handicapped child by extended family members.

Training Grandparents of Children with Special Needs. This project, funded under Section 631(c) of P.L. 98-199, the EHA Amendments of 1983, provides for the training of grandparents to meet the special needs of their handicapped grandchildren. The project has three components. The first is a series of six annual Grandparent Workshops which offer grandparents opportunities to meet other grandparents and develop supports, as well as to meet with professionals who can provide information and direct grandparents to local resources to meet their family's needs. The staff of the Seattle Grandparent Workshops have reported on the often high levels of instrumental and expressive support which grandparents provide the family of their handicapped grandchild, and the grandparents' strong interest in meeting with and sharing their experiences with other grandparents (Vadasy, Fewell, & Meyer, in press).

The second component of this project is the Helping Grandparent Program in which experienced grandparents are trained to provide support to grandparents of newly diagnosed children. Modeled upon the Parent-to-Parent Support programs developed by the King County ARC in Seattle, the Helping Grandparents will be available to offer one-to-one support to grandparents matched on selected family characteristics. The third component is the grandparent newsletter, *Especially Grandparents,* which is disseminated quarterly to grandparents and professionals interested in grandparent concerns.

The Maternal Grandmother's Role

When a family is faced with a crisis, the role of individual extended family members may take on additional significance. Given the paucity of information on the relationship between the extended family and families of handicapped children, it seems crucial to investigate the effect the handicapped child may have on particular extended family members, and to ascertain the role that an individual may play in the care and support of such a child. One such attempt was a qualitative exploration of the maternal grandmother's role in families with young handicapped children (Sonnek, 1983).

The purpose of this particular study was to describe the maternal grandmother's role in families with a handicapped child between birth and three years of age. Eight mother-adult daughter pairs who are grandparents/parents of such a child were interviewed individually about what grandmothers do for their daughters, grandchildren, and handicapped grandchild, as well as how grandmothers feel about being a grandmother and having a handicapped grandchild. Each unstructured interview was audiotaped and transcribed. The responses of the mother-adult daughter pairs were divided into statements on discrete topics.

These statements were sorted into categories according to similarity of theme, meaning, or content.

An analysis of the response showed that the maternal grandmother's role could not be described by a single set of activities. Rather, these grandmothering activities were more frequently characterized by: (a) circumstances that create the need for grandmothering activities, (b) limits which determine the type of activities or the circumstances creating the need for grandmothering, and (c) factors which facilitate the continual involvement of grandmothers in grandmothering activities. In order to accommodate this expanded perspective of the maternal grandmother role, four categories were generated to reflect these various influences.

Grandmothering activities. Central to the maternal grandmother's role was the category called "Grandmothering Activities." This category incorporated 18 possible activities which grandmothers might engage in with or for their daughters, grandchildren, or handicapped grandchild. Table 4.1 lists a sample of the activities with examples from the interviews. There did not appear to be separate activities for grandmothering nonhandicapped grandchildren versus grandmothering the handicapped grandchild, although there tended to be more references to the activity "Teacher/Therapist" in regard to grandmothering the handicapped grandchild. What did emerge was that grandmothering appeared to be intricately intertwined with the help patterns of mothers for their daughter. For example, one mother said: "She'll (grandmother) watch them (grandchildren) when I work some. She watches them two or three times a week while I work, which helps out financially." A grandmother reported: "She (daughter) tells me the kinds of things (activities) they (teachers) do. And then, when she (daughter) was in the hospital, every time I changed (handicapped grandchild), we'd do a few little things (prescribed activities)."

Table 4.1. Samples from *Grandmothering Activities*

Activities	Example
Source of Assistance	If they're (daughter and husband) going to get groceries or if they're going, you know, someplace during the day where it's not convenient to have a babysitter. (grandmother babysits). (grandmother interview)
Caregiver	I'm the babysitter, par excellence. (grandmother interview)
Gift-giver	I get them (grandchildren) gifts at Christmas-time and holidays. (grandmother interview)

Playmate	(When) they're (grandchildren) at our house, we'll (grandparents) play games with them, inside games. . . .They like to do those sort of things. . .mostly games, little kids' kinds of things.
	(grandmother interview)
Teacher-Therapist	I do talk plain to him (handicapped grandchild); I talk slow to him. I try to get him to pronounce his words.
	(grandmother interview)

Circumstances. A second category was added because mothers and adult daughters often provided information about the events or situations precipitating particular activities. This category was called "Circumstances." It contained 32 opportunities, events, or incidents which were cited as creating the need for one or several of the grandmothering activities. The data showed that the need for any grandmothering activity could be created by the daughters, the grandmothers, the nonhandicapped grandchildren, the handicapped grandchild, or the demographics of the mother's or daughter's environment. Thus, the occasions for grandmothering were grouped according to the source. Table 4.2 contains a sample of the occasions with examples from the interviews.

Table 4.2. Samples from *Circumstances*

Occasions	Example
Financial Problems	She loans me money if I need it.
	(mother interview)
Grandmother Visiting Grandchildren	Sometimes I don't get to bed for hours and hours when I'm down there (visiting grandchildren in North Carolina) because I have to read to them (grandchildren).
	(grandmother interview)
Requests of Grandchildren	She spoils them (grandchildren). She gives them anything they ask for.
	(mother interview)
Birth-Diagnosis of Handicapped Child	When (handicapped child) was born, Mom took (sibling) for the first week because (handicapped child) stayed in the hospital so I came home. She kept (sibling) which gave me a lot of time to get myself back together and figure where we were going to go from here.
	(mother interview)
Overlapping Lifestyles	We belong to the same church circle and the same church organizations. We do those things together.
	(grandmother interview)

Parameters. The data showed that there were limits to the activities in which grandmothers participated. Twenty-six types of limits were identified and incorporated under a category "Parameters." These limits could stem from daughters, grandmothers, nonhandicapped grandchildren, the handicapped grandchild, or family demographics, and they were grouped accordingly. Table 4.3 contains a sample of these limits with examples from the interviews.

Table 4.3. Samples from *Parameters*

Limits	Example
Personal Obligations	(Mother-daughter relationship has changed) I think just because of children in general. I have my own family now. And I have my own responsibilities. I can't take off when I want to or when she (mother) wants to come. I can't just go. (mother interview)
Preference in Grand-mother Acitivites	Well, I don't bake cookies for them. (grandchildren) (grandmother interview)
Age of Grandchildren	She gives them (grandchildren) little jobs. Well, the older one (child); (handicapped child's) too young for that. (mother interview)
Seasonal-Weather Variables	In the winter weekends, I'm quite avaiable (to babysit) and on evenings I'm available. (grandmother interview)

Fostering Grandmothering. The final category was designated as "Fostering Grandmothering." Again, the data indicated that mothers and adult daughters had described some factors that appeared to facilitate the continuing involvement of grandmothers in the daughter's family, although these factors did not appear to have a direct impact on the circumstances when grandmothering occurred or the type of activities engaged in by grandmothers. Because most of the factors represented a possible continuum of response (e.g., "Degree of Satisfaction with Grandmothering Activities-Daughter," "Grandmother's Feelings about Grandchildren," "Efforts to Maintain Contact Between Mother and Daughter"), any of the 37 variables incorporated in Fostering Grandmothering had the potential for expanding or diminishing the maternal grandmother role. As was the case in Circumstances and Parameters, the variables in Fostering Grandmothering could be grouped by daughters, grandmothers, nonhandicapped grandchildren or family demographics. Table 4.4 contains a sample of these variables with examples from the interviews.

Table 4.4. Samples from *Fostering Grandmothering*

Variables	Example
Degree of Satisfaction with Grandmothering Activities	She doesn't spoil them (grandchildren) really bad and I'm grateful for that. I think that it makes it a lot harder when there's a lot of spoiling done, even though they are her only grandchildren. (mother interview)
Degree of Satisfaction with being Grandmother	I was 38 when I was a grandma and I loved it. I just thought it was great. (grandmother interview)
Attitude of Grandchildren	The kids want to see Grandma and Grandpa. (mother interview)
Overlapping Lifestyles	The town she lives in is where we go to the bank. (mother interview)

Thus, the maternal grandmother's role appears to evolve from the integration and interaction among a multitude of variables which could be divided into four major categories. The composite of these four categories—Grandmothering Activities, Circumstances, Parameters, and Fostering Grandmothering—represent the milieu for the maternal grandmother's role. The dynamic nature of this role is illustrated in Figure 4.1.

This study (Sonnek, 1983) can only be considered a preliminary effort in understanding the relationship of the extended family and the handicapped child. The study confirms the complexity of the maternal grandmother's relationship with her adult daughter's family, including the handicapped grandchild. The results of the study—a better appreciation of the variables which influence the maternal grandmother's role—may be useful in organizing data in other studies of other extended family roles.

Conclusion

The study of the extended family is beset by an array of complexities. First of all, the term "extended family" has many different interpretations. It may be defined broadly to include all persons, regardless of sex or bloodline, who are related to a nuclear family; it may include only those persons of a particular bloodline or sex (e.g., maternal grandparents or aunts, uncles); or it may refer to both a particular bloodline and sex (e.g., paternal grandfathers).

Demographic variables also influence the role of extended family members. Some of these variables include age; sex; marital status;

number of grandchildren, children, nieces, and nephews; socioeconomic status; educational level; and geographic proximity.

The presence of a handicapped child becomes yet another variable adding to the complexity of the extended family role. The type and severity of the handicapping condition, as well as the effect of the child on the nuclear family and the extended family members themselves, are factors that will influence the roles extended family members play.

Despite parameters established for the study, the findings by Sonnek (1983) highlight the complexity of the maternal grandmother's role. The presence of the young handicapped child was only one of many and varied factors that were found to influence the maternal grandmother's role. Future research efforts in the area should be sensitive to the complexity of the extended family member roles. Investigations on the role of other extended family members may clarify the relationship between the extended family and the nuclear family. This study suggests that grandmothers engage in activities from which all family members receive either direct or indirect benefit. The results suggest that successful programs for extended family members should focus on supporting the entire family, rather than only the handicapped child, and on utilizing existing helping patterns within the family. By proceeding in this direction, professionals who are working with families of handicapped children may provide a clearer perspective of how such families function on a day-to-day basis, and may suggest ways to support family functioning.

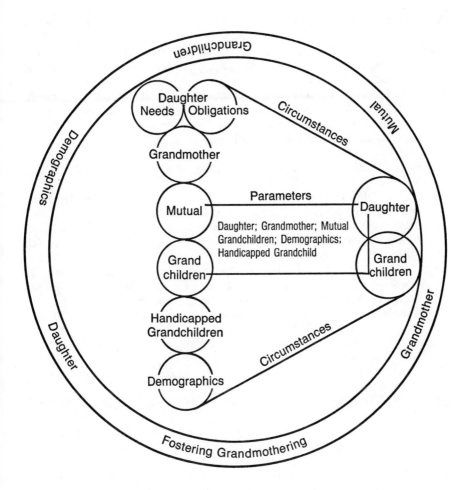

Figure 4.1. Influences on Maternal Grandmother's Role.

References

Adams, B. (1968). *Kinship in an urban setting*. Chicago: Markham.

Alan Guttmacher Institute (1976). *Eleven million teenagers: What can be done about the epidemic of adolescent pregnancies in the United States*. New York: Author.

Albrecht, R. (1954). The parental responsibility of grandparents. *Marriage and Family Living, 16*, 201-204.

Apple, D. (1954). *Grandparents and grandchildren: A sociological and psychological study of their relationship*. Unpublished doctoral dissertation. Cambridge, MA: Radcliffe College.

Atcheley, T. (1977). *Social forces of later life* (2nd ed). Belmont, CA: Wadsworth.

Bell, C. (1968). *Middle-class families*. London: Routledge and Kegan Paul.

Berger, M., & Fowlkes, M.A. (1980). Family Intervention Project: A family network model for serving young handicapped children. *Young Children, 35*, 22-31.

Birenbaum, A. (1970). On managing a courtesy stigma. *Journal of Health and Social Behavior, 11*, 196-206.

Borden, B. (1946). The roles of grandparents in children's behavior. *American Smith College Studies in Social Work, 17*, 115-116.

Boyd, R.R. (1969a). Emerging role of the four-generational family. In R.R. Boyd & G.C. Oakes (Eds.), *Foundations of practical gerontology*. Columbia, SC: University of South Carolina.

Boyd, R.R. (1969b). The valued grandparent: A changing social role. In W.T. Donahue, J.L. Kornbluh, & B. Power (Eds.), *Living in the multigenerational family*. Ann Arbor: Institute of Gerontology, University of Michigan.

Brotman, H.B. (1977). Every tenth American. *Sourcebook on aging*. Chicago: Marquis Academic Media.

Cohler, B.J., & Grunebaum, H.U. (1981). *Mothers, grandmothers and daughters*. New York: Wiley.

Davis, D.R. (1967). Family processes in mental retardation. *American Journal of Psychiatry, 124*, 340-350.

Ehlers, W.H. (1966). *Mothers of retarded children*. Springfield, IL: Charles C Thomas.

Farber, B. (1959). Effects of a severely retarded child on family integration. *Monographs of the Society for Research in Child Development 24*(2), Serial No. 71.

Gabe, T. (1981). *Social characteristics and economic status of the U.S. aged population*. The Library of Congress, Congressional Research Service. Report No. 81-32EPW.

Gabel, H., & Kotsch, L.S. (1981). Extended families and young handicapped children. *Topics in Early Childhood Special Education, 1*, 29-35.

Harris, C.S. (1978). *Fact book on aging: A profile of America's older population*. Washington, DC: The National Council on the Aging.

Harris, L., & Associates. (1975). *The myth and reality of aging in America*. New York: National Council on Aging.

Hetherington, E.M. (1979). Divorce: a child's perspective. *American Psychologist, 34*:851-858.

Hill, R. (1949). *Families Under stress*. New York: Harper.

Johnson, E.J., & Bursk, B.J. (1977). Relationship between elderly and their adult children. *Gerontologist, 17,* 90-96.

Kahana, B., & Kahana, E. (1970). Grandparenthood from the perspective of the developing child. *Developmental Psychology, 3,* 98-105.

Kahana, E., & Kahana, B. (1971). Theoretical and research perspectives on grandparenthood. *Aging and Human Development, 2,* 261-268.

Kivnick, H.Q. (1982). Grandparenthood: An overview of meaning and mental health. *Gerontologist, 22,* 59-66.

Komarovsky, M. (1962). *Blue-collar marriage.* New York: Random House.

LaBarre, M.B., Jessner, L., & Ussery, L. (1960). The significance of grandmothers in the psychopathology of children. *American Journal of Orthopsychiatry, 30,* 175-185.

Leichter, H. J., & Mitchell, W.E. (1968). Jewish extended families. In R.F. Winch & L.W. Goodman (Eds.), *Selected studies in marriage and family.* New York: Holt, Rinehart & Winston.

Litwak, E. (1960). Geographic mobility and extended family cohesion. *American Sociological Review, 25,* 385-394.

Lopata, H.Z. (1973). *Widowhood in an American city.* Cambridge, MA: Schenkem.

McAndrew, I. (1976). Children with a handicap and their families. *Child: Care, Health, and Development, 2,* 213-237.

McDowell, J., & Gabel, H. (1981). *Social support among mothers of mentally retarded infants.* Unpublished manuscript. Nashville, TN: George Peabody College of Vanderbilt University.

Neugarten, B.L., & Weinstein, K.K. (1964). The changing American grandparent. *Journal of Marriage and the Family, 26,* 199-204.

Nimkoff, M.F. (1961). Changing family relationships of older people in the United States during the last 50 years. *Gerontologist, 1,* 92-97.

Pieper, E. (1976). Grandparents can help. *Exceptional Parent, 6,* 7-10.

Radcliffe-Brown, A.R. (1952). *Structure and function in primitive society.* London: Cohen & West.

Rhoades, E.A. (1975). A grandparent's workshop. *Volta Review, 77,* 557-560.

Robertson, J.F. (1975). Interaction in three-generation families, parents as mediator: Towards a theoretical perspective. *International Journal of Aging and Human Development, 6,* 103-110.

Robertson, J.F. (1976). Significance of grandparents. *Gerontologist, 16,* 137-140.

Robertson, J.F. (1977). Grandmotherhood: A study of role conceptions. *Journal of Marriage and the Family, 39,* 165-174.

Schell, G.C. (1981). The young handicapped child: A family perspective. *Topics in Early Childhood Special Education, 1,* 21-27.

Schorr, A. (1960). *Filial responsibility in the modern American family.* Washington, DC: U.S. Department of Health, Education and Welfare.

Select Committee on Children, Youth and Families, (1983). *U.S. children and their families: Current conditions and recent trends.* 98th Congress, House of Representatives. U.S. Government Printing Office, 20-830-0.

Shanas, E. (1960). Family responsibility and health of older people. *Journal of Gerontology, 15,* 408-411.

Shanas, E. (1962). *The health of older people: A social survey.* Cambridge, MA: Harvard University Press.

Shanas, E. (1967). Family help patterns and social class in three countries.

Journal of Marriage and the Family, 29, 257-266.

Shanas, E. (1979). Social myth as hypothesis: The case of the family realities of old people. *Gerontologist, 19,* 3-9.

Sonnek, I.M. (1983). *The maternal grandmother role in families with young handicapped children.* Unpublished doctoral dissertation, Bloomington: Indiana University.

Strauss, C.A. (1943). Grandma made Johnny delinquent. *American Journal of Orthopsychiatry, 13,* 343-346.

Stryker, S. (1955). The adjustment of married offspring to their parents. *American Sociological Review, 20,* 149-154.

Subcommittee on Human Services of the Select Committee on Aging. (1982, December 16). *Grandparents: The other victims of divorce and custody disputes.* 97th Congress, House of Representatives, December 16, 1982.

Susser, P. (1974). Parents are partners. *Exceptional Parent, 4,* 41-47.

Sussman, M.B. (1953). The help pattern in the middle class family. *American Sociological Review, 18,* 22-28.

Sussman, M.B. (1959). The isolated nuclear family: Fact or fiction. *Social Problems, 5,* 333-340.

Sussman, M.B. (1960). Intergenerational family relationships and social role changes in middle age. *Journal of Gerontology, 15,* 71-75.

Sussman, M.B. (1962). Kin family network: Unheralded structure in current conceptualizations of family functioning. *Marriage and Family Living, 24,* 231-240.

Townsend, P. (1957). *The family life of old people in East London.* London: Routledge and Kegan Paul.

Troll, L.E. (1971). The family of later life: A decade review. *Journal of Marriage and the Family, 33,* 263-290.

Troll, L.E. Miller, S., & Atcheley, R. (1979). *Families in later life.* Belmont, CA: Wadsworth.

U.S. Bureau of the Census. (1976). *Current population reports, special studies series P-23,* No. 59.

U.S. Bureau of the Census. (1979a). *Marital status and living arrangements: March 1978,* Series P-20, No. 338.

U.S. Bureau of the Census. (1979b). *Statistical abstract of the United States 1979* (100th ed.).

Uzoka, A.F. (1979). The myth of the nuclear family: Historical background and clinical implications. *American Psychologist, 34,* 1095-1106.

Vadasy, P.F., Fewell, R.R., & Meyer, D.J. (in press). Grandparents of children with special needs: Insights into their experiences and concerns. *Journal of the Division for Early Childhood.*

Vollmer, H. (1937). The grandmother: A problem in child-rearing. *American Journal of Orthopsychiatry, 7,* 378-382.

Young, M. (1954). The role of the extended family in a disaster. *Human Relations, 3,* 383-391.

Young, M., & Willmott, P. (1957). *Family and kinship in East London.* London: Routledge and Kegan Paul.

Zero Population Growth. (1976). *Teenage pregnancy: A major problem among minors.* Washington, D.C.

5

Mothers of
Deaf-Blind Children

Patricia F. Vadasy and Rebecca R. Fewell

What is it like to be the mother of a child with a severe handicap? When a mother has a child who is deaf-blind, whom does she turn to for support and strength? How does her life change as her child grows older? Are her thoughts about the future a source of comfort or fear? These are some of the questions that stimulated the study that is reported in this chapter. The follow-up study surveyed female guardians of 92 deaf-blind children who were served between 1970-78 at a treatment and evaluation center for the deaf blind. Most of the children were born during the last rubella epidemic and are now adolescents. Results of the 41 surveys that were returned are reported.

This chapter also discusses the context in which these parents' experiences have taken place, and in which they now find themselves. A parent's experiences will not only be influenced by the immediate family and the social supports that help the parent provide the extra care and face the difficult questions and worries that the child's handicap occasions; the family will also be influenced by the broader social and political context in which policies for handicapped children and their parents are developed. It is these broad ecological settings (Bronfenbrenner, 1977) in which the family functions that are also a critical part of this story. In this sense, this chapter is also a study of transitions, of the transition in mothers' concerns for their school-age children as they approach adulthood, the transition of children from the school into the community, and of the transition in policies for children with low-incidence handicaps.

Background To This Study

The Maternal Rubella Syndrome

The majority of children in this study are victims of congenital rubella, contracted by their mothers during pregnancy. Rubella, or German measles, was first recognized as a mild childhood illness in the early nineteenth century. However, it was not until 1941 that Gregg, an Australian ophthalmologist, recognized the association of maternal rubella infection during pregnancy with the occurrence of congenital cataracts and heart disease in the infants in his practice (Krugman, 1983). Maternal rubella syndrome is caused by an RNA virus of the arbovirus group. When contracted by the mother in the first trimester, it causes various congenital abnormalities. The likelihood and severity of these defects increase the earlier in pregnancy the mother contracts the virus. The rubella virus reduces embryonic cell division and also stimulates the fetal immune system. The resulting inflammation causes cell damage (Vernon, Grieve, & Shaver, 1980).

The primary effects of the virus upon the fetus are: visual defects; hearing defects; microcephaly and mental retardation ranging from mild to profound; cardiac defects, including patent ductus arteriosus, ventricular septal defects, and pulmonary stenosis. The most common visual impairments are due to congenital cataracts, retinal pigment epithelium (rubella retinitis), glaucoma, and corneal clouding (Seelye, 1979).

In 1962, the rubella virus was isolated, leading to development of a live, attenuated rubella vaccine. Following a cycle of six to nine-year outbreaks, with major epidemics in 1935, 1943, 1952, and 1958, a major rubella outbreak occurred in 1963-65, resulting in the births of an estimated 20,000 infants with congenital rubella. In 1966, a vaccine was developed, and following clinical trials, was licensed in June 1969. To date, more than 100 million children have been immunized, and no major outbreak has occurred in this country since that of 1963-65 (Krugman, 1983).

The pattern of the epidemic is of some interest. The crest of the epidemic appears to have occurred in 1964-65, but there was a movement of the epidemic from the east to the west coast of the country. Evidence of this wave of rubella is the greater number of hearing-impaired school-age children in Regions IX and X (the West and Northwest) than in the rest of the country. For example, of the hearing-impaired children born in 1966-68 in Region III (Washington D.C. and surrounding states) who were surveyed by Gallaudet College Office of Demographic Studies, only 7% were rubella victims, whereas 24% of students in Region IX (including Arizona, California, and Nevada) and 19% of students in Region X (Alaska, Idaho, Oregon, and Washington) who were born in 1966-68 were rubella victims (Office of Demographic Studies, 1980).

During the epidemic years, rubella births occurred on a cyclical basis, with most births occurring between September and January (Trybus, Karchmer, Kerstetter, & Hicks, 1980). This pattern reflects the increased prevalence of rubella in the winter and early spring months.

The effects of the virus on the unborn child varied with the timing of the mother's exposure, and individuals who work with the deaf-blind population have described the range of handicaps. Brewer and Kakalik (1974) of the Rand Corporation estimated that about 60-75% of the deaf-blind population 21 years of age and under were "middle trainable and below," 5-10% were "middle educable and above," and 15-25% were "upper trainable to lower educable." They projected the following: In 1980, only 500 individuals would be middle educable and above, while 3,500 would fall into the lowest functioning category. They estimated that the cost of serving 5,400 deaf-blind children and youth in 1980, at an average of $5,000 per person, would be $27 million. During 1980, the cost of serving deaf-blind children through the federal, regional, and state Centers and Services for Deaf-Blind Children (described below) was about $14 million.

More recently, Hicks (1982) reported that 1,000-1,500 children born during the epidemic are now being served in programs offered through the federal Regional Centers for Services to Deaf-Blind Children and Youth Program (see below). Most of these children have at least two additional handicaps, the most common being mental retardation and heart disorders. Vernon et al. (1980) in their review found that about 73% of rubella victims have hearing losses; from 35-76% have heart disorders; 33% have visual defects; more than half have urogenital disorders; 42% are mentally retarded; 7% are autistic; and 15-40% have diabetes mellitus by adolescence.

The wide range of handicaps these children may experience has made it difficult for educators to plan standard services for the deaf blind. This difficulty in planning appropriate services is compounded by the lack of accurate data on the actual numbers of individuals who are affected by the various possible combinations of handicaps.

Legislation and Programs for the Deaf-Blind Rubella Population

The 1963-65 rubella epidemic stimulated the development of the rubella vaccine and a national vaccination program. In 1966, the live, attenuated rubella vaccine was developed, and, after clinical trials confirmed its safety and effectiveness, the vaccine was licensed in 1969 (Krugman, 1983). Under Public Law 89-749, Section 314 (e), $41,600,000 was authorized for the Rubella Immunization Program.

In 1968, P.L. 90-247 was passed to provide federal support for a number of regional centers for deaf-blind children across the country. As Brewer and Kakalik (1974) point out, federal support was sought because at that time individual states could not meet the specialized needs of this low-incidence handicap group. In 1969, eight regional centers were allocated $1 million to provide direct and support services to this group. Two centers were added in 1970 when P.L. 90-247 was amended by P.L. 91-230, the Education of the Handicapped Act. Title VI-C, Section 622 of this Act set forth the services that would be provided by these centers. These services were to include at least the following:

1. Comprehensive diagnostic and evaluative services for deaf-blind children;
2. A program for the adjustment, orientation, and education of deaf-blind children which integrates all the professional and allied services necessary therefore; and
3. Effective consultative services for parents, teachers, and others who play a direct role in the lives of deaf-blind children. (P.L. 91-230, Part C, Section 622d.1)

Since 1969, as many as 16 regional and single state centers have been funded to serve deaf-blind children and their families under contract with the former Office, and present Department of Education (Dantona, 1974).

In 1975, P.L. 93-380 authorized funding of the Deaf-Blind Centers and Services Program, administered today by the Special Education Programs (SEP) branch of the Department of Education. The Deaf-Blind Program has administered the allocation of Title VI-C funds through 5-year contracts with 15 regional and state centers.

In 1983, there were eight multi-state and seven single-state centers which were in their fifth and final years of their current contracts with the Department of Education. Total funding for these centers over the 5-year period was $69,624,072. One of the main responsibilities of the regional centers was to determine whether a child was eligible for programs and services for the deaf blind. The following definition served as a guideline for the centers, and for other Department of Education projects which served this group:

The term 'deaf-blind children' means children who have auditory and visual handicaps, the combination of which causes such severe communication and other developmental and educational problems that they cannot be properly accommodated in special education programs for either the hearing handicapped child or for the visually handicapped child. (Federal Register, 40(35), Feb. 20, 1975, Section 121c.37)

If the regional center provides an evaluation and finds that the child does not meet this criteria, the center is responsible for acting as an advocate to find a suitable placement for the child. The centers are authorized to serve deaf-blind children from birth to age 22. As mentioned earlier, national data on the deaf-blind population are not widely available, and descriptive data are more easily obtained from studies by researchers working with small groups of these children.

Characteristics of Deaf-Blind Rubella Victims

Several Gallaudet College studies of children with hearing impairments include data that help define the deaf-blind and their needs. Jensema (1974) sampled 43,946 students enrolled in special education programs for the hearing impaired (about 75% of the total number of students enrolled in these programs), and found that those children for whom maternal rubella was reported as the cause of their hearing loss had more severe hearing losses than children in the "other causes" group: 83% of the rubella group had a hearing loss greater than 70dB (which is within the critical range for speech comprehension), compared to 69% of the other group. Multiple handicaps were also more common in the rubella group (38%) than in the other group (27%). Visual problems were the most commonly reported (15%), followed by emotional-behavioral problems (11%), heart disorders (8%), and mental retardation (7%). The low rate of mental retardation in Jensema's study most likely reflects the fact that the programs surveyed by Gallaudet served the higher functioning rubella population. Earlier, Vernon (1967) had found that 54% of his sample of 129 rubella-deafened children had multiple handicaps. Both Vernon (1967) and Jensema and Trybus (1975) reported emotional-behavioral disorders in their populations. Vernon used three criteria to evaluate emotional adjustment: teacher's ratings, psychological evaluations, and school reports of behavior. The postrubella group had significantly more (p < .001) ratings of maladjustment than the contrast group who were deaf from genetic causes. School records revealed that 18% of postrubella children were dismissed from school for emotional disturbances, and psychologists' ratings of 103 of the 129 rubella children classified 27% of the children as emotionally disturbed. Jensema and Trybus (1975) also examined reports of emotional-behavioral problems in children served in programs for the hearing impaired. They found a higher rate of these problems in students who were born during the years of the rubella epidemic. The overall rate of reported problems was 7.9%, while the rate for children born in 1964-65 was 9.4%. Not surprisingly, children with multiple handicaps were more often reported to have emotional-behavioral problems. Only 5.3% of children with no additional handicaps were reported to have emotional-behavioral problems, whereas the rate for children with two additional handicaps was 22.8%. Educationally significant emotional-behavioral problems were most commonly reported in conjunction with perceptual-motor problems and with brain damage, two conditions found in many rubella victims.

Another recent report (Stein, Palmer, & Weinberg, 1980) on 101 deaf-blind children who were evaluated at the Siegel Institute of Michael Reese Hospital and Medical Center between 1972 and 1979 indicated that 68% of the children had severe-to-profound hearing losses (loss greater than 80dB in middle and high frequencies); 31% of the children had no functional vision. Head circumference, EEG findings, and neurological exams revealed a high incidence of neurological handicaps in the group: 40% of the children were microcephalic or macrocephalic; 55% had abnormal EEGs; and 40% had some type of neuromuscular disorder such as cerebral palsy, poor muscle motility, or hypotonia. Based upon standardized test results (several measures were used), and examiners' observations, 79% of the children were classified as functioning in the "middle trainable and below range," a category including children who can communicate basic needs, may be able to attain some self-help skills, but will require some form of direct care into their adult lives. The authors concluded that most of these children will require supervised care for the rest of their lives.

In addition to the handicaps that the majority of school-age deaf-blind children are found to experience, it has been suggested that they are susceptible to the late onset of endocrine disorders, particularly diabetes, and other vision problems, such as glaucoma, cataracts, and detached retinas (Hicks, 1982).

The uncertain futures of these children stimulated the Rehabilitation Services Administration (RSA) and Special Education Programs (SEP) of the Department of Education to contract a one-year study of the demographic characteristics of the U.S. deaf-blind population and the services that are available for them. The authors of the resulting report (Wolf, Delk, & Schein, 1982) interviewed a sample of federal officials and administrators of regional centers and special education programs, parents, and deaf-blind adults regarding their satisfaction with programs and their needs. These authors described the size and characteristics of the total deaf-blind population, and used National Center for Health Statistics definitions to distinguish four categories of deaf-blind individuals: those with no usable hearing for speech and no useful vision in either eye, those with no usable hearing for speech and severe visual impairment in both eyes, those with severe hearing impairment and blind, and those severely impaired visually and auditorily. The rubella group is distributed across those categories.

Although Wolf et al. (1982) do not report demographic data on the rubella group, they do describe additional handicaps of children up to age 21 who were served in programs administered by their respondents. Of the total group of 585 students, 81% were mentally retarded, 10% had emotional problems, and 16% had heart disorders. These figures are similar to those obtained in the studies of the rubella group that were described earlier (Hicks, 1982; Stein et al., 1980; Vernon et al., 1980). Table 5.1 summarizes the findings of the major studies of deaf-blind children.

In conclusion, then, these separate studies indicate that the diverse effects of the rubella virus upon the affected children results in a combination of visual, auditory, neurological, and intellectual handicaps. Consequently, as Hicks (1982) has pointed out, there is no typical profile of a child with rubella which can be used to plan educational and support services, and professionals must tailor interventions to each child's needs. Studies conducted on groups of deaf-blind children enrolled in special education programs or programs for the hearing impaired tend to portray a less seriously involved child than studies limited to rubella victims. It is important to keep in mind the etiology of deaf-blindness as well as how it is defined, as there are significant differences in definitions as well as in etiology which have implications in planning appropriate services.

Table 5.1. Studies of Deaf-Blind Children

Study	Population	Hearing Impaired	Visually Impaired	Mentally Retarded	Emotional/ Behavior Problems	Neurological Handicaps	Heart Disorders	Multiple Handicaps
Vernon, 1967	129 rubella victims (applicants to Calif. School for Deaf, 1954-1964)	mean loss 82.3 dB in speech range (severe-profound)		8% (n=98)	22% aphasic; 18% dismissed from school for emotional disturbance; 27% classified as emotionally disturbed by psychologist.			54%
Jensema, 1974 (Gallaudet ODS sample)	43,946 children in special programs for hearing impaired (3,840 rubella)	83% loss greater than 70dB (n=3,840)	15%	7%	11%		8%	38%
Stein, Palmer, & Weinberg, 1980	101 deaf-blind children	68% loss greater than 80dB (n=99)	31% no functional vision (n=96)	79% middle trainable and below (n=85)		55% abnormal EEGs (n=80); 40% abnormal head size (n=88); 40% neuromuscular disorder (n=90)		

Study	Population	Hearing Impaired	Visually Impaired	Mentally Retarded	Emotional/ Behavior Problems	Neurological Handicaps	Heart Disorders	Multiple Handicaps
Korn, Chess & Fernandez, 1978	243 rubella children, 3-6 years	75%	33%	23% (10% mild-moderate, 13% severe-profound) 11% no estimate possible ($n=171$)	7% autistic 12% reactive behavior disorder 3% cerebral dysfunction	33%	33%	19%=2 handicaps 19%=3 handicaps 11%=4 handicaps
Vernon, Grieve, & Shaver, 1980	Review of the literature	73%	33% (4% glaucoma, 12%–50% cataracts)	42%	7% autistic	35–76%		
Wolf, Delk, & Schein, 1982	585 deaf-blind children			81%	10%	23% cerebral palsy; 56% brain damage; 17% epilepsy	16%	

Children and Policies in Transition

Most of the the deaf-blind children for whom the specialized services described above were originally planned are now adolescents. Their educational needs, as well as the context in which appropriate services are provided, have changed. Most of the direct services that were not available in the states at the time that P.L. 90-247 was passed are now mandated under P.L. 94-142 (the Education of All Handicapped Children Act of 1975). Yet, as a recent report underscores (Scott, Campeau, Wheeler, & Ferrara, 1982), the adequacy of P.L. 94-142 funds for meeting the needs of deaf-blind children, and the appropriateness of generic services for the deaf-blind population are being questioned. Although as Scott et al. determined in their interviews with SEA and Deaf-Blind Center staff, adequate direct services for the deaf-blind might be available if the authorized funds for P.L. 94-142 were appropriated, the deaf-blind children would lose access to many of the indirect services that they have received under Title VI-C funds if those funds were ended. Any decrease in Title VI-C funds would be likely to have an impact on the prevocational and vocational training services now most needed by these adolescents, and would have a particularly negative impact on the rubella group and their families. Without Title VI-C funds, parents of deaf-blind children would not receive many of the indirect support services that have been available to them, and that may have made it easier for their families to cope with the needs of a severely multi-handicapped child. As others have pointed out, few groups of handicapped individuals and their families have been targeted for as comprehensive an array of specialized services as this relatively low-incidence group. This fact should be kept in mind as policies are developed for the transition of these children into adult programs.

Scott et al.'s recent report on the deaf-blind centers and service program which was contracted by the Department of Education indicates that decreased use of Title VI-C funds for the education of deaf-blind children is a growing trend. Another indication of decreased future federal support for specialized deaf-blind services may be the change in the number of deaf-blind centers funded in 1983 (*Federal Register,* *48*(98) 22612), when only six regional centers were funded. The Education of the Handicapped Act Amendments of 1983 (P.L. 98-199) respond to the changing needs of the now late-adolescent rubella group by making available to deaf-blind youth, upon age 22, programs and services to facilitate their transition from educational to other services. The manner in which these services are to be provided may be influenced by the 1984 program priorities for Services for Deaf-Blind Children and Youth:

> To: (a) ensure the provision of services to deaf-blind children and youth while phasing down Federal support for provision of direct services

under this program, and (b) provide technical assistance to States to build their capacity to expand services to deaf-blind children formerly served through other means. (*Federal Register, 49*(84) 18418)

As the data from this study will indicate, these changes reflect the increasing need of the deaf-blind rubella group for adult services. The manner in which these services are provided will have a significant effect upon the lives of these individuals and their families.

Research Rationale, Goals, and Results

The following study was initiated against this backdrop, which silhouettes a unique group of multihandicapped children and a network of specialized service programs which are in a state of transition. One of the goals of this study was to gather data on the placements and experiences of a selected group of these deaf-blind children and the experiences and expectations of their mothers. As noted above, the Deaf-Blind Regional Centers have subcontracted with numerous public and private agencies to provide services mandated under P.L. 91-230. Between 1970 and 1978, the Deaf-Blind Treatment and Evaluation Center at George Peabody College for Teachers subcontracted to provide direct and support services to about 400 deaf-blind children and their families. In March 1983, a follow-up study was initiated to determine the current status of 92 of the children and their mothers who were served at the Peabody Center between 1970 and 1978. For most families, 10 years had elapsed since the time they were served by Peabody staff. Questionnaires were mailed to the mothers or female guardians of 92 children who had documented visual and auditory impairments at the time they were served by Peabody staff. Most of the children (66%) were born during the 1963-65 rubella epidemic and were adolescents (between the ages of 17 and 20) at the time of the study. Two of the more pressing immediate needs of this group are reported to be prevocational and vocational services, and life-planning strategies (Scott et al., 1982; Wolf et al., 1982). These are needs that are currently being addressed in specially funded projects for the deaf blind and through the indirect services provided by the regional centers. In order to provide some information on those needs, a questionnaire was designed to gather information on the child's present placement, level of functioning, vocational training and experiences, and future prospects.

Like many rubella children, the children in this study were often multihandicapped at the time of their initial diagnosis and evaluation. Besides having severe visual and auditory impairments, many of the children were mentally retarded and had emotional disorders and heart problems. One goal of the study was to determine how mothers were affected by their child's handicaps. Research on families indicates that the parents' marriage (Farber, 1959; Gath, 1977; Love, 1979; Tew & Lawrence, 1973), employment (Dunlap & Hollinsworth, 1977; Moore, Hamerlynck, Barsh, Spieker, & Jones, 1982), and levels of stress and depression (Breslau, Staruch, & Mortimer, 1982; Tew & Lawrence, 1973) are affected by the presence of a handicapped child. Data were therefore gathered on mothers' life experiences; their perceptions and satisfaction with their child's present placement and training; their expectations for the child's future; and their access to and need for supports throughout their child's life.

Procedures

Questionnaires and a cover letter and consent form were mailed to the mothers or female guardians of 92 deaf-blind children. Nineteen of the questionnaires were returned because they could not be delivered, and none of these families were able to be located. After one follow-up mailing, a total of 41 (45%) of the surveys were returned. Replies were received from 34 natural mothers (83%), 3 foster mothers (5%), and 4 adoptive mothers (10%).

The Findings

Characteristics of deaf-blind subjects. The sex distribution of the subjects was approximately equal, with 19 males and 22 females. The deaf-blind children came from families that ranged in size from one to nine children. The median family size was three children ($n = 38$). The birth order of the subjects varied from only child ($n = 4$) to seventh-born child ($n = 4$). Twenty percent ($n = 8$) of the subjects were 6-15 years old; 68% ($n = 28$) were 16-18 years old; and 12% ($n = 5$) were 20-28 years old. Sixty-six percent ($n = 27$) of the children were born within the period of the last rubella epidemic, between 1963-1966. Rubella was the etiology of deaf-blindness in 34 (83%) of the cases. As was the case with most rubella births, 32 of the subjects (78%) were born between the months of October and January. Thirty-one of the deaf-blind subjects were listed on the registry maintained by the Southeast Regional Center for Deaf-Blind Children in Talladega, Alabama. Deaf-blind individuals who are over 21 years of age are not listed on state or regional registries.

Degree of impairment. Mothers rated all 41 subjects as multiply handicapped, having two or more handicaps (including hearing, visual, mental retardation, emotional-behavioral, heart disorder, cerebral palsy); 56% of subjects were impaired in each of the first four areas. The area in which most subjects were rated most severely impaired was in their hearing, where 27 (71%) subjects were rated by mothers as profoundly impaired. Four subjects (11%) were rated as mild-to-moderately hearing impaired, and five mothers did not specify the degree of their child's hearing loss. Fourteen subjects (34%) were reported as having no functional vision, and 24 (59%) as having limited but functional vision. Mothers reported that 73% ($n = 30$) of the children had some degree of mental retardation. Nine (25%) subjects were rated as severely retarded, 9 as moderately retarded, and 7 (19%) as mildy retarded. Mothers of 30 subjects (83%) indicated their child had emotional-behavioral problems, a higher proportion than that reported in other studies (Jensema, 1974; Korn, Chess, and Fernandez, 1978; Vernon, 1967; Wolf, et al., 1982) of deaf-blind children (Table 5.1). Mothers of two subjects (5%) rated these problems as severe; mothers of nine subjects (25%) rated them as moderate; and mothers of 14 subjects (39%) rated them as mild. In addition, 15 subjects (37%) had heart disorders, and four subjects (11%) had cerebral palsy. Two subjects had scoliosis, and two subjects had cleft lip-cleft palate. Mothers rated 15% of subjects as very dependent on others for personal needs; 45% were rated as somewhat dependent; and 40% were rated as independent in personal care.

Placement. Eighty-three percent ($n = 34$) of subjects were under the care of their natural parents; four subjects were cared for by adoptive parents; and three subjects were cared for by foster parents. At the time of the survey, 16 (39%) of the subjects were living at home, and 25 (61%) were living outside of the home, two (5%) in a state institution, four (10%) in a residential school for the blind, three (7%) in a residential school for the deaf, 10 (24%) in a residential school for the deaf and blind, and three (7%) in a group home. One subject was attending a community college and living alone in his own apartment. The etiology of this subject's multiple handicaps was rubella with retinitis pigmentosa. According to his mother's ratings he was profoundly hearing impaired, had limited vision and no other handicaps. Fourteen (34%) of the subjects had always lived at home with parents or guardians. Three mothers (11%) were dissatisfied with the child's present living situation, and 81% of the mothers said they were satisfied with the child's present placement.

Mothers were asked to indicate where they expected their child would live as an adult. Twelve percent ($n = 5$) indicated their child would most likely live in an institution; 3% ($n = 1$) indicated the child would live in a foster home; 16% ($n = 6$) indicated that the child would live in a group home; and 24 mothers (60%) said that their child would live at home. Although 20 mothers expected their child would be mostly independent in personal care (eating, toileting, dressing, grooming), only five of these mothers thought their child would live in a group home; 12 of these mothers expected their child to live at home. Several mothers commented that they worried about what would happen to their child when parents would no longer be able to care for the child at home. Other mothers indicated that their child would probably live at home for lack of a better placement.

> (She will live) at home if parents are able to care for her — otherwise in an institution.

> We will not put him in an institution and there are no group homes for him in our city at this time.

> I would like to see him stay in a group home but at present there is none, so he will stay at home after his schooling ends at age 21.

> At home as long as I live — afterwards, I don't know.

> I would like to make arrangements about his care if I should get disabled or die. I want him placed in a home where he won't be treated wrong, because he is human and he has always had the best of care at home.

> Our state is going through a transition period. Group homes and day activity might be available when our son is 21-22. He could live at home if activity would be available.

Pearson product-moment correlations revealed a significant relation between the child's expected adult residence and the severity of the child's handicaps ($r = .34$; $p = .025$) and between the child's expected adult residence and the number of the child's handicaps ($r = -.34$; $p = .029$). More severely handicapped children were more likely to be expected to live at home.

Most mothers expected that their child would remain single as an adult; only three mothers (7%) expected their child to marry. These three children were all rubella victims, two of them had profound hearing losses, limited vision, and no other handicaps according to mothers' ratings. The third child was totally blind and had other handicaps, the severity of which were not specified by the mother.

Children's income and vocational training. Forty percent (16) of the mothers reported that their child had no independent income source and depended entirely upon parents for financial support. Fifty-seven percent (23) of the mothers reported their child received some type of government support, primarily Supplemental Security Income (SSI). Sixteen children (39%) had a gross monthly income that was $25 or less; eight children (20%) received $100-200 per month; and eight children (20%) received $200-300 per month. Nine mothers (22%) thought their child would remain financially dependent upon the family in the future; 25 mothers (61%) thought their child would be eligible for government support. Two mothers expected their child would have earnings above minimum wage. Eleven mothers (30%) were dissatisfied with their child's future income.

Twenty-three mothers (56%) reported that their child had never received any vocational training. Of the 16 children who were reported to have received vocational training, eight were trained in a specific task like sorting and in assembly work. When they were asked about their child's future employment, ten mothers (24%) reported they did not expect that their child would ever be able to work; 12 mothers (29%) thought their child might be able to attend a day activity center; 11 mothers (27%) thought their child would be able to work in a sheltered workshop; and two mothers (5%) thought their child could be competitively employed. Fourteen mothers (37%) were dissatisfied with their child's vocational future.

Mothers' experiences. As we noted at the beginning of this chapter, we were interested in mothers' experiences over the course of their child's development, and in supports which may help mothers meet the multiple needs of a child who is deaf and blind.

Data were gathered on the mothers' age, marital status, education, and employment experience. Mothers' age at the index child's birth ranged from 11 years to 40 years. Eighteen (44%) of the mothers were married to the child's natural father at the time of the survey. Six mothers (15%) had never been married to the child's father. Three mothers (7%) were separated from the child's father, and 10 mothers (24%) were divorced from the child's father. Of those mothers who were divorced, five mothers (50%) had remarried. The younger the mother and the child at the time of the mother's divorce, the greater the likelihood of the mother's remarriage. The average age of those mothers who did remarry was 28 years.

It is not surprising that the family income of married and divorced mothers differed significantly: married mothers had a higher average family income than divorced or separated mothers ($p = .0001$). Thirteen mothers (32%) were not working outside the home at the time of the survey: 34% were working full time, and 10% were working part time. Approximately 54% ($n = 22$) of the mothers had been employed full time at some period since their child was born, and about 34% ($n = 14$) worked part time. When mothers' employment rates throughout their children's lives were examined, the proportion of mothers who reported working full time decreased somewhat with the increasing age of the child. Fifty-one percent ($n = 21$) of the mothers confirmed that they had wanted to work at one time but were unable to because of their deaf-blind child's needs.

> I have never been able to get a full-time job because of my daughter's handicaps. There are very few people who want to take care of handicapped children.

In their survey of 448 families of handicapped children in Washington State, Moore, et al. (1982) also found that 27% of single mothers and 21% of married mothers reported that they were unable to work because of the child. In our study, mothers of the deaf-blind children who were living at home were less likely to be working than mothers of children who were placed outside the home ($p = .06$). There was no difference between the employment status of those mothers who were married and those who were divorced or separated at the time of the study.

Important supports for mothers. Mothers were asked to identify the individuals and services that helped them while their child was growing up, as well as supports that were most helpful at the time of the survey. They were also asked to identify supports that would have made it easier for them to care for the child, both while the child was growing up and now.

When mothers were asked to rank supports that were most important while their deaf-blind child was 0-10 years old, 24 mothers (59%) identified their spouse and 6 mothers (15%) identified the child's grandmother as the most important support. Daughters, teachers, and grandmothers were also frequently reported to be less important supports.

Family supports were also examined in one of the author's study of 80 mothers of children with Down syndrome (Fewell, 1984). In that study mothers with greater family support reported they received support from more individual sources than mothers with less family support. Mothers with higher family support also perceived themselves as having more support from family and community groups and were more satisfied with the availability and quality of those supports than mothers with less family support. Fewell also found that mothers with lower levels of education (high school education or less) reported they received significantly more support from families, relatives, and their religion ($p < .05$) than mothers with more than a high school education.

When mothers were asked to identify three things that would have made it easier for them to care for their deaf-blind child, 11 mothers (27%) desired more family support, five mothers (12%) wanted supplemental income, and four mothers (10%) desired a day activity center for their child and more parent training. Special education was most frequently selected as the second-most desired support ($n = 7$, or 17%), as well as the most frequently selected third-most important support ($n = 8$, or 20%). Thirteen mothers (32%) identified spouses as the most important immediate support, and about 15% of mothers indicated that teachers and school staff were the most important supports at the present time.

Thirty-two mothers (78%) reported that they belonged to an organized religion. Of the 31 mothers who noted their religious affiliation, 13 identified themselves as Baptists, and 6 as Methodists. Twenty-four mothers (59%) said that they attended church once a week or more often; 36 mothers (88%) said that their religious beliefs had helped them care for their handicapped child. Fewell (1984) also found that mothers of children with Down syndrome who have high religious support also have more support from family and friends and are more satisfied with those supports (*p.* < .05) than mothers with low levels of religious support. She found that mothers with a Protestant upbringing reported significantly more support and satisfaction from their religion than mothers raised as Catholics.

Finally, mothers were asked to indicate what would make it easier to care for their adolescent child. Ten mothers (24%) rated vocational training for their child as most important. Five mothers (12%) each rated support from spouses, placement change, and in-home aides as most important.

Future needs of children and their mothers. Mothers were asked whether they had made any plans for their child in the event of the parents' death or disability. Twenty-four (59%) mothers had made no plans. Three mothers commented that they were either worried about the future, or they asked the authors for advice about making plans.

Because most (80%) of the children involved in this study were at least 16 years old and approaching the age at which they will no longer be eligible for special education services, we asked mothers if they thought their child's needs could be adequately met in programs that serve other types of handicapped children as well as deaf-blind children. This question was also of interest for mothers of younger deaf-blind children in light of possible shifts in policy which would reduce the specialized services that would be available for this low-incidence handicap group once the large rubella group approaches age 21. Twenty-six mothers (63%) felt their child needed special services that were specifically planned for the deaf-blind; six mothers (15%) thought that their child's needs could be met in generic programs for the handicapped. There were no differences between mothers of older and younger children on this question. These results suggest that changes in policies for deaf-blind children and their families may require some adjustment on the part of parents, who have become accustomed to receiving specialized services for their child.

Implications

Mothers and Their Supports

These findings indicate that as their deaf-blind children were growing up, mothers relied upon supports within their families and perceived these supports as helpful in caring for their children. In most cases, someone in the mother's immediate family (spouse, daughter, son) provided what the mother felt was her most important source of assistance. Grandmothers were mentioned frequently, and their importance to the mothers in this group may reflect the important role of the grandmother in a rural family's life (Gabel & Kotsch, 1981; German & Maisto, 1982). Extended family support may have been more available and influential for these mothers, many of whom (46%) lived in rural areas of the Southeast, than it would have been for a group of urban mothers. Fewell (1984) also found that mothers of children with Down syndrome who lived in rural areas reported significantly more family support from parents and relatives than mothers from urban areas. While their geographical location may have provided some of these mothers with the advantage of a more cohesive and supportive extended family environment, it may also have had several disadvantages. Mothers in this study often commented on the difficulty of finding access to professionals in their community who had expertise and training in the needs of deaf-blind children, and families sometimes traveled long distances to transport their child to medical and educational services. Opportunities for employment may also have been more limited for mothers in this study who lived outside of large metropolitan areas, and this may have had an effect on maternal employment and family income.

The survey results reiterate the problem underscored by Gallagher (1984) that unlike most stresses, those related to raising a severely handicapped child will not go away after the child turns 21 years old. The fact that most mothers (60%) expect that their child will live in the parents' home as an adult suggests that families will need continued services to make home placement beneficial for the adult child, as well as to ease the burden of care for parents who have already fulfilled what society generally accepts as a parent's responsibility to her child. Parents of handicapped children, in effect, are often held to a different standard than parents of nonhandicapped children who are permitted to consider that their duties to their child end when the child turns 21, 18, or even 16. Wikler (1983) has recently reported on the increased stress families of mentally retarded children experience when the child approaches adulthood. She has pointed out the simultaneous support needs of both the handicapped individual and the family at this transition.

Extrafamilial supports become more important for parents of older children with severe handicaps for whom familial support often becomes less accessible. Not only are parents older and often have fewer financial resources and less energy than parents of younger children, but siblings are often grown and no longer living at home. Grandparents are very old or deceased. Parents of necessity must often look outside the family for assistance with their adult child.

It is not only that norms may be different for parents of a handicapped child than for parents of nonhandicapped children. Their choices may also be quite limited. If appropriate alternative placements are not available, parents who have spent many years making great personal sacrifices to seek specialized medical treatment and educational services for their deaf-blind child may have no alternative but to take their child back into their home at age 21. Only five of the children in this study were expected to live in an institution as adults, and all of these children were living in an institution or at a residential school at the time of the survey. As Seltzer and Krauss (1984) have observed, in some states community placement priority is given to individuals who were previously institutionalized. What this means is that parents of children who have never lived in an institution may have a more difficult time finding an out-of-home living option for their adult children than parents of children for whom a community placement would be considered deinstitutionalization.

Institutionalization and the likely loss of hard-won gains for their child was not regarded as an option for most mothers. Several mothers commented that their child did not retain skills if the child was removed from a program for any length of time, and other mothers lamented the lack of alternative placements for the adult deaf-blind individual.

> She has accomplished a great deal in self-help but does not retain it if removed from her program for more than a short time.

> I am concerned about his training when he can no longer attend because of his age.

> If he isn't eligible for the state school for the blind, there is nothing in our area but day care.

> I would like to see more vocational challenges for her, and also for her to go off campus to work some.

After reviewing studies on out-of-home placement for severely retarded children, Seltzer and Krauss (1984) conclude that there are two major obstacles to adequate services for these children: the level of retardation, and placement of the child with the natural family. The authors note that despite the policy emphasis on family placement, children who are in nonfamily placements receive more services. These findings and those of this study suggest the need for a shift from a substitute child welfare model to one that is supportive and supplements the family's efforts.

Looking to the Future

Most of these mothers (54%) whose children were living at a residential school for the deaf, the blind, or the deaf-blind face a major transition. Taking their child back into their home at age 21 will often demand that they learn how to respond to the very different needs of a deaf-blind adult. Kershman (1982) has reported that the training needs of parents of deaf-blind children who have less than monthly contact with their child are greater than needs of parents who see their child more frequently. She has suggested that these parents of older (17 - 21 years) children report greater training needs because they anticipate the child's return home. For the parents of residentially placed children in this study, most of whom (76%) see their child once or twice a month or less often, the child's return home at age 21 will mean caring for a child who no longer spends most of the day in an educational program. In most cases (56%), it will mean caring for a child who has had no vocational training. For almost one fourth of the group, it will mean caring for a child whom mothers expect will never be able to work. According to the mothers' estimates, 15% of these children were very dependent on others for all their personal care needs, and 44% of the children were partially dependent. Even those mothers who were more optimistic about their child's abilities and who estimated that their child would be able to attend a day activity center (30%) or work in a sheltered setting (27%) will not necessarily have access to these options in their community. Limited access to services was a particular problem for families in rural areas, a finding that was also reported in Moore et al.'s study (1982), in which 46% of rural families compared to 28% of urban families had difficulty finding services near their home.

> Our state is not geared to the severely handicapped living and working in the community.

> I'm satisifed with her training, but her vocational future is bleak.

> He has none (vocational future).

> This is a rural area, and there aren't a lot of services available.

> (We need) the development of adequate training and work facilities for our child as an adult.

> By the time she has completed schooling hopefully there would be some type of vocational training she could get into.

> What we feel we need is help with how we can best help him to have some life ahead of him after his schooling at the age of 21 ends. Everyone who works with him agrees he does have the potential to work in a sheltered workshop and be semi-independent in a group home, but at this time there seems to be no such program in this state, and no plans for any.

> The only thing I wish would happen when she finishes school at 21 is that she will be placed in a job.

> I am happy to have her in a school where she can get some training. What worries me is what will happen to her after she turns 21 and there is no place for her to go. I am afraid she will forget what she knows. I would like her to stay in some kind of program, if only for part time.

> The major concern is what happens to us and our son when he turns 21.

> We wish there could be further education available for our child as

she appears to be at a stage that she really wants to learn more, and seems more interested to learn.

About half of the deaf-blind children in this study were 18 years old and within several years will no longer be eligible for educational services. This group, like the rest of the rubella group, has an imminent need for varied adult support services. The adult who is deaf-blind as a result of rubella will have quite different and more extensive needs than those of adults with Usher's syndrome, for whom most deaf-blind adult services have been planned in the past. The comments of the mothers that are summarized in Table 5.2 reflect the diversity of these needs.

Table 5.2. Immediate and Future Needs of Mothers of Deaf-Blind Adolescents

	n
Greater access to information about deaf-blindness	5
More help in the home	5
Living option for the child after parents' death	3
Vocational training for the child	4
More options for the child after age 21	4
Access to group home	2
Financial help	4
Access to professionals with specialized training	7
Continued educational services for child after age 21	2
Communication training	1
Summer programs	2
Transportation	2
Access to sheltered workshop, other employment	5
Respite care, trained sitter	4
Health insurance for child	1
Opportunity for continued education for parent	1
Access to day activity center	1

As Moroney (1981) has pointed out in his discussion of public policies for families of the handicapped, community care and placement of the handicapped demand that families who are expected to provide that care, particularly for the dependent, severely handicapped child, have access to services needed to keep the handicapped individual in the home. Problems arise when community-based care is translated into reductions in the services needed to make less restrictive placement viable for the families of the handicapped individuals. A model policy for families of the severely handicapped would be one that offered parents the option of supports for in-home care of their child as well as choices of short-

or long-term residential placement outside of the home (Yando & Zigler, 1984). Seltzer and Krauss (1984) review many of the obstacles to home placement of the severely retarded child. They note that the severely retarded child's family may be excluded from the respite care programs that can help sustain family members and offer temporary relief. They also note the high rate of institutionalization for severely retarded individuals and the lack of community options for these families. For example, supportive alternatives to institutionalization for these individuals may include part-time foster care, weekday residential placement, and community residences staffed with the trained personnel needed to care for clients with significant medical, self-care, and supervisory needs. Yet, as the mothers in this study indicate, these alternatives are often unavailable.

Systems theory indicates that families need to readjust their roles and expectations as children make transitions into new stages of development. Families of rubella children now face a major transition as their child approaches adulthood. A Department of Education preliminary policy statement on the school-to-adult life transition acknowledges the impact of this experience on families.

> Students in transition from school are leaving a somewhat organized provider system and entering a more complex and confusing world, not fully understood by most service professionals, much less parents or consumers. (Will, 1984)

Fortunately, increased attention is being directed to the adolescent rubella group, and some (Scott et al., 1982; Wolf et al., 1982) have begun to delineate immediate and future needs of this group. The Department of Education, in recognizing these needs, has established funding priorities for special projects for severely handicapped children that specifically address the needs of the pre-adult deaf-blind. For example, one of these priorities will support projects to develop total life planning for deaf-blind children and youth, and another will support projects that design prevocational and vocational programs for the deaf-blind. Approximately $10,140,000 is expected to be available to support the deaf-blind centers and technical assistance and other special projects for the deaf-blind in fiscal year 1984 (*Federal Register*, *49*(85), 18684). These special projects include providing transitional services to deaf-blind youth after age 22, a pressing need for many of the families in this study. Continued federal commitment to provide for this group is demonstrated in these appropriations, which respond to needs identified by Wolf et al. (1982) in their study, contracted by the Department of Education, of the needs of deaf-blind individuals, and to Scott et al.'s (1982) recommendations. Those authors recommended extended educational services to deaf-blind students beyond age 21, education and respite care for parents, job placement, alternative living programs, and federal support for indirect services not provided by the states. These are policies that are also congruent with the needs that were expressed by the mothers who responded to this survey.

Increased Need and Decreased Availability of Services

Yet changes in how these services are provided are likely. As noted, only six one-year contracts for regional centers were awarded in 1983 to replace the 15 centers whose 5-year contracts expired the previous year. This reduction may reflect a slowly changing federal policy toward serving this low-incidence handicap group. The Deaf-Blind Program was established in the late 1960s at a time when direct services were not available in the states to meet the special needs of the rubella group. Since that time, P.L. 94-142 was passed and mandated a free and appropriate education for all handicapped children. In theory, the direct services that the Deaf-Blind Program has provided could and should now be provided by the states. In fact, however, P.L. 94-142 appropriations have never met authorized levels. As Scott et al. (1982) point out, most State Education Agencies (SEAs) and Deaf-Blind Center staff agree that P.L. 94-142, if adequately funded, would provide for the direct needs of the deaf-blind 0-21 group. However, full funding is unlikely in the present economic climate. Further, even if direct services were assured through full funding, P.L. 94-142 does not mandate the very specialized indirect support services that the Deaf-Blind Program provides, including additional teacher aides, prevocational and vocational programs, weekend and summer programs, specially trained staff, and parent counseling. Based upon their interviews with SEA and Deaf-Blind Center staff, Scott et al. (1982) concluded that without the federal Title VI-C funds, states would have to eliminate these supplemental services. Yet the respondents to this study often reported that these services were extremely beneficial when their child was young, and they indicated a continued, and in some cases, greater need for these support services as their children approach age 21. Scott et al. pointed out parents' particular need for training in transitional skills as their children reach prevocational and vocational levels, a need also reported by the mothers who responded to this survey. This training, the authors noted, would not be available without federal support.

About one fourth of the mothers indicated that supplemental income would have made it easier for them to provide care during their children's early years. As these children return to their parents' homes at age 21, one might anticipate that mothers will experience economic burdens similar to those experienced when the child was young, if not greater strains as parents begin to retire and no longer maintain their peak income level. While their incomes may decline, most of these families will probably not fall below poverty level; yet, as Moroney (1981) stresses, most social services that would support these families, such as Medicare, Medicaid, and other income maintenance programs, are income related, with poverty being the primary criterion for benefits and services. More flexible income and tax policies should be considered which would take into account the already great financial expenditures these parents have incurred.

> The state of Alabama gives no financial support at all. This support would be very helpful.

> I am having problems trying to put her on insurance. Her income is so little, and my earnings are too. I have to take some of her money to help with the bills, and I don't think it is fair. She needs her money in case anything should happen to her before she is eligible to join an insurance, which is 20 years old.

Thirty-eight percent of Moore et al.'s (1982) sample reported that they were not eligible for services they needed because their incomes were too high. This problem was most common in the middle-income group and was rated as more stressful by that group than by the other income groups. Others (Boggs, 1979; Roth, 1979; Tapper, 1979) have argued for the need to provide cash subsidies to parents who wish to care for their severely handicapped child in their home. Two strong arguments for cash subsidies are that they would cost the government less than institutionalization, and that they would allow for optimal child and family functioning.

Coordination of Services

Finally, unlike services for school-age deaf-blind children which continue to flow through the children's educational programs, services for the deaf-blind rubella adult will require careful coordination. The needs of the deaf-blind adolescents in this study who have multiple and severe handicaps and are at least somewhat dependent on others, are typical of the needs of the rubella group. Ideally, a transition from school-based to community-based service delivery should begin immediately, while these children are still eligible for educational services, can be assessed by school personnel, continue to be identified on state or regional registries, and, in many cases, are receiving vocational training that offers them the potential for some type of community placement. Once these children leave these programs and return to their parents' homes at age 21, they will be more difficult to locate. Furthermore, since many of them will lose vocational skills without continued practice, the longer they are without training or employment, the more difficult it will be for them to find an appropriate job or living placement.

This transition from school- to community-based service delivery will require careful planning for two reasons. First, the role of the federal government, which until now has been the primary agent in serving this group, seems likely to decrease. As Scott et al. (1982) note, a few states have already decreased their use of Title VI-C funds to serve the deaf blind, with one state committing itself to full funding of direct program costs (p. 26). Second, as the role of the federal government declines, the number of programs and agencies which serve these adult clients is likely to increase. Wolf et al. (1982) noted the diversity of relations that exist between state education and rehabilitation service agencies. For example, in some states an agency for the blind also serves the deaf blind, whereas in other states the deaf blind are served through an agency for the deaf. Agents that will need to be involved in planning services for the adult needs of the rubella group include those community agencies for the blind that have traditionally served the deaf blind, vocational rehabilitation agencies, sheltered workshop staff, and individuals responsible for planning and supervising group homes and other community residences. The deaf-blind clients these agents have worked with in the past have had quite different needs and abilities from the rubella group. The resources and approaches to serving the more severely impaired deaf-blind client are more highly developed today as a result of federal support to develop methods and materials for the deaf blind. As Wolf et al. (1982) recommend in their suggested policies, vocational rehabilitation counselors will need to become familiar with both the abilities of the deaf-blind client as well as with the types of training and vocational experience to which the client has already been exposed. Finally, the diverse needs and family environments of these deaf-blind children make it vital that parents participate in formulating the policies and programs that will also affect their futures. The commitment and the family and personal contributions that the mothers in this study have demonstrated make them highly motivated and deserving partners in whatever planning occurs to provide for the adult needs of this special population of severely handicapped individuals.

References

Boggs, E.M. (1979). Allocation of resources for family care. In R.H. Bruininks & G.C. Krantz (Eds.), *Family care of developmentally disabled members: Conference proceedings* (pp. 47-62). Minneapolis: University of Minnesota.

Breslau, N., Staruch, K.S., & Mortimer, E.A. (1982). Psychological distress in mothers of disabled children. *American Journal of Diseases of Children, 136*, 682-686.

Brewer, G.D., & Kakalik, J.S. (1974). Serving the deaf-blind population: Planning for 1980. In C.E. Sherrick (Ed.), *1980 is now: A conference on the future of deaf-blind children* (pp. 19-24). Los Angeles: John Tracy Clinic.

Bronfenbrenner, U. (1977). Toward an experimental ecology of human development. *American Psychologist, 32*, 513-531.

Dantona, R. (1974). Demographic data and status of services for deaf-blind children in the United States. In C.E. Sherrick (Ed.), *1980 is now: A conference on the future of deaf-blind children* (pp. 25-33). Los Angeles: John Tracy Clinic.

Dunlap, W.R., & Hollinsworth, J.S. (1977, July). How does a handicapped child affect the family? Implications for practitioners. *The Family Coordinator,* pp. 286-293.

Farber, B. (1959). Effects of a severely retarded child on family integration. *Monographs of the Society for Research in Child Development, 24* (Serial No. 71).

Federal Register, 40(35), February 20, 1975.

Federal Register, 48(98), 22612-22614. May 19, 1983.

Federal Register, 49(84), 18418. April 30, 1984.

Federal Register, 49(85), 18684. May 1, 1984.

Fewell, R.R. (1984). *Sources of support for mothers of children with Down syndrome.* Paper presented at the Conference on Research on Mental Retardation and Developmental Disabilities, Gatlinburg, TN.

Gabel, H., & Kotsch, L.S. (1981). Extended families and young handicapped children. *Topics in Early Childhood Special Education, 1*, 29-36.

Gallagher, J.J. (1984). Foreword. In J. Blacher (Ed.), *Severely handicapped young children and their families: Research in review* (pp. xiii-xv). Orlando, FL: Academic Press.

Gath, A. (1977). The impact of an abnormal child upon the parents. *British Journal of Psychiatry, 30*, 405-410.

German, M.L., & Maisto, A.A. (1982, February). The relationship of a perceived family support system to the institutional placement of mentally retarded children. *Education and Training of the Mentally Retarded,* pp. 17-23.

Hicks, W. (1982). *Deafness, associated and unassociated disorders.* Gallaudet College, Washington, DC.

Jensema, C.J. (1974). Post-rubella children in special educational programs for the hearing impaired. *The Volta Review, 76*, 466-473.

Jensema, C., & Trybus, R.J. (1975). *Reported emotional/behavioral problems among hearing impaired children in special educational programs: United States, 1972-73.* Gallaudet College, Office of Demographic Studies, Washington, DC.

Kershman, S.M. (1982). The training needs of parents of deaf-blind multi-handicapped children. Part two: Factors associated with parental responses. *Education of the Visually Handicapped, 14*, 4-14.

Korn, S.J., Chess, S., & Fernandez, P. (1978). The impact of children's physical handicaps on marital quality and family interaction. In R.M. Lerner & G.B. Spanier (Eds.), *Child influences on marital and family interaction: A life-span perspective* (pp. 299-326). New York: Academic Press.

Krugman, S. (1983). The conquest of measles and rubella. *Natural History, 1*, 16-20.

Love, H. (1979). *The mentally retarded child and his family*. Springfield, IL: Charles C Thomas.

Moore, J.A., Hamerlynck, L.A., Barsh, E.T., Spieker, S., & Jones, R.R. (1982). *Extending family resources*. (Available from Children's Clinic and Preschool, 1850 Boyer Avenue East, Seattle, WA, 98112)

Moroney, R.M. (1981). Public social policy: Impact on families with handicapped children. In J.L. Paul (Ed.), *Understanding and working with parents of children with special needs* (pp. 180-204). New York: Holt, Rinehart & Winston.

Office of Demographic Studies. (1980). *Rubella and non-rubella deaf students by region and state*. Gallaudet College, Washington, DC.

Roth, W. (1979). An economic model of social and psychological factors in families with developmentally disabled children. In R.H. Bruininks & G.C. Krantz (Eds.), *Family care of developmentally disabled members: Conference proceedings* (pp. 39-46). Minneapolis: University of Minnesota.

Scott, A.C., Campeau, P.L., Wheeler, J.D., & Ferrara, S. (1982). Evaluability Assessment of the Deaf-Blind Centers and Services Program. (Available from American Institutes for Research in the Behavioral Sciences, P.O. Box 1113, 1791 Arastradero Rd., Palo Alto, CA 94302)

Seelye, R.R. (1979). The deaf-blind child as a visually functioning person. *Proceedings: Workshop for Serving the Deaf-Blind and Multihandicapped Child*. Sacramento: Southwestern Region Deaf-Blind Center.

Seltzer, M.M., & Krauss, M.W. (1984). Placement alternatives for mentally retarded children and their families. In J. Blacher (Ed.), *Severely handicapped young children and their families* (pp. 143-178). Orlando, FL: Academic Press.

Stein, L.K., Palmer, P., & Weinberg, B. (1980). Characteristics of a young deaf-blind population. *The Siegel Report 10*. David T. Siegel Institute for Communicative Disorders, Michael Reese Hospital and Medical Center, Chicago.

Tapper, H. (1979). Barriers to a family subsidy program. In R.H. Bruininks & G.C. Krantz (Eds.), *Family care of developmentally disabled members: Conference proceedings* (pp. 79-86). Minneapolis: University of Minnesota.

Tew, B., & Lawrence, K.M. (1973). Mothers, brothers, and sisters of patients with spina bifida. *Developmental Medicine and Child Neurology, 15*, 69-76.

Trybus, R.J., Karchmer, M.A., Kerstetter, P.P., & Hicks, W. (1980). The demographics of deafness resulting from maternal rubella. *American Annals of the Deaf, 125*, 977-984.

Vernon, M. (1967). Characteristics associated with post-rubella deaf children: Psychological, educational, and physical. *The Volta Review, 69*, 176-185.

Vernon, M., Grieve, B., & Shaver, K. (1980). Handicapping conditions associated with the congenital rubella syndrome. *American Annals of the Deaf, 125,* 993-997.

Wikler, L. (1983). *Periodic stresses in families of children with mental retardation.* Paper presented at the American Association on Mental Deficiency Annual Convention, Dallas, TX.

Will, M. (1984). Bridges from school to working life. *Programs for the Handicapped, 2,* 1-5.

Wolf, E.G., Delk, M.T., & Schein, J.D. (1982). *Needs assessment of services to deaf-blind individuals* (Final report, U.S. Department of Education Contract No. 300-81-0426. Available from Redex, Inc., 1110 Fidler Lane, Suite 821, Silver Spring, MD, 20910)

Yando, R., & Zigler, E. (1984). Severely handicapped children and their families: A synthesis. In J. Blacher (Ed.), *Severely handicapped young children and their families: Research in review* (pp. 401-416). Orlando, FL: Academic Press.

6

The Effect of Professionals on the Family of a Handicapped Child

Cathleen Tooley Moeller

Initial Experiences

I am a parent. Anyone who has ever approached parenthood knows well the anticipation and small fears that cross your mind as you await the birth of your child. I fully expected that my third child would be born beautiful and healthy and would have just as brilliant a future as our first two sons. The very worst I expected from my third pregnancy was the disappointment that I would have another son rather than the daughter we dreamed of having.

Our child was born beautiful and healthy, with ten fingers and ten toes. Nothing was missing, including the magic that displaced whatever disappointment I had that he was another boy.

I was soon shocked, however to learn that our seemingly normal, healthy, beautiful child, because of an extra chromosome, number 21, was also a statistic—1 child out of 750 who is born with Down syndrome. Our precious baby had not been in this world five hours when this shattering news was delivered by a genetic specialist, a person whom to this day I would not recognize if she stood face to face with me. After I received the news, I secretly prayed that the genetic specialist was wrong. Even when she announced the diagnosis, I insisted that she explain to me just how sure she was. She explained that, based on her expertise, she was 98% certain of her initial diagnosis. I clung desperately to that small 2% percent of uncertainty, but somehow in my heart I was afraid that she was right. The joy we felt briefly as new parents was extinguished by a person who never even bothered to introduce herself to us by name. My life, my husband's life, our marriage, and the lives of our children would never be the same again. From the moment we received the diagnosis, we would never again be a "normal" family.

Once we received the chromosome test results that confirmed our little Matthew did have Down syndrome, trisomy 21, there was no longer a shred of hope that the doctors could possibly be mistaken. Our instincts then drew us together as a family. Strange doctors, including the nameless genetic specialists, outsiders to our family, had just given us brutal news, wounding our family in the most personal way. To us, their clinical language and impersonal talk of statistics were weapons that threatened an innocent baby—more important, our precious baby! We huddled together to protect ourselves against the intense pain and grief we were experiencing.

It's difficult to give a time or date when the hurting stopped, but in its place came an enormous strength. Nevertheless, the pain reminds me of a chronic bad back. You never know when it's going to flare up and suprise you, and remind you how vulnerable you still are.

Our first step in protecting ourselves from further pain was to become informed about our child's disability. This information not only protected us from the fear and confusion we experienced in our encounters with medical professionals, but it also made us feel a sense of control. We read everything possible on the subject. We prepared ourselves with information on the very best we could expect for our son's life, and the very worst. As we broke the news to friends and family, we felt we had sufficient information to answer any and all of their questions.

I believe inside all parents there resides a strength that is born out of love for their child. The more we got to know our son and become knowledgeable about his disability, the more the pain eased. When we fell in love with him, we came to the realization that no matter what, we would survive, and then the pain all but disappeared. The grief we felt for the loss of the perfect baby we wanted diminished as we realized that Matthew *was* our real child and we ceased to compare him to the imaginary child we thought would be born to us. The pain returns occasionally, but once most parents come to terms with their child's disability, they take the first step in the process of putting their lives back in their own control. Each time the pain brings on the familiar feelings of sadness, fear, and doubt, we as parents draw on our most potent reserves, the love we feel for our child.

In the time just after we received the diagnosis, we tried to use special family members and very close friends as a support system to alleviate our painful grieving. We expected that our pain would diminish as we shared our grief with loved ones—that their strength and love would ease our burden. We were, however, frustrated when this sharing did not ease the pain. In fact, the more we talked to family and friends who were close to us, the more we tended to take on their shock, pain, and upset at our situation. We were, as we soon discovered, creating a vicious circle of grief! Their pain added to our pain, and as a result, our entire family floundered emotionally. We needed to step outside this vicious circle we had unknowingly created and draw some strength and guidance from others who were not caught up in the emotional experience of Matthew's birth.

It was difficult and discouraging to find that the people we loved and trusted most could not help us in our time of greatest emotional need. We knew we needed support from others who had been where we were now, groping for bits and pieces of information that somehow enabled them to survive.

Professional and Parent Support Networks

At this point we were fortunate to be put in contact with a variety of professionals who, as it turned out, would influence every aspect of Matthew's life as well as our own reactions and ability to help him. As these experts slowly entered his life and the lives of everyone in the family, we began to absorb their hope, their honesty, and their encouragement, and to regain our strength as a family.

The doctors with whom we had been in contact when Matthew was still in the hospital led us to believe that we should feel lucky that people with Down syndrome now have life-spans that are almost as long as normal, and that they are no longer being institutionalized. "Lucky" was not how our family felt, however, during those first few days in the hospital. We were soon fortunate to meet a very kind nurse from the hospital who referred us to a parent-to-parent support group. The family coordinator and head of the group, Ann, called me, and before long, seemingly worked miracles. She had a grown child with Down syndrome who was actually living on her own! This wonderful woman gave me tangible information, and I clung to her every word. Ann helped me understand our child's disability in ways books could never relate. I learned that my child could learn almost anything if someone took the time and patience to teach him. He would be able to attend regular schools, like my other two children, and get appropriate school services in a special education program. I glanced down at my tiny sleeping baby knowing he too would one day wave goodbye to me, lunchpail in hand, while climbing on board a big yellow schoolbus. That knowledge somehow seemed so important to me that I cried tears of sheer relief. This other mother had convinced me that our family could look forward to living a full, happy life with our handicapped child. I listened eagerly as Ann went on to tell me that her daughter even kept track of her own checking account, and Ann said she knew of a few adults with Down syndrome who actually had their driver's licenses! Ann gave me hope and the strength to face the world. We shared a certain common bond, because she knew without a doubt exactly the feelings I was experiencing. I was one of over a hundred mothers with a disabled child that she had counseled, but because of her understanding, my family and I will always have a special place for her in our hearts. She helped us to feel hope, and although we realized it was just the beginning, we saw that we would be able to survive.

Ann also put my husband in touch with the leader of a program designed just for fathers and their handicapped children. The man to whom my husband spoke was a teacher of handicapped toddlers, and also the parent of a preschooler with Down syndrome. Through this program my husband also began to feel that he wasn't alone. This fathers' program offered a series of informative lectures dealing with every aspect of our child's life, from infancy to adulthood. The lectures provided information on medical and legal issues, and sibling and family problems. The fathers learned how to offer emotional sustenance to the immediate family, as well as to help extended family members adjust to the handicapped child. My husband speaks highly of the two men who run the program, and feels a certain unspoken intimacy and sense of gratitude towards these men, who he feels put him back in touch with reality.

> I feel a lot more relaxed about the love I feel for my son. I realize now that the whole family does not have to sacrifice their lives for the sake of the handicapped child. Having a father who has a handicapped child head the fathers program definitely gives the program credibility. He knows how I feel.

Our Child's Infant Program

When Matthew was an infant, we enrolled him in an early intervention program in a university setting where he was seen by a special education teacher, as well as a physical therapist. This marked the beginning of our relationship with a great many professionals who would enter our lives through their involvement with our son.

When I placed Matthew into a strange woman's arms on his first day in the infant program, I didn't know what she hoped to accomplish with my 4-week-old baby. I watched her as she checked his reflexes and conferred with the therapist. She cooed softly to him, and smiled proudly when he accomplished certain tasks, such as following an object with his eyes. I had no idea that first day of what the teacher and therapist expected of Matthew and myself; all I knew was that I began to feel safe in their presence. I trusted them, and I sensed from the start the difference between the negative and critical tone of our conversations with doctors, and the positive tone of these women's observations and comments. In those first few weeks, I was mesmerized as I watched the teacher and the therapist. They would hug my baby and praise him with baby talk after a "workout." As the weeks and months passed, I sensed my baby's growing attachment to his teacher, and his response to her obvious delight whenever he accomplished a new feat. I, too, unconsciously formed my own attachment to her. I began to share with her small anecdotes about his cute or funny behaviors at home, my feelings about his handicap, problems with his brothers' reactions to a new baby — even confiding to her the new-found closeness I was experiencing in our marriage since Matthew's birth.

I soon found myself looking forward to the sessions with the teacher and physical therapist. I felt I had finally found a place where my child and I could really feel safe. Other mothers to whom I spoke shared the same feelings, and as one mother put it:

> I found myself feeling proud of my child. Her teacher was so thrilled to hear of everything she did at home, and was almost as delighted to learn when she first sat up as we were! We called and told her even before we told the grandparents. We felt she had a right to be one of the first to know.

These sessions were a place where my child was not judged on what he could *not* do, but rather on what he could and would eventually be able to do. It was clear that we were all working together to make him the very best person he could possibly be. When I later asked the infant teacher how she was able to make new parents, who were often quite devastated and still in shock, feel so positive about their child, she replied:

> In the very beginning, I realized that I am that baby's first teacher, and the parents are still in a great deal of pain. So I keep stressing positive statements about the baby, as a way of comforting the parents. Every baby has potential, and it is important for parents to know that right away.

Professionals who work with families in the early months of the child's life can have a profound influence on parents. A mother may hear the first hopeful words about her child from the teacher or therapist. And those words and assurances can become the basis of strong attachments, acknowledged or unrealized, between parents and program staff.

Parent and Professional Roles and Relations

The school terms went by, and my child was soon assigned to a new teacher and a new therapist. I was emotionally unprepared for this change, because I felt devastated and bitter that these people who had spent so much time with our baby, as well as with us, could desert us. I definitely felt an emotional void in my life, and I could see Matthew was confused as to the whereabouts of his old friends. It was difficult to remember that these people did not drop out of the heavens into our lives only, but rather were trained to do a certain job. When they had finished their work, they would refer my child to the next set of professionals who would meet his changing needs. It was equally hard to keep in mind that these people worked not only with my child, but with a dozen or so babies a week. I had a conversation with one mother and I was relieved to hear her say out loud the same feelings I had secretly harbored.

> I had to change my daughter's therapy session because she had been sick, so I ended up coming on a different day than usual. I walked in the room and was so taken aback to see her (teacher) with another infant, holding and talking to him just as she did my child! I was crushed. I thought we were her favorites — I was actually jealous.

Every mother I interviewed, when asked, expressed the same feeling. We all had attached ourselves so steadfastly to these first teachers and therapists that it was difficult to realize they could have similiar feelings for all the babies they saw. As one of the mothers interviewed by Winton and Turnbull (1981) has described, these professionals became a substitute family for us, and we felt as possessive about their relationships with our individual children as we would feel if an aunt or uncle took on a strange child and showed the same love and affection they had shown for their nieces and nephews. My son's first teacher, who understood the importance of the child's first teacher in the parents' lives, has made a few ground rules for her student teachers to protect everyone's feelings.

> I insist student teachers work in the classroom for at least two quarters, because the transition for parents, when teachers are switched more often, is just too difficult for parents emotionally.

This emotional attachment is a two-way street: teachers and therapists also become emotionally involved with the children, and sometimes much more than they anticipate.

I used to worry late into the night about a particular baby I was working with, or a family that I felt wasn't coping well. I'd become preoccupied with the emotional well-being of everyone concerned with that baby. I soon found that I didn't have a life outside of my job. I had to draw the line in order to survive as a person. It was a painful learning experience, not something they taught us in school.

I have tried to reflect back to the time of my son's infant program, and reconstruct how this attachment between parent and teacher formed. I remember my first year in the early intervention program. While the teacher was working with my child, I would talk to her and ramble on and on about one thing or another concerning my son's disability, mostly about how we, as a family, were or were not adjusting. I remember that she used to glance up at me occasionally and nod her head to let me know she was listening, but rarely, if ever, did she reply. She told me much later that she felt that if she reponded to my personal concerns, she would have jeopardized the quality of our parent-teacher relationship, allowing it to become an emotionally dependent one, and further, one that she did not feel she was trained or prepared to handle. Looking back on the situation now, I remember that I felt grateful she was such a good listener, and I simply thought that she was just a very quiet person. I now know why she was so quiet.

The Quality of the Parent-Professional Relationship

I have spoken to a variety of families of handicapped children, all of whom have known professionals who have played an important part in their lives and the life of their child. These people include doctors, teachers, physical therapists, speech therapists, occupational therapists, communication disorders specialists, nurses, lawyers, and administrators of the programs that eventually mainstream our children into the world. The families spoke of these people with varying degrees of like and dislike: their judgments, however, seemed to be based on the professionals' emotional response to their handicapped child.

> I felt she (the teacher) was a very knowledgeable and highly trained individual as far as her profession went, but we made the decision to change teachers because we didn't feel she was sensitive to our child. She should have held him and talked to him more lovingly — after all he's just a baby. He often cried after she worked with him. I thought her manner with him was rather brusque.

The quality of the parent-professional relationship is one of crucial importance. Parents need technical information, skills training, counseling, and support services so that the handicapped child, as well as the family, can live as normal a lifestyle as possible. This learning process is one that cannot be accomplished solely by reading books (what parenting skills can?), nor can books provide the confidence parents need to feel comfortable making important decisions for their child. This is where professionals can help the family by sharing their knowledge and experience.

The professionals who are in constant touch with the handicapped child must develop a rapport with parents that is based on trust and genuine caring. Guilt is, unfortunately, a burden almost all parents carry with them in one form or another, and parents of handicapped children are even more likely to experience it. We ask ourselves: "Am I doing enough?" "Should I spend more time with him?" "Am I expecting too much?" and of course, "Are my expectations too low?" We feel at times that we are too preoccupied with our handicapped child, and then turn around and feel that we are not worried enough. It's a difficult job being a parent, especially if our child has special needs.

When we get together in parent meetings, or we are observing our children at school, we all go through the feelings that I've just described. At those times, the parents who are feeling particularly "up" seem to be of great help to those that are down. Our group exhibits a see-saw syndrome. The message that we seem to be trying to share with one another, however, is to take care of ourselves, learn to be a little selfish, cherish our spouses, and make time for the things we want to do instead of the things we feel we *have* to do. We never absorb the advice all at once, but keep passing it around to whoever needs it the most. A couple who were more guilt-ridden than most of us experienced the most positive effects of our group's encouragements.

> We went on vacation and after a lot of agonizing, left the girls with my parents. In that one week alone with my husband, we shed all the negative feelings we'd been harboring, and realized life was to be enjoyed. Our handicapped child was doing the very best possible. We realized that as parents that was the ultimate goal we could hope for — in any of our children! We finally quit looking at life so seriously. It was a wonderful burden to shrug off.

Professionals who are sensitive to these parental feelings can offer the parents guidelines to help them evaluate their level of involvement with their child. When parents reflect upon their experiences with professionals, the first thought that often comes to mind is the quality of their relationship with the professional, and their feeling of being respected. The sensitive professional respects the dignity and integrity of the parent's role, and regards the parent's input about the child as unique, useful, and worthy of respect.

When the relationship between parent and professional flourishes, it is one of the most rewarding and satisfying relationships a parent could have. One family I interviewed has become so close to their child's physical therapist that she is often a dinner guest in their home. Their opinion of her is strongly influenced by the therapist's attachment to their child.

> I like her very much. I felt that in the first months she was undergoing some transitions in her personal life, and she often seemed disorganized and confused. But as soon as she held my baby, she was able to get her to do anything. I feel she was as attached to my baby as an aunt would be. . .I knew she cared deeply.

Parent and Professional Expertise

Next to the parent, the teacher is probably the most important person in a child's life. The parents view the teacher as the "expert," looking to the teacher for direction, information, and assurance. The relationship is one of heartfelt intensity. The teacher must maintain an open, honest relationship with both parent and child. The teacher's impact and responsibility is indeed profound, but teachers should also keep in mind that they have much to learn from the parents. The parent is the best asset a teacher can have in understanding and helping a handicapped child, and unfortunately the least used.

> I argued with the teacher until I was so frustrated I wanted to cry. My son was being placed in a program with other children who were academically too advanced for him. I couldn't make this teacher understand how far my son had come emotionally and mentally since the previous year. He is supposed to be a special education teacher, but he argued state funding with me while I was just trying to tell him that Timmy needed more time before he was ready for this program.

Professionals tend to take on an authoritative role in the life of the family with a handicapped child. It is only natural that we parents view professionals as experts, and naturally we assume they know what programs are best for our child. The parents tend to feel somewhat helpless and in awe of the professionals they come in contact with, especially during the child's preschool years. The parent is often reluctant to argue or disagree with the professionals, fearing that the child's program or special services might be jeopardized. This, of course, is not the case, and parents need to understand this. Professionals also need to keep in mind that parents are most understanding of their child's needs, and to let parents know they value their unique insights. One mother of a blind child has described the effect that her son's nursery school staff had on her and her husband by acknowledging their contributions:

> They restored our parental expertise by consulting us about how we handled specific situations in the home that were problems in the classroom. They made a point of telling us when we were doing something right. . . . We were finally given the chance to pull together as a family, to begin to heal. (Stotland, 1984, p.73)

One of the professional's most important responsibilities is to provide direction. There may be a difference of opinion about the services a child needs. The services that are available to the parent may not all be equally effective or successful. Parents are often referred to various sources for answers, and they must determine how best to select the services that are available to them. While parents have individual ways of adjusting to life with a handicapped child, they all have one thing in common: They all want to find the most appropriate services for their special-needs child. Parents who have experienced a lack of response to their child's needs will be overwhelmingly grateful to a helpful professional. Parents' vulnerability to inadequate information and supports is reduced by the formation of parent advocacy groups, and increased public awareness of their needs; however, the struggle for parents is hardly over. Professionals in the legal, medical, and educational professions must remember their influence on the lives of parents of handicapped children and do whatever they can to support parents in their unique role.

Keeping Parent Needs in Mind

The parents of a handicapped child experience many of the same feelings as parents of "normal" children, while at the same time they cope with the overwhelming parenting demands imposed on them by a child who has special needs. A handicapped child needs *more* time, *more* energy, *more* patience, and *more* money than a normal child. Often these parents give more of themselves, and get less for their parent egos in return. It is vital that teachers and therapists keep this in mind when prescribing exercises or extra tasks for the parent to practice at home. One parent expressed her frustrations this way:

> I have three children at home, all preschool age, and my youngest is handicapped. It takes all the physical energy I have to cope. I was supposed to work on his fine motor skills at home for an hour each day between therapy sessions. I felt so inadequate that I didn't have the nerve to tell the teacher I couldn't even begin to find the extra time.

Teachers and therapists are sometimes so caught up in their enthusiasm to put a new theory into action that they don't stop to think about the additional demands they are placing on a family that is already struggling to cope. One fairly outspoken mother finally could no longer stand the pressure of having to work with her child so often at home; she felt her life was revolving entirely too much around her handicapped child, at the expense of the other family members who also needed her.

> I can't solve all his physical problems. I feel like telling the teacher, "You know the job, you're the expert — you make it work." I get tired

of trying to be so many different people and be good at all of them. . .wife, mother, special mother, employee. I can't make it all work, and I don't pretend to know how. I feel like a lot should get done in the three hours she (the teacher) has him. I expect her to make my life easier, not harder.

The parents to whom I spoke said that they preferred that their involvement with their child's teacher be informal and give-and-take in nature. They felt that the teacher's role was more properly that of decision-maker for their child's educational needs. While the parents felt very strongly that they wanted to have input concerning their child's program and that their information should not be taken lightly, they felt that educators should finally determine the goals, objectives, and methods of instruction for their child. On the other hand, parents preferred to have total control in deciding what types of records should be kept, what medical services should be provided, and when the child should be transferred to another school. For the most part, there is a joint responsibility for decisions affecting the child, with teachers and parents contributing more or less, according to their expertise. There is, of course, a question as to whether active and joint decision-making on the part of parents and educators is a realistic expectation when applied to *all* parents.

Keeping the lines of communication open between parents and professionals is, of course, essential, both for the success of the child's program and the parent-professional partnership. When working with a child, professionals have to keep in mind the expectations parents have for their child. These expectations can help the professional decide upon a program that is best suited to all three involved: parent, professional, and child. I asked parents to share what they thought were the best questions that professionals had asked them, or questions that they wish had been asked, and the following is a result. Questions similar to these were presented to parents prior to an IEP meeting in a study done by Goldstein and Turnbull (1982).

- What skills do you think your child should be performing?
- Are there problems at home (behavioral, physical, verbal) that can be helped by work at school?
- What kinds of a discipline and rewards have you found to be effective?
- How does your child best use his social skills at home with friends and neighborhood children?
- Does your child have any problems dealing with other peer groups?
- What do you feel are your child's strengths and weaknesses?

Questions like these encourage parents to share the kind of information teachers do not have access to concerning the child's home life, and to share insights that parents gain in their unique relationship with their child. Professionals who ask these questions also acknowledge the parents' expertise and help parents become aware of their potential to contribute to their child's school program.

Father-Professional Relations

Professionals who work with the young child and the family often tend not to include fathers fully. I had a very enlightening interview with the father of a toddler with Down syndrome who had just recently recovered from open heart surgery. He related the strong feelings he had towards the professionals he had come in contact with in his child's life. His first contact was with his child's pediatrician when he learned of his daughter's disability.

> I felt like an outsider. I remember the doctor came into the room and looked right at my wife and told her that it had been confirmed by the genetic specialist that Paula had Down syndrome. I was devastated. I love my daughter too. The worst part of it was that the doctor only managed to catch my glance as he left the room.

This couple went on to learn that in addition to their child's genetic defect, she also had a life-threatening heart problem. They had to make a series of difficult decisions that would affect their child's future, and they decided, against their doctor's advice, that their child should undergo the heart surgery. The father recalls this terribly emotional time for their family:

> When we went into the surgeon's office to discuss Paula's surgery, we had to make a life or death decision based on the information he was about to give us. But in the entire time he talked, he looked directly at my wife. I kept trying to ignore the situation and just listen. But it was just too important. I finally had to stand up and demand that he look at me when he spoke. It was obvious by his surprise that he was totally unaware of his insensitivity.

The father recounted similar experiences when he occasionally accompanied his wife and child to school or therapy sessions. He noticed that when they went down the halls and encountered a professional who worked with the family on a regular basis, the teacher or therapist would always look at his wife first, and only later look at him. I first thought that the father had probably overreacted, and was especially sensitive. I did, however, mention the conversation to my husband, and asked about his experiences. He too remarked that he felt a bit awkward about attending a therapy session or just showing up at school.

> Even as his father, I feel more like a visitor than a parent. I guess I've just relied on second-hand information about our child that the professionals give the mother.

One father to whom I spoke has a special-needs child of high-school age. He felt that fathers are often cast into a back seat role, beginning with the child's birth. As a result, professionals often overlook the needs and potential contributions of these other parents.

> Back when our son was born, it was still common practice that the mother was put out for the birth, and the father waited in a smoke-filled room. The doctor came in and told me that our son was not "right," and explained his handicap in somewhat clinical terms. I was so shocked that I couldn't muster the energy to ask any questions. The pain I felt at that moment made my heart ache with sadness. The doctor went on to remind me how strong I would have to be for my wife, who was not yet aware of the situation. I tried very hard to comfort her, and still remember how selfish I felt that I wished I had someone to comfort me.

The fathers to whom I spoke said that they tended to remain silent or passive in situations involving their child where they normally might have been more aggressive. When I pressed them for reasons, I got the following reply from a father who seemed to speak for the majority of fathers I spoke to:

> I have never before been involved with so many professional people. . . . The statements and advice they gave us concerning our child seemed so final and infallible. I was fearful that I would show my ignorance if I challenged them, after all, they have been to school for years, learning all about my child's disability, and we had only heard a small sampling of information over the past six months. I felt inadequate, and figured they had to know best.

Professionals do, certainly, know their various fields of expertise, but the input and information that parents, including fathers, can offer should be valued no less than the information the professional can offer the family.

Parent as Teacher

Just as a disabled child's world is limited, so too are the child's educational experiences. The day comes when the child is no longer eligible for school services and must make the transition to the adult world. If the parents and professionals have worked as a team, the parents should be prepared to teach their child the additional skills the child will need to exist in a world outside of the family's home. In his book, Albert T. Murphy (1981) describes parents' feelings about successful relationships with their child's teachers and therapists. They expressed their feelings, and the special skills they learned, as follows:

> They included me in the activity planning right from the start.
>
> She not only did her own job but always tried to keep me informed

of all the other services and agencies we'd be needing. She'd go out of her way — was really concerned.

She helped me to feel better about my son and about myself without kidding anybody — I mean, she helped us see the limits too. She helped me to get beyond "whose fault" to "nobody's fault."

I learned that I could really do something, not just hope and wait for others to act. (p.149)

The positive experiences with professionals these parents report prepare parents to teach their child the life skills that the child learns at home and will later generalize in other settings.

There are a variety of skills and values that are most appropriately taught by the family. Sondra Diamond (1981) has outlined five of these skills: acceptance of the disability, decision-making, freedom of choice, risk-taking, and a sense of privacy. The first is the ability to accept a disability. Parents begin to teach their child this acceptance as soon as the child realizes that he or she is different—for some children this may be when they are as young as three years of age. The parent must then begin to teach the child how to live with a handicap in a world of non-handicapped people. Learning this acceptance is a lifelong task for the child. In order to help their child cope with his or her differentness, parents need to make the child feel a sense of worthiness. A child who feels loved and accepted by those around him will find it easier to accept his handicap because he will not feel that it separates him from those he cares for and who care for him.

The child also needs to learn decision-making skills. These skills are fostered by the child's exposure to a variety of social situations. At home, the child learns to make decisions by being given choices: What should you wear today—your red sweater or your blue sweater? What do you want for dinner—hamburgers or hot dogs? There are endless choices even a young child can be asked to help make, and as a result, the child learns to use whatever information is available to make a choice. As the child gets older, the decisions become more complex, but hopefully, the child will have learned how to use information to make a decision. These decisions include how to protect oneself, whether to play in the street or in the yard, and whether to talk to strangers. We take for granted that we must teach our nonhandicapped children these basic decision-making skills, yet we sometimes forget that our handi-capped children must also learn these skills.

Related to learning how to make decisions is learning how to exer-cise freedom of choice. When a child learns his limitations, he sometimes feels that there are no choices left for him to make. A child who is mentally retarded will not be president, and a child in a wheelchair can-not choose to be a professional boxer. We as parents must teach our children all the things they *can* do, so that when the time comes, they can make appropriate choices for themselves. This begins when we as parents learn to respect the choices they do make. For example, if a child does not want to visit a relative, we can try to convince the child why he or she should go, but rather than force the child, we must respect the child's final choice. The child who does not feel forced to engage in a socially desirable activity may find it easier to participate later.

In the process of learning and developing their potential, children will need to take risks. The child who falls while learning to walk learns what mistakes *not* to make. Learning comes from experiencing failure and disappointment as well as success, and risk-taking is required in all new endeavors. The benefits of taking risks are learning how to succeed and perform new skills; if a child knows emotionally and physically what the pitfalls are, he or she will have learned how to avoid them, and in the process learned a little about personal survival.

A handicapped person's privacy is often invaded. People feel free to stare at the child in public, and to touch or move the child without waiting for the child's approval. This can lead to a distorted self-image. Parents must show the child that he or she is entitled to privacy and personal space. The handicapped child must also, in turn, respect others' personal space and need for privacy.

Families have their own ways of teaching their child these life skills and values. These are skills that are most effectively taught in the context of the child's home and community. The child will gain from these skills whatever effort the family puts into teaching them. This is most easily accomplished when parents value the skills and feel comfortable teaching them. And in this process of preparing their child for a future independent life, family members often find that the child has much to teach them about the dignity and strength that are often underestimated in handicapped individuals in our society.

Future Concerns

I have yet to speak to any parent of a handicapped child who does not, in some shape or form, dread the future. In the very early stages of our lives with a handicapped child, we are taught discipline—we force ourselves to live in the present. If you are a parent, you can imagine just how very difficult this can be. Before a child is even born, we pick out a variety of names and imagine the personality the named child will have, and the possible future the child will have. Every mother, for at least a fleeting moment, imagines that her son or daughter might someday be president, or have a career of some grandeur. We imagine and we project our fondest wishes and dreams on a child we have yet to meet. When that child is born handicapped, those joys and dreams instantly go up in smoke. We don't yet know the child's potential or degree of impairment—we only have the name of a syndrome or anomaly or illness to go on. We have, too, professionals' guarded and generalized predictions: "These children usually. . ." or "Our studies have found that most children. . ." These are shaky statements on which to build our child's future. We, from the very beginning, often know all of the futures our children will *never* have—they most likely will never be doctors, lawyers, presidents, business tycoons, or professors. And the list goes on. It is etched painfully in the heart of every parent of a young handicapped child. We are left only with the question of what will our child be able to do? What career can we hope for them? Will they ever live on their own and earn a living? Can they ever marry and have their own family? These questions can only be answered as we watch our children grow, and as we observe what special talents they have. So, in order to survive, we are forced to live one day at a time, and not plan too far into the future. We guard ourselves against the fear that the original pain of the initial diagnosis will creep up and catch us unaware, and in a small way, we lose a little bit of the control we try to bring to our lives. When this happens, the familiar feelings of despair and fear haunt us once again, only, as time goes on, we often have more resources to help us accept setbacks, to get back on track, and take one day at a time.

My son is still only a toddler, and right now I find it difficult to even think of visiting group homes and checking out what kind of life he'll have in them. I have just enough strength inside to contemplate his move from his early intervention program into the public school system. And even that transition raises fears about what the future will bring.

Of all the families I have talked to, not one said they felt they had the future settled as far as their handicapped child was concerned. These children ranged in age from infants to adults 26 years of age. This mother expresses the uncertainty that even parents of a handicapped adult face.

> My daughter finally got her own apartment and could take care of her finances. Paying her rent, balancing her checkbook. She has Down syndrome (age 26) and has been taught a variety of skills, but she had no interest in getting a job. I didn't want to push her, but prayed that she would find something to do with all her free time. I was so worried, and only annoyed her with my fears. Finally she joined a church, and now is so busy with the church activities—the sewing club, the garden club, cooking for functions—that she's never home. I went to bed thanking the good Lord for allowing me some peace of mind in my life!

Parents also worry about a husband or wife's dying and leaving the child's care up to the surviving parent, or worse yet, leaving the child alone. In the back of every parent's mind is the hope that he or she will outlive the handicapped child. In order to reduce that fear of the unknown, we as parents must learn to begin planning for the future needs of our young special child, and to begin to establish expectations for our child's future. The best skill I believe we can teach our children that will enable them to have the very best future possible, is to learn to love themselves, to learn self-esteem and to cherish it dearly. We begin to teach our children this basic life skill when they are very young. We must make them feel a sense of worthiness, and to wear it like a badge of courage. It is the most valuable skill we all possess because it helps us to get the most out of our lives.

Conclusion: The Growth of Trust

As parents of a handicapped child, we are extremely vulnerable. We must accept that ours will never be a typical family, and that we will always be thought of as different from most families. We will almost always interpret a smile from a passerby first as one of pity and then, perhaps, of friendliness; our emotional guard is always up. In light of this heightened sensitivity and resulting vulnerability, it is no wonder that we parents develop close bonds to the professionals who work with our handicapped children. First of all, they are so knowledgeable, and in this knowledge, the source of hope for our children. Second, they are so accepting of our children. We can relax in their presence; they are safe people, whereas contacts with others outside the immediate family circle are often uncomfortable and occasions for anxiety or embarrassment.

> I found myself dreading taking him to the supermarket. I didn't know if people smiled at my child because he's cute, or because they knew he's retarded, and they felt sorry for me. . .

I feel that we as a family of a handicapped child need more than anything else the security these professionals offer us. We need to believe, to trust in these professionals when they tell us that their physical therapy will enable a child to walk more like a "normal" person, and therefore to be more readily accepted in society. That speech therapy will enable our child to master our language, and in turn, make it easier to communicate with others. That certain work programs will prepare our child for a job that will provide him with an income and self-esteem, and will relieve our family and society of the financial burden of caring for him throughout his adult life. Most of all, we need to believe firmly that our child will grow to be loved just as he or she loves, and to be accepted as a worthwhile human. Finally, we need to believe that all the studies, interviews, and reams of paper we volunteer to complete for their research will help professionals plan for a richer and more rewarding life for our child and others like him. I as a mother, my husband as a father, and my two other children as his brothers, all depend on the knowledge of every professional we come in contact with. We look to them to give us something more we can believe in that will give our less-than-perfect child a more perfect life. It is no small wonder, in light of these expectations, that we regard each and every professional with great feeling—after all, we are placing our hearts into their hands.

References

Diamond, S. (1981). Growing up with parents of a handicapped child: A handicapped person's perspective. In J. L. Paul (Ed.), *Understanding and working with parents of children with special needs* (pp. 23-50). New York: Holt, Rinehart & Winston.

Goldstein, S., & Turnbull, A. P. (1982). Strategies to increase parent participation in IEP conferences. *Exceptional Children, 48*, 360-361.

Murphy, A. T. (1981). *Special children, special parents.* Englewood Cliffs, NJ: Prentice-Hall.

Stotland, J. (1984). Relationship of parents to professionals: A challenge to professionals. *The Journal of Visual Impairment and Blindness, 78*, 69-74.

Winton, P. J., & Turnbull, A. P. (1981). Parent involvement as viewed by parents of preschool handicapped children. *Topics in Early Childhood Special Education, 1*, 11-19.

7

Roles and Support Networks of Mothers of Handicapped Children

Carl J. Dunst, Carol M. Trivette, and Arthur H. Cross

Fundamental to a life-span perspective of development is the description and explanation of change over time, either in relationship to age or biocultural determinants, or both (Baltes, Reese, & Nesselroade, 1977). Age-related changes are generally described in terms of major time periods including prenatal development, infancy, childhood, adolescence, adulthood, and old age. Biocultural changes are generally described in terms of major life events and transitions such as the birth of a child, entry into school, puberty, entry into the workforce, marriage, and parenthood. In addition to behavior description and explication, a life-span orientation to development also concerns itself with optimizing human development by identifying the types of events and experiences that can affect behavior in desirable ways.

In this chapter we describe the roles and support networks of mothers of young handicapped children in relationship to both age-related and two particular biocultural differences: employment and marital status. We also present evidence concerning the direct and indirect effects of social support and role-sharing on personal well-being, family integrity, and child functioning. Finally, we suggest a need to redefine intervention practices in social systems terms so that the broad-based impacts of intra- and extrafamily support can be determined.

To place our own research in proper perspective, we begin with a review of the literature on (a) the age-related characteristics of maternal roles and support, (b) the effects of biocultural factors (employment and marital status) on maternal roles and support, and (c) child, parent, and family outcomes which are mediated by roles and support.

Roles and Support of Mothers of Nonhandicapped Children

Inasmuch as the discipline of life-span development itself is still in its infancy (Goulet & Baltes, 1970), empirical research with a clear focus on life-span changes in roles and social support networks is relatively scarce. Available data, however, strongly indicate that maternal roles and support vary as a function of age, biocultural factors, and life stages.

Ballenski and Cook (1982) provide evidence that parents' role demands vary as a function of the age of their children. Additionally, availability and satisfaction with informal sources of support are found to differ as a function of the life cycle stage of the subjects (Tamir & Antonucci, 1981). There is some evidence that maternal social support and role satisfaction are interrelated (Abernethy, 1973). Taken together, available evidence points to the fact that both maternal social support and maternal roles vary across the life cycle. We now turn to a description of these types of changes and differences.

Life-span Characteristics

Parenting roles are generally described in relationship to seven major maternal role stages: *pregnancy*—the prospective mother formulates notions about "good" mothering behavior; *infancy*—the mother cares for, protects, and nurtures the child; *toddlerhood*—the mother instills a sense of restraint while at the same time fosters independence in her child; *preschool years*—the mother prepares the child for separation and entry into school; *school years*—the mother fosters proper values in her child; *adolescence*—the mother prepares for the child's transition into adulthood and eventual separation from the family; *adult years*—the mother serves as a source of support to her offspring (Ballenski & Cook,

1982; Duvall, 1971; Lamb, 1978).

A number of researchers have found that maternal roles, as well as role characteristics (satisfaction, competence, and demands), vary as a function of the age of the child, mother, or both. Ballenski and Cook (1982) examined both maternal roles and mothers' perceived role competence at five child age levels, from birth to 18 years, and found that although mothers generally considered themselves competent in their parenting skills, particular roles as well as role demands changed considerably as a function of their child's age.

Ragozin, Basham, Crnic, Greenberg, & Robinson (1982) found that parenting roles were significantly related to both maternal age and role satisfaction. As mothers matured, they became more satisfied with parenting and more committed to parenting roles. Role structure was also related to maternal age. Compared to younger mothers, older mothers demonstrated increased caregiving roles and less time away from their child.

Comparative studies of role division among husbands and wives (Gallagher, Cross, & Scharfman, 1981; Pearlin, 1975; Sanik & O'Neill, 1982; Schaefer & Edgerton, 1981) show that mothers perform the bulk of traditional household chores and child-care responsibilities, and that fathers perform primarily provider roles. Life cycle comparisons as well as comparisons of different groups of parents reveal that over the past 20-30 years, mothers have continued to perform primarily traditional female and maternal roles. Thus, although there are age-related changes in the nature of maternal roles across the life span, the types of roles mothers perform have remained relatively stable across different groups of mothers.

Taken together, available data suggest both age-related and life cycle changes in maternal roles. This type of evidence has been used to describe the life-span characteristics of role continuity and stability (Duvall, 1971; Rossi, 1968). These data provide a foundation for describing life-span stability as well as changes related to age and life cycle.

There is some evidence to suggest that social networks and social support have life-span characteristics. Shulman (1975) examined social support in relation to two life-span variables: age and life stage (single; married, no children; married, with children; and widowed, separated, or divorced), and found that social support varied as a function of both variables. Support became more stable (that is, it was provided by the same individuals) with increased age, and persons named as social network members changed in relationship to one's life cycle. For example, whereas blood relatives and other kin were less likely to be perceived by single adults as sources of support, the opposite was true for married adults and for widowed, separated, or divorced individuals. Overall, the results showed that "personal (social) networks. . .varied with age and life stage, in composition, stability, and degree of involvement" (p. 813).

Tamir and Antonucci (1981) examined change and continuity in social support in relation to seven life stages: single, married (childless), parent of preschool child, parent of school-age child, parent of school-age and high school-age children, and parent of child(ren) over 18. The extent to which neighbors, friends, and relatives were perceived as sources of support and were sought out in times of need were the dependent measures. Mothers at the younger life stages reported neighbors and friends as being more supportive than relatives in times of need and crises, while at older life stages mothers expressed more satisfaction with the support they received, regardless of its source. These studies provide evidence to indicate that social support varies as a function of age and life cycle stage.

Biocultural Determinants

Two important determinants of maternal roles and social support are marital and employment status. A number of researchers have examined how roles vary as a function of marital and employment status. For example, a number of studies (see Vadasy, Chapter 9) indicate that single mothers, as a result of the multiple roles they must fill, often have a greater need for family and community support, yet receive less support than married mothers or male members of the household.

A mother's employment status appears to affect some roles but not others. With regard to traditional household roles (food preparation, housework, etc.), working mothers generally do less cooking, less housework, and entertain visitors less often than do nonworking mothers. To a small degree, husbands assume additional responsibilities in households where the wife works, although the amount of time husbands commit to traditional female roles is quite limited (Sanik & O'Neill, 1982). Mothers, regardless of employment status, assume most of the duties and responsibilities for child care. Thus, working mothers, in general, do not receive spousal support in performing household and child-care roles. Rather, household chores are simply less likely to get done or are done less often, and working mothers continue to assume primary responsibility for child-care roles despite added employment commitments.

Marital status is also related to role satisfaction and social support. In investigations of nonmarried mothers (Bowen, 1982; Brandwein, Brown, & Fox, 1974; Glasser & Navarre, 1964), support from members of the mothers' social networks is generally unrelated to maternal role satisfaction. This has not been found in studies of married mothers. Abernethy (1973) and Bott (1971) found married mothers who were members of "tightly knit" social networks to experience increased role satisfaction, both domestic and maternal. Evidently, intrafamily roles and responsibilities of single mothers are unaffected by availability of extrafamily support. Other studies indicate that the mother's employment status as well as her marital status may influence the amount of support available to her. For example, Weinraub and Wolf (1983), in a study of mothers differing in both employment and marital status, found "single mothers. . .to be more socially isolated than married mothers. They worked longer hours and received less emotional and less parental support. . .(and). . .they tended to have less stable social networks" (p. 1297). It may not be surprising that single mothers who receive little support report that it has a minimal impact on their lives.

Marital status may also be related to the nature of support at a particular point in time. Longino and Lipman (1982) examined the support provided by family members and friends to currently married, formerly married, and never-married females. There were no significant differences among the groups in terms of support provided by friends. However, married and formerly married females reported receiving significantly more support from family members compared to never-married respondents.

In a comparative study by Brim (1974) of married and nonmarried females, marital status was found to be differentially related to general life satisfaction and extrafamily support. Brim found a significant relationship between satisfaction and extrafamily support for nonmarried women, but not for married women. There was, however, for married women, a significant relationship between life satisfaction and intrafamily support from one's husband. Brim concluded that for married women, the presence of a stable conjugal relationship decreased the need for extrafamily support as a mediator of general life satisfaction, but for nonmarried women, the need for extrafamily support is almost a necessity for well-being.

This brief review of two selected biocultural determinants indicates that both roles and support are affected by mothers' marital and employment status. Thus, in addition to being related to the age and life cycle variables, roles and support are also influenced by at least these two biocultural factors. Together, the results of these studies suggest an interaction between age-related and biocultural factors, although to the best of our knowledge, this relationship has not been empirically examined.

Mediating Influences of Intra- and Extrafamily Support

Social systems theory postulates that support from members of social networks influence, both directly and indirectly, the behavior, knowledge, attitudes, and expectations of parents and their offspring (Bronfenbrenner, 1977, 1979; Caplan, 1976; Cochran & Brassard, 1979; Hobbs, 1975; Holahan, 1977; Mitchell & Trickett, 1980).

A sizable body of literature indicates that social support has positive mediational effects on personal and familial well-being (Bott, 1971; Dean & Lin, 1977; McCubbin et al., 1980; Mitchell & Trickett, 1980). Recent work has demonstrated that social support not only mediates life events and individual well-being, but that social support both directly and indirectly influences attitudes toward parenting (Crnic, Greenberg, Ragozin, Robinson, & Basham, 1983), styles of interaction parents manifest with their children (Crnic et al., 1983; Crockenberg, 1981; Embry, 1980; Giovanoni & Billingsley, 1970; Hetherington, Cox & Cox, 1976, 1978; Philliber & Graham, 1981; Weinraub & Wolf, 1983), parental expectations and aspirations for their children (Lazar & Darlington, 1982), and child behavior and development (Crnic et al., 1983; Crockenberg, 1981). Taken together, these findings demonstrate positive relationships between social support and personal, family, and child functioning. Additionally, the evidence strongly suggests that social support represents one form of intervention that might be used to optimize development, alleviate negative outcomes, and strengthen members of a child's family. As we suggest later, it may be worthwhile to rethink early intervention in social systems terms (see Dunst, in press) and apply these findings in ways that will have the greatest benefits.

Roles and Support Networks
of Mothers of Handicapped Children

We now describe the roles and support networks of families of handicapped children, factors related to maternal roles and social support, and the extent to which intra- and extrafamily support mediates outcomes in a manner similar to that reported in studies of families with nonhandicapped children.

Maternal Roles

Role division in families of handicapped children has been found to parallel that found between wives and husbands of nonhandicapped children (Cross, 1980; Gallagher et al., 1981; Schaefer & Edgerton, 1981). Husbands, for the most part, perform traditional provider and home maintenance tasks, whereas wives assume traditional housework and child-care roles. Such traditional role division appears to have some negative impact upon mothers. Evidence from a study by Trivette (1982) revealed that increased burdens associated with the care of a handicapped child remain essentially the responsibility of the mother, and result in increased maternal time demands and decreased personal well-being.

In the one study that has examined the age-related characteristics of roles in families of handicapped children (Schaefer & Edgerton, 1981), the performance of general household roles was found to be significantly correlated with the child's age. Fathers' participation increased with the increasing age of the child. Thus, as children became older, mothers received some additional assistance from their husbands in performing household chores. However, with regard to child-care roles, mothers assumed major responsibility, and the amount of time they devoted to these roles remained the same regardless of the child's age. This indicates that responsibilities for routine child care, as well as increased demands related to the specific handicaps of the children, were met primarily by mothers with minimal help from their spouses.

Although no researcher has examined the life-span characteristics of the roles of mothers of handicapped children, one would expect to find some deviations in their life cycles compared to mothers of nonhandicapped children. Most life cycle changes in families with nonhandicapped children have relatively clear boundaries when roles can be expected to change following certain life events and transitions. For example, a child's graduation from high school is generally followed by the child's separation from the family (Duvall, 1971). For families of handicapped children, life transitions are delayed, or, in the case of a severely and profoundly retarded person, may never occur at all. Parents, and most often mothers, are faced with the prolonged and sometimes lifelong responsibility for child care that normally would decrease with the child's increasing age. These conditions cannot but have some negative impact on the child's caregivers, usually the mother. Studies examining the impacts of deviations in life cycle transitions are sorely needed if we are to fully understand the implications of role changes and stability in families of handicapped children.

Social Support

A number of investigators have found that families of handicapped children have less social support available to them compared to families of nonhandicapped children (Friedrich & Friedrich, 1981; McAndrew, 1976; McDowell & Gabel, 1979; Stagg & Catron, Chapter 11). For example, McAndrew (1976) found that following the birth of a handicapped child, friends and relatives oftentimes isolated themselves from the family, withdrawing or failing to extend support. McDowell and Gabel (1979) found that mothers of retarded children reported having fewer social network members (relatives and friends) compared to mothers of nonretarded children. These investigators concluded that: "Mothers of retarded infants appear to be a more isolated group, even though they, like other parents of handicapped children, need more than the usual amount of friendship, advice, consolation and other support" (p.6). Stagg and Catron (Chapter 11) found that mothers of retarded children reported differences in their satisfaction with social support, depending on their child's age. Mothers of preschool retarded children reported less satisfaction than mothers of nonretarded children, but mothers of teenage retarded children reported more satisfaction than the mothers of nonretarded teenagers.

To the best of our knowledge there have been no studies that have specifically examined either the age-related or life cycle changes in social support among families of handicapped children. However, Gourash's (1978) help-seeking model provides a basis for predicting the types of social support that parents might seek in response to the birth and rearing of a handicapped child. According to Gourash, there are four ways personal social network members influence decisions about help-seeking. These include: "(a) buffering the experiences of stress thus obviating the need for help, (b) precluding the necessity for professional assistance through the provision of instrumental and affective support, (c) acting as screening and referral agents to professional services, and (d) transmitting attitudes, values, and norms about help-seeking" (p. 516). Evidence from the mental health field (Mitchell & Trickett, 1980) suggests that the first two influences often alleviate the need for professional help in dealing with most day-to-day crises and stresses. Granovetter (1973) found that the second two influences come into play whenever needed information or support are not available through one's personal social network. In terms of Gourash's (1978) help-seeking model, one would hypothesize that because less social support is available to families of retarded and handicapped children than families of nonhandicapped children, personal support networks are less likely to buffer the stresses and demands of the birth and rearing of a retarded or handicapped child. Moreover, because extended family members and members of the parents' kinship units are less likely to be knowledgeable about retarded and handicapped children (Gabel, 1979), one would hypothesize further that families of handicapped children would be more likely to seek help from nonmembers of their personal social network. Consequently, one would expect to find considerable variations in the support provided to families of handicapped children across the life cycle as they seek outside help to meet their changing needs.

Determinants and Mediating Influences

Schaefer and Edgerton (1981) conducted one of the most illuminating studies of the relationships between parenting roles and demographic and biocultural determinants. The subjects were 46 mother-father dyads. The parents had two children, one of whom was handicapped. The Parent Role Scale (Gallagher et al., 1981) was used as the independent measure of parenting roles. The scale includes 20 items (14 general roles and 6 child-care roles) which respondents rated in terms of "who currently performs" each role. Ratings were made on a 5-point scale ranging from

Mother Does It Alone (1) to Shared Equally (3) to Father Does It Alone (5). A comparison of working and nonworking mothers revealed no differences in terms of performance of child-care roles, but some differences with regard to general roles. Working mothers had higher ratings on items involving monetary roles (earning money, making decisions about how money should be spent, and financial obligations), and lower ratings for general household chores, including cooking, food buying, and housework. Thus, division of labor between husbands and wives, although quite traditional, was affected by mothers' employment status in a manner much like that found in families of nonhandicapped children. Neither SES (occupation, education levels, or income) nor race was associated with role division.

As we report later in this chapter, we have found a number of differences in parenting roles for working and nonworking mothers, but few differences in types of support available to mothers differing in employment status. In contrast, our data indicate a number of significant differences between married and nonmarried mothers in terms of their social support networks. Together, these findings suggest differential influences of marital and employment status on maternal roles and support. The specific nature of these differential impacts are described in more detail below.

There have been two investigations that have examined the mediating influences of role characteristics in families of handicapped children (Schaefer & Edgerton, 1981; Trivette, 1982). Schaefer and Edgerton (1981) found a significant relationship between marital satisfaction and maternal role demands. Mothers who reported that their husbands shared in both general household and child-care roles indicated greater marital satisfaction. Trivette (1982) found role satisfaction rather than role accumulation (number of roles performed) was the best predictor of a number of personal and family outcomes. Greater satisfaction with how roles were performed was significantly related to fewer maternal time demands, more social support, greater family integration, and more family opportunities.

Other researchers have investigated the influences of social support among families of handicapped children. Friedrich (1979) found that mothers who had more supportive social networks and enhanced well-being reported fewer stress-related reactions to their children's handicaps. Better physical and emotional well-being, fewer time demands, less devastating family effects, and more family integration were reported in a study by Dunst (1982). Similar results were found in a subsequent and more extensive study by these investigators (Dunst, Trivette, & Cross, 1985).

Although evidence suggests that less social support is available to families of handicapped children than families of nonhandicapped children, it appears that the support available has a positive effect on child and family functioning. This strongly suggests that support can be used as an intervention to achieve positive results in family functioning.

An Empirical Investigation of Maternal Roles and Support

In this section we present results from a study designed to examine a number of aspects of maternal roles and social support networks. The following dimensions of roles and support were examined: (a) structural and organizational features, (b) age-related characteristics, (c) biocultural determinants, and (d) the mediational influences of intra- and extra-family support.

Conceptual Framework

Life-span developmental psychology (Baltes et al., 1977; Goulet & Baltes, 1970), ecological psychology (Bronfenbrenner, 1977, 1979; Cochran & Brassard, 1979), and social network theory (Caplan, 1976; Holahan, 1977; Mitchell & Trickett, 1980) were used as the theoretical and conceptual framework for describing change and stability in roles and support, and examining how support mediates child, parental, and family functioning.

According to Baltes et al. (1977), life-span developmental psychology concerns itself with behavior *description* and *explication* in relationship to age and biocultural determinants, as well as identifying ways to optimize behavior change. In the present study, we sought to (a) describe how age influences maternal roles and support, (b) identify other factors that affect roles and support, and (c) determine how intra- and extra-family support mediates parent, family, and child outcomes.

Bronfenbrenner's (1979) articulate formulation of an ecology of human development makes explicit that if social support is to be implicated as either a mediational or causative factor, it is necessary to control for potentially confounding variables and to examine the mutual contributions of other explainer variables. In addition, Bronfenbrenner notes the importance of determining the bidirectional influences of persons, settings, and their characteristics on outcome measures. He maintains that studies of the ecology of human development should not obtain outcome measures only on a single subject (e.g., the child), but that the influences of mediational factors be determined for the child, parent, and family, as well as for other relevant network members.

In the present study, we examined social support as a mediational variable influencing not only parent, but also family and child functioning. Moreover, we simultaneously examined the influences of a series of family, child, and biocultural characteristics to determine how they influenced family outcomes. We hypothesized that, after controlling for these factors, social support would both directly and indirectly affect child, parent, and family functioning. The major tenet of our research was that social support would have major effects beyond those attributable to other explainer variables, and that social support would have both stress-buffering and positive mediational influences. To the extent that different types and dimensions of support could be identified that affected behavior in desirable ways, the types of experiences (interventions) that could be used to optimize the course of development would be strongly indicated.

Method

Subjects. The subjects were 96 mothers of mentally retarded, handicapped, and developmentally at-risk infants and preschoolers. The mean age of the sample was 28.98 (SD = 8.52) years. On the average, the mothers had completed 11.50 (SD = 2.57) years of school. The majority (68 %) of the mothers fell within the two lowest classes of socioeconomic status (Hollingshead, 1975). A total of 74 mothers were married, and 22 were unmarried (single, separated, divorced, or widowed); and 51 were working and 45 were nonworking. All mothers and their children were participants in an early intervention program (Dunst, 1982, in press).

The children's mean chronological age was 37.52 months (SD = 13.75); mean mental age was 22.90 months (SD = 12.70); mean intelligence quotients was 63.88 (SD = 26.10); and their mean social quotient was 70.70 (SD = 27.98). Twenty-nine of the children were diagnosed as mentally retarded, 38 were physically impaired, and 29 were developmentally delayed or at-risk for developmental problems. The etiologies of the children's handicaps included: cerebral palsy (24%), mental retardation due to unknown prenatal influences (23%), language impairment (18%), developmentally at-risk due to environmental factors (12%), cranial anomalies and spina bifida (12%), and chromosomal aberrations (6%). Fifty-seven percent of the children were male and 43% female.

Procedure. The mothers completed four questionnaires as part of their participation in the study: *Family Support Scale* (Dunst, Jenkins, & Trivette, 1984), *Parent Role Scale* (Gallagher et al., 1981), *Questionnaire on Resources and Stress* (Holroyd, 1973, 1974), and the *Parent-Child Interaction Rating Scale* (Dunst, 1984).

The *Family Support Scale* (FSS) measures how helpful 18 different sources of support have been to parents in caring for their preschool-age child. The sources of support include both individuals (spouse, parents, friends, physician, etc.) and groups (church, school, day care, etc.) at the different ecological levels posited by Bronfenbrenner (1979). Respondents indicate whether the source of support is available to them and the extent to which each source is helpful to them. Helpfulness is rated on a 5-point scale ranging from Not At All Helpful (0) to Extremely Helpful (4). Coefficient alpha computed from the average correlation among the 18 scale items is 0.77. Test-retest reliability of the total FSS scores, taken one month apart, is 0.91.

The *Parent Role Scale* (PRS) includes 20 roles which are generally performed in households with young children. The scales include 14 household roles and six child-care roles. Respondents indicate who currently performs the role (accumulation), who they would like to see perform the role (congruence), and how satisfied they are with role performance (satisfaction). The role accumulation and role satisfaction scores were used as independent measures of intrafamily support in the present study. Interrater reliability of the role-accumulation and role-satisfaction scores average, respectively, $r = 0.79$ and $r = 0.91$ (Cross, 1980).

The *Questionnaire on Resources and Stress* (QRS) was used as one outcome measure of child, parent, and family functioning. The scale is a true-false questionnaire which includes seven personal respondent scales, three family-functioning scales, and five perceptions-of-child-capabilities scales. Selected subscales were used in the present study as outcome measures. The discriminative validity of the QRS has been demonstrated in studies of the differential influences of handicapping conditions on parent, family, and child outcomes (Holroyd, 1974; Holroyd & Guthrie, 1979; Holroyd & McArthur, 1976).

The *Parent-Child Interaction Rating Scale* measures how many different "games" parents play with their child, and how often. Ratings are made for 24 different games which parents typically play with their preschool-age children (e.g., pat-a-cake, "this little pig," pretend phone conversations, repeating the alphabet). The 24 games are subdivided into four groups of six games, with each group corresponding to games generally played with children aged birth to one year, one to two years, two to three years, and three to four years of age, respectively. Ratings are made on a four-point scale ranging from Do Not Play At All (0) to Play Almost Every Day (3). The dependent measures of parent-child interaction were the number and frequency of games played by the parent and child. Frequency was computed as the total of the ratings for the 24 individual scale items. Coefficient alpha computed from the average correlation among the 24 scale items is 0.95. Test-retest reliability for the individual items, taken one month apart, averaged 0.74 (SD = 0.17).

Data Analysis

Role and support structure. Principal components factor analysis using varimax rotated solutions was used to discern the structural features of maternal roles and support. Analyses were performed separately for the 20 PRS roles and the 18 FSS sources of support. The correlational matrices were factored with unities in the diagonals, and factors with eigenvalues exceeding 1.0 were retained for rotation. Items with factor loadings of 0.40 or higher were used to determine factor membership.

Age-related characteristics. The age-related changes and stability in maternal roles and support were examined using a series of six groups one-way analysis of variance. The independent variable was the mental age level of the children. The subjects were divided into mental age groups of 1 to 11.9, 12 to 17.9, 18 to 23.9, 24 to 29.9, 30 to 37.9, and 38 to 65 months. The mean mental ages of the six groups were, respectively, 5.93 (SD = 2.66), 15.15 (SD = 2.27), 21.47 (SD = 1.13), 27.00 (SD = = 2.42), 34.46 (SD = 2.02), and 47.34 (SD = 8.01) months. The dependent measures included the individual items on both the PRS (role accumulation and role satisfaction) and FSS scales, and the total PRS and FSS scale scores. Correlational analyses were also performed to determine relationships between the child's and mother's chronological age and maternal roles and support.

Biocultural determinants. The extent to which maternal roles and support varied as a function of marital and employment status was tested using a series of t-tests. The two independent measures were marital status and employment status. The dependent measures were the same as described for the age-related characteristics of roles and support.

Mediational influences. Hierarchical multiple regression analyses by sets (Cohen & Cohen, 1983) were used to assess the mediational influences of intra- and extrafamily support. Four covariate sets were first entered into the analysis before the effects of support were assessed: family characteristics (SES and gross monthly income), child characteristics (chronological age, intelligence quotient, and diagnostic group), marital status, and work status. In each analysis, the increments (I) in R^2 were determined to assess whether the different sets of independent measures accounted for a significant proportion of variance in the dependent measures. The analyses were performed separately for maternal roles and maternal support. The dependent measures included: personal well-being, maternal time demands, family integrity, family opportunities, frequency and types of parent-child interactions, and several different aspects of child functioning and behavior.

180   *Dunst, Trivette, and Cross*

Results and Discussion

Detailed accounts of the findings reported in this section may be found in Dunst, 1985; Dunst and Trivette, 1984; Dunst, Trivette, and Cross, in press; Trivette and Dunst, submitted for publication.

Roles and support structure. The factor analysis of the PRS items yielded six orthogonal components. All but one was directly interpretable. Factor 1 included predominantly traditional female roles— both household chores and child-care responsibilities. Factor 2 was a financial factor that included both adequacy of resources as well as decisions about financial expenditures. Factor 3 included items that tapped predominantly interpersonal relationships and decisions. Factor 4 was not readily interpretable. Factor 5 was a home maintenance factor, and included traditional male roles. Factor 6 was a social relations factor. Together, the six factors accounted for 65% of the variance.

The factor analysis of the FSS items yielded six orthogonal components accounting for 65% of the variance. Factor 1 included primarily individuals comprising one's personal social network, Factor 2 was a social groups/organization factor, Factor 3 was a "kin-by-marriage" factor, Factor 4 included specialized professional services, Factor 5 was a generic professional helpers factor, and Factor 6 was a "blood relative" factor.

The findings from the factor analyses indicate that both intra- and extrafamily support are not unitary constructs but rather are comprised of various components and independent dimensions of social support. Similar findings for the PRS were reported by Schaefer and Edgerton (1981), and by Dunst et al. (1984) and Fewell (1984) for the FSS.

Age-related characteristics. The findings of the analyses of maternal roles yielded no significant differences in either role accumulation or satisfaction in performance of roles as a function of the child's developmental status. Thus, the number of roles performed as well as role satisfaction remained relatively stable among the subjects.

The correlational analyses yielded several age-related effects. The child's chronological age was significantly related to child discipline ($r = 0.18, p < .05$). Mothers assumed less responsibility for disciplining their children as the children became older. Maternal age was significantly correlated with several dimensions of role accumulation and role satisfaction. Mothers, with increasing age, assumed less responsibility for maintaining financial records ($r = 0.19, p < .05$), engaged in less maintenance of household appliances ($r = 0.17, p < .05$), and assumed more responsibility for meal preparation ($r = -0.25, p < .01$). Mothers, with increasing age, also reported being more satisfied with teaching their child(ren) preacademic skills ($r = 0.20, p < .05$), and with managing the financial resources of the family ($r = 0.20, p < .05$). Thus, whereas the child's developmental status and chronological age were generally unrelated to maternal roles, a number of role characteristics were found to be significantly related to the mother's age.

The results of this portion of our analyses indicate that at least until the child reaches school age, maternal roles remain relatively stable. These findings are consistent with those reported by Schaefer and Edgerton (1981). Maternal age proved to be the best correlate of parenting-role characteristics. The particular results are similar to those reported by Ragozin et al. (1982) who also found that parenting roles were related to maternal age. Tentatively, it would appear that mother's age rather than the child's developmental status is the age-related dimension along which maternal roles vary in families of young handicapped children.

Close inspection of the data revealed some noteworthy trends in role division among the mothers and their child's father. The results show a clear trend toward division into traditional female and male roles. The data indicate that mothers assume primary responsibility for child care. In contrast, traditional male roles (financial provider, protector, outside maintenance, and equipment maintenance) are performed by the husband-mate. Likewise, nearly all other household roles are primarily the responsibility of the mothers. What is most significant about these findings is not the traditional division of roles, which has been reported by others (Gallagher et al., 1981; Pearlin, 1975; Sanik & O'Neill, 1982; Schaefer & Edgerton, 1981), but rather the fact that the mothers of both the nonhandicapped and handicapped children have the major responsibility for these child-care and household chores.

Across-age comparisons revealed considerable stability in the helpfulness of support from the various sources. The only support source that changed as a function of the child's developmental status was school-day care center ($F [5, 90] = 2.62, p < .03$). This type of child care was perceived as being more helpful as children became developmentally older. The extent to which school-day care was considered helpful was also the only FSS item that correlated significantly with child chronological age ($r = 0.28, p < .01$). This source of support was considered more helpful as a child became older.

A number of significant correlations were found between ratings of helpfulness of support and mother's age. Maternal age correlated significantly with helpfulness from one's own parents ($r = -0.18, p < .05$), husband ($r = 0.23, p < .05$), offspring ($r = 0.31, p < .01$), family/child's physician ($r = 0.20, p < .05$), social groups ($r = 0.19, p < .05$), and the church ($r = 0.32, p < .01$). The findings indicated that these different sources of support were rated as being more helpful with mothers' increasing age except for the mothers' parents, who were rated as being less helpful as the mothers became older. The findings for the FSS correlational analyses are much like those for the PRS results.

Maternal age rather than child age was found to be the variable most associated with provisions of support. Shulman (1975) reported similar findings. Just as maternal roles varied with the mother's age, her social support also appears to vary with age.

Biocultural determinants. A comparison of the total number of maternal roles performed by working and nonworking mothers found that the latter performed significantly more teacher (t [95] = -2.20, p < .05), child care (t [95] = -2.15, p < .05), and meal preparation (t [95] = 2.03, p < .05) roles. In contrast, working mothers contributed more financially to the family's income (t [95] = 5.28, p < .001), and had more responsibility deciding how money would be spent (t [95] = 2.74, p < .01) compared to nonworking mothers.

In terms of role satisfaction, all the significant differences between working and nonworking mothers favored the latter. Nonworking mothers indicated that they were more satisfied with how the following roles were performed: resource divider, home maintenance, social host, teacher, nurse, transporter, and clothing selecter (t [95] = -2.20 to 3.61, p < .05 to .001). Likewise, there was a significant difference between groups in terms of overall degree of role satisfaction (t [95] = 2.13, p < .05). Nonworking mothers were generally more satisfied than working mothers with how roles were being performed in their households.

Comparisons of the number of roles performed by the married and unmarried mothers found significant differences on the following roles: provider, resource divider, bookkeeper, protector, home maintenance, moral leader, and personal confidant (t [95] = 2.40 to 4.22, p < .05 to .001). All the differences for individual roles favored the unmarried mothers, indicating that the latter performed more roles compared to their married counterparts. There was also a significant difference between the groups for the total role accumulation scores (t [95] = 2.30, p < .05), with unmarried mothers indicating they performed more roles. Of particular note is the fact that that there were no differences between groups in terms of child-care roles. This indicates that parenting roles, regardless of maternal employment status, remain primarily the responsibility of mothers.

There were several differences between groups in terms of satisfaction with performance of child-care roles. Unmarried mothers were more satisfied with how roles were being performed relative to the married respondents. Significant differences were found between groups for three child-care roles: nurse (t [95] = -4.65, p < .001), transporter (t [95] = -2.48, p < .01), and clothing selector (t [95] = -3.51, p < .001). Thus, even though unmarried mothers have more responsibility for performing roles, they are, in some instances, more satisfied in how roles are performed.

Taken together, our findings replicate previous results which indicate that employment status (Sanik & O'Neill, 1982) and marital status (Weinraub & Wolf, 1983) have differential effects on maternal role responsibilities and role satisfaction. Our results partially replicate those of Schaefer and Edgerton (1981). In both investigations, performance of general household chores differed as a function of the mothers' employment status. We found some differences between working and nonworking mothers' child-care responsibilities, whereas Schaefer and Edgerton did not. However, certain methodological differences in the two studies would appear to account for the inconsistent findings. In our study, only mothers' PRS responses were used, whereas Shaefer and Edgerton included both mothers' and fathers' responses.

Comparisons of sources of support yielded only one significant difference between working and nonworking mothers. Working mothers indicated that they were more satisfied with the help they received from their husband-mate (t [95] = 2.24, $p < .05$).

A number of significant differences were found between the married and unmarried mothers. Not surprisingly, unmarried mothers, compared to married mothers, indicated that their child's father (t [95] = 6.28, $p < .001$), the father's parents (t [95] = 4.06, $p < .001$), and the father's relatives (t [95] = 3.09, $p < .01$) were less helpful in terms of support received. This lack of support was, in part, compensated for by support from the unmarried mother's parents (t [95] = -2.23, $p < .05$), as well as by extrafamilial support from health departments and other social service agencies (t [95] = -4.54, $p < .001$). The findings concerning the influences of marital status on support replicate those of Brim (1974) and Longino and Lipman (1982). Less support from certain sources is typically compensated for by more support from alternative sources. This type of compensatory support is very consistent with Gourash's (1978) help-seeking model, which postulates factors that are likely to influence help-seeking decisions.

Social support and family functioning. Next, we undertook a closer examination of how social support contributed to specific aspects of family functioning. This was done through a series of hierarchical multiple regression analyses by sets, entering first, in order, the four covariate sets (family characteristics, child characteristics, marital status, employment status); second, qualitative measures of support; and third, quantitative measures of support. For the PRS and FSS, respectively, the qualitative measures of support were total role-satisfaction scores and the total helpfulness scores. The quantitative measures of PRS and FSS support were, respectively, total role-accumulation scores and total number of sources of support. At each step of the analysis, the Increments (I) in R^2 were determined to assess whether the particular set of independent variables accounted for a significant amount of variance in the dependent measures.

Before discussing the results, the analytical strategy used in this investigation deserves comment to place the findings in proper perspective. The method of analysis employed to assess the effects of social support discerned the unique and nonshared variance accounted for in the dependent measures. The hierarchical model partialled out (in an ANCOVA sense) the shared variance between the seven separate convariates and the social support measures before the unique contributions were determined. Thus, small but statistically significant amounts of variance accounted for by social support may be considered particularly robust.

Emotional and physical well-being. The dependent measure of personal well-being was the physical and emotional health scale on the QRS. Significant proportions of variance in the dependent measure were accounted for by: child characteristics ($I = 0.10$, $F[4, 89] = 2.48$, $p <$ .05), employment status ($I = 0.03$, $F[1, 87] = 3.28$, $p < .07$), and role satisfaction ($I = 0.04$, $F[1, 86] = 4.62$, $p < .05$). Enhanced well-being was associated with having a child with a higher IQ, with not working, and with higher role-satisfaction scores.

Time demands. The dependent measure was the QRS time-demands scale. This scale measures the extent to which excessive time demands are placed upon the respondent by the handicapped child. Significant proportions of the variance in the dependent measure were accounted for by: family characteristics ($I = 0.12$, $F[2, 93] = 6.46$, $p < .01$), child characteristics ($I = 0.09$, $F[4, 89] = 2.48$, $p < .05$), role satisfaction ($I = 0.09$, $F[1, 86] = 11.00$, $p < .01$), and support satisfaction ($I = 0.06$, $F[1, 86] = 7.50$, $p < .01$). Excessive time demands were associated with respondents who had low incomes, children with low IQ scores, low role-satisfaction scores, and low support-helpfulness scores.

Family integrity. The QRS family integration scale was the outcome measure. The scale measures the extent to which a family functions as an integrated unit. The child characteristics ($I = 0.14$, $F[4, 89] = 3.86$, $p < .01$) and role satisfaction ($I = 0.09$, $F[1, 86] = 10.81$, $p < .001$) sets accounted for significant proportions of the variance. More integrated units were associated with families of children with higher IQs and with mothers who reported higher role-satisfaction scores.

Family opportunities. The dependent measure, the QRS family opportunities scale, measures the extent to which the family is limited by the handicapped child. The family characteristics ($I = 0.08$, $F[2, 93] = 3.77$, $p < .05$) and role satisfaction ($I = 0.11$, $F[1, 86] = 12.91$, $p < .001$) sets were significantly related to the dependent measure. Increased family opportunities were associated wtih higher incomes and higher role-satisfaction scores.

Number of parent-child interactions. The dependent measure was the number of different "games" the mothers generally played with their child (Dunst, 1984). Significant proportions of variance were accounted for by employment status ($I = 0.04$, $F[1, 87] = 3.47$, $p < .07$) and number of sources of support ($I = 0.05$, $F[1, 85] = 5.05$, $p < .05$). Engagement in a greater number of games occurred among nonworking mothers and mothers with a larger social support network.

Frequency of parent-child interactions. The frequency at which mothers played different games (Dunst, 1984) with their child was the dependent measure. Significant proportions of variance were accounted for by employment status ($I = 0.03$, $F[1, 87] = 3.13$, $p < .08$) and the aggregation of the two social support scores ($I = 0.04$, $F[2, 85] = 3.54$, $p < .07$). Nonworking mothers and mothers with larger degrees of social support interacted with their children on a more frequent basis.

Child behavior problems. The dependent measure was the QRS behavior difficulty scale. This scale measures the extent to which the respondent perceived her child's behavior as difficult and troublesome. Child characteristics ($I = 0.15$, $F[4, 89] = 4.17$, $p < .01$) and satisfaction with support ($I = 0.04$, $F[2, 85] = 4.10$, $p < .05$) accounted for significant proportions of variance. Mothers perceived their children's behavior as less troublesome if their children had higher IQs, and they were more satisified with the social support available to them.

IQ difference. The child's IQ/DQ at the time the mothers completed the questionnaires for this study minus the child's IQ/DQ one year earlier was used as one measure of child behavior and development. Significant proportions of variance were accounted for by child characteristics ($I = 0.31$, $F[4, 89] = 10.73$, $p < .001$) and role accumulation ($I = 0.03$, $F[1, 85] = 4.54$, $p < .05$). Smaller IQ decreases (or in some instances larger IQ gains) were associated with children who had higher IQ scores to begin with, and with mothers with fewer roles to perform.

Child progress. The dependent measure was the amount of progress the child made during the year preceding the study. Child progress was computed as the difference between MAs at the two measurement occasions divided by the corresponding differences in CAs [$MA_2 - MA_1)/(CA_2 - CA_1)$]. The family characteristics ($I = 0.07$, $F[2, 93] = 3.34$, $p < .05$), child characteristics ($I = 0.54$, $F[4, 89] = 30.98$, $p < .001$), and role satisfaction ($I = 0.03$, $F[1, 86] = 3.40$, $p < .07$) sets accounted for significant proportions of variance. Greater child progress was related to higher income, higher SES, higher child IQs, and greater role satisfaction.

Taken together, the findings from the analyses examining the mediational influences of social support provide evidence that parental, family, and child functioning are affected by both intrafamily role sharing and help from extrafamily sources. The results add to previous findings concerning the broad-based impacts of social support. Specifically, our findings demonstrate that aspects of personal well-being, several dimensions of family functioning, quantitative and qualitative characteristics of mother-child interactions, parental perceptions of child behavior, and actual behavior progress of handicapped children, were influenced both directly and indirectly by social support beyond that attributable to other explainer variables. The findings also indicate that specific types of support are related to different outcomes. For example, whereas family integrity and family opportunities were affected by intrafamily role satisfaction, parent-child interactions were affected by broader based provisions of support (i.e., larger social support networks). Thus, different types of social support have differential rather than global impacts. In terms of the implications for intervention, the results suggest that specific types of support should be mediated to produce different outcomes.

It was not unexpected that family as well as child characteristics would be related to the dependent measures. The specific nature of the findings, however, are worth noting. Family income, but not SES, and child level of intellectual performance, but not diagnostic group or chronological age, were the two consistent predictors of parent, family, and child outcomes. Of particular note is the fact that marital status was not significantly related to any dependent measure. Employment status, however, was related to several outcome measures (well-being and parent-child interactions) in an expected manner. Of theoretical and pragmatic importance were the findings that intra- and extrafamily support accounted for significant proportions of variance in outcomes beyond that attributable to the other independent measures. The latter finding indicates that social support, in fact, has mediational effects on personal, family, and child functioning.

Summary and Implications for Early Intervention

The major findings of our investigation of maternal roles and support can be summarized as follows: (a) role enactment and social support are not unitary constructs but rather are comprised of various components and independent dimensions; (b) both role characteristics (accumulation and satisfaction) and social support varied, in part, as a function of maternal age, but not as a function of child age or child developmental status; (c) family roles were generally divided into traditional female and traditional male roles; (d) both role accumulation and role satisfaction differed as a function of maternal marital and employment status; (e) social support differed as a function of marital status but not employment status; and (f) intra- and extrafamily support had mediational influences on parental, family, and child functioning beyond that due to other explainer variables.

These findings suggest the need to rethink early intervention in social systems terms. As noted in the introductory section, a life-span perspective of development concerns itself with not only behavior description and explication but also with optimizing development. The results of our study on intra- and extrafamily support, as well as the review of related research, strongly suggest the types of experiences that might be used as interventions to affect personal, family, and child functioning.

Early intervention has generally been defined either at the level of program involvement (i.e., involved vs. not involved in a particular early education program) or in terms of provision of certain therapeutic or educational treatments. Social systems theory suggest a broader based conceptualization and definition of early intervention as well as a set of decision rules for specifying the dimensions and aspects of intervention that are likely to have cause-effect and mediational impacts. According to Dunst (in press), early intervention, when conceptualized in social systems terms, can be defined as the *"provision of support to families of young handicapped children from members of informal social support networks that impact both directly and indirectly upon parental, family, and child functioning."* That is, early intervention can be considered an aggregation of the many different types of help, assistance, and services that are provided to families and their handicapped children by individuals and groups. Involvement in a preschool special education program is one type of early intervention, but so is compassion from a friend, advice from a physician, respite from relatives, and role-sharing between a husband and wife. To the extent that these different types of support have positive effects, either cumulatively or in interaction with one another, the efficacy of early intervention is substantiated.

The types of support one would provide or mediate to affect positive changes are tentatively suggested by existing research. For example, the results of this study indicated that family functioning was almost entirely affected by intrafamily support rather than extrafamily support. Consequently, if the integrity of the family unit is threatened by the birth and rearing of a handicapped child, then efforts to intervene at the level of the nuclear family are indicated. Likewise, if the nature of parent-child interactions are influenced by broader based provisions of support, and affecting changes in the parent-child dyad are indicated, then efforts toward mediating extrafamily support might be attempted. Increased interest in social systems research with families of handicapped children should begin to identify the specifc types of support that will likely produce specific outcomes.

In addition to suggesting a broader based definition and approach to early intervention, social systems theory suggests broader-based out-comes of early intervention efforts. Dunst (1985) provides a tentative list of possible outcome measures. They include: personal well-being and coping; family integrity; parental attitudes, aspirations, and expectations; parental self-concepts and locus-of-control; aspects of parent-child interactions; and specific dimensions of child behavior and development. This list is suggested by evidence which indicates that different types of social support directly and indirectly influence and mediate personal, family, and child functioning.

Discerning the effects of social support (independent variable) on personal, family, and child functioning (dependent variables) while controlling for other explainer or confounding variables (covariates) could be done using the type of multiple regression procedures employed in the study described above. This type of analytical strategy provides a basis for answering two questions: "What dimensions and types of support (early intervention) are related to different outcome measures?" and "How much variance do different types and forms of support account for beyond that attributable to other explanatory variables?" To the extent that an aggregated set of measures of social support account for a significant proportion of variance beyond that attributable to competing independent variables, we would have evidence documenting the unique impact of early intervention. To the extent that different types and forms of support account for significant proportions of variance, the differential impacts of early intervention would be discerned.

Bronfenbrenner (1975), Foster, Berger, and McLean (1981), and Zigler and Berman (1983) among others, have been major proponents of an ecology of early intervention. Social systems theory suggests a need for a broader based definition of early intervention, expansion of the goals and objectives of intervention, and more sensitive methods for discerning the unique and differential impacts of intervention efforts. In this chapter we offered one perspective for applying social systems theory for research and intervention purposes.

References

Abernethy, V. (1973). Social network and response to the maternal role. *International Journal of Society and the Family, 3,* 86-92.

Ballenski, C.B., & Cook, A.S. (1982). Mothers' perceptions of their competence in managing selected parenting tasks. *Family Relations, 31,* 489-494.

Baltes, P.B., Reese, H.W., & Nesselroade, J.R. (1977). *Life-span developmental psychology: Introduction to research methods.* Monterey, CA: Brooks/Cole.

Bott, E. (1971). *Family and social networks.* London: Tavistock Publications.

Bowen, G.L. (1982). Social network and the maternal role satisfaction of formerly-married mothers. *Journal of Divorce, 5,* 77-85.

Brandwein, R.A., Brown, C.A., & Fox, E.M. (1974). Women and children last: The social situation of divorced mothers and their families. *Journal of Marriage and the Family, 34,* 498-515.

Brim, J.A. (1974). Social network correlates of avowed happiness. *Journal of Nervous and Mental Disease, 158,* 432-439.

Bronfenbrenner, U. (1975). Is early intervention effective? In B. Friedlander, G. Sterritt, & G. Kirk (Eds.), *Exceptional infant (Vol. 3): Assessment and intervention* (pp. 449-475). New York: Brunner/Mazel.

Bronfenbrenner, U. (1977). Toward an experimental ecology of human development. *American Psychologist, 32,* 513-531.

Bronfenbrenner, U. (1979). *The ecology of human development: Experiment by nature and design.* Cambridge MA: Harvard University Press.

Caplan, G. (1976). The family as a support system. In G. Caplan & M. Kililea (Eds.), *Support systems and mutual help* (pp. 19-36). New York: Grune & Stratton.

Cochran, M., & Brassard, J. (1979). Child development and personal social networks. *Child Development, 50,* 601-606.

Cohen, J., & Cohen, P. (1983). *Applied multiple regression correlation analysis for the behavioral sciences* (2nd ed). Hillsdale, NJ: Erlbaum.

Crnic, K., Greenberg, M., Ragozin, A., Robinson, N., & Basham, R. (1983). Effects of stress and social support on mothers of premature and full-term infants. *Child Development, 54,* 209-217.

Crockenberg. S. (1981). Infant irritability, mother responsiveness and social influences on the security of infant-mother attachment. *Child Development, 52,* 857-865.

Cross, A.H. (1980). Parental characteristics of family adaptation to a handicapped child. Unpublished doctoral dissertation, University of North Carolina, Chapel Hill.

Dean, A., & Lin, N. (1977). Stress-buffering role of social support. *Journal of Nervous and Mental Disease, 165,* 403-417.

Dunst, C.J. (1982). *Social support, early intervention, and institutional avoidance.* Paper presented at the annual meeting of the Southeastern Association on Mental Deficiency, November, Louisville, KY.

Dunst, C.J. (1984). *Parent-Child Interaction Rating Scale: Reliability and validity.* Unpublished paper, Family, Infant and Preschool Program, Western Carolina Center, Morganton, NC.

Dunst, C.J. (in press). Rethinking early intervention. *Analysis and Intervention in Developmental Disabilities.*

Dunst, C.J., Jenkins, V., & Trivette, C. (1984). *Family Support Scale: Relability and validity.* Paper submitted for publication.

Dunst, C.J., Trivette, C.M., & Cross, A. (1985). Mediating influences of social support: Personal, family and child outcomes. *American Journal of Mental Deficiency, 90,* (Vol. 4).

Dunst, C.J., Trivette, C.M., & Cross, A. (In press). Social support networks of Appalachian and nonAppalachian families with handicapped children. In S.E. Keefe (Ed.), *Mental health in Appalachia.* Lexington: University of Kentucky Press.

Duvall, E. (1971). *Family development.* Philadelphia: Lippincott.

Embry, L. (1980). Family support for handicapped preschool children at risk for abuse. *New Directions for Exceptional Children, 4,* 29-58.

Fewell, R.R. (1984). *Sources of social support for mothers of children with Down Syndrome.* Paper presented at the 62nd annual convention of the Council for Exceptional Children, Washington, DC.

Foster, M., Berger, M., & McLean, M. (1981). Rethinking a good idea. *Topics in Early Childhood Special Education, 1,* 55-65.

Friedrich, W.N. (1979). Predictors of the coping behaviors of mothers of handicapped children. *Journal of Consulting and Clinical Psychology, 47,* 1140-1141.

Friedrich, W.N., & Friedrich, W.L. (1981). Psychosocial assets of parents of handicapped and nonhandicapped children. *American Journal of Mental Deficiency, 5,* 551-553.

Gabel, H. (1979). The Family, Infant and Toddler Project: Early intervention for rural families of retarded children. In R. Schalock (Ed.), *MR/DD rural services...It is time* (pp. 86-96). Washington, DC: Institute for Comprehensive Planning.

Gallagher, J.J., Cross, A., & Scharfman, W. (1981). Parental adaptation to a young handicapped child: The father's role. *Journal of the Division for Early Childhood, 3,* 3-14.

Giovanoni, J., & Billingsley, A. (1970). Child neglect among the poor: A study of parental adequacy in families of three ethnic groups. *Child Welfare, 49,* 496-204.

Glasser, P., & Navarre, E. (1964). Structural problems of the one-parent family. *Journal of Social Issues, 21,* 98-109.

Goulet, L.R., & Baltes, P.B. (1970). *Life-span developmental psychology: Research and theory.* New York: Academic Press.

Gourash, N. (1978). Help seeking: A review of the literature. *American Journal of Community Psychology, 6,* 499-517.

Granovetter, M. (1973). The strength of weak ties. *American Journal of Sociology, 78,* 13-60.

Hetherington, E., Cox, M., & Cox, R. (1976). Divorced fathers. *Family Coordinator, 25,* 427-428.

Hetherington, E., Cox, M., & Cox, R. (1978). The aftermath of divorce. In J. Stevens & M. Mathews (Eds.), *Mother-child, father-child relations* (pp. 149-176). Washington, DC: National Association for the Education of Young Children.

Hobbs, N. (1975). *The futures of children.* San Francisco: Jossey-Bass.

Holahan, C.J. (1977). Social ecology. In I. Iscoe, B. Bloom, & C. Spielberger (Eds.),

Community psychology in transition (pp. 123-126). New York: Wiley.

Hollingshead, A.B. (1975). *Four factor index of social status.* Unpublished paper. Department of Sociology, Yale University, New Haven, CT.

Holroyd, J. (1973). *Questionnaire on Resources and Stress.* Unpublished instrument. Center for the Health Sciences, University of California, Los Angeles.

Holroyd, J. (1974). The Questionaire on Resources and Stress: An instrument to measure family responses to a handicapped family member. *Journal of Community Psychology, 2,* 92-94.

Holroyd, J., & Guthrie, D. (1979). Stress in families of children with neuromuscular disease. *Journal of Clinical Psychology, 35,* 734-739.

Holroyd, J., & McArthur, D. (1976). Mental retardation and stress on the parents: A contrast between Down's syndrome and childhood autism. *American Journal of Mental Deficiency, 80,* 431-436.

Lamb, M. (1978). Influence of the child on marital quality and family interaction during the prenatal, perinatal, and infancy periods. In R. Lerner & G. Spainer (Eds.), *Child influences on marital and family interaction* (pp. 137-164). New York: Academic Press.

Lazar, I., & Darlington, R. (1982). Lasting effects of early education. *Monographs of the Society for Research in Child Development, 195,* 47 (2-3).

Longino, Jr., C.R., & Lipman, A. (1982). The married, the formerly married and the never married: Support system differentials of older women in planned retirement communities. *International Journal of Aging and Human Development, 15,* 285-297.

McAndrew, I. (1976). Children with a handicap and their families. *Child: Care, Health and Development, 2,* 213-237.

McCubbin, H., Joy, C., Cauble, A.E., Comeau, J., Patterson, J., & Needle, R. (1980). Family stress and coping: A decade review. *Journal of Marriage and the Family, 42,* 855-871.

McDowell, J., & Gabel, H. (1979). *Social support among mothers of mentally retarded infants.* Unpublished manuscript. George Peabody College of Vanderbilt University, Nashville, TN.

Mitchell, R.E., & Trickett, E.J. (1980). Task force report: Social networks as mediators of social support. *Community Mental Health Journal, 16,* 27-43.

Pearlin, L.I. (1975). Sex roles and depression. In N. Datan & L. Ginsberg (Eds.), *Life-span developmental psychology: Normative life crises* (pp. 191-208). New York: Academic Press.

Philliber, S., & Graham, E.H. (1981). The impact of age of mother on mother-child interaction patterns. *Journal of Marriage and the Family, 43,* 109-115.

Ragozin, A.S., Basham, R.B., Crnic, M.A., Greenberg, M.T., & Robinson, N.M. (1982). Effects of maternal age on parenting role. *Developmental Psychology, 18,* 627-634.

Rossi, A. (1968). Transition to parenthood. *Journal of Marriage and the Family, 30,* 26-39.

Sanik, M.M., & O'Neill, B. (1982). Who does the family work? *Journal of Extension, 20,* 15-20.

Schaefer, E. & Edgerton, M. (1981). *Role division.* Unpublished manuscript. Frank Porter Graham Child Development Center, Chapel Hill, NC.

Shulman, N. (1975). Life-cycle variations in patterns of close relationships.

Journal of Marriage and the Family, 37, 813-821.

Tamir, L.M., & Antonucci, T.C. (1981). Self-perception, motivation, and social support through the family life course. *Journal of Marriage and the Family, 43,* 151-160.

Trivette, C.M. (1982). *The study of role division and stress in families with handicapped children.* Unpublished master's thesis. Appalachian State University, Boone, NC.

Trivette, C.M., & Dunst, C.J. Characteristics and influences of role division and social support among mothers of handicapped preschoolers. Manuscript submitted for publication.

Weinraub, M., & Wolf, B.M. (1983). Effects of stress and social supports on mother-child interactions in single- and two-parent families. *Child Development, 54,* 1297-1311.

Zigler, E. & Berman, W. (1983). Discerning the future of early childhood interventions. *American Psychologist, 38,* 894-906.

Author's Note

Appreciation is extended to Ms. Pat Condrey for her assistance in preparation of this manuscript. Research reported in this chapter was supported, in part, by grants to the first author from the National Institute of Mental Health (MH38862) and the Research Section, Division of Mental Health, Mental Retardation, and Substance Abuse, North Carolina Department of Human Resources (#83527).

8

Three Mothers: Life-span Experiences

Margaret Roberts

This chapter contains the first-hand experiences of three mothers of handicapped children. These are the stories of typical parents of not quite typical children. Each mother relates her personal experiences—some of joy and discovery, and most of strain and frustration. Each of their stories is unique, yet they share common threads, including their reactions and adaptations to their child's disability.

The parent experience has been well documented in book-length accounts written by individual parents of disabled children. For example, Josh Greenfeld (1972) in *A Child Called Noah,* and Elizabeth Pieper in (n.d.) *Sticks and Stones: The Story of a Loving Child,* candidly describe both the terrible demands they experience as a result of their child's handicap, as well as the feelings and experiences they share in common with all parents. Most often, these first-person accounts are considered "extra reading" by students and professionals, for whom the accounts provide a means of becoming familiar with parent concerns. An understanding of the parent experience, however, requires first-hand encounters with parents, and even these encounters often fail to convey the extended impact the child has on family members throughout the family's life. This chapter endeavors to address that theme.

The testimony of the following three mothers reflects their experiences and insights into what it is like to learn that your child is handicapped, and how a parent learns to live with the knowledge. Each of the mothers shares her reactions upon first learning about her child's problems. The children's handicaps differ—one is a child with Down syndrome, one has cerebral palsy, and one has an undiagnosed developmental disability. The mothers represent different stages of the family life cycle—one is the mother of a 15 month old, one is the mother of an 8 year old, and one is the mother of a 15 year old. The reader will find that although the mothers' situations differ, they face similar questions and experience similar needs. These accounts describe their individual ways of coming to terms with their child's needs, and their own needs and those of their family.

Karen: Coping During the Child's Early Years

Karen Walker talks quietly with the other mothers who are waiting in the family room of Ashwood Center, a developmental disability center which serves disabled children birth to 3 years old. This is a typical Wednesday morning for Karen. One mother waits for her 2-year-old son's preschool class to let out. Another mother's child is in speech therapy. Karen waits for the physical therapist and her 15-month-old daughter, Lisa, to return from their "workout." The mothers are there for similar reasons; each is a parent of a handicapped child.

Karen questions one mother, who, like herself, has a daughter with Down syndrome. At what age did Elizabeth start crawling? When did you take her off the bottle? How do your other children react to Elizabeth?

From the first day Karen brought Lisa to Ashwood, nearly 12 months ago, she reached out to other parents. Karen gently probed for their feelings and insights about having a disabled child. She candidly expressed her own concerns. "I'm a pretty open person," Karen freely admits. "I guess talking is my own form of therapy, and I like to know what other parents are thinking." Karen's candor frequently broke the ice during parent meetings as she expressed concerns many other parents felt but did not feel comfortable sharing. She questions without intimidating, and she talks about her own feelings openly, and honestly, without defense.

Receiving the Diagnosis

Like any expectant mother, Karen dreamed about a perfect baby. Her

2-year-old daughter, Kelly, would soon have a playmate and they would be a happy family of four. Although there was a history of Down syndrome in the family (Karen's husband, John, had a younger sister with Down syndrome), the thought of having a handicapped baby never occurred to Karen.

When it came time to deliver, Karen found herself in a high-risk situation. Not only was Lisa born one month ahead of schedule, but Karen's water broke three days before she actually delivered Lisa. Karen recalls vividly her days in the hospital.

> Everybody was there. An obstetrician specializing in high-risk deliveries, my pediatrician, an intern. Lisa's first cry sounded funny to me. But I had no idea there was anything wrong with her! My pediatrician, Dr. Collins, saw Lisa right after she was born, but he didn't say anything to me! I suppose he wanted me to have a good night's sleep before he dropped the bomb. I think that was wise, now. I hadn't had any sleep for two nights.

Yet the manner in which the doctor gave Karen the news of her new baby was less than optimal.

> The way the doctor told me about Lisa left a little to be desired. John wasn't with me. It was seven in the morning. I came back from the bathroom and Dr. Collins was sitting in my room. He immediately told me he had some concerns about Lisa. Then he started listing off a few characteristics of Down syndrome. He said, "Have you ever heard of Down syndrome?" Well, I almost fell off the bed! I told him I had, and that my sister-in-law had Down syndrome. He said, "I'm over 50% sure that your child has Down syndrome, but just to make sure I'm having a genetic specialist come out today at noon." Then he said, "I'm really sorry." He came over, gave me a kiss on the cheek, and left the room. I was all alone.

John was at work, so Karen called him and told him to come to the hospital immediately. Karen's eyes widen as she describes her initial reaction. "I was in shock. I had no emotion. When John arrived, we called our pastor. He was there in 10 minutes and our first questions were why? Why has this happened to us?"

The pastor told John and Karen there were a lot of imperfections in the world due to Original Sin. And having a handicapped baby was one example. The pastor's explanations, however, were far from comforting. Karen felt Lisa's Down syndrome was a punishment from God for Karen's lack of acceptance towards her own sister-in-law, Jennifer.

> John's sister, Jennifer, was 20 at that time. We would visit her occasionally. She was really the first handicapped person I knew. I had mixed feelings toward Jennifer. While I recognized that she was a loving person, there were also some unattractive sides to her. I never dreamed of actually having a child with Down syndrome. There was

already one in the family, and this just couldn't happen! So, when Lisa was born, my first reaction was that I was being punished because I wasn't charitable enough in my own heart toward my sister-in-law. In order to make me into the person I should be, I had been given a child with Down syndrome. Now this is a terrible burden to put upon yourself, but this was my initial feeling in the hospital. I worked with this feeling for a long time.

During the remainder of her stay in the hospital, Karen felt alone, isolated, shattered. Karen remembers, "Part of me was thinking, I want this to be just a bad dream. I want to wake up tomorrow and have this not be a problem for us and have our baby normal." Yet Karen was only reminded of the reality when 24 hours later, she had to repeat the news for her gynecologist.

When my gynecologist came into the hospital room to see how the new mom was doing, he said, "Hi, how are you today?" He was real sunny, with a bright smile. I said, "You mean you haven't heard? My child has Down syndrome!" And he said, "Well my wife has a cousin with Down syndrome. As far as I know, he holds a menial job, and he's supposed to be a really nice person." Then he kind of backed out of my room and left. I just felt awful. Some comfort he was!

Important Early Supports. Twenty-four hours after Lisa's delivery, Karen left the hospital. Feeling isolated and still in shock, Karen spent the next few days seriously considering giving Lisa up for adoption. Knowing what her husband's family had sacrificed because of Jennifer, she saw Lisa's birth as a life sentence. Through it all, John was supportive and caring. However, the ultimate decision was left to Karen since she would be the primary caregiver. After three days of prayer and personal questioning, Karen made her decision. They would take Lisa home.

Karen speaks fondly of two individuals who "saved her life" during these first months following Lisa's birth. The first was a young pediatrician, Dr. Helen Davis, who worked at the children's hospital. Because Lisa had feeding problems and Karen and John needed a few more days to make their decision, Lisa remained in the hospital after Karen went home. Helen Davis noticed Lisa and questioned why she was still in the hospital. Dr. Collins explained the situation to her. Karen recalls, "Helen offered to take Lisa home for a few weeks while we decided what we would do. We met Dr. Davis at the hospital and took an immediate liking to each other. We would go over to see Lisa every night, and Helen would take Lisa on her rounds during the day. Helen was basically Lisa's first mother. Our relationship has grown into a deep friendship. I adore Helen." Karen pauses, deep in thought, "And, you know, Helen's professional acceptance of Lisa helped me, because she saw value in Lisa that I couldn't see for a long time."

Another important person to enter Karen's life around this time was

Nina Bloom. Nina had a 6-year-old son with Down syndrome and was actively involved in the local Advocates for Retarded Citizens Parent-to-Parent Support Program. Karen explains how she and Nina initially met.

A friend of my mother-in-law was involved in the local ARC's Parent-to-Parent Program. She asked my mother-in-law if it was okay to give them my name. Someone contacted me from Parent-to-Parent and asked me how we were doing. I said, "Everything was fine." I was really still in shock. Nina and I had been matched up. We were the same age and she also had a child with Down syndrome. A few days later Nina called and talked to John. It turned out that Nina's husband and John were acquaintances in college years ago. Within a week, I called her back when I came out of my shock. Lisa was about three weeks old. I was hurting so much, I decided I needed to talk to someone who had been there. I wanted to get through the pain and to know how to deal with it as soon as I could. Nina came over with her son, Alan. When I saw Alan, that was the last straw to opening my eyes to the reality.

From then on Nina and Karen established the groundwork for a mutually trusting and supportive friendship. Karen describes the importance and timeliness of Nina's presence. "Nina's availability to me was wonderful. Whenever I needed to talk, she knew exactly where I was. Nobody I knew—my friends, even the professionals who worked with Lisa—really knew how I was feeling. They hadn't been through it. Nina saved my life that first year."

Adjusting to the Diagnosis

For a moment, Karen steps out of the past and back into the present, reflecting on her own experience as a new parent.

Brand new parents who have just been told they have a handicapped child are just shattered. It's difficult for you to come to grips with the fact that no matter how many neat people come to your rescue with thoughtful words, words of encouragement, words of support and love, nothing is going to change the fact that your child has Down syndrome. People can try to comfort you with spiritual insights and messages. Other parents can come and say, "I know it's hard at first, but our child has become a blessing in our life, and our whole family has benefited," the whole concept of "every family should have one." A new parent can't see that. You can't begin to imagine that this is going to work out for the good, because it is such a setback.

I know a lot of damage has been done when parents with handicapped kids try to do somebody else a favor by marching in to a new parent's home with their older handicapped child to show as an example. You know, it can destroy a brand new parent to see an older child with the handicap just because it hits home—this is what I have. When you first learn about your child's handicap, you have a tremendous sense of wanting to get out of the problem, to run away, to avoid the situation.

I really admire brand new parents who feel an immediate bonding with their handicapped child, because that was not my experience. All I could feel was, I didn't want this, I didn't deserve this. I didn't want people to tell me how great these kids were, because I had seen my sister-in-law's efforts, and my in-laws' involvement in raising her, and some of the joys and very real burdens that her life presented to them.

Karen pauses, then continues to describe her initial feelings as well as her more recent thoughts about Lisa. The seriousness in her eyes and voice reflect the freshness of the grief she describes.

The whole grieving process is a bittersweet thing that new parents have to grow into. I think parents should be made aware of what this grieving process is. I think somebody told me that I would go through a grief process, but I didn't know what that meant. I didn't know what it was until I was actually *in* it. You think you're losing your mind, your grip, but it's actually a real part of life. I think if parents are made aware that it could take months, a year, 18 months, and all that is acceptable and within the realm of being a normal person, then it would ease their fears about having to maintain sanity and their ability to cope. It's painful. Right after Lisa was born, all I could think about was getting pregnant again, to right a wrong, to cover up Lisa whom I looked at as a mistake. I wanted something normal and on a happier note. As time went along, I realized I wanted to love Lisa completely and for being who she is. I still want another child, but I want to give Lisa a chance first. I want to end my childbearing years on a positive note. I suppose I'm saying that my life will feel more complete by having another normal child, that there is still an ache there, that, because of Lisa, there's something missing.

Karen spent the first few months feeling devastated, out of control. She was neither prepared nor able to confront the dilemma which faced her. Karen compensated for her feelings of lack of control by keeping her life organized, her emotions in check. Karen smiles as she describes her behavior.

During the first six months, my pace was frenetic. I couldn't stop. Everything had to be spic-n-span. I had to be totally organized and in control. I washed and cleaned and would constantly be picking everything up! I thought Lisa was out of my control. I was trying to make up for that terrible shock to my system by having everything else in my life totally ordered. I also had to show my friends, and people with whom I came in contact, that they could approach me, that I was going to be open and that this hadn't destroyed me. I didn't want people to feel uncomfortable around me and think "What do we say to her? How do we react to her?" So, I found the burden was even intensified because I had to be the strongman. I had to show people that, yes I still am me, and I'm happy. This has been a setback, but we love our child and we're coping, so please don't leave me alone. I need you to still be my friend.

Despite Karen's efforts to appear in control to her friends, she was not able to lessen the pain she felt or sort out her own confusion. The stress and confusion Karen felt affected her emotionally, mentally, and physically.

I'd get up in the morning or go to bed at night and I'd ask, when is the heartache and pain going to leave? It was not just an emotional disappointment, but a physical pain. Physically, I felt like my heart was breaking. I got sick all the time. I got colds right and left. You don't realize that to be sick at heart can make you sick in the body. That's grief. Every time I would look at Lisa I couldn't escape the fact that she had Down syndrome. I could never isolate Lisa from her Down syndrome and just say, you precious little child, I just love you.

In her desperate attempt to maintain control over her situation, Karen spent a few months studying everything she could about healing. She read books. She took Lisa to people who had healing ministries. Karen recollects this time of her life with a smile. "Of course I felt frustrated each morning when I would run into Lisa's room and find that she still had Down syndrome." There were also the feelings of guilt to deal with each time Lisa wasn't healed.

I accept now that Lisa will have Down syndrome all her life. But that was one more stage of getting through the grief and accepting who she is. I went through many things to reach for the stars for Lisa. It all sounds very exhausting, and it is when you're the person who is going through it. It's mentally and emotionally draining.

Accessing Supports and Continuing to Adjust

During the time Karen was coming to terms with her own feelings about Lisa, she took full advantage of the services the Ashwood Developmental Disability Center had to offer. Until Lisa was about a year old, Karen and her two daughters would bundle up and drive to Ashwood in order to attend the weekly Parent-Infant class, a parent meeting, or physical therapy for Lisa. Karen liked to talk to the other mothers. She particularly looked forward to getting to know and comparing notes with the mothers who had children with Down syndrome.

This year Karen brings Lisa to preschool, twice weekly, and to physical therapy once a week. So much of her time is given to Lisa that Karen has had to learn to use her few hours of free time well. Karen had been concerned about the lack of attention and quality time alone she had been able to give to Kelly. Therefore during Lisa's class, one afternoon a week, she and Kelly go to McDonald's for lunch.

In addition to the therapy and preschool classes at Ashwood, a physical therapist from the Elks club works with Lisa twice a week in their home. Although Karen assumes primary responsibility, John also plays an active role in Lisa's education by serving as a member of Ashwood's board of directors. In addition, every other Saturday, John and Lisa attend the fathers' program at the local university. Not only does the program provide an opportunity for John and Lisa to spend time together, but it also allows Karen time for herself.

The support and acceptance Karen receives from other parents and professionals help to lift her spirits on days when she feels down. Karen shares her opinions about the professionals with whom she has come into contact.

> My pediatrician always enjoys Lisa when she's there. He always has a word of encouragement like, "You're doing a great job. She's doing well." Just the acceptance he conveys makes me feel good, like I am doing something special here. It's so important for professionals who work with your child to be positive about your child, and show that they enjoy your child. It makes your day! Parents want to get through the grief. They want to get through the hard times.

Karen candidly admits the hard times and grieving have not dissipated completely.

> I think the grieving process takes on different forms all the time. In the first year, it was very intense. It was constant. Now I feel grief, but it's much more low key. It's most intense when I'm put in situations when the facts hit me in the face. Like an IEP conference. I can spend weeks with Lisa, just loving her, and then I forget about the fact that she is slow. It's not as obvious because she's just a little person I live with. She's just who she is. The painful part comes from being reminded of your child's deficiencies, or meeting strangers who can't take their eyes off of Lisa and start asking questions. The grieving process takes on a different form when you start to compare your handicapped child with another. Like when Ellen, another child with Down syndrome, was getting around at 15 months and Lisa was not. Then I need to look at myself and ask, "Why does this matter to me? Big deal. Does that make her any less because she isn't crawling and Ellen is?" This is one more obstacle to overcome. You've got to readjust your expectations for your child. You have to throw out the window all the values of society. In a few years, when my friends' babies wander off to kindergarten, or drive off in cars, or go off to college, there will be an ache, I suppose. But I think I can choose whether I want to wallow in that, in self-pity. Or I can continually keep that acceptance current, and appreciate who Lisa is and what Lisa can do. It's best to just live each day for what it is. I really can't control anything. I can provide the best environment I can for Lisa.

I can't worry too much about the future but hope that the effort I make each day will make her future brighter.

Kate: Adjusting Through the Child's School Years

The eight-year-old Jenkins twins, Erik and Geoff, are both attractive boys of medium height whose Star Wars sweatshirts and Darth Vader lunch boxes announce their current interests. Erik is friendly but reserved like his mother. In a crowd, Erik will most often sit quietly and absorb all that is going on around him. Yet bring up a topic such as basketball and Erik's voice fills with enthusiasm, his face shines with excitement. Suddenly he's off—describing the most important plays of his team's last basketball game. Geoff is less reticent than Erik. He'll frequently initiate a conversation by showing a friend his new shoes, or by asking his mother to fix the string on his ukulele. Because Geoff's speech is unclear, it is almost always difficult to understand him.

Geoff was diagnosed at six months as having brain damage and cerebral palsy. His delayed development became obvious to his parents, Kate and Tim, early on, as Erik proceeded to reach his developmental milestones on schedule and Geoff didn't.

Geoff has demanded more time and energy from his parents throughout the years than has Erik. Although Kate is not certain about the hidden impact that having a retarded twin may have had on Erik, there have been incidents which indicate its complexity. For example, one day Kate and Erik were looking at a newspaper picture of a mother and her three newborn triplets. Erik immediately asked, "Which one is handicapped?" Kate usually doesn't think of Erik and Geoff as twins because they have been developmentally so different from the time they were infants. Occasionally, Kate is hit with the realization that the twins are the same age and yet very different.

Last year, Erik played basketball with the Boy's Club. Geoff and I would go to a game every week. At one of those games, I was just sitting there and all of a sudden I realized that here was Geoff sitting with me watching the other boys play. Yet he was the same age as all these other kids; he should have been out there playing basketball and he wasn't. For some reason, it hit me really hard, instantly. Every now and then something like that will happen when I feel the pain all over again, even though I think that I'm well adjusted and am accepting everything. Sometimes it will trigger other things where I have to readjust all over again.

It's different though. It's easier to get over things now. I can't really compare it to a pin prick, but I can work out of it sooner because I guess I have enough background. Whereas in the beginning, with the early diagnosis and lack of practice, I can remember thinking that

I just had this black cloud over me. It reminded me of the character in Li'l Abner who was always followed by a black cloud. I felt as if it were going to be there the rest of my life. I just couldn't see how I was going to live the rest of my life as depressed and unhappy as I was. I did work out of it. So, when this happens now, I don't feel that things will never be good again. Now I can see an end to the bad feelings.

Searching for a Diagnosis

When the twins were born, Tim and Kate's elation was undercut by some major complications: Geoff had to be resuscitated, and at six hours old he started having seizures.

The doctor came and told us he had taken a look at the situation. He told us the seizures were indicative of brain damage. Brain damage was a really scary thing to hear. It made us think of all the really weird cases we'd ever seen or heard of.

The next day was the absolute worst day of my entire life. I can remember sitting in my room at the hospital all day—that was all I did—that's all I remember. I suppose I probably ate some meals, and they brought Erik in and I held him. But all I can remember is sitting there crying because the nurse said Geoff was still having seizures and they were working on controlling them. We had been concerned about prematurity when I was pregnant, and I had endured 2 ½ months of bedrest to reach full term, so it was devastating to feel we'd made it only to encounter something worse. We felt totally helpless and powerless, after trying our best to make it all turn out right. That period was the bottom. Nothing after that was quite as bad.

Kate and Tim brought Erik home from the hospital, and soon after Geoff's seizures were under control, he joined them. "We still had this really hazy idea that there had been brain damage," explains Kate, "but there was a possibility that Geoff might be okay." Hospital visits, however, did not end with the twins' delivery. Because of all the unknowns, Kate and Tim brought Geoff to the neurology clinic once a month. The hint of irritation in Kate's voice, as she describes the initial hospital visits, reflects her attitudes towards the doctor's behavior.

During each visit a neurologist would come in with a colleague and they would measure his head. That's the first thing they would always do was measure his head. Doctors were always measuring his head. Lots of times they wouldn't even speak to Tim and me! They wouldn't tell us anything. We'd just go in and he'd be weighed and measured and his head would be measured again. They'd say "We're measuring this because, if it's small, it indicates a lack of brain growth." And it was small, so we'd say, "Well, would you say that his brain is not growing?" Then they'd say, "Well it's possible, but we really don't know." No answers. It was really hard having no answers and feeling that they weren't telling us all they knew.

When Geoff was about six months old, Kate and Tim finally met a doctor who was honest and direct. After taking a skull x-ray, the doctor told them that Geoff's brain was not growing properly and that they could expect significant mental delays. Doctors had previously mentioned the possibility of cerebral palsy. While cerebral palsy was hard to face, the thought of Geoff being mentally retarded was even more difficult to accept. Kate describes her reaction to the doctor's diagnosis.

Cerebral palsy was bad, but for some reason a physical disability wasn't as bad as being retarded. I can remember saying to people, "We know that Geoff has cerebral palsy, but we don't know yet if he's retarded." Even though no one actually told us that he was retarded, I was certain inside myself. But it was hard for me to say out loud that he was retarded. I didn't like what that told me about my attitudes either, because I always thought that I was an accepting kind of person. But when I didn't want my kid to be retarded more than I didn't want him to be physically handicapped, it just made me feel ugly inside. The doctor who told us never actually said the word "retarded" either. He told us that Geoff would have "mental delays." Looking back, our adjustment process had a lot to do with learning to accept terms such as "brain damaged" and "mentally retarded," and to regard them as medical diagnoses rather than as social stigmas.

I can remember coming out of that appointment and feeling, not really refreshed, but as if somebody had finally told us something and we knew what we had to work with. He'd been blunt, but he told us the truth.

Accessing Early Services

The doctor also told Kate and Tim about a school which served disabled children. At the time, Kate was taking Geoff to a parent-infant program at the local community college, but he really wasn't fitting in there. During the class Geoff spent all of the time sitting in his infant seat, whereas the other children were all crawling around. The doctor suggested Oakdale School, a program which served Geoff's specific needs.

I just felt relieved that there was something for Geoff. He was six months old. At that point, all the school offered for children Geoff's age was an hour of home therapy a week. So that was all we were doing, but it was a good opportunity for me to learn, too. The physical therapist would come twice a week, and I would sit and pick her brain while she worked with Geoff. I found out so much more about what was happening than I had from the doctors! At last I felt I was learning what I needed to know, and helping my child too.

Kate also had participated in a mothers' discussion group at Oakdale. The monthly speakers provided her with some answers to her questions, and she and the other mothers built strong friendships which have lasted over the years. Years later, Kate would remember this group as an important part in her own adjustment to having a handicapped child in the family.

It was so helpful for me to get to know other parents. I think that the parent support I felt at Oakdale was just as important as the help Geoff was getting there. This was a low time in my marriage. My husband and I weren't communicating well. Although we overcame that, at the time the other moms filled a very real need. And I found I could talk about "bad" feelings like resentment and even a sort of dislike toward my disabled son, and they had had similar feelings. I didn't feel so much like an unnatural mother. We helped each other and cried together and took our kids out together, so that we didn't feel like the only ones who had a disabled child. That really helped.

Coping with Feelings of Guilt

Despite the support she was receiving from the parent group, there were times during that first year Kate felt overwhelmed by the stress. She now had three boys to look after, and there was still so much they didn't know about Geoff's condition. What concerned Kate the most were the guilt feelings which gnawed at her.

I felt a lot of guilt because I worried about Geoff living at home for the rest of his life. I needed to accept the fact that at some point in time he would live someplace else. He would eventually be someone else's concern. I needed to face that, in order to lose that black cloud, that oppressed feeling. But, at the same time, it brought on guilt because, as his mother, I should love him enough to take care of him the rest of his life, right? Another side to my guilt was that I felt, in a way, that because of the nature of Geoff's brain damage, because his placenta had separated early and caused oxygen distress, that I had let my child down—that my body had somehow betrayed him by letting that happen. And if I couldn't "do it all" and be Supermom, I was still letting him down.

Finally, Kate decided there was too much for her to work out by herself. She decided to seek some counseling.

I used to pretend that I had it in me, and I finally did reach the point where I realized it was okay to decide that Geoff wasn't going to live with me the rest of his life. I wasn't going to do that and I didn't feel like I *had* to do that. I had my own life to think about. So that was a really important decision that this counselor helped me come to terms with. That was my guilt acceptance.

Obtaining Information and Educational Services

The counselor suggested that Kate take Geoff in for a complete evaluation so that she could have some answers to her questions. The evaluation was very depressing. Kate recalls, "I remember them saying Geoff had severe delays. All I could think was 'severely handicapped.' "

Following the evaluation, Kate met with Susan, the woman who evaluated Geoff. Susan was one of the most honest and direct professionals Kate met during those early years. As Kate recalls, "Susan gave me the bad news, but then we went on and worked with what was there." Kate was concerned about other issues—problems she saw with the other boys. Susan helped Kate with a lot of parenting insight and technique. Kate reached the point where she could work out the burdens she was feeling. "I finally felt that I wasn't being buried by the three children. Susan was a big factor in helping me adjust."

When Geoff turned three, the time came for him to leave Oakdale and move on to the public schools. Kate had learned a lot about Geoff's problems and child development. She had also established close friendships while Geoff had been at Oakdale. After the small, close environment at Oakdale, the public school system was yet another unknown. Kate felt slightly uneasy when preschool started in the fall. Any fears were quickly assuaged when she met Geoff's teacher, whom she immediately liked and trusted. The family's major difficulty that year was the long hours of school. Geoff was used to an hour of therapy a week and a 4-day-a-week 1 ½ hours-a-day program. Now he was spending five hours - five days a week at school! The strain was too much. Geoff came home every day crying and feeling totally exhausted.

Geoff stayed in the preschool for almost 3 years. During that time Kate discovered how much better Geoff behaved and how much more he learned when he spent time with children functioning higher than himself. When the opportunity to integrate Geoff into a normal kindergarten arose, Kate welcomed it with excitement.

For the past two years now Geoff has been fully integrated into a normal classroom. Every year, however, Kate realizes that it may be the last year of integration. His delays and obvious handicaps become more and more noticeable, and as he grows, his continuing need for one-to-one help is incompatible with a placement in a "normal" classroom.

While Kate has been generally pleased with Geoff's education in the public schools, she also feels a parent must constantly "stay on top of the situation," especially when it comes to her son's yearly Individual Education Plan.

> The IEP process was something that was really hard for me to accept and to get into because I'm not, by nature, an assertive person. In a group I don't speak up that much, but as a parent in an IEP conference, I have to. I have to be totally prepared. I may have a lot

of confidence in the staff that's working with him; they're all great people. But I have to know what each of them is doing with Geoff and where they're headed with him. I need to review my concerns when I go to the conference, to speak up, and really be his advocate. I have to do that. I think the parent is the one who has the best whole concept of the child, with regard to where he's been and where he's going. And the parent has a lot to offer the staff members in knowledge and understanding of the child.

Family and Future Concerns

Kate's involvement in Geoff's education has not prevented her from noticing the effect Geoff has on her two other boys. Kate was made well aware of this issue years ago, when Derek, who was six years old, brought home a new friend. Geoff was three years old at the time. While Derek was showing his friend around the house he said, "And this is my brother Geoff. He can't walk, and he can't talk, and he can't do *anything*." Kate talks openly with her sons in order to provide them with accurate information about Geoff and to clarify any misperceptions or angry feelings which might come up. In addition, Derek and Erik have attended a number of Sibling Workshops, designed especially for children who have a disabled sibling.

Kate has also begun to think about the future and what it will hold for Geoff and the rest of the family.

I feel like Geoff is in a sort of transitional period, and he's laying groundwork for what comes later. Now I am really starting to think more about things like adolescence, sexual development, and his adult life, things that I just didn't want to think about for a long time. So I can't really say that I think now just about eight-or nine-year-old type concerns. It's more concerns like what he gets at school now and what he's going to need as an adult, so that he can have as full a life as possible, learn to get along with other people, all kinds of people, and can fit into society as an adult.

I think that after eight years, I've come far enough to see that there were things that I didn't want to think about five years ago that I am starting to think about as time goes by. As they get closer, they're not as scary to me.

What I would like for Geoff is a group home. I would like him to work in a sheltered workshop. I see Geoff as a person who will be able to function in that kind of environment, although I feel too that it will require a lot of work on my part, given the lack of good group homes and living and working situations for handicapped adults. I think that in a few years, I will have to get much more involved in that search. Now I'm willing to go look at more places and be more interested. Whereas, for a long time, I didn't take the time.

The boys mentioned that when they grow up they want Geoff to live with them — they feel very responsible. They don't understand yet why I feel it would be best if Geoff had his own place.

I realize that I'll reach the point when I can think about things that I can't face now. Somewhere down the road. I don't want to think about when I'm not here anymore and Geoff will live on and someone else will have to be his advocate and look out for him. I can't think about that. That's one that I haven't been able to tackle emotionally. We have wills that will resolve his situation, good wills drawn up by knowledgeable lawyers; it's our own emotional adjustment that hasn't happened.

Although Kate has come to terms with many difficult decisions during her eight years of living with Geoff, she observes that there will always be new problems and, given her experience, recurring emotions to cope with. However, Kate is confident that the time will come when she can face the difficult decisions that lay ahead.

I think I go in and out of phases. One example is my positive attitude. Most often I feel like Geoff has enough to work with, that he'll lead a good life. Socially, he's a happy person, and I think that he'll be a happy adult. He'll lead a life that he'll be satisfied with. So people don't have to feel sorry for him, because he's content and fulfilled and that's what counts. Most of the time I feel that way, and I don't view him as a tragedy at all. But there are times, like when I realize that he should be one of the kids on the basketball court and he's not, that I'm reminded of his limitations.

I think that acceptance and a positive attitude can come and go. You can imagine how difficult he is at times. Most of the time he's not hard to take places, but every now and then he'll get upset and be so conspicuous. He's getting big enough where he's very difficult to handle, and then I'll go through a phase of resenting him.

I also think the grief phase is ongoing. Even after you reach acceptance, there are still times when I experience aspects of grief, especially as Geoff gets older. For example, about a month ago we were coming out of a McDonalds, and he didn't want to leave and started having a tantrum. A couple of boys went by and made fun of the way he looked. So, as a handicapped child grows older and his differences stand out more, you have to face the handicap all over again, the fact that you do have a funny-looking kid and people are going to stare at him. Even though *you've* accepted the way he is, and he's part of the family, and you're living with it, every now and then you come up against stumbling blocks and you have to readjust everything.

Julie: The New and Ongoing Concerns of the Mother of an Adolescent

A typical weekday morning begins at the Rossman household when the alarm clock rings at six a.m. Julie Rossman knows she must get up, prepare breakfast for her family, and get her three children off to school. Julie readily admits, however, that she frequently waits until the last possible minute to drag herself out of bed. In her typical low-keyed, relaxed manner, Julie laughs at her morning behavior. She is not alone in her procrastination. Shaking her head, smiling, she succinctly explains, "We just aren't a morning family."

Once Julie is up however, the household activity begins. Judy, the youngest daughter is first up. At five-and-a-half years old her enthusiasm for school is still apparent. Liz, the middle daughter, like her mother, sleeps until the last possible moment. Occasionally there will be a minor crisis: no clean socks for Judy; the blouse Liz had planned on wearing needs ironing.

At 15 years old, Monica is the oldest of the three girls, and because of her developmental delays, Monica requires a little more help to get ready in the morning than either of her younger sisters. Julie describes a typical morning's routine. The matter-of-fact tone in her voice implies that one morning varies very little from the next.

I know that when I wake up in the morning Monica needs more assistance to get ready than Liz does. I'll say to Liz, "Get your bottom out of bed, let's get going." And, after I've said that seven or eight times, why, there she is. . .out of bed and all sunny, dressed! When Monica gets up, we usually go through this thing about, "What day is it?" and she thinks about it and she thinks about it and says what day it is, and she always knows what special thing is going to happen that day. It's real important for her to think about that. If she hasn't had a shower, I frequently have to wrestle to get her into the shower. Monica hates showers (until she's in) and you know, at 15 years old she's not a tiny kid anymore. It's sometimes a struggle to get her into the shower. I always know that it's going to take a little more personal effort on my part to get Monica ready and out the door.

By the time her husband Bob has left for work and the children are off to school, the busy activity of the morning has subsided. But Julie's day continues: completing household chores; attending Board of Director's meeting of the developmental disability center for which she serves as president; watching her daughter's basketball games; and this month, volunteering to help out at Special Olympics practices with Monica.

Early Suspicions

Throughout her pregnancy, Julie had many dreams of the baby she wanted to have. When Monica was born, she certainly appeared to be the "normal, healthy, Ivory Snow baby" Julie had envisioned.

I had what I considered to be a textbook delivery at that time. I had gotten up in the morning with some minor cramping and spent the day in a rocking chair playing cards. I went to the hospital about 3:30 and Monica was born about 7:30. I thought the birth was miraculous. I remember Bob saying that he thought Monica was the most beautiful thing in the world.

Monica continued to fulfill Julie's image of the "Ivory Snow baby" during that first year. There was nothing that signaled trouble, and no reason to think there might be something wrong with her child.

I was real comfortable with kids. I had babysat a lot and I didn't have the kind of new-mother jitters that is so common. I just felt comfortable having a child and taking care of her.

Monica was just fine as a baby, and when we started looking for developmental milestones, she was always within the normal range. If the textbook said your baby will sit up between four and six months, Monica did it, but just at the end of that time. And, if the book said, whatever it was between x and y, she would be right there at y. Instead of crawling, Monica tended to roll places, but that was okay, because that's a legitimate way of getting from here to there when you're a few months old. And, when she was 12 months old, Monica would walk around a coffee table, but she wouldn't walk on her own. At 14 or 15 months she would walk holding someone's hand, but would fall if she let go. I never worried. I was aware of the fact that different children developed at different rates. Besides, Monica had a wonderful, sunny disposition. She was cheerful and happy and adorable. And the doctor never gave me the faintest clue that he perhaps had some suspicions.

While Julie was busy enjoying her daughter, Julie's mother began voicing her suspicions that something was wrong with Monica.

My mother started saying, "There's something the matter." Now my mother is a pessimist. My mother-in-law is an optimist. My mother-in-law would say, "She's fine. Don't worry." Then my mother would say, "There's something the matter with her."

Being an optimist herself, Julie chose to listen to her mother-in-law and set aside her mother's concerns. Her 14-month-old daughter didn't do any of the usual things that warranted suspicion. She didn't have a strange gait; she didn't exhibit any bizarre behaviors.

Around the time Monica was 15 months old, however, Julie began to share her mother's concerns. Monica's speech was limited, and she still wasn't walking independently. Perhaps, Julie thought to herself, she should check with her doctor, just in case.

I took Monica to Dr. Ellensburg and said, "Well, we have some concerns. She doesn't seem to be beginning to talk." And he said, "Does Monica seem to hear all right?" and I said, "Yes." And he walked around behind her and clapped his hands and she turned around and he said, "Well, her hearing is fine." That was the hearing test. I said "She's also slow in walking." He said, "Can she ride and pedal a trike?" Well, she could, so I said, "Yes." He said, "Well then her large motor skills are just fine." That was the extent of it. Well, I didn't know any different so I didn't say, "No, I want a complete workup!" I was satisfied with that. If he's not sweating it, why should I?

Julie took Monica home with renewed optimism. Bob's family kept saying "Oh, don't worry—she'll do this," or "Cousin Davy didn't do that until he was so old." Family members also told Julie, "You do too much for her. Of course she doesn't ask for milk; all she has to do is point to the refrigerator and grunt, and you give it to her." The family's comments allayed any suspicion Julie had about Monica.

Looking back on that time, Julie thinks about how her physician could have taken a more active role in helping Julie provide him with the information about Monica that would enable him to confirm or deny her suspicions. Julie describes her strong belief in early intervention and her feelings about the role the physician should take in helping parents.

If a parent is taking a child to a pediatrician and the pediatrician has a suspicion about some area of that child's development, then it is that pediatrician's absolute responsibility to help the parent, in a nonalarmist manner, find out whether in fact a problem exists. I think it's necessary because, although parents live with their kids and see their kids every day, they don't observe their kids, and there's a distinct difference. If parents don't know what to look for, they are not going to know what to report. And if the doctor can't get an accurate report, then he or she is going to miss something. I don't think it will terrify a parent if the doctor says to you, "Gee, the baby is so cute, I think I'd like to see her again in three months, and why don't you see how she seems to be doing with eating Cheerios. I'd like you to observe how she's playing with her toys, especially the small toys, and how she's picking up small objects. Then let's talk about that again when she comes in."

Okay, maybe that will raise some suspicions on the part of the parent, but the doctor can say it in a nonthreatening way, and give the parents some guidelines for things to look for. Then the doctor can get somewhere. Now let's take that a step further and assume that the parent comes back in three months and the doctor does have some serious questions. Then he or she can share those concerns with the parent. The doctor can say, "I have some concerns because your child doesn't seem to be doing this, and it's something that most children can do at this age. Let's see if maybe we can give little Sally some additional stimulation. I know of a couple of programs that might be good for your child. Now I don't want you to get upset. I'm not saying that there's something the matter, but I'm saying let's not just ignore this but try to start some extra help now." And the doctor can then direct the parent to any one of a number of places where this child can get some extra stimulation or therapy once a week. One of two things will happen. Either the doctor's suspicions will turn out to be ill-founded, and the child will have gone to a preschool, been involved in a program for a few months, learned some skills, and will certainly not have been damaged in any way by that exposure. Or, the doctor's suspicions will be confirmed and in that case, the child will have had early intervention, and the time that would otherwise have been lost isn't. Now show me what's bad about that, except for possible hurt feelings on the part of the parent, which can be dealt with. Why waste that time?

If someone had raised those kinds of suspicions, Monica could have been in school a year and a half earlier. Now I'm not saying it would make a difference between her life now and being a college professor. I'm not saying that. But it would have been helpful to her. It would have been helpful to me too. It might have saved her from developing poor speech habits. Or, it may have helped develop her facial muscles at an earlier age so that her speech might be clearer today. I think that's a legitimate possibility.

The doctor to whom Julie was telling this disagreed altogether. The approach he favored was not to say anything until the parent was ready to hear it. He would decide a parent was ready when the parent asked, "Is something the matter with this child?" Julie feels, however, that the emotional blow to parents is something they can work through, and that early intervention is too valuable to the child to delay diagnosis.

When Monica was around 18 months old, Julie enrolled her in a toddler program at the local community college. Both Julie and Monica enjoyed the teacher and the activities, but it was hard for Julie not to compare Monica to the other children. "It became obvious to me that Monica was slower than the other children—they were beginning to talk and she wasn't. They were walking all by themselves and she still needed to grab onto something. But again, she was cheerful and had this wonderful personality. It just really covered up a lot of things."

Julie wasn't the only one to notice that her daughter was different from the other children. In the spring of that year, Monica's teacher had a parent-teacher conference with the group of mothers from class. The news Julie was to hear was worse than she could have imagined.

We all sat around and the teacher went over all these general things. There was a group of maybe 20 women there. When the conference was about over, she looked at me and said, "And you, stay after. I want to talk to you privately."

So, I stayed after and she said, "Your child has problems you've got to do something about. All these other kids are learning to play cooperatively and your child is still playing parallel to the other children." Then she said, "Your child will never catch up by herself; she'll never catch up by kindergarten. You've got to do something."

She just went on and on. I was devastated. I felt like I needed to call an ambulance to have my daughter taken home from school that day! This woman painted such a dismal picture. I had no idea what to do with this information.

Julie immediately called her own doctor and told him what the teacher had said. He told her to wait, everything would be fine. And, for a short while everything was fine. That summer Liz was born. With the joy and excitement of a second child, any anxiety Julie may have felt about Monica temporarily vanished. The summer was spent "just being a happy family."

The Search for a Diagnosis

In the fall, however, Bob and Julie decided they needed more specific information about Monica's problems. Where to go and who to see were the big questions. Julie says she finds it hard to recall exactly what she and Bob did to seek help during the next few months, adding "Maybe I'm just shutting out a lot of unpleasant memories." Bob and Julie finally decided to make an appointment with a well-known psychologist in town. He would evaluate their daughter and finally they could get some answers. The psychologist's evaluation, however, was hardly what Julie expected. After interviewing both Bob and Julie and playing with Monica for 15 minutes, he presented a depressing report. Their daughter's potential, he concluded, was extremely limited.

Angry and depressed, Julie and Bob left the office. Refusing to accept the psychologist's grim diagnosis, Julie began an exhaustive search to get more definitive answers to her questions.

It was real difficult for us to know what to do next. At this point, I had changed pediatricians. Our new pediatrician was more helpful. He ran some tests and sent us over to Children's Hospital for more exhaustive tests. I remember one thing the doctor did. He took scrapings from the inside of Monica's mouth to run some cellular tests. He said there were certain kinds of developmental disabilities that resulted because the child was not the sex that everybody thought he or she was when the child was born. I just about died! I could handle the disability and the developmental problems, but how was I to explain to her grandmother that her granddaughter was a grandson! It just blew my mind! Well, it turned out, thank God, that she really was still a girl.

Despite the many tests and evaluations, the doctors were unable to come up with any answers to explain Monica's developmental lag.

We went to Children's Hospital and the doctors tested Monica. They came up with all these results that said it didn't appear to be this, and it didn't appear to be that, and it didn't appear to be any of the genetic problems that they were able to screen for. It was horrible.

Julie pauses a moment, the tone of her voice is more serious than usual as she describes her frustration with the lack of any definitive answers.

Here I had been living with my kid for years, and she was coming along okay, and now suddenly they were placing these limits on her life, but they couldn't put a label on the problem! It was a real strange kind of thing. Everybody was telling me she might be slow, but nobody could tell me *specifically* what was wrong with her. I wanted some black-and-white answers. I didn't want to be left in the gray zone.

I was told that what most likely happened is I had a virus while I was pregnant. But I had a perfectly healthy pregnancy. I don't think I sneezed once in nine months. So the virus didn't affect me, but it affected the baby? I don't happen to buy that, but that's okay. For a long time I thought it was oxygen deprivation, but recently a doctor whom I respect very much told me that he didn't think that that was the case.

Early on, I really wanted to attach a name to it. I wanted to know that my child had xyz syndrome because then it would be more tangible, I could do something about it.

Seeking Information and Services

If Julie's search for answers to her daughter's problems was both frustrating and time consuming, her search for a preschool was even more so. When Monica was three years old, Julie decided it was time she started school. Julie spent the next few months going from one preschool to another. Each time the teacher's response was the same. "I'm terribly sorry, but this is not the right program for your daughter." Julie's search led her to Fernhill School, a preschool specifically serving handicapped children. "I went over there, and I saw this school. It was real sobering, because *my kid* didn't look like *those kids*." Julie talked with the staff, and they decided that Monica was functioning at a much higher level than the other children, and that they could not evaluate her and work up some kind of program until the end of the school year. Not even a school for handicapped children would accept her daughter! Julie's efforts seemed in vain. The Fernhill staff recommended that Julie enroll Monica in a preschool program in the public school system that served children with needs similar to Monica's. Finally, the search had ended.

When Monica started summer school I felt that finally something was being done. The kids there had a wide range of disabilities. I remember one of the first children I saw there, he was probably a thalidomide baby. He was a cute little boy, and he just had flippers. When I saw him, it was just heartbreaking. I thought, "Oh, that poor child, he can't use these things, these appendages." Then I saw him a few minutes later and he was stacking these 1-inch blocks. It was all Monica could do to get one block on top of another, and she was older and all put together physically! This little kid was stacking the blocks one on top of another without any problem. A few minutes later I saw him at snack time and he was drinking from a cup. That really told me you can't make too many assumptions.

During the next three years, Julie became actively involved in her daughter's program. She volunteered in the classroom and became president of the parent group.

Julie has fond memories of Monica's preschool years for both herself and her daughter. Julie liked Monica's teacher, Sally, who showed a genuine interest in her daughter.

During the past eight years of Monica's schooling, Julie has been relatively pleased with Monica's teachers and program. Each year counts for a lot, according to Julie, and she candidly admits that she is constantly "watchdogging" Monica's program more than her other children's. "My other girls will survive if they have a lousy teacher one year, but for Monica, it's important for her to have a good year, every year."

Three years ago, Julie and Bob once again found themselves searching for specific reasons for Monica's delays.

When Monica was about 12, she had a seizure. We went to a neurologist who said, "Ah, look at this, she's got tuberous sclerosis." And, on one level, I felt liberated from the gray zone I had been living in all these years! I knew I had a kid who had a syndrome. I ran to the books and read everything I could! Then I thought, "Oh God!" The books I read were very outdated, but they described how the syndrome results in these growths all over the face and brain. I read how Monica would lose everything she's ever gained. She would forget how to talk, and would go blind and deaf. I thought, this is just horrible. I just fell apart!

Then, we took Monica to Children's Hospital for genetic tests. Fifteen doctors there told me that the neurologist was wrong. He had based his diagnosis on three things: the fact that Monica was retarded, that she had had a seizure, and that she has what had been diagnosed before as a skin problem. Evidently, patients with tuberous sclerosis frequently have areas without pigment on their skin in the shape, strangely enough, of an ash leaf. We had a lot of work done; kidney scans on Bob and me, and other tests. Well, the doctors at Children's said it's just not so.

So we were back into the gray zone. But it was okay. I think that finally you reach a point where you don't have to know. The thing that's important is where your kid is now, and how can you best help that child to develop to his or her full potential. That's what really counts. It doesn't matter what they've got, or what the label is. But it took time to get to that point.

Present and Future Concerns

When asked what her concerns are for Monica now as an adolescent, Julie mentions two things: day-to-day life, and preparing for the future.

Most of the time you don't spend a whole lot of emotional energy thinking in terms of "I've got a child with a disability." You grow away from that being your constant focus. At the same time, there are days when I get into the car to go out to dinner and I think, "Oh, it's been such a struggle just to get these three kids ready for me to leave." Some days I can easily see that it will be fine to leave the kids. Other days, if Monica is really off the wall, I have to hire somebody, and go through that whole hassle. It's a real luxury for parents not to have to worry about getting a babysitter. So a disability will affect what you're doing in an evening, and will involve you in all kinds of other arrangements and considerations.

You also find that your emotional involvement changes. At one point in time you might be going through the grieving process, and at some other time you might be in what I call the "crusader rabbit syndrome," you know, you feel like "Now that I've got my act together, I've got to help all these other parents who haven't got their act together yet, who are just learning about their kids."

Julie finds that her own expectations for her daughter are still being challenged and are constantly readjusting.

There are a lot of day-to-day frustrations, even now. Judgmental things. We gave her a camera for Hanukkah, a Polaroid instant picture camera, so Monica won't have to wait for the pictures. Patience is not her long suit. Well, she just loved the camera. Film for the camera is very expensive. I tried to explain that to Monica, but she doesn't understand. The first three days she had the camera she used four rolls of film. She takes pictures of the bird cage and the light fixture, real important things! But, she's really proud of it, and it's something that she can accomplish. But it's real frustrating because we're trying to teach her how to do it right and she just wants it now — immediately.

There's some other things that are difficult on a daily basis. She doesn't like crowds, and this becomes hard for me because I really like our family to do things together. If the family is invited somewhere, it's really hard for me to separate family members and not all do the same thing. But it's something that I have to do, and it's something you have to do anyway when your kids get older and your teenager doesn't want to go along. Well, I've got a teenager too, and she's certainly physically developed and has the emotional ups and downs that a 15 year old would have, but she has the judgment of somebody many years younger, and so it's kind of a juggling act.

We recently were invited to a brunch at someone's home where we knew there would be about 75 people. I thought, this is not going to work for me. Monica will be miserable and I'll be miserable. Liz will be embarrassed because it's her friend, and if Monica uses a loud voice, which she commonly does, it will be embarrassing. That's unfair to Liz. So, I said, "Gee, we were invited to Rebecca's bas mitzvah brunch." Monica said, "I don't want to go." I said, "Okay, I'll make other arrangements for you." Monica wanted to stay home alone, and although I've left her home alone for real short periods of time, like a half an hour at maximum, I'm not ready to leave her alone for three hours. She didn't want a babysitter. She wanted to do something else. So we made other arrangements for her. That's my problem. I have to be open enough for her to make some choices.

I think that on a day-to-day basis you just think about day-to-day things. Of course, you have to think of major life issues some time. But you can't think about them every single day—you'd go crazy. It's frustrating sometimes, when I ask Monica something 67 times and she still doesn't do it. She takes care of her things like a much younger child. Half the time if she's in the bathroom she says, "Come and wipe me." I know darn well she can wipe herself.

There are times when you're thinking in terms of the big picture. You're thinking in terms of longer range needs or goals. For example, now that Monica is 15, it's time for us to start thinking in terms of a group home for her, of a more independent living situation for her. So, that's the kind of long range issue that we discuss and are very involved with at this moment.

But this morning when I woke up, I didn't think anything other than, "Hey, she's got to get out to the bus."

Conclusion

The testimonies of the three mothers reflect their insights and experiences regarding the impact a disabled child has on mothers and their families. Common themes appear in each of these profiles, and patterns of experience and response begin to emerge. This section examines these common themes which include: adjustment and readjustment, the cycles of emotions, information-gathering, and the parent-professional relationship. These themes merit serious attention in ongoing efforts to understand the extended impact a disabled child has on parents throughout parents' lives.

Adjustment and Readjustment

Many writers have used the notion of stages to describe parents' changing responses to a child's handicap (Baum, 1962; Klaus & Kennel, 1976; Richmond, 1973). Still others describe specific emotions parents experience. For example, Helen Featherstone in her well-known book

A Difference in the Family (1980), discusses four types of emotion: fear, anger, loneliness, and guilt. The purpose of this chapter is not to support one particular theory, but rather to acknowledge that parents travel through periods and phases of adjustment and readjustment throughout their lives.

As is illustrated in the mothers' narratives, parents grope towards their own individual solutions. What works for one parent may be unacceptable to another. Almost always, parents report they are numb with pain in the early stages of adjustment. The initial shock of the disability seems to obscure everything else. As one of the mothers explains, "Our world had been shattered." Or, when Kate had finished reading the draft of her own story she exclaimed, "I had forgotten how truly depressed I was!"

As time proceeds, parents begin to look at their child's disability a little differently. The balance of pain and pleasure eventually and gradually shifts when the disabled child becomes interwoven into the fabric of family life. For most families, life becomes more positive, as each of the three mothers testifies.

Parents do not speak about a linear cycle of emotional stress. The grief, pain, and stress parents experience ebb and flow over time. Critical periods, however, may be identified. These are times when parents experience renewed emotional upheaval. Wikler (1981) identifies five critical periods. These occur when expectations for the disabled child's development are discrepant to those for a normally developing child. For example, Wikler states that grieving and stress often increase when a disabled child should have begun walking or talking by a certain age. The mothers' experiences confirm this notion. As is also illustrated in the profiles, the beginning of public school and the onset of puberty are periods of increased stress. Other events which caused renewed emotional upheaval were the actual diagnosis of mental retardation; an exacerbated behavior or health problem (e.g., a seizure or a tantrum outside of a restaurant); and the discussion of placement of a disabled child outside the home (e.g., deciding on wills and trusts, the future). Once again, each of the mothers were confronted with many of these issues, and each dealt with them in the way which best fit their needs and the needs of their family.

An awareness of the recurrence of stress — which may assume various forms: anger, depression, frustration, or grief — as well as parents' predictable periods of vulnerability, is necessary for professionals to enable them to plan appropriate interventions with families.

Information Gathering

One of the first lessons one learns as the parent of a disabled child is that clear, honest, and responsive information is hard to come by. Physicians, psychologists, reading specialists and other professionals diagnose a child's problems in technical language — and then explain their diagnoses in vague, sometimes frightening terms. Mystery and confusion about the child's problem persist even after it has been identified.

Parents' need for solid information is painfully clear from the start. Parents do, of course, look to the appropriate professionals for help, but frequently they find little satisfaction. The frustration they experience often ends only when they find relief, comfort, and guidance from others who have already "been through it" — other parents. It is through this informal network — the friend of a friend, the next door neighbor, the local parent group — that parents finally get useful information, information that relates to them and to their disabled child stated in words they can understand and in terms they can apply. This is the information they trust.

Given that many parents speak of other parents as their most credible and knowledgeable resource, continued efforts should be made by professionals to organize parent groups and to refer parents to local and national parent groups such as Advocates for Retarded Citizens and Closer Look.

The Parent-Professional Relationship

Professionals play a large role in the lives of disabled people and their families. Yet mothers' anecdotes portray the parent-professional relationship in negative and unsatisfactory terms. Professionals, however, can and should help families in many ways. Parents speak most often about the need for honest information from professionals, particularly at the time of the diagnosis and during their child's early years. Parents need information about their child's problems. They want to know as much as possible about the origin of the disability and its implications for their child's life and their family's future. Parents complain that doctors fail to respond candidly and honestly to their concerns. While questions cannot always be answered immediately, and the prognosis for many children is unclear, some professionals postpone informing parents even when a problem is apparent. Parents relate experiences about doctors politely excusing themselves or retreating into medical jargon, in an effort to avoid a difficult situation.

Parents have dual needs. One is to express their concerns openly. The second is to be given honest medical data in a form they can understand. Both needs are rarely met. When a physician provides an honest and clear evaluation, although the news is emotionally traumatic, parents usually breathe a sigh of relief. One mother describes her feeling after having finally met a doctor who gave her specific information: "I can remember coming out of that appointment feeling, not really refreshed, but like somebody *finally* told us something and we knew what we had to work with. He'd been blunt, but he told us the truth." Parents need information for many reasons: to understand the cause and nature of a handicap and the implications of a diagnosis, to set reasonable expectations for the future, and to begin to regain some control over their lives.

In addition to the need for honest information, parents need to express their grief, shock, and anger. Parents must often control these emotions when they interact with professionals, from whom they seek information and expert advice. Parent workshops and regular parent groups, however, provide parents with needed opportunities to share these feelings with other parents who can offer support and the benefit of similar experiences.

Parents talk fondly of the professional who shows respect to them and their child: the doctor who compliments a mother for the great job she is doing with her daughter, the teacher who treats the parent as an integral and knowledgeable partner in the child's educational program. As one of the mothers observed, "I think the parent is the one who has the best whole concept of the child. . .the parent has a lot to offer." Professionals must recognize the parents' potential to contribute information and reactions that are uniquely their own, accumulated over years of day-to-day involvement with their disabled child.

Parents appreciate the professional who genuinely likes and respects their child as well. One mother's anxiety about her daughter entering the public school was quickly assuaged when she realized, "the teacher really liked Monica." Another mother describes the benefit she experienced from a professional's positive attitude towards her handicapped daughter. "Dr. Davis' professional acceptance of Lisa helped me because she saw value in Lisa that I couldn't see for a long time."

Parents seek out help from different professionals at different times in their disabled child's life. In the early years, parents rely primarily on doctors rather than educators for guidance. When the child reaches the age of three, parents begin to have more contact with educators. In these interactions parents indicate that they look for professionals to provide straightforward and honest answers to their questions, and information that can be understood and applied. Finally, parents look for professionals not only to show respect for their feelings, but also to respect their child's needs and feelings. As the mothers in these interviews indicated, these kinds of positive professional attitudes can significantly contribute to the parent's adjustment, particularly when a parent is not able to see the light from the depths of stress and depression. The professional's positive attitude toward the child can also provide the parent with a model and an alternative to focusing only on the child's problems and overlooking the child's unique characteristics.

References

Baum, M.H. (1962). Some dynamic factors affecting family adjustment to the handicapped child. *Exceptional Children, 28*, 387-92.

Featherstone, H. (1980). *A difference in the family.* New York: Basic Books.

Greenfeld, J. (1972). *A child called Noah.* New York: Holt, Rinehart & Winston.

Klaus, M., & Kennell, J. (1976). *Maternal and infant bonding.* St. Louis: C.V. Mosby.

Pieper, Elizabeth. (n.d.) *Sticks and stones: The story of loving a child.* Syracuse, NY: Human Policy Press.

Richmond, J.B. (1973). The family and the handicapped child. *Clinical Proceedings, 29*, 156-164.

Wikler, L. (1981). Chronic stresses of families of mentally retarded children. *Family Relations, 30*, 281-288.

9

Single Mothers: A Social Phenomenon and Population in Need

Patricia F. Vadasy

This book focuses upon a special group of families — the most basic social units — families of handicapped children. The perspective that these chapters reflect is that families are interrelated systems in which all members are not only affected by a child's handicap, but also have the potential to contribute, in large and in small ways, at different points in time, to the person that child will become. Family relations are reciprocal, and the system is dynamic, with family members' needs and experiences changing over time. The system is often multigenerational, including siblings, their parents, and their grandparents, as well as other extended family members. The level of analysis or intervention, however, is most frequently the child's immediate family, and the model for that unit is most often the two-parent family.

Yet in a growing number of families, a single parent is responsible for child-rearing. In these families, all components of the family system are affected by the absence of one parent, most often the father, and the resulting stress. Single parents of handicapped children will experience even greater stresses in their family system than parents in two-parent families. This is intuitive, although there is a small body of data to support that single parents of handicapped children face more problems than married parents or single parents of nonhandicapped children. Those data will be reported, but they are meager and are not the focus of this chapter. Rather, this chapter will attempt to shed light on single mothers of handicapped children by describing the growing total population of single mothers and their experiences. The data on the demographics and the special needs which single-parent families share provide a context in which to consider the impact a child's handicap may have upon a single parent.

As Gorham (Ross & Sawhill, 1975) has pointed out in a study of female-headed families, a study of single parents is a study of transitions. At the level of the individual, the single parent is often in a transition between marriages (Bane & Weiss, 1980; Wattenberg & Reinhardt, 1979), or between married and nonmarried states. At a broader social level, single-parent families represent a transition from a two-parent family model in which the husband is the chief economic resource, to a more egalitarian family model in which both spouses share in making physical and economic contributions to the family unit. Gorham notes that our social institutions have not yet adapted to respond to the needs of these new family forms. In the meantime, public policies towards families are also in transition, and often favor intact families.

It should be noted that for practical purposes, this chapter will focus on single mothers. Most of the literature on single parents describes single mothers, a bias perhaps, but one that can be justified both by the relatively small numbers of single fathers (although they are growing), as well as the multiple problems single mothers, by virtue of their gender, experience. Where it is appropriate, generalizations will be made for single fathers, and future study should certainly be dedicated to their experiences and needs. Most single parents are single mothers, and many of their experiences derive from the feminization of poverty in our society. Only 2% of all children lived in father-headed families in 1982 (Select Committee on Children, Youth, and Families, 1984). In 1980, 65% of children under six years of age living in female-headed families were poor (Select Committee on Children, Youth, and Families, 1984). In light of these numbers it is surprising to note that one third of female-headed single parent families never receive welfare, and that most who receive welfare are assisted for less than five years (Schorr & Moen, 1979). This figure speaks of the significant personal resources these mothers bring to their roles.

But first of all, we will present a brief overview on the changing American family structure which will help readers better understand these growing numbers of families, their characteristics, and their needs. Then we will go on to suggest what happens to these single-mother family systems when they include a handicapped child.

Single Parents in America Today

In whatever ways they differ. . .all single parents suffer from public images of the ideal family. (Schorr & Moen, 1979, p.16)

The single-parent family is a permanent part of American life. (Select Committee on Children, Youth, and Families, 1984)

The most dramatic change in the American family over the past 20 years is the increase in single-parent families. Many readers will probably recall the one or two unmarried mothers they knew during the time they were growing up. In 1960, about 13% of U.S. families were one-parent families, while today about 22% of all U.S. children live in single-parent families (U.S. Bureau of the Census, 1984). The number of single-parent families increased from 3.3 million in 1970 to 6.8 million in 1983 — an increase of 107%. The number of children living in single-parent families increased from 8.4 million in 1970 to 13.7 million in 1982. The vast majority of these children live with their mothers. In 1970, only 1.1% of children lived in single-father homes; by 1982 this increased to 1.9%, or 1.2 million children (Select Committee on Children, Youth, and Families, 1984).

Many of these single-parent families are the result of separation and divorce, and an increasing proportion are the result of births to unmarried women. In 1970, 956,000 one-parent families were headed by a divorced woman. The number of these families increased by 1983 to 2.8 million families. The number of one-parent families headed by divorced fathers in 1983 was 428,000. These changes are accompanied by a decrease of 5% in the total number of two-parent families between 1970 and 1983 (U.S. Bureau of the Census, 1984).

Other single-parent families result from out-of-wedlock births, which have increased 50% in the last decade. In 1982, 715,227 babies were born to unmarried women, accounting for about 20% of total births (National Center for Health Statistics, 1984). Between 1960 and 1970, out-of-wedlock births account for 9% of the growth in female-headed families with children for whites, and 21% for nonwhites (Ross & Sawhill, 1975). This trend has been related to improved health care for young pregnant mothers and infants, and increased sexual activity, as well as to the high unemployment and underemployment rates for young black men, and the predominantly urban nature of the black population, which seems less conducive to family stability than suburban environments.

What these numbers convey is that "single parenthood is a normal and permanent feature of our social landscape" (Schorr & Moen, 1979). In their study of single fathers, Rosenthal and Keshet (1981) argue that the two-parent model of the family is no longer appropriate, and that instead, the parent-child unit be considered the core of the family, rather than the marriage bond. The result is that the single parent is not regarded as part of a broken family unit, but as one half of the smallest possible, but most enduring, family unit. Although the individual situations of single-parent families vary considerably, many single mothers share special problems that place many of them and their children at risk for stresses resulting from their marital status. Single mothers who are black, poor, and who have low levels of education face even greater problems. Whereas one out of three white children today will spend some part of their childhood in a single-parent home, three out of four black children will do so. This is due, in part, to the growing number of out-of-wedlock births to black women, which has increased from 38% of all black births in 1970, to 55% in 1979. In comparison, the percentage of white out-of-wedlock births during that period rose from 5.7% to 9.4% of all white births (National Center for Health Statistics, 1981).

Many of these single-parent families are the result of divorce. Glick and Norton (1973) point out that the increase in the number of divorce decrees has resulted in more children being affected. Further, the number of divorces which involve children has increased by 69% between 1960 and 1970, while the number of divorces involving no children increased only 40% (National Center for Health Statistics, 1978). High divorce rates are associated with low levels of education and income, and with minority status. The stress resulting from divorce is also associated with high rates of illness and accidents.

Single-parent status has an immediate effect on the living arrangements of these families, but it may have a wider impact upon their extended family networks as well. In a recent series of reviews of U.S. Bureau of the Census data on fertility and household and family characteristics, Bane and Ellwood (1984a,b) report some noteworthy trends on single mothers and their children's living arrangements. The authors found that among white women, an increase in marital dissolutions was the most important factor contributing to the increase in the number of unmarried women with children, whereas among black women, there has been a much larger increase in never-married women who head households with children. Between 1970 and 1982, there was a 63% increase in the number of black never-married women with children, compared to an 8% increase for white women. On the other hand, during the same time there was a 120% increase in the number of divorced, separated, or widowed white women of childbearing age with children, compared to an increase of 55% for black women. When Bane and Ellwood looked more closely at the changes for younger women ages 18-24, they found that between 1970 and 1982, the percentage of unmarried female family heads with children had increased from 28.9% to 33.3% for black women (a 15% increase), but only from 6.2% to 6.7% for white women (an 8% increase). At the same time, the authors found that the proportion of unmarried young mothers who do not head their own households has also increased, suggesting that many of these young unmarried mothers are living with other family members (1984a).

Bane and Ellwood (1984b) used data from the Panel Study of Income Dynamics (Survey Research Center, 1984) to calculate probabilities for transitions into and out of non-two-parent situations and concluded that at present, about 33% of white youth and 73% of black youth spend some part of their childhood in a non-two-parent situation, and that 10 years from now, the proportions are likely to increase to 46% for whites and 87% for blacks. Bane (1976) has estimated that the average duration for one-parent situations is 5 to 6 years, which is the average duration between divorce and remarriage.

Not surprisingly, most of these single-mother family heads are employed. Bronfenbrenner (1976) has pointed out that the highest labor force participation rates for women are for single mothers. In 1981, two thirds of single mothers of children between the ages of 6 and 17 years were employed, and one half of single mothers of children under age six were employed (U.S. Department of Labor, 1983). The poverty rate for these families is higher than that for the general population. In 1980, 44% of all families headed by women lived in poverty, compared to 7% of married couples with children (U.S. Department of Labor, 1983). These trends are not unique to this country. The financial difficulties of single mothers were also noted in a large British follow-up study (Ferri, 1976; Ferri & Robinson, 1976), in which the authors underscore the fact that the single mothers' poverty contributes to their isolation. This isolation often makes it difficult to involve the mothers and their children in activities outside the home—activities, as the authors point out, which may be particularly beneficial to these families. This study suggests the circular relationship between poverty and the social isolation which makes it difficult for many single mothers to change their circumstances.

In this country, family income differentials make clear the economic disadvantage of single mothers. The median family income in 1980 for families maintained by women was $7,652 compared to $23,930 for married-couple families, and $14,249 for families maintained by men. During the past two decades, the proportion of white female-headed families living in poverty increased from 15% to 26%; among blacks the proportion increased from 24% to 59% (U.S. Bureau of the Census, 1983). The economic status of many single mothers makes it difficult for them to afford many of the extras that would make it easier to raise a child, including adequate housing, day care, babysitters, quality education programs, and educational toys and materials. Not only is it difficult for them to afford many "extras" for their children, but it is also often difficult for them to spend the amount of time, or the "quality" time, with their children that enhances a child's development.

It has been pointed out that most children spend only part of their childhood in a single-parent home, that the average time between marriages for the single mother is about 5 years. But as Bane and Weiss (1980) remind us, "this may be a relatively brief interval for an adult, but it is a significant one in a child's life" (p. 11). Most single-parent families, as Polit (1980) observes, make adaptive, integrative, functional transitions, and should indeed be regarded as "families in process" rather than families in crisis (p. 12). When a child requires many special materials, however, as well as added time and attention, as many children with handicaps do, the single mother and her child are at greater risk. In these families the single mother may find it extremely difficult to meet her child's needs, and the child may suffer more than a nonhandicapped peer from the absence of a second parent.

Findings Reported on Single Mothers of Handicapped Children

Unfortunately, the empirical data on single mothers with handicapped children are scarce, and they reflect a bias on the part of researchers. Of those available, older studies tended to focus on the impact of marital status on the child's placement, whereas more recent studies have described the particular stresses single mothers experience.

In earlier studies of families of handicapped children, the family characteristics predicting institutionalization or home placement of the handicapped child were often the outcomes of interest. In several of those studies, single-parent status was often found to be associated with the child's placement in an institution (Appell & Tisdall, 1968; Bayley, 1973; Farber, 1968; Graliker, Koch, & Henderson, 1965; Hobbs, 1964; Saenger, 1960; Shellhaas & Nihira, 1969). This finding was also reported in a more recent study of mothers of mentally retarded children by German and Maisto (1982), where over half (54%) of the residential children came from single-parent families, and only one fourth (26%) of the home-reared children lived in single-parent families.

Not surprisingly, when the marital status of mothers of handicapped children has been examined, single mothers are reported to experience more negative outcomes than married mothers. In her study of mothers of handicapped infants, Beckman (1983) found that single mothers reported significantly more stress than married mothers on the *Questionnaire on Resources and Stress* (Holroyd, 1974) and the *Schedule of Recent Experiences* (Holmes & Rahe, 1967). In an earlier study, Holroyd (1974) also found that single mothers of handicapped children, compared to married mothers, reported having too many time demands and stifled personal development, as well as feeling that their family had many problems and was not integrated. They also reported more financial problems than married mothers. These findings are not surprising when viewed in light of the demographics of single-mother families reviewed above.

In a nonrandom study of 20 single mothers of children with mental retardation, Wikler (1979) examined the mothers' need for and use of both formal and informal support services. She found that the single mothers reported the greatest need for respite or child care, the next greatest need for financial assistance, and the third greatest need for personal-social supports. In comparison, a group of matched controls, single mothers with nonhandicapped children, reported just the opposite, ordering their needs as being first for personal-social supports, then for financial assistance, and lastly, for respite or child care. She found that the single mothers with retarded children were less likely to be employed than the mothers in the control group, and that they used more than one formal organized support group significantly more often than the controls. Wikler found that 73% of the mothers with handicapped children were receiving at least one type of social welfare support, yet this did not include respite care, their greatest stated need. She cited the benefits that families in a pilot respite care study experienced when they received as little as eight hours a week of trained respite services. Finally, Wikler reported that 80% of the women with retarded children reported they did not expect to remarry. Although Wikler does not report the remarriage expectations of the controls, this finding can be compared to the .71 probability that women between the ages of 15 and 44 years whose first marriage ends in divorce will remarry within five years after divorce (National Center for Health Statistics, 1980).

Wikler's findings indicate one way in which a handicapped child may affect the single mother's marital status, by reducing her chances for remarriage. In a survey of 448 parents of handicapped children, Moore, Hamerlynck, Barsh, Spieker, and Jones (1982) reported that single mothers reported substantial marital strains that suggested the disabled child contributed to the parents' separation. Moore et al. also found that the married mothers were more likely to report they had the option to work compared to single mothers, who would not have the back-up support of a husband for child care. As the single mother of a 4-year-old moderately handicapped child and two nonhandicapped children reported:

> Caring for my child cut into the amount of time I could spend at work, until my employer simply had to cut my hours back to less than half time.

Studies of single mothers of nonhandicapped children report that optimal mother-child interaction is predicted by hours of employment (Weinraub & Wolf, 1983), and that the likeliness of the mother's full-time employment was related to family size (Polit, 1980). One would expect that a single mother with a handicapped child would face difficult problems maintaining a job, attending to the child's needs, and sustaining her personal and emotional life.

The Single Mother's Experiences

Two-parent families are more likely than single parents to be able to meet the extra care demands of raising a handicapped child in the home. In a two-parent family, the mother has access not only to the physical and practical assistance the father may provide in feeding, changing, carrying, babysitting, and playing with the child, but also to the care-taking he provides for the other children, and to the financial support from his income. The single mother's family structure affects both how she will manage the daily demands of caring for her child, as well as what resources she can access to support her efforts. The single mother's economic status will be a major variable in the demands she must meet and the resulting stress she experiences. The economic strains the single mother experiences are closely related to the family functions the single mother must assume.

The term "family functions" describes how the family unit meets the needs of its individual members. In the past, families filled many more functions than they do today, and many of those functions have been taken over by nonfamily agents or groups, or have been redistributed within the family. For example, whereas the family used to be solely responsible for educating its children and producing food and clothing, those social and productive functions have been taken over by the public schools and a highly organized agricultural and manufac-turing system. Whereas husbands used to function as the family's chief economic resource, working wives now contribute to the family's income, and their position in the family has changed significantly (Ross & Sawhill, 1975). Although family functions have changed over the past century, families continue to meet their members' basic economic, physical, and emotional needs.

In two-parent families, the responsibilities for these functions have often been divided between husband and wife, or more recently, are being redistributed between them. For example, in traditional families, the husband has primary responsibility for meeting the family's economic needs, whereas the wife sees to the family's physical needs. Social changes, including the women's movement and the increased employment of married mothers, have brought about a greater sharing of these roles.

In the single-parent family, these functions must be met without the support of a spouse, either by the single parent alone, or with help from other sources, including family, friends, or social agencies. When the single parent is the mother of a handicapped child, her ability to meet her family's needs is severely strained. In his study of support systems, Caplan (1974) has identified three characteristics of enduring supports such as families. These supports first of all provide the individual with material or financial assistance in coping with a situation; second, they share the persons's tasks; and third, they help the person bear his or her emotional burdens. In the case of single mothers with handicapped children, all three of these types of assistance become extremely important for the well-being of both the mother and the child.

The Single Mother's Economic Needs

As Bianchi (1981) has noted in her study of social differences in families' economic well-being, "living arrangements and economic relationships are so intertwined that the two must be considered in conjunction if reasonable social policy is to be formulated" (p.5). She notes that female-headed families with children are characterized by precarious financial circumstances: In 1981, 35% of female-headed families lived in poverty, more than three times the rate for all families. When Bane and Weiss (1980) studied the economic effects of marital disruption on mothers, they found that the women's family incomes dropped significantly when their married status changed—43% for divorced women, 51% for separated women, and 30% for widows. Only with remarriage do the income levels of these mothers approach the levels they had before their marriage ended.

Poverty is often associated with single-parent status for women, and it has often been questioned whether it is low income or the father's absence that is the major cause of stress for single mothers. In her study of 72 divorced and married mothers, Colletta (1983) found that low-income divorced mothers differed from moderate-income divorced mothers in overall stress, financial stress, child-rearing stress, stress associated with using community services, employment, and living arrangements. The mothers in Colletta's study worried about the effects of their employment on their children, and described how little time they had for themselves.

The question of how maternal employment affects single-mother families is important, because most single mothers with children now work—two thirds of mothers of school-age children, and one-half of mothers of preschool-age children. The presence of a handicapped child would seem to jeopardize seriously the single mother's ability to work, particularly when the child has many physical and health-care needs, and when trained caretakers are unavailable. Breslau, Salkever, and Staruch (1982) reported some rather surprising findings regarding the employment of mothers of severely handicapped children. Not surprisingly, they found that the mother's income and race and the severity of the child's disability were significantly related to the mother's employment. Low-income and black mothers of disabled children were less likely to work than mothers who were white and who had an income above the median, and mothers of more severely disabled children were less likely to work than mothers of less severely disabled children. However, the authors found that the presence of a disabled child had no impact on the labor force activity of single parents. The authors speculated that this may have been due to the small sample of single mothers in their study and the restricted variability of the group. Or it may be that the single mothers, because of their greater economic needs, may not be able to respond to the extra care demands of a disabled child by reducing their work hours. Their role as provider may also mean they have less time and energy to devote to their child's extra needs.

> I don't have time, since I work, to take part in his therapy, or to talk to his teachers.

These findings suggest that single mothers of handicapped children may have even less choice about whether or not to work than other single mothers. This would seem to place single mothers with handicapped children at an economic disadvantage. Yet work often offers single mothers noneconomic rewards as well as an income, these rewards including social and emotional respite and enhanced self-esteem. A national survey (National Opinion Research Center General Social Service Survey, cited in Weiss, 1979b) of married and unmarried working women found that working single mothers were more likely than married working mothers to say they would continue to work even if they didn't have to. As one single mother stated:

> I went to work because I needed the money. But partly I went to work for the sake of my sanity. (Weiss, 1979b, p. 21)

The respite from child care that work offers many single mothers is likely to be very important for the single mother of a handicapped child. Not only are the handicapped child's demands likely to be greater when the mother and child are together, but the child may not be able to contribute to satisfying parent-child interactions which reinforce the mother's efforts. As a result, the mother may not receive the emotional reinforcement that gives her the energy to sustain full-time involvement with the child.

The single mother's ability to work, if she has a preschool-age child, depends upon the availability of child care. The difficulty working mothers experience in arranging dependable, quality child care is well documented in anecdotal literature (Kamerman, 1980; Select Committee on Children, Youth, and Families, 1984). Even if a single mother is able to find specially trained, experienced child care for a handicapped preschool child, she may not be able to afford it. As the single mother of a handicapped infant explained:

> I tried to get someone else to care for her. . .but it was absolutely prohibitive. Through a private employment agency, the minimum salary for a baby nurse is about $85 a week. If I wanted someone like a trained nurse with real experience, the salary was closer to $150. Well, that was just out of the question. (Klein, 1973, p. 148)

Or even if the single mother can afford child care, she may not be able to find it.

> My ex-husband gives us sufficient money. I have enough leisure time—just not enough child care. His (the child's) grandparents feel he's too much for them. Occasionally other mothers with handicapped kids will trade with me, but I still worry about my sanity.

The single mother may find that she is able to cope with the caretaking and economic demands of raising a handicapped child only by living with parents or relatives, but, as one single mother notes, these living arrangements have their disadvantages.

> I live with my parents to make things easier for me, but my mother and I often disagree on what is best for my daughter.

The resources and motivation a single mother must have if she wishes to improve her ability to provide for her children are often more than an overly stressed mother is able to muster.

> I am going to school, so I have little time for anything but school and my child. I will finish school even if I have to drop out for a while because of my child's extended hospital stays.

The Single Mother's Physical Needs

Families also provide for the physical needs of members, particularly children. These responsibilities include meeting the child's needs for food, clothing, and medical care, as well as educating the child. The single mother's available time, energy, and financial situation will determine to a large extent how easily she can meet these needs. When a child is ill or is handicapped, these physical needs increase, and the single parent's ability to fill them may be taxed to the limit. In their British follow-up study of single mothers, Ferri and Robinson (1976) looked at the impact of illness on the family. They documented single mothers' often exaggerated fears about their children's health, which the authors attributed to the mothers' isolation.

> You worry about small things that you would never give a second thought to if you have a husband to share problems with. (p.50)

Weinraub and Wolf (1984) also reported the lower levels of parenting support and lower levels of satisfaction with that support in single mothers compared to married mothers. The single parent's sense of isolation may be heightened by fears about the child's health. The single mother of a handicapped child may experience chronic fears about her child's health. Without a spouse or an intimate source in whom to confide, it becomes very important that the single mother has others to turn to in order to manage her child's daily needs. This is supported by findings that parenting is positively associated with social support (Colletta, 1979; Pascoe, Loda, Jeffries, & Easp, 1981). In one of the few studies of single mothers, Weinraub and Wolf (1984) found that increased parenting support predicted optimal mother-child interaction in single-parent families. As Belsky (1984) has pointed out, these findings are important because the kinds of parenting that supported parents are found to provide has been related to child competence.

Responsive parenting is always a desirable goal but it may be particularly important for a young child with special needs. Infants with handicaps may present confusing signals to the parent, who may be uncertain how to respond, jeopardizing the parent-child relation. Young children with developmental delays often require extra stimulation or therapeutic interventions. Parents who are confident in their roles can better provide the extra patience and sensitivity these children need for optimal development (Cochran & Brassard, 1979). As the child matures, this parent confidence will manifest itself in the parent's ability to negotiate the maze of special education programs, and to find appropriate services for the child. As one divorced mother observed about her experiences:

> The most successful approach I've had as a parent is being persistent and knowledgeable. My most unsuccessful approach has been to be too emotional.

The Single Mother's Added Role Demands

In two-parent families, both parents contribute to the child's early education and socialization. Single mothers often have sole responsibility for these tasks. Studies on the effects of father absence upon child development report mixed findings, but there appears to be an association between paternal absence and poor cognitive performance in children. Possible mediating variables include low SES levels, high levels of anxiety in the home, and low levels of parent-child interaction (Ross & Sawhill, 1975; Shinn, 1979). In Herzog and Sudia's (1973) review of studies of father-absent families, many negative consequences of being raised in a fatherless family were found to be primarily due to the economic deprivation resulting from the father's absence. In some cases, the effect of the father's absence on the very young child's cognitive and social development may not be great, or, as Shinn (1979) states, "permanent father absence is simply the low end point on a continuum of father-child interaction" (p. 321). Other studies that report fathers spend surprisingly little time with their infants and young children (Ban & Lewis, 1974; Pleck, 1979; Robinson, 1977; Walker & Woods, 1976) suggest that young children in single-mother families may not experience significantly less paternal attention than children in two-parent families. Rather, the young child of the single mother may suffer more from maternal rather than paternal deprivation, because the single mother must often divide her time among many tasks in addition to child-rearing (Brandwein, Brown, & Fox, 1974). For example, divorced mothers have been found to spend less time with their children than mothers in intact families (Hetherington, Cox, & Cox, 1975). Based on their review of studies on the effects of father absence, Ross and Sawhill (1975) conclude that pathology is not a necessary consequence of a broken home. Evidence that financial hardship contributes significantly to a mother's ability to compensate for a father's absence and to negative child outcomes (Cashion, 1982; Ferri, 1976; Jauch, 1977; Robinson, 1977) strongly supports policies that would provide economic compensation to single mothers to offset the hardships and risks that have been reported.

Single mothers will experience added role demands within their families resulting from the absence of the child's father. It appears that their ability to provide financially for the family is likely to create the greatest stress, affecting their ability to meet their child's physical and emotional needs. McLanahan (1983) has reported that single mothers are more likely to experience chronic stress due to low income than male family heads. Her review of data from the Michigan Panel Study of Income Dynamics also revealed that female-headed families experience lower levels of social support, more acute stress from major life events, more negative self-images, and more negative views about the future than male family heads. Whereas some of these stresses may be associated with the transition from a married to a single state, other stresses are not time related but appear to be a function of the mother's single status.

Individuals will bring different personal resources to the role of the single mother, and some mothers may be able to cope with these role-strain stresses better than others. In Chapter 7, Dunst, Trivette, and Cross report that despite the increased role responsibilities the unmarried mothers in their sample experienced, the unmarried mothers also reported more satisfaction with how family roles were being performed than married mothers. The task remains for professionals to identify the practical aids and supports that some single mothers need to maintain their self-esteem and sense of competence in meeting their family's basic needs.

The Single Mother's Emotional Needs

Families not only provide for their members' physical needs for food, clothing, shelter, and education. They also meet each other's needs for affection, guidance, affirmation, and emotional nurturing. In the single mother's family, one adult becomes almost solely responsible for providing emotional support. This reduction in the sources of emotional sustenance within the family will affect both the mother and the child.

At the nuclear level, the child of a single mother experiences the loss of the paternal influence, including the contributions fathers have been found to make to the child's social and cognitive development (Shinn, 1979), as well as the second-order effects the child experiences from the father's influence on mother-child interactions. For example, fathers are found to positively influence the interactions of mothers with their premature infants (Hawthorne, Richards, & Callon, 1978; Herzog, 1979; Minde, Morton, Manning, & Hines, 1980; Tinsley, Johnson, Szczypka, & Parke, 1982), and in their absence, single mothers may be less responsive to a difficult-to-care-for child.

Single Mothers' Shifts in Support

Family size has effects upon the child as well as the single mother, and mothers of handicapped children are particularly vulnerable to the lack of a spouse's support. Parenting is influenced by the availability of personal supports, and the marital relationship appears to be a positive influence upon both parents' relations with their children (Belsky, 1984). In their study of mothers of pre-term and full-term infants, Crnic, Greenberg, Ragozin, Robinson, and Basham (1983) found that the availability of and the mothers' satisfaction with intimate support from their spouses was the most significant predictor of a married mother's positive attitude toward parenting, and the affect she demonstrated in face-to-face interaction with her infant. Cochran and Brassard (1979) have also pointed out the contributions fathers in two-parent families make to the family's available social networks; friends and relatives of the fathers often serve as social partners for children, and as models of nonparent adult behavior. These social influences are readily available in the two-parent family, whereas the single mother may have to make a greater effort to provide her child with adult role models and opportunities for varied social interactions.

Single mothers lack the intimate support from a spouse, but they may find supports from other family members and friends. In Chapter 7, Dunst, Trivette, and Cross report that the unmarried mothers compensated for a loss of support from the child's father and his family by finding alternative sources of support.

Because the single mother lacks the intimate support usually provided by the husband, she may turn toward her child to meet this need, and not surprisingly, strong bonds may develop between parent and child in the single-parent family. Elkind (1982) observes that single parents may be more likely than married parents to use their children as confidants. This may reduce the single parent's stress and isolation, but at the same time, increase the child's emotional burden. Weiss (1978) suggests that child and parent roles are affected by the single-parent family structure. Whereas parents in two-parent households provide each other with emotional and daily living support, parents in single-parent families depend on their children for some of this support. Polit (1980) also found that the divorced mothers she interviewed reported they derived important emotional support from their children during their initial separation from their husbands, and that they shared their feelings and problems with their children.

Based on interviews with over 200 single parents, Weiss (1979a) observed that children in single-parent families tend to grow up a little faster than children in two-parent families. Children in single-parent families more often assume roles as partners in decision making, as confidants to parents, and they assume household responsibilities that peers in two-parent families often do not assume until they are older. Weiss points out that these child changes are often functional for the parent, helping single parents cope with isolation, stress, and the burden of household chores. Weinraub and Wolf's (1984) study of 14 single mothers of preschool children and a group of matched married controls indicated that single working mothers were likely to place greater maturity demands on their children than employed married mothers. The single parent of a handicapped child will not be able to make these kinds of demands of her child, and rather than accepting that her child is more mature than peers in two-parent families, the single mother of a physically or mentally handicapped child must accept that her child will eventually fall behind peers in certain skills and domains.

Although the handicapped child may not be able adequately to fill the roles of confidant, partner, and helper to the single mother, the child's increased needs nonetheless contribute to high levels of cohesiveness in a single-parent family. Mink, Nihira, and Meyers (1983) studied 115 trainable mentally retarded children and their families to identify lifestyle patterns that could be related to family and child characteristics. They found that single-parent families tended to be child-oriented and expressive. They scored high on factors related to the child's well-being, such as pride, affection, warmth, language stimulation, and nonuse of physical punishment. They scored low on moral-religious emphasis, control, and concordance. Mink et al.'s (1983) findings indicate that the single parent may be able to provide a very nurturing environment for the handicapped child, although, in the process, the parent risks becoming highly enmeshed and isolated. The single mother of the handicapped child may need to sacrifice her personal development as the price for providing her child with the extra time, attention, and resources the child needs. As one divorced mother of a 12-year-old son with Down syndrome described:

> He loves to swim, to play ball, and he's terrific when we're doing things. But he only wants to be with me, and I'm worn out.

Although single mothers lack the intimate support married mothers share with their spouse, the single mother-child relationship may meet the mother's needs for affection and warmth, especially as the child grows older and is able to share more experiences with the mother. The handicapped child may not be able to provide that emotional feedback. Murphy (1981) shares the insights of a widow and mother of a 17-year-old retarded daughter, illustrating the isolation the single mother may experience.

> Speaking selfishly, what I miss is having someone around who loves me, who cares. My daughter has *me*. . .(she) still has her friends, but for me, well, here it is Saturday and another night at home. (p.183)

Friends and other family members may become important resources for the single mother, who may turn to them for help in child care and household chores, and for moral support. An unmarried mother of a child with cri-du-chat syndrome commented on her need for this personal support:

> It's not really the time I really need from them, but just that they care, that they ask about my daughter. . . . I think I'd like to have another child, but with a husband. I could have really used that moral support. But I have become stronger.

Or as the divorced mother of a child with Down syndrome confessed:

> I'm at the end of my rope. I'm not despondent, but I need to regroup my forces and pull myself together. In fact, I'm going to be selfish and insist one of my older children bail me out and take care of my son occasionally. I just wish I could have a week alone to pull myself together.

Peer support can be extremely valuable, yet as this divorced mother demonstrates, very difficult for a single parent to obtain.

> I have no other adult to get support from at this point. When I was divorced, the group of parents we worked with and saw frequently seemed to step back. It was almost as if they were afraid it would happen to them, and they'd be faced with raising their handicapped child alone. It was easy to give support when it was a problem we had in common.

Stress and the Single Mother

Like all roles, the parent's role has its associated role strains which are, in part, a function of the parent's and the child's changing needs. In two-parent families, these role strains are shared, and one parent may offer the other either instrumental or moral support when crises occur. Many parents experience role strains related to their child's developmental milestones—the colicky infant, the terrible two-year-old, the increasingly independent school-age child, the rebellious adolescent. When the child is handicapped, parents experience stress in the absence of these developmental milestones. The child does not walk or talk at the normal age, or requires individual therapy or extra attention to learn basic skills. Or the parent must accept that the child will never attain certain skills. The stresses triggered by these developmental and transition crises have been well described (see Blacher, 1984 for review). In the two-parent family, husband and wife face these chronic stresses and crises together. Both parents can work together to locate appropriate services, for example, and the advocate role is one that is often shared in families with handicapped children, if only because it often requires unflagging energy and commitment to meet a handicapped child's changing needs. The physical demands alone can be overwhelming, as the single mother of a 17-year-old severely handicapped daughter relates:

> The lifting in and out of wheelchairs, beds, and toilets is becoming an enormous problem as she gets bigger.

Behavior problems may compound the stress the parent of a handicapped child experiences. The mother of a 12-year-old child with Down syndrome candidly reflects:

> My son is spoiled and now I'm paying the price. His brothers and sisters spoil him too, but there's no one around to discipline him. He started acting up when he entered puberty, which was also when his father and I were divorced. Now he raises hell and acts as if he hates me. It's often a battle — very unpleasant, and not working. I'm worried about the mess I've made of him — he's gotten to be a brat.

Negotiating the maze of educational programs for a handicapped child can add to the single parent's stress:

> My concerns about her educational progress are already causing me nightmares. My daughter is in a program that's too advanced and she knows it. So in addition to my personal problems, I have a child whose self-esteem is going downhill, at home and at school. I haven't got enough of me left to keep her going and myself. I keep waiting for a second emotional wind. It was so much easier when she was small.

The single mother faces these stresses and strains alone. If the mother is separated or divorced, she may receive some support from the child's father, or she may receive support from relatives or friends. But she faces the daily routine stresses alone, including the underlying fears about the future and occasional doubts about her child's progress that all parents experience.

> My husband walked out and never ever gave a second thought to the continuing problems and decisions I'd have to deal with — he refuses to help.

> I had this friend with a daughter about Sally's age. For a while I didn't like her calling me up all the time and telling me what her daughter was doing. My daughter wasn't walking, and she would call and tell me how June was walking. I thought she was being really insensitive, but now it doesn't bother me.

In addition to the stresses the single mother faces in caring for her children, she may also face the stresses of a divorce or a separation. A study by Polit (1980) suggests that divorced mothers of only children experience their postdivorce transition with less stress than divorced mothers with two or three children. Polit's interviews with 90 divorced mothers revealed that the single mothers with only one child had fewer child-care problems, a greater likelihood of having a full-time job and correspondingly fewer financial problems, and less depression and anxiety than the divorced mothers with two or three children. Polit's findings have implications for mothers of handicapped children, who present greater than average demands on the mother's time and finances, as does a larger family. As Polit observes, small families are more manageable and make it easier for the mother to adjust to a divorce.

Divorce requires a similar emotional adjustment on the part of both husband and wife; in many cases, however, the wife faces significant economic stresses. Hill (1983) notes that long-term separated mothers rely more heavily on public assistance, whereas divorced mothers rely upon their own earnings (Bane and Weiss, 1980). Divorce often means a change in women's working status, with the percentage of mothers working increasing from 66 to 90% after divorce. Yet, despite this change in the mother's employment status, nearly one fourth of children who lose a father through separation or divorce fall into poverty (Duncan & Morgan, 1976). One single mother of a two-year-old handicapped child and two other children describes her dilemma:

> Without SSI and welfare, I wouldn't be able to afford my child's surgery, so I worry about being able to afford what he needs when I start working.

Implications for Policies for Single Mothers

Any work on families written today would be incomplete without a discussion of single mothers, because of their increasing numbers and the difficult problems many of them face. This chapter provided a profile of these families and the most urgent problems faced by the growing population of single mothers. Limited data on single mothers of handicapped children were reviewed, and anecdotal data were presented to draw attention to their special needs. From this brief review, implications for general policies for single mothers emerge which would also address the more complex needs of single mothers with handicapped children. In addition, research priorities are suggested which would clarify the particular needs and strengths of single mothers with a handicapped child, as well as support the benefits of policies implemented to support their roles. A high priority for future research would be to determine the numbers of families with handicapped children that are headed by single parents, and to use these data as a base for planning. More detailed demographic data on these families, such as the mothers' employment status and income levels, are needed to better understand what specific programs, such as income allowances or subsidized child care, will be of most benefit. Future research on this growing population and its needs will contribute to informed and responsive family policy.

Kamerman (1983) makes the important point, in her review on family policies which support expanded roles for fathers, that a responsive social policy for families must value the family as a major social institution—"all families, not just one particular type, be it single-parent families, inadequate families, poor or deprived families" (pp. 29-30). She suggests an agenda for an androgynous family policy, which she describes as "one addressing family needs and roles, including parenting, rather than specific concerns for fathers or mothers" (p. 30). According to Kamerman, a public policy for families should: (a) support the economic roles of parents, and (b) support the nurturing and caretaking roles of parents. Further, policy-makers must recognize that most parents today must find ways to fill both roles. Kamerman's agenda certainly applies as well to policies for the single mother. Her agenda would encourage social service professionals to recognize single-mother-headed families as legitimate family forms, and to appreciate the particularly heavy responsibilities these mothers face.

Economic Roles

The demographic data make clear that the single mother's economic position is often a difficult one. As was pointed out in the 1984 Select Committee's report on children and families, female family heads who work full time, year-round have a median income that is 58% of the median income for married-couple families. Bianchi (1981) has stressed that families' living arrangements and economic relationships are so inseparable that they must be considered together in formulating social policy. She concluded that the precarious position of female-headed families merits governmental action to insure the financial support of children in these families. She described the disadvantages of the most widely available source, Aid to Families with Dependent Children, and suggested alternatives, including a taxed, guaranteed maintenance payment to all single-parent families, or tax incentives that would enable a parent of a young child to pay back an annual government loan through higher taxes spread out over a lifetime. Bianchi notes the quite developed economic policies for single-parent families in many European countries that merit closer examination by U.S. policymakers. Bane, Wilson, and Baer (1983) in their analysis of public spending on children and families have suggested that the United States should have a large-scale insurance program for children, similar to those in place in European countries, or to the Social Security program that provides for the elderly in this country. Family housing allowances which have been implemented in Sweden and in France would also assist many middle- and low-income single parents, for whom housing costs represent a major family expense. These programs should be neutral in the sense that they would not favor a particular family style, but would insure the welfare of all children.

The majority of mothers today work. What this means for these women is increased stress and pressures which they must meet by reducing the time they could otherwise spend with their children, on household tasks, or on leisure activities. The stress increases with the single mother's increased economic needs, and, with the presence of a handicapped child, with the child's increased caretaking needs. Policies which would reduce sex discrimination in employment and decrease the wage differentials between male and female workers would significantly benefit these families. These are policies that would reflect that women today are no longer secondary earners, but either contribute significantly to a two-parent family income or are solely supporting their family. Moen, Kain, and Elder (1983), in their analysis of how economic conditions affect family life, describe findings on how economic change affects a parent's sense of personal control. Increasing income levels for working women is a long-term goal that will have an immediate effect on women's self-esteem and, as Moen et al. (1983) point out, an indirect effect upon parent-child interactions.

Other policies would reduce the burdens that single working mothers experience. Flexible working hours, and employee benefits such as sick leave, vacation entitlements, and health insurance, not only enhance the quality of life for the single-parent family; these supports and benefits often determine whether a single mother is able to support her family on her income or must seek welfare. These policies would also acknowledge the working mother's responsibilities to her family, and this recognition alone on behalf of employers would provide intangible support. Finally, divorced or separated mothers would benefit from increased contributions from the child's father, based upon his ability to pay child support.

Nurturing and Caretaking Roles

The majority of single mothers work and therefore require some type of child-care services. A wide range of affordable quality child care is probably the most pressing need for these families. This would include licensed family day care for young infants, center-based preschool programs, after-school programs for school-age children, and supervised after-school programs for the often overlooked latchkey children ages 11 and older. Kamerman (1980) has documented, in parents' own words, the very difficult task of locating and affording child care. In the Select Committee's (1984) report, it was noted that U.S. Department of Agriculture studies found that day care costs represent 8-9% of the average single mother's expenses. The single working mother's efforts to secure reliable day care are almost always much more difficult than the married working mother's, because her income is more limited, she does not have a husband who can help out when arrangements fall through, and she often has a job that offers minimal or no sick leave, vacation, or health-care benefits. In many cases, children in these families lack access to adequate medical care, particularly when the mother is not Medicade-eligible and lacks group coverage through an employer-sponsored health plan. This results in poor preventive care and other high, unplanned, out-of-pocket expenses.

The young unmarried working mothers with minimal education who work in the hospitality, health-care, or service sectors of the economy face the added challenge of arranging day care outside the traditional 8 to 5, Monday through Friday time-frame. Employer-sponsored on-site day care is certainly one solution to this problem. Not only would this permit mothers to spend time with their child during commuting and during the day (their lunch hours, coffee breaks), it would also reduce their transportation time and costs to and from a day care site, and increase the total time available for themselves and their children. These are not insignificant matters in families that must ration time and money very carefully. Increased subsidized child care that is available on a sliding-fee scale is also needed to assist low-income mothers. Most important, as the Select Committee on Children, Youth, and Families (1984) recommended, parents should have child-care options to choose from to meet each family's needs and preferences.

The single mother of a handicapped child will have special child-care needs. The most obvious needs concern the handicapped child, and enrollment in an early intervention program or school-based program, together with respite care, are most often provided through state or federal programs for the developmentally disabled. Respite care is always a high priority for single mothers, as the research has indicated, and service providers, in their efforts to locate trained respite services for the handicapped child, often overlook the need to coordinate this with child care for other children in the family. The single mother needs some time away from all of her children, as well as time out from caring for her handicapped child, and she is often unable to afford this luxury.

Kamerman (1983) emphasizes that working parents most urgently need support balancing their dual roles. As examples of responsive policies, she notes the liberal parental leave policies of European countries, including annual paid sick leave to care for a sick child. Also included in this area are flextime, part-time jobs, alternate work schedules, and flexplace for workers in fields where the technology permits them to do some of their work at home.

Special Considerations for Single Mothers of Handicapped Children

Policies for families of handicapped children are often designed to help parents in their roles as caretakers and educators for the handicapped child. Yet these parents also assume multiple roles. In two-parent families, these roles are often shared between the mother and father, whereas the single mother will be primarily responsible for all of these roles—she is parent of the handicapped child, parent of her other non-handicapped children, housekeeper, cook, and chief or sole economic provider. Policies that are designed with the needs of the handicapped child in mind are often not coordinated with those that would enable the single mother to fulfill her other roles. Because the single mother must often so delicately balance these roles, it is particularly important that her multiple responsibilities be kept in mind. For example, transportation to and from her children's schools or day care, or housekeeping or laundry assistance may be critical needs if she is to maintain a full-time job. Yet these are services that are often unavailable. The strains of running a household without help have been documented in several studies of divorced mothers (Colletta, 1983; Hetherington, Cox, & Cox, 1976), and these are strains that will be more severe when the mother cares for a handicapped child. As Wikler (1979) has pointed out, single mothers should be given a priority for respite care. To reduce risks of extreme isolation, support groups should be made available to single parents, again keeping in mind the special accommodations that will be have to be made for working mothers, including scheduling and child care. Some single mothers may find that existing parent support groups meet their needs, whereas other single mothers may welcome opportunities to discuss their special concerns with other single parents. Due to the small numbers of single mothers in any single program, staff may try to form support groups which serve the single parents from clusters of child programs within a region.

Research Needs

Finally, as Kamerman (1983) notes, there is a need to evaluate new and revised policies to determine how they influence the quality of life for single mothers and their children. As she points out, supportive policies are assumed to have positive consequences, but their differential impact on families of various income levels, employment status, and family size is far from understood. For example, the needs of younger never-married single mothers may differ from those of separated or divorced single mothers, as resources will differ and their support systems are likely to include different constellations of family members. As Polit's (1980) study of divorced single mothers suggests, the mother's experience is likely to be influenced by the number of children, and family size will have an even more powerful effect on the single mother of a special-needs child, as well as upon the child's siblings. Differences in mothers' education and employment status will strongly influence their ability to meet their family's economic needs.

The mother's role orientation will also influence the kinds of supports and networks a single mother will find most beneficial. In their interviews with 45 divorced mothers, McLanahan, Wedemeyer, and Adelberg (1981) found the effects of the mothers' social supports and family network structure on their psychological well-being was mediated by their role-orientation. Mothers who were classified as stabilizers and who wished to maintain their predivorce roles found the most support from close-knit networks, whereas changers, mothers who were trying to establish a new identity, fared better in loose-knit networks. The authors noted that the mother's role-orientation will change over time, and that supports and services should be tailored to the individual's needs.

Policies also need to be evaluated for the broader impact they will have on extended family systems. For example, although most single mothers are heads of their households, Bane and Ellwood's (1984a) recent analyses show that an increasing number of young unmarried mothers are living with family members. It is not known how many single mothers with handicapped children fall into this category, but when they do, the strains that are involved in caring for a child with special needs will be distributed across the household. This phenomenon demonstrates the adaptiveness of families in the face of unusual economic and emotional pressures. Rather than penalize mothers who have access to a nurturing, cohesive family, policies should aim to strengthen the single mothers in these subfamilies so that the entire family system can continue to sustain itself. This trend in living arrangements underlines the impact the handicapped child may have upon a family's composition and economic situation, the interplay of which Moen, Kain, and Elder (1983) have described. Public policies often have unforeseen effects upon living arrangements, as Ellwood and Bane (1984) concluded. They estimated models to study aggregate state data over time, controlling for unmeasured state effects, and examined the association between AFDC benefit levels and living arrangements, divorce and separation, and childbearing. They found that a $100 increase in AFDC benefit levels would have a very minor impact on family structure, but a more significant impact on family living arrangements. A $100 AFDC increase was estimated to result in an increase of only 5% in births to unmarried women. A $100 increase in benefits, however, was predicted to reduce the number of children living with their single mothers in a subfamily arrangement by 25% to 30%. Ellwood and Bane's conclusions have implications for deciding social policies that will affect single mothers, and they bear repeating:

> We have found that welfare does influence behavior. . .more when the significance of the family or living arrangement is small. . . . The next step seems to be to understand the significance of those events which welfare does indeed influence. . .[because] policy can play a major role in the living arrangements of single mothers. Policymakers need to know what difference living arrangements make to both mother and children. With such knowledge, policies can be designed which may help single mothers and their offspring. (pp. 67-68)

Ellwood and Bane's analysis demonstrates the value of an ecological social research perspective, one that takes in the family system in any study of an individual family member's behavior and experiences. This perspective is needed to generate the information for planning policies to support single mothers and the family and community networks in which they are imbedded. Single mothers most obviously lack the major family support of a male parent. Yet if we focus only on how these single-parent families differ from traditional two-parent families, we may set ourselves up to find pathology and deviance, and may overlook their successful and innovative adaptations. For example, Polit (1980) notes that she and her colleagues approached their research on single-parent families with the important assumption that the woman's family role can no longer be defined solely in terms of her relationship with men, lest we overlook the woman's strengths and adaptiveness. The degree to which single mothers adapt to their family configuration will determine their needs and suggest positive coping strategies that can be applied by other single mothers. Then, where intrafamily and community supports are inadequate, professionals can propose direct services and interventions that reflect the actual needs of these new family systems.

References

Appell, M.A., & Tisdall, W.J. (1968). Factors differentiating institutionalized from non-institutionalized referred retardates. *American Journal of Mental Deficiency, 73*, 424-432.

Ban, P.L., & Lewis, M. (1974). Mothers and fathers, girls and boys: Attachment behavior in the one-year-old. *Merrill-Palmer Quarterly, 20*, 195-204.

Bane, M.J. (1976). Marital disruption and the lives of children. *Journal of Social Issues, 32*, 103-117.

Bane, M.J., & Ellwood, D. T. (1984a). *The dynamics of children's living arrangements* (Working paper supported by U.S. Department of Health and Human Services, Contract No. HHS - 92A-82). Harvard University, Cambridge, MA.

Bane, M.J., & Ellwood, D.T. (1984b). *Single mothers and their living arrangements* (Working paper supported by U.S. Department of Health and Human Services, Contract No. HHS-100-82-0038). Harvard University, Cambridge, MA.

Bane, M.J., & Weiss, R.S. (1980, May). Alone together: The world of single-parent families. *American Demographics,* 11-15, 48.

Bane, M.J., Wilson, J.B., & Baer, N. (1983). Trends in public spending on children and their families. In R.R. Nelson & F. Skidmore (Eds.), *American families and the economy* (pp. 109-144). Washington, DC: National Academy Press.

Bayley, M. (1973). *Mental handicap and community care.* Boston: Routlege & Kegan Paul.

Beckman, P.J. (1983). Influence of selected child characteristics on stress in families of handicapped infants. *American Journal of Mental Deficiency, 88*, 150-156.

Belsky, J. (1984). The determinants of parenting: A process model. *Child Development, 55*, 83-96.

Bianchi, S.M. (1981). *Household composition and racial inequality.* New Brunswick, NJ: Rutgers University Press.

Blacher, J. (1984). Sequential stages of parental adjustment to the birth of a child with handicaps: Fact or artifact? *Mental Retardation, 22*, 55-68.

Brandwein, R.A., Brown, C.A., & Fox, E.M. (1974, August). Women and children last: The social situation of divorced mothers and their families. *Journal of Marriage and Family,* 498-514.

Breslau, N., Salkever, D., & Staruch, K. (1982). Women's labor force activity and responsibilities for disabled dependents: A study of families with disabled children. *Journal of Health and Social Behavior, 23*, 169-183.

Bronfenbrenner, U. (1976). The family circle: A study in fragmentation. *National Elementary Principal, 55*, 11-25.

Caplan, G. (1974). *Support systems and community mental health.* New York: Behavioral Publications.

Cashion, B. G. (1982). Female-headed families: Effects on children and clinical implications. *Journal of Marital and Family Therapy, 8*, 77-85.

Cochran, M., & Brassard, J. (1979). Child development and personal social networks. *Child Development, 50*, 601-616.

Colletta, N. (1979). Support systems after divorce: Incidence and impact. *Journal of Marriage and the Family, 41*, 837-846.

Colletta, N.D. (1983). Stressful lives: The situation of divorced mothers and their children. *Journal of Divorce, 6,* 19-31.

Crnic, K.A., Greenberg, M.T., Ragozin, A.S., Robinson, N.M., & Basham, R. (1983). Effects of stress and social support on mothers and premature and full-term infants. *Child Development, 54,* 209-217.

Duncan, G.J., & Morgan, J.N. (1976). Young children and "other" family members. In G.J. Duncan & J.N. Morgan (Eds.), *Five thousand American families—Patterns of economic progress* (Vol. 6, pp. 155-182). Ann Arbor, MI: Institute for Social Research.

Elkind, D. (1982). Parental stresses: Their detrimental effects on the emotional well-being of children. *International Journal of Sociology of the Family, 12,* 275-283.

Ellwood, D.T., & Bane, M.J. (1984). *The impact of AFDC on family structure and living arrangements* (Working paper supported by U.S. Department of Health and Human Services Contract No. 92A-82). Harvard University, Cambridge, MA.

Farber, B. (1968). *Mental retardation: Its social context and social consequences.* Boston: Houghton Mifflin.

Ferri, E. (1976). *Growing up in a one-parent family: A long-term study of child development.* Windsor, Great Britain: NFER Publishing.

Ferri, E., & Robinson, H. (1976). *Coping alone.* Windsor, Great Britain: NFER Publishing.

German, M.L., & Maisto, A.T. (1982, February). The relationship of a perceived family support system to the institutional placement of mentally retarded children. *Education and Training of the Mentally Retarded,* 17-23.

Glick, P.C., & Norton, A.J. (1973). Perspectives on the recent upturn in divorce and remarriage. *Demography, 10,* 301-314.

Graliker, B., Koch, R., & Henderson, M. (1965). A study of factors influencing placement of retarded children in a state residential institution. *American Journal of Mental Deficiency, 69,* 553-559.

Hawthorne, J.T., Richards, M.P., & Callon, M.A. (1978). A study of potential visiting of babies in a special care unit. In F.S.W. Brimblecombe, M.P.M. Richards, & N.R.C. Robertson (Eds.), *Early separation and special care nurseries* (Clinics in Developmental Medicine). London: SIMP/Heinemann Medical Books.

Herzog, R., & Sudia, C.E. (1973). Children in fatherless families. In B. M. Caldwell & H. N. Ricciuti (Eds.), *Review of child development research* (Vol. 3). Chicago: University of Chicago Press.

Herzog, J.M. (1979). Disturbances in parenting high-risk infants: Clinical impressions and hypotheses. In T.M. Field (Ed.), *Infants born at risk: Behavior and development.* New York: S.P. Medical & Scientific Books.

Hetherington, E. M., Cox, M., & Cox, R. (1975, April). *Beyond father absence: Conceptualization of effects of divorce.* Paper presented at the meeting of the Society for Research in Child Development, Denver, CO.

Hetherington, E.M., Cox, M., & Cox, R. (1976). *The aftermath of divorce.* Paper presented at the meeting of the American Psychological Association, Washington, DC.

Hill, M.S. (1983). Trends in the economic situation of U.S.families and children: 1970-1980. In R.R. Nelson & F. Skidmore (Eds.), *American families and the economy: The high costs of living* (pp. 9-58). Washington, DC: National Academy Press.

Hobbs, M.A. (1964). A comparison of institutionalized and non-institutionalized mentally retarded. *American Journal of Mental Deficiency, 69,* 206-210.

Holmes, T.H., & Rahe, R.H. (1967). The Social Readjustment Rating Scale. *Journal of Psychosomatic Research, 11,* 213-218.

Holroyd, J. (1974). The Questionnaire on Resources and Stress: An instrument to measure family response to a handicapped member. *Journal of Community Psychology, 2,* 92-94.

Jauch, C. (1977). The one-parent family. *Journal of Clinical Child Psychology, 6,* 30-32.

Kamerman, S.B. (1983). Fatherhood and social policy: Some insights from a comparative perspective. In M.E. Lamb & A. Sagi (Eds.), *Fatherhood and family policy* (pp. 23-37). Hillsdale, NJ: Erlbaum.

Kamerman, S.B. (1980). *Parenting in an unresponsive society: Managing work and family.* New York: Free Press.

Klein, C. (1973). *The single parent experience.* New York: Walker.

McLanahan, S. (1983). Family structure and stress: A longitudinal comparison of two-parent and female-headed families. *Journal of Marriage and the Family, 45,* 347-357.

McLanahan, S. S., Wedemeyer, N. V., & Adelberg, T. (1981). Network structure, social support, and psychological well-being in the single-parent family. *Journal of Marriage and the Family, 43,* 601-612.

Minde, K.K., Marton, P., Manning, D., & Hines, B. (1980). Some determinants of mother-infant interaction in the premature nursery. *American Academy of Child Psychiatry Journal, 19,* 1-21.

Mink, I.T., Nihira, K., & Meyers, C.E. (1983). Taxonomy of family life styles: I. Homes with TMR children. *American Journal of Mental Deficiency, 87,* 484-497.

Moen, P., Kain, E.L., & Elder, G.H. (1983). Economic conditions and family life: Contemporary and historical perspectives. In R.R. Nelson & F. Skidmore (Eds.), *American families and the economy* (pp. 213-259). Washington, DC: National Academy Press.

Moore, J.A., Hamerlynck, L.A., Barsh, E.T., Spieker, S., & Jones, R.R. (1982, December). *Extending family resources.* (Available from Children's Clinic and Preschool, 1850 Boyer Avenue East, Seattle, WA 98112).

Murphy, A.T. (1981). *Special children, special parents: Personal issues with handicapped children.* Englewood Cliffs, NJ: Prentice-Hall.

National Center for Health Statistics. (1978). Divorces and divorce rates, United States. *Vital and Health Statistics,* Series 21, No. 29. Washington, DC: U.S. Government Printing Office.

National Center for Health Statistics. (1980). Remarriages of women 15-44 years of age whose first marriage ended in divorce: United States, 1976. *Advance Data, 58,* February 14. Public Health Service, U.S. Department of Health, Education, and Welfare.

National Center for Health Statistics. (1981). Advance report of final natality statistics, 1979. *Monthly Vital Statistics Report, 30*(6), Supplement.

National Center for Health Statistics. (1984, September). Advance report of final natality statistics, 1982. *Monthly Vital Statistics Report, 33*(6). Supp. DHHS

Pub. No. (PHS) 84-1120. Hyattsville, MD: Public Health Service.

Pascoe, J.M., Loda, F.A., Jeffries, V., & Easp, J.A. (1981). The association between mother's social support and provision of stimulation to their children. *Developmental and Behavioral Pediatrics, 2,* 15-19.

Pleck, J.H. (1979). Men's family work: Three perspectives and some new data. *The Family Coordinator, 28,* 481-488.

Polit, D.F. (1980). *The one-parent/one-child family: Social and psychological consequences.* (Available from the Institute on Women and Families, American Institutes for Research, 22 Hilliard St., Cambridge, MA, 02138).

Robinson, J.P. (1977). *How Americans use time.* New York: Praeger.

Rosenthal, K.M., & Keshet, H.F. (1981). *Fathers without partners: A study of fathers and the family after marital separation.* Totowa, NJ: Rowman & Littlefield.

Ross, H.L., & Sawhill, I.V. (1975). *Time of transition: The growth of families headed by women.* Washington, DC: The Urban Institute.

Saenger, G. (1960). *Factors influencing the institutionalization of mentally retarded individuals in New York City: A study of the effects of services, personnel characteristics, and family background on the decision to institutionalize.* Albany, NY: New York State Department of Health Resources Board.

Schorr, A.L., & Moen, P. (1979). The single parent and public policy. *Social Policy, 9,* 15-21.

Select Committee on Children, Youth, and Families. (1984). *Children, youth, and families: 1983 a year-end report.* Washington, DC: U.S. House of Representatives.

Shellhaas, M.D., & Nihira, K. (1969). Factor analysis of reasons retardates are referred to an institution. *American Journal of Mental Deficiency, 74,* 171-179.

Shinn, M. (1979). Father absence and children's cognitive development. In S. Chess & A. Thomas (Eds.), *Annual progress in child psychiatry and child development.* New York: Brunner/Mazel.

Survey Research Center. (1984). *User's guide to the panel study of income dynamics.* Ann Arbor, MI: Institute for Social Research.

Tinsley, B.R., Johnson, P., Szczypka, D., & Parke, R.D. (1982, March). *Reconceptualizing the social environment of the high risk infant: Fathers and settings.* Paper presented at the International Conference on Infant Studies, Austin, TX.

U.S. Bureau of the Census. (1983). *American women: Three decades of change* (Special Demographic Analyses, CDS-80-8). Washington, DC: U.S. Government Printing Office.

U.S. Bureau of the Census. (1984). *Household and family characteristics: March 1983* (Current Population Reports Series P-20, No. 388). Washington, DC: U.S. Government Printing Office.

U.S. Department of Labor. (1983). *Children of working mothers* (Bureau of Labor Statistics, Special Labor Force Report, Bulletin 2158).

Walker, K., & Woods, M. (1976). *Time use.* Washington, DC: American Home Economics Association.

Wattenberg, E., & Reinhardt, H. (1979, November). Female- headed families: Trends and implications. *Social Work,* pp. 460-467.

Weinraub, M., & Wolf, B.M. (1983). Effects of stress and social supports on mother-child interactions in single- and two-parent families. *Child Development,* 54, 1297-1311.

Weiss, R. S. (1979a). Growing up a little faster: The experience of growing up in a single-parent household. *Journal of Social Issues, 35,* 7-111.

Weiss, R.S. (1979b). *Going it alone: The family life and social situation of the single parent.* New York: Basic Books.

Weiss, R.S. (1978). *Single-parent households as settings for growing up.* Paper presented at the National Institute of Mental Health Conference, Washington, DC.

Wikler, L. (1979). *Single parents of mentally retarded children: A neglected population.* Paper presented at the American Association of Mental Deficiency, Miami, FL.

Author's Note

The author would like to thank Ms. Judith A. Moore, Director of Children's Clinic and Preschool for sharing comments of single mothers who participated in the Extending Family Resources Project (Moore, Hamerlynck, Barsh, Spieker, & Jones, 1982); the single mothers who participated in workshops sponsored by the Supporting Extended Family Members (SEFAM) programs; Cathleen Tooley Moeller for sharing her interviews with single mothers; and Dr. Joseph R. Jenkins for his thoughtful review and comments.

PART II

Extrafamilial Supports

10

Family Support in Public School Programs

Linda Espinosa and Marsha Shearer

Subsequent to the enactment of Public Law 94-142, the Education for All Handicapped Children Act, the public schools have become responsible for providing an appropriate educational program and required related services to all school-age children with handicapping conditions. The vast array of services included under the rubric of "related services" extends to "transportation, and such developmental, corrective and other supportive services. . .as may be required to assist a handicapped child to benefit from special education" (Sec. 4A, Section 602). The specific services identified under this provision of the federal law include: early identification and assessment, school health services, social work services, and family counseling if needed.

The school is viewed as the institution responsible for managing the child's entire educational program and guaranteeing that if the child or family is in need of additional supportive services, such as family counseling or parent training, the school district will arrange for those services without charge to the parents or student. Thus, under state and federal laws, public schools are responsible for many services which could be classified as family support services. The purpose of this chapter is to discuss both the theory and the reality of family support provided through the public schools.

In Part 1 of this chapter, we will describe the context in which families receive support from public school programs. This description will include a discussion of the kinds of supports that schools provide, the factors affecting supports parents receive from schools, and the changing nature of families' needs for supports. As we will point out, and as others in this volume document more fully (see Chapters 1 and 2 by Fewell and Meyer, respectively), family needs are not static. The needs of a family of a preschooler are quite different from those of a family of a teenager. In Part 2 we will focus on the specific educational supports to which parents and children have access.

Part 1. The Context of Family Support

A public school program or local educatioñal agency (LEA) is a tax-supported institution governed by local, state, and federal educational rules and regulations. It is a local and state responsibility, under both state and federal constitutions, to guarantee that every child residing within district borders receives an educational program. According to Marion (1981), the primary function of education in the United States is to prepare citizens for occupational roles. In addition, the educational mission includes the preservation of culture and preparation for participation in the democratic process.

Families with handicapped children have many social, medical psychological, and educational needs. They also have rights and are entitled to certain services and protections under federal law. The Education for All Handicapped Children Act, P.L. 94-142, provides for parents' participation in their child's educational program through guaranteeing the following rights:

1. *Due process*: All parents are provided protection in the identification, evaluation, and placement of their children. Parents may challenge the educational decisions made by school officials.
2. *Individualized educational program (IEP)*: Parents have the right to be involved in the development of the IEP for their child, which must include individualized short- and long-term educational goals, describe all services to be provided, and be reviewed at least annually.
3. *Notification and consent*: Parents must be notified of all evaluation and placement decisions, and have the right to give or withhold consent for initial evaluation and placement.
4. *Access*: Parents have the right to review all relevant school records pertaining to their child's educational program.

5. *Participation*: Parents have the right to participate on state advisory boards and in public hearings on state rules and regulations and state special education plans.

States or local school systems that are found in noncompliance with the provisions of P.L. 94-142 may have their federal special education funds withheld.

As is evident, the federal law is designed to guarantee every handicapped student equal protection and equal educational opportunity. The law identifies the parents of the student as critical participants who can and should be involved in educational decision-making. The intent is to form a partnership between parents and school officials where the guiding principle is the child's welfare. Many of the provisions respond to the historical neglect and discriminatory treatment of children with handicapping conditions in this nation's school systems.

P.L. 94-142 is a product of this context of historical grievances, and its legalistic framework and requirement of extensive parent involvement are attempts to correct inequalities in educating the handicapped. It is not surprising that these guidelines for an enlightened educational system have often resulted in legal disputes, with school officials lined up on one side, and parents on the other. Thus, while the intent and provisions of P.L. 94-142 should guarantee that families of handicapped children receive extensive support from the school system, the implementation has been less than perfect. Federal funding has never reached the originally authorized levels.

The Education for All Handicapped Children Act was passed in 1975 and was to be fully implemented by 1980. We have had five short years to measure the law's impact on services to families of handicapped children. There is some evidence that implementation in the early stages was more troublesome than in more recent years. As parents became aware of their rights and identified needed supportive services for their children, they often requested services that many school districts were not prepared or responsible to deliver. School districts have had to develop administrative procedures, hire and train a wide variety of specialists, implement new educational models, and find the fiscal resources to make necessary changes in their special education programs.

Consequently, the research reported before 1982 in the literature and reviewed below identifies many more problems and concerns related to how the schools provide support to parents than does more recent research. This trend became particularly striking when parents of children with special needs were interviewed during the preparation of this chapter. The experiences of parents of adolescents whose children began school 8-12 years ago are much different than the experiences of parents whose children are currently enrolled in a preschool or early primary program.

Factors Affecting Public School Support

The amount of support that a parent of a handicapped child receives from a public school agency will vary according to a complex set of inter-related factors. A parent in Boston, Massachusetts is necessarily going to have different experiences with a large eastern, urban school system than a parent in a rural mountain town. These differences occur despite standardized federal guidelines which all educational agencies must follow.

Size and location of district or school. School districts with a large student population and a correspondingly large funding-base are usually able to offer more specialized resources than smaller districts in the education of handicapped children. It has been estimated that 1.5 million handicapped children live in America's rural areas (Halpern, 1982). These small, sparsely populated districts have historically had difficulties providing educational and related services for handicapped children. Halpern has identified the following areas as particularly troublesome to rural districts:

- recruiting and maintaining qualified staff (often salaries are lower in rural areas than in urban areas)
- transporting children over long distances
- meeting the needs of children with low-incidence handicaps
- providing highly trained specialists
- meeting higher per-child costs

There is some evidence (Hodge, 1980) that rural districts have significantly increased both the number of children being served and the amount of related services provided to those children. Small rural districts still face unique problems in fully implementing P.L. 94-142, often because of the higher costs associated with providing specialized services to a small number of children (Halpern, 1982). In her survey of 200 rural school systems, Helge (1984) found that the major problems special education administrators reported were funding inadequacies (74%), difficulties recruiting and retaining qualified staff (66% and 64%), and transportation inadequacies (60%).

Although families in rural areas must often face these problems of access to local services, higher poverty levels than nonrural areas, and more expensive service costs than urban families, they also may benefit from closer family and community ties that help them cope (Helge, 1984). Fewell (1984) compared mothers of children with Down syndrome living in rural areas (population less than 2,600) to mothers living in urban areas (population greater than 2,600). First, she found urban mothers ($n = 59$), reporting on a questionnaire, had significantly higher scores ($p < .05$) on items related to frustration in obtaining and using educational services than did rural mothers ($n = 18$). Second, rural mothers reported significantly greater ($p < .01$) family support from parents and relatives than urban mothers.

In addition, there are certain precedents and mandates that have developed within states, counties, and localities that affect the types of services that are available. A state may have identified parent counseling and education as a priority and may have set aside discretionary funds to hire social workers. Within that state, parent counseling may be readily available and frequently provided. Local districts may also apply for special state and federal funds to operate model programs.

Many model or demonstration programs emphasize the need to provide additional parent and family supports. For instance, all of the 40-60 federally funded Handicapped Children's Early Education Projects (HCEEP) have extensive parent involvement and parent training-education components. Therefore, a parent in a southern California city may receive counseling, parenting classes, and free babysitting by virtue of a special state or federal grant, while a northern California parent may be offered very little support from the school system. Although the HCEEP projects are mandated by law to provide for parent participation, the nature of parent involvement across projects varies considerably. Hocutt and Wiegerink (1983) surveyed third-year HCEEP projects to determine the actual implementation of this parent involvement component. The operational definition of parent involvement included four services for parents: direct parent training; passive educational and therapeutic activities (parents receiving reports, counseling related to child); active educational and therapeutic activities (parents acting as change agents for their child); and planning, development, operation, and evaluation of the project. The authors found that the 28 projects surveyed reported highest involvement in the passive educational and therapeutic activities (59% of parents participating) and parent-training activities (59%), and lowest involvement in planning, development, operation, and evaluation activities. Projects sponsored by public schools had lower levels of involvement than those sponsored by private, nonprofit organizations. The authors relate this finding to the fact that the public schools tend to focus on the child rather than the family, and to emphasize practices that enhance professional development. When the authors surveyed project parents regarding their satisfaction with project services, they found that the projects with the highest proportions of least satisfied parents were affiliated with public schools and were parents of multiply handicapped children. A much higher proportion of the more satisfied parents (73%) reported that they had an ability to influence their child's school program compared to the least satisfied parents (6%). Hocutt and Wiegerink's findings suggest that parents are often excluded from decision-making activities that influence their child's educational program, and that parents who are given a role in these activities are more satisfied, and perhaps more involved, in turn, than parents who are excluded from decision-making or policy concerns.

Funding structure of district or state. All states have a funding formula that governs the disbursement of educational funds for local districts to provide educational programs for handicapped students. The eligibility criteria and method of determining the rate of funding vary widely among states. The funding ratios will determine, to some extent, the number of teachers, psychologists, counselors, aides, and other support personnel who will be available to students and families. The additional local revenue that may be generated in any given city also varies widely according to local and state law.

American school systems have been affected by the recent tax revolts, economic recession, and shifting federal role in educational funding. It is clear that fully implementing P.L. 94-142 is costly (Price & Goodman, 1980), and that in an era of budget austerity school systems often cannot provide a full range of supportive services. It is also clear that state and local funding priorities shape and influence the resources available to handicapped children and their families. Therefore, the level of resources allocated for special education, the method of distributing those resources, and the identified priorities will all influence whether or not a family receives support, and the level of support available. For example, as Vadasy and Fewell point out in Chapter 5, federal funds may be targeted to serve certain groups of handicapped children in special programs that may not be available to other groups of handicapped children.

School district personnel characteristics. The initial human contact between a parent and a school official often sets the stage for future interactions. Parents can be either encouraged or rebuffed, reassured or intimidated, listened to or ignored (Schulz, 1982). The attitudes and personalities of school personnel are critical in determining whether or not the parents will seek additional supports and participate in their child's program (Lavelle & Keogh, 1980). (See Chapter 6 for examples of parent experiences with professionals.)

When school staff focus primarily upon the child's deficits, they are likely to neglect the role of the family in promoting the child's development, and to discourage parents from assuming an equal rather than a minor role in the child's education. Schaefer (1983) has proposed an ecological model for parent and professional interaction which emphasizes the contributions of parents and professionals across child-care settings and recognizes the important parental roles that are exercised in the home as well as in the school.

Professionals can and often do communicate to parents a sense of blame and guilt (Karnes & Teska, 1980). A lack of rapport between parents and school officials can be attributed to several factors: (a) most school personnel have not been trained, nor do they feel comfortable working directly with parents; (b) parents may be viewed as threats or troublemakers (Karnes & Teska, 1980); (c) parents and professionals may have conflicting goals; (d) professionals may feel that they are the "experts" (Schulz, 1982); or (e) the school official may be ill-equipped to deal with the emotional and psychological needs of a parent of a handicapped child (Turnbull & Turnbull, 1978; 1982). Seligman (1983) notes that professionals often lack the training in interpersonal skills that is needed for successful interactions with parents. Often lacking too is an understanding of the impact of the child upon family members which makes the professional sensitive to parent needs.

Several researchers have identified desirable characteristics for special education professionals who work with parents:

- "human qualities of acceptance, understanding and warmth; the professional attributes of objectivity, confidence and knowledge, as well as the technical skills of listening and talking to people under stress" (Lillie & Trohanis, 1976)
- the ability to generate confidence and respect
- the ability to provide clear and accurate information and feedback (Karnes & Teska, 1980)
- the need to be sensitive and flexible (Turnbull & Turnbull, 1978).

Not only may the school district officials' personal characteristics promote or undermine the parent-school relationship, but school officials can also be more or less effective in generating and allocating resources, promoting school morale, and collaborating with other agencies to secure related services. Collaboration among districts and other community agencies may be particularly necessary to provide special education services in rural areas, particularly services for children with low-incidence handicaps. As Helge (1984) points out, however, collaborative arrangements may have certain drawbacks, including a cumbersome bureaucracy, confusion about staff accountability, staff burnout due to grueling travel demands on itinerant staff, and uneven quality of services across districts which share personnel.

The administration sets the tone for school-wide activities and effectiveness (Gearheart & Wright, 1979). School officials who actively and energetically seek out additional revenue sources and who develop cost-efficient delivery systems will be best able to provide supportive services to families of handicapped children. Desirable school characteristics include: flexible budgeting and cross-agency planning (Semmel & Morrissey, 1981); specific interagency agreements (Craig, 1981); and strong leadership (Semmel & Morrissey, 1981).

Family history and demographics. There is some evidence that a family's socio-economic status influences their level of involvement and participation in the school system (Lynch & Stein, 1982). It is reasonable to assume that parents who are better informed and more knowledgeable about the rights and the guarantees of P.L. 94-142 will be more likely to argue for and receive a higher level of services. It has been well documented that parents are often passive participants in the IEP process and reluctant to ask for additional services such as counseling or therapy (Goldstein, Strickland, Turnbull, & Curry, 1980; Lynch & Stein, 1982). Parents' reluctance to be more aggressive is not surprising; even when professionals in the special education field suddenly find themselves in the parent's role, they find it a "shocking and traumatizing" experience to locate and organize appropriate services for their handicapped child (Turnbull & Turnbull, 1978). Many educators have addressed the need to train parents so that they can work more effectively with school personnel (Lavelle & Keogh, 1980; Lynch & Stein, 1982). Seligman (1983) has also described the interpersonal skills which professionals should develop to increase parent-professional communication and collaboration.

The number of additional family pressures and stresses will also influence how effectively parents can advocate for their children. For instance, a single working mother with four children, one of whom is hearing impaired, will have little time and energy to locate, schedule, and take advantage of support services. If a service such as mental health counseling is questionable and costly, and if a parent does not specifically request it, the schools are unlikely to provide that particular service to that particular family.

Parents who have developed advocacy skills or who participate in parent support networks are likely to be more effective in acting on behalf of their children than parents without these kinds of supports. As one of the mothers in Chapter 8 relates, the parent may have to make an effort to become more assertive in assuming a role in the handicapped child's educational programming and monitoring ongoing progress.

Severity of disability and age of child. It is obvious that multiply handicapped children with extensive medical needs are going to require more related services than mildly handicapped children. Ideally, the level of support provided by a school system should correlate highly with the level of need. There is some evidence that parents of more severely handicapped children are more actively involved in their child's IEP (Morgan, 1980) and are therefore more likely to receive additional support than parents of less severely impaired children. Other research supports the claim that parents of mildly handicapped students (McKinney & Hocutt, 1982) are not as actively involved and therefore less likely to request additional services than parents of severely impaired students. Fewell and Gelb (1983) have reviewed the literature on the response of nondisabled persons to the moderately handicapped, and noted that by virtue of their marginality — being classified sometimes as "normal" and other times as "abnormal" — moderately handicapped children may fail to receive appropriate services. It appears that all parents, regardless of the severity of their child's disability, may experience difficulties obtaining needed services for their child.

Parent involvement has been found to decrease as children approach adolescence (Lynch & Stein, 1982; Morgan, 1980), and this decreased involvement may influence the services their teenage child receives. One very articulate mother of a teenager complained about the lack of appropriate services for adolescents, such as sex education, training in social skills, and opportunities for socializing. She said she felt that parents of older children often expected their children to be self-sufficient, and were therefore less involved in advocating for them. Mothers who were previously unemployed when the child was young may take a full- or part-time job when the child is a teenager, and consequently have less time to work with the school. Parents who have devoted considerable time and energy to their child's preschool and elementary school programs may experience some "burnout" by the time the child is an adolescent. Yet parents may need to be especially active on behalf of their adolescent child if appropriate vocational and adult living skills are not being taught in the child's school program. As Kiernan (1983) has noted, planning for the handicapped adolescent's future requires a longitudinal perspective as well as horizontal integration of all of the educational options that may prepare the student for employment and residential and support-service options. The teenage handicapped student often begins to play a more active role, together with parents and educators, in planning for future independence.

Types of Support Provided by Educational Agencies

Educational agencies may be required to provide a wide range of services to handicapped students and their families. Some services, such as parent counseling, are specifically defined in regulation; other services, such as emotional support, cannot be mandated. The most salient types of support school agencies provide that are not considered specifically "educational," are: a shared concern for the child's welfare, emotional support, information and technical advice, professional expertise, and assistance in identifying other resources.

Shared responsibility for welfare of child. As Marion (1981) points out, the American school system, in cooperation with parents, shares primary responsibility for the welfare of the child. When the child leaves the nucleus of the family to attend school, the parent shares with the schools the responsibility for the child's well-being. Inherent in this act is the parent's belief that the school's decisions will be guided by an overriding concern for the child's welfare. For most parents, faced with the 24-hour-a-day task of caring for a child with special needs, the opportunity to share this responsibility comes as a great relief. Ideally a parent will establish a partnership with the school system — a joint endeavor built upon communication, mutual respect, and appreciation (Mopsik & Agard, 1980)—which results in optimal educational services for child and family.

In addition to shared responsibility, the schools offer an extremely valuable and rare service to stressed families — respite care. During the child's hours of school attendance, parents and other family members have time to become employed, learn a skill or trade, pursue a hobby or recreational activity, run a house, or simply rest and restore vital energies. All parents need time away from their children. For parents of children with handicapping conditions who may require additional medical attention, constant surveillance, and unlimited patience, the child's time away from home during the school day may be critical to the family's well-being, and may make it possible for the family to maintain the child in the home.

Gorham (in Gorham, Des Jardinas, Page, Pettis, & Scheiber, 1975), a parent of a severely handicapped child, believes parents are grateful to school systems for the respite care they provide. In some cases, however, parents need more than respite assistance: they need to find a residential placement for a severely impaired child. This is a decision which school staff can assist parents in making, both by helping parents obtain information about possible placements and by supporting the parents' final decision.

Ironically, the more crisis laden the child and family, and the greater their need for support, the more difficult is their search for help and respite care. Gorham et al. (1975) cite a mother's letter as an example: "My past experiences in finding appropriate services for my son, now aged fifteen, were for the most part discouraging" (p.181). The mother describes three early placements, then continues, "At the age of nine, he started at the [local] Educational Center and learned how to show his anger in aggressive ways. We had no contact with the school and lived in daily fear that he would be expelled. He finally was expelled at the age of thirteen and a half, and then followed probably the most traumatic six months of my entire life." The mother describes their family's frantic and desperate search for agency assistance, being told her son was "too psychotic for an institution for the retarded and too retarded for a mental hospital" (p. 181). At last, political pressure was exercised to get their son admitted to a state hospital. The impact of this experience on the family was draining, emotionally, physically, and financially. Although parents ultimately must make these kinds of decisions regarding their child's placement, professionals who provide information and support can make the parents' task much easier.

Emotional support. When professionals are sympathetic and understanding, parents are supported in their attempts to accept and adapt to their child's condition (D'Arcy, 1968; Emde & Brown, 1978).

Many researchers have found that parents feel isolated after the birth of a handicapped child (Roskies, 1972; Walker, Thomas, & Russell, 1971). Often friends, neighbors, and family members will stay away or choose to not see or hold the baby (Fraiberg, Smith, & Adelson, 1969). These acts of denial or rejection can add to the parents' difficulty in accepting and adjusting to their child's condition.

The professional educator who possesses any or all of the characteristics described by Lillie and Trohanis (1976) (e.g., acceptance, understanding, and warmth) can provide the parent with emotional support during a time of critical need. Again, the extent to which the professional educator will be able to extend emotional support will depend, in part, on previous training, experience, and professional priorities. These helping and caring attributes need to be valued by a school system, and acquired by the teaching and support staff.

Only recently have teacher training programs begun to include courses in which students learn the skills and techniques of interacting with parents. The need for this training has increased immensely as parents have become more active participants in their child's educational programs. While all staff members now have more exposure to parents, it is ultimately the teacher who is asked to assume a number of roles in relation to parents (Reynolds & Birch, 1982). The parent-teacher relationship is not as simple and straightforward as it might appear. The relationship is affected by what each participant brings to the interaction and how they view each other. Seligman (1983) notes variables that affect the parent-teacher relationship:

> 1) personality of the parent(s); 2) personality of the teacher; 3) problems presented by the nature of the child's handicap; 4) parental reactions to their handicapped child; 5) relationship between parents of the handicapped child, and between the parents and the child; 6) stereotypes teachers may have of parents of exceptional children; 7) anxieties teachers experience (often related to stereotypes); 8) the treatment parents have received from other professionals. (p. 450-451)

In their research, Wittmer and Myrick (1974) and Aspy and Roebuck (1967, cited in Seligman, 1983) found that it was difficult for teachers to practice what they knew to be good theory about working with parents. Aspy and Roebuck (1967) noted the following characteristics of effective teachers:

> 1) see other people as being worthy rather than unworthy; 2) do not regard others as threatening but rather as essentially well intended; 3) regard people as important sources of satisfaction rather than as sources of frustration and suspicion; 4) are good listeners; 5) have empathy (ability to truly comprehend someone else's circumstances); 6) show care and concern; 7) are genuine (not phony); 8) are knowledgeable. (in Seligman, 1983, p. 452)

Ineffective teachers were characterized by Wittmer and Myrick (1974, cited in Seligman, 1983) as: "1) insensitive; 2) cold, disinterested; 3) authoritarian; 4) ridiculing; 5) arbitrary; 6) sarcastic; 7) punitive" (p. 452).

Fortunately, persons are generally attracted to a career in education because they like to help others. Effective work with exceptional children will require an understanding of the dynamics of the child's family, including the roles and values and interactional patterns of family members, their needs, and the expectations of the teacher and the school system, and their ability to relate to all family members in a warm and understanding manner.

Finally, school staff, in their concern to meet the family's emotional needs, should not overlook the practical problems which families experience and with which staff may provide assistance. Several authors (Blackard & Barsch, 1982; Dunlap & Hollinsworth, 1977; Gath, 1973; Sullivan, 1976) have reported on the logistical and financial difficulties parents of handicapped children experience, and school staff are often the most accessible sources of information to parents in time of need.

Information and technical knowledge. Parents have ongoing needs for reliable, accurate information about their child's condition, educational alternatives, and long-term outlook (Karnes & Teska, 1980; Lavelle & Keogh, 1980). Schools, in cooperation with the medical community, represent parents' single greatest source of information and technical knowledge about their child's handicapping condition.

As Lavelle and Keogh (1980) have pointed out, parents need continuing support and guidance as they pass through the stages of adaptation. In Chapter 13, Mallory notes that during the child's early years, medical professionals play a major role in informing parents and acting as case managers. School staff assume that role for the school-age child. They are most effective when they offer support by providing honest communication, rather than confusing, ambiguous statements, by listening carefully to understand the parent's concerns and experiences, and by sharing information with parents.

All schools are required to inform parents of their rights, and these discussions provide school staff with an opportunity to encourage full parent participation and to establish parent-school rapport. At the initial contact with parents, and throughout the child's school career, the schools can and should provide information—information on the child's performance, on alternative educational options, on community groups and services, on expanded training and educational opportunities, and on the child's progress.

Professional expertise. In its teachers, administrators, psychologists, social workers, therapists, and support personnel, the educational community possesses the greatest collection of professional expertise in the field of special education. This professional training and experience is available to be shared with parents and family members. Professionals can offer support to parents through their knowledge of child development, educational alternatives, evaluation and diagnostic procedures, rules and regulations, and school policies and practices (Schulz, 1982). Professionals fill certain unique roles by virtue of their training and expertise. However, as Schaefer (1983) points out, they also share certain roles with parents—these include the roles of advocate, planner-organizer, case manager-coordinator, and collaborator. Schaefer's ecological model of parent- professional inter-action stresses the shared and reciprocal roles of parents in areas that have often been viewed as the sole responsibility of professionals.

Most often, parents view the school officials as "the experts." These are the people who have been trained specifically to deal with their child's learning disabilities, mental retardation, behavior disorders, or sensory impairments. Unfortunately, professional training is often narrowly focused and does not prepare the professional to anticipate and respond to parents' increasing desire for information. Parents have a right to be informed about their child's needs (Turnbull & Turnbull, 1978). It is, however, extremely important for parents to hear from the professionals that their child can succeed and has succeeded, that there is hope for the future, and that they are not to blame for their child's handicap. This type of emotional support is just as important for parents as the technical support school staff provide. However, because many teacher training programs have not included this type of parent-interaction training, teachers have often regarded this as a low priority. In addition, the pathological perspective most professionals have acquired emphasizes negative findings on family adaptation and fails to consider the positive contributions parents make to their child's development. The effective professional uses his or her combined training and experience to build upon families' strengths and help parents be most effective in their roles.

Resource network. In addition to providing parents with professional and technical information, schools also help parents identify parent support groups, community resources, and, ideally, other agency supportive services. The school, as the key agent responsible for managing educational programs and identifying related services, should put parents in contact with other agencies and groups that could be of assistance. This includes referring parents of young children to Parent-to-Parent support groups, where parents of newly or recently diagnosed children can seek the advice and reassurance of peers who can share their similar experiences and coping strategies. It includes informing parents of social service agencies that can help families meet their financial needs. And, as one mother of a blind child urged, it includes being candid with parents when school staff are not able to help parents obtain needed support.

If you cannot think of a way to help the parents, please say, "I don't know." That at least gives us hope to continue searching for someone who does know or hope that someone may know in the future. Try and refer parents to other parents and professionals who may know of other resources. (Stotland, 1984, p. 74)

A critical element in most special education programs is parent involvement. Successful early child-development programs, for example, appear to be those that support the parental role as the child's primary teacher, and that work toward strengthening rather than supplanting the parent-child relationship (Bronfenbrenner, 1974). Programs often provide family members with the opportunity to specify objectives and activities they see as important, to learn teaching techniques, to problem-solve and share experiences with other families, and to develop coping skills that will enhance the child's learning and the family's interaction.

As Hocutt and Wiegerink's (1983) surveys suggest, however, parent involvement should not be limited to participation in IEP development, or to direct participation in their children's educational or therapeutic programs, but should also include opportunities for parents to share in making decisions which influence their child's program. And, equally important, parents should be given the option to not be involved when other family needs are more pressing.

Part 2. Supports Directly Related to Education

Schools are charged with the task of identifying and locating all handicapped children, including those who are unserved or underserved from birth through age 21 (P.L. 94-142, 121 a. 11, 128). In carrying out this responsibility, most school systems conduct a wide variety of child identification activities. These can include development and dissemination of materials, media announcements, free preschool screening clinics, review of school records, team staffing, and ultimately, comprehensive evaluation. Through each step of the process, parents and other family members can and should be receiving emotional support, accurate information, and the benefit of guidance from a group of experts.

Identification and Evaluative Services

Prior to conducting a comprehensive evaluation, schools must notify parents, request their permission, and provide them with a description of tests and procedures to be used, as well as inform them of their rights (P.L. 94-142: 121 a. 504). Often, parents will request a prediagnosis conference to clarify the procedures and better understand the need for an evaluation. During this conference, school officials have an opportunity to: share information regarding the child's school performance and educational needs, describe any educational interventions that have already taken place, listen to the concerns and experiences and the goals and desires of the parents, and explain the need for the recommended testing (Mopsik & Agard, 1980).

When this initial session increases rapport and mutual respect, it sets the stage for increased parent involvement and shared educational decision-making. However, as one parent put it, "Those meetings are only as good as the person running them." An unsympathetic, hurried, unresponsive professional may intimidate or discourage the most well-adjusted and informed parent. When the family is non-English speaking, or when there are significant class or racial differences between parent and teacher, the chances that the parents' experience will be negative increase.

In our work with parents, we often found that parents of older children with learning disabilities and mild handicaps were frustrated and discouraged during their child's screening and prediagnosis. Reports from more satisfied parents of younger children suggested that significant improvements have been made subsequent to the enactment of P.L. 94-142. Parents of young children were more apt to speak of "sympathetic, caring administrators who listen." What once was a long, slow process that schools were ill-equipped to carry out has now become, in most cases, a carefully prescribed process in which administrators must adhere to reasonable time lines and due process procedures.

To determine whether or not a child is in need of a special education placement, schools must provide a comprehensive multidisciplinary evaluation that is nondiscriminatory, includes more than one test or procedure, and includes all relevant medical information (P.L. 94-142, 121 a. 531, 532). The relatively recent phenomenon of providing complete identification and assessment for all children who are experiencing substantial academic difficulties, at no cost to the parents, has provided parents the opportunity to be better informed about their child's education than ever before. With the advent of due process safeguards, the need to obtain informed consent from parents, and the emphasis on parent involvement in all school decisions, the family is now cast as a leading player in the school-home drama.

The assessment conference can be a time of crisis for parents. If it is handled correctly, it can enhance the child's educational prospects. Unfortunately, the literature is replete with examples of parents who have been turned off by professional jargon (Karnes & Teska, 1980), received cold, unresponsive, and punitive treatment from professionals (Embry, 1980), or been talked down to and bullied by poorly trained professionals (Turnbull, 1983). We have heard parents complain, "We couldn't even get an evaluation until I threatened to sue."

Nevertheless, great strides have been made, and when the minimum provisions of P.L. 94-142 are carried out, the child and the family are assured of a free, unbiased, and complete assessment.

Individualized Education Program

Each child who has been evaluated and determined eligible for special education must have an individualized education program (IEP). The IEP is to be developed at a conference that includes the parents, the child's teacher, a representative of the school administration, and in some cases, the child (P.L. 94-142, 121a. 130, 341,345). At the IEP conference, "the child's evaluation results are reviewed; educational needs, goals, and objectives are selected; procedures for reviewing progress are established; a tentative placement is selected; and the necessary instructional and supportive services are designated" (Mopsik & Agard, 1980, p. 125). This process—the development of an individualized program specifically designed to allocate resources to meet the needs of a child—is probably the single most important event for the parents. As Turnbull (1983) notes, the IEP conference is the key forum for the shared decision-making outlined in P.L. 94-142.

It is at this time that parents should expect to have their questions answered, and their observations about and their goals for their child seriously considered. Unfortunately, evidence suggests that there have been problems in carrying out this procedure, particularly in the child's early years.

The IEP conference may be an overwhelming experience for parents, who may be presented with stacks of technical information about their child that they have no way to evaluate. As Stotland (1984), a mother, points out, parents need time to review assessment data prior to the meeting, and need to know their rights as participants. Stotland also notes several logistic and practical suggestions that can promote cooperation and successful interactions at these meetings, including giving a parent adequate time in between scheduled parent meetings. Teachers' attitudes and their attempts to prepare parents for these meetings can do much to make the IEP conference a positive experience.

Several research studies have found that teachers and other IEP team members did not encourage parent involvement and felt that parents should play passive roles (Lynch & Stein, 1982; Tudor, 1977). Parents have not been perceived as partners by school officials, nor have they been expected to actively participate in decision-making (Lynch & Stein, 1982). It is not surprising, therefore, that many parents have low levels of participation, and when they do participate, are more comfortable giving information rather than actively participating in the decision-making (Lynch & Stein, 1982).

Ann Turnbull (1983) has recently reviewed the research on the role of parents in IEP conferences. She found that although P.L. 94-142 sets forth the policy that parents be involved as equal participants in deciding how to meet their child's needs, in practice, parents are quite often passive participants who more often give and receive information rather than share in decision-making. Further, Turnbull found that parents often prefer that teachers assume the responsibility for their child's program. Moeller, in Chapter 6, reports that parents she interviewed also preferred that the teacher make the educational decisions. Turnbull recommends that professionals receive training to help them facilitate equal participation by parents who wish to be involved, and that a more flexible policy be developed that allows for all levels of parent participation, including minimal involvement, according to the family's changing needs.

Educational Programming

Handicapped children are entitled to receive all the educational services, special adaptations, and materials indicated in their IEP. The primary educational service is direct, intensive academic instruction provided by a specially trained teacher. It should also include small classes, individual attention, individually designed and paced exercises, and a well-managed learning environment (Mopsik & Agard, 1980). Corrective or supportive personnel and materials may be required, as well as opportunities to participate in all regular education support services available to nonhandicapped students (i.e., physical education, career education, vocational education, employment opportunities, and extracurricular activities). Transportation services must also be provided, if needed.

The parents have the right to request their child's placement in a private school, nonpublic school agencies, and to the provision of special equipment. If the school agrees that these are needed, then these placements or services must be provided at no cost to the family.

Related services. As stated in the introduction to this chapter, educational agencies must provide any related services that are required for the child to benefit from the special education program. Related services could include: speech therapy, occupational or physical therapy, audiological services, mobility instruction, special driver's education, and parent counseling, education, or training. Medical costs, including those for psychiatric evaluations and examinations by other specialists, are paid for by the school if they are incurred for diagnostic purposes rather than for treatment. There are many gray areas that are not clearly defined, regarding services which various agencies must provide. Some areas of debate include: amount and type of psychological counseling, room and board expenses at a private facility, medical attendants for students who are physically incontinent, major and costly building renovations (e.g., special air conditioning or sterile rooms).

One analyst (Craig, 1981) believes that "fewer students may actually be receiving related services now" (p. 11) than before the passage of P.L. 94-142. She contends:

> Thus the intent of the law, which is to enhance and expand the availability and provision of necessary services for the handicapped through the coordination of all available resources by providing incentives to identify the need for and assure the provision of related services, has actually created disincentives for schools to identify those student needs. (p. 12)

From a parent's perspective, related services such as parent education and transportation may be essential to the family's well-being. From the school's point of view, any nonacademic service that will stretch an already thin budget is regarded cautiously, at best. Craig (1981) notes that effective coordination between schools and private agencies which provide related services is needed to insure that children are adequately served. She observes that when schools are uncertain about their fiscal liability for related services, they are reluctant to recommend them in a child's IEP, making it critical that parents know their rights. Parents also need to be aware of the school's dilemma in attempting to fulfill the promise of P.L. 94-142 in the context of competing demands for limited resources.

Throughout the school year, both at regularly scheduled IEP and parent conferences and at annual IEP reviews, as well as during impromptu parent-teacher conferences, parents should meet with their child's teacher and other support staff. At these formal and informal conferences, parents can share valuable insights about their child's skills and interests, learn teaching techniques they can implement in the home, and generally review their child's progress. As one mother has written, parents have much valuable information they can share with their child's teacher.

> We developed a method of helping teachers cope. . .I told them I was comfortable answering any questions they might have and I would find out the answers to specific questions from specialists working with David. I encouraged them to ask David how he can do something if they are not sure. Moreover, I ask them not to lower their expectations simply because David may need to approach an assignment from a different perspective. (Stotland, 1984, pp. 73-74)

Although it is often assumed that educational agencies must have and make available all required educational and related services deemed necessary for each and every handicapped child, it is also true that schools cannot do all things for all children, particularly in times of fiscal conservatism. The services and supports that an individual child or family actually receive will often be a measure of parents' knowledge, assertiveness, and persistence, as well as the resources that the school can provide.

Parents' Roles

Parents have the right, and some might say the duty, to be involved in all aspects of their child's educational program. Schaefer (1983) has proposed a useful matrix of parent roles in the regular school setting which includes the unique roles parents play as well as the roles they share with professionals. These parent roles are: volunteer-fund-raiser, paraprofessional, observer-student, and decision-maker. Shared roles are: advocate, planner-organizer, case manager- coordinator, and collaborator. Although Schaefer was not attempting to describe the special roles of parents of handicapped children, his matrix successfully describes the roles these special parents fill.

One way parents can be involved is to volunteer to assist in the classroom, the school building, the play yard, the office, or on special trips. Many parents have found that by volunteering their time and energy, they have been able to learn first-hand what kind of program their child is receiving, as well as how to apply techniques in the home. Parent volunteers often become exceptionally knowledgeable about school procedures, legal regulations, school personnel networks, and procedures for making changes for handicapped students.

Parents may also serve as paid or unpaid staff for special projects. With the emphasis on parent involvement, school districts throughout the country have applied for and received funding for model special education projects. Often, a state will set aside a portion of their P.L. 94-142 discretionary funds to support a special parent involvement project. It is not uncommon to hear of parents who began as volunteers when their children were young and moved on to paid employment within the project or school system. Through these efforts, schools offer parents training, meaningful involvement, and the possibility of employment.

Parents may also wish to regularly observe their child's program as a means of monitoring the child's progress and keeping informed of new techniques and activities in which the child is involved. The benefits of this observation may include continuity in the child's school program resulting from the parent's implementation of classroom strategies in the home.

Finally, parents may serve on committees and in support groups formed to develop and enhance children's school programs. All schools must afford parents the opportunity to be involved in the development and review of their district and state special education plan. Most school districts have parent advisory councils, parent support groups, and other coalitions designed to provide parents with information and support. However, as Hocutt and Wiegerink (1983) note, parents are more often offered opportunities for involvement as direct change agents with their child than as decision-makers. When parents do have opportunities to influence educational programming, they report increased levels of satisfaction and improved programs for their children (Cartwright, 1981; Hocutt & Wiegerink, 1983).

In addition to these roles which parents of handicapped children share with all parents, they have certain responsibilities as advocates and case managers, roles they share with the school staff. The need to assume these oversight roles is underscored by a mother of a blind child:

> I feel righteously indignant if the school does not give me the best it has to offer because Jed's success is subject to a much greater risk than any other child's. (Barton, 1984, p. 67)

The level of parents' involvement in advocacy, planning, and case management may vary over time. For example, Winton and Turnbull (1981) found that parents may sometimes want the option of not being involved in activities when this is in the family's best interests. Most important, however, is that professionals give parents first the opportunity to assume as many of these roles as they wish, and second the support to work most effectively in these roles towards their child's education.

Parent Needs Across the Life-span

Parents, as well as teachers, school administrators, state officials, and university faculty were interviewed during the preparation of this chapter. Repeatedly, some very basic human needs were identified as critical to the family-school partnership. These needs included: respect for parents as individuals; consideration and empathy for each family's particular circumstances; honest, open communication; and continuity in parents' relationship with the school system. As Turnbull and Turnbull (1978) so eloquently stated:

> . . .parents need respect for their privacy and individual dignity. . .don't treat them casually and clinically. . .parents don't want flippant and self-righteous answers. . .parents want honesty and openness—if you don't know, say so. (p. 134-135)

The need for parents to be treated in a sensitive and caring fashion cannot be overstated. Family members have often complained that professionals didn't listen to them, talked down to them, made them feel guilty, or recommended totally unrealistic home treatment plans (Bennett, 1978). It has been demonstrated that parents who receive initial emotional support from professionals are more likely to accept the reality of their child's condition (Emde & Brown, 1978).

Parents are first and foremost human beings who desire a normal family life, not a life consumed by the activities of advocating for their handicapped child. Their self-respect, dignity, and privacy are all threatened with the arrival of a child with special needs. It is imperative that school officials recognize the emotional needs of parents and offer basic human understanding.

The literature and our parent interviews underscore family members' need to know. They need to know as much as possible about their child's condition, about services available through the school, about other community resources, about parent networks, and also about their rights. They need advice on how to handle their child at home, and how to handle behavior problems (Karnes & Teska, 1980). They want to know the implications for the future, and whether or not self-sufficiency is a realistic goal for their child. Families look to the schools as the "experts" and the "authorities"; and, as such, regard the schools as their primary source of information about their child's condition.

A family's need for emotional support, information, and educational guidance varies during the course of their child's development and the parents' stages of acceptance. Marion (1981) has identified four periods of crisis for parents of handicapped children:

1. *Initial diagnosis* — parents need emotional support and understanding, and basic information;
2. *Entry into school* — parents must learn about services and programs most appropriate for their child;
3. *Puberty* — parents need information on sex education and social expectations;
4. *Vocational decisions* — parents need help in preparing their child for employment.

Both parents and school officials have voiced the concern that the active parent-school collaboration that often exists during the preschool and early primary years dissipates during the child's teenage years. Parents have stated that their increased levels of employment and pursuit of deferred activities, as well as their growing expectations for their child's independence contribute to this decline in their school involvement.

Yet this decreasing parent involvement comes at a time when young students are beginning to expand their social contacts and have a sexual identity. Few schools have well developed programs to assist handicapped children in this area. The topics of dating, sexual relationships, self-defense, employment, and social counseling are very real concerns of parents of teenagers with handicapping conditions—concerns that should be legitimately addressed by parents and school staff, and concerns that demand their effective cooperation.

Many parents also voiced a particular need for additional vocational training for their handicapped teenage children (also see Chapter 5 by Vadasy and Fewell). The ultimate goal of economic self-sufficiency for the handicapped can only be realized if our vocational programs are expanded, well-integrated, and correspond to the needs of the employment market. The child's ultimate independence requires a planning process that begins while the child is still in school, and it involves a partnership which includes the family, professionals, the handicapped child, and representatives from the community. Together these individuals can review all of the available options both within and outside of the school system which will match the child's long range needs (Kiernan, 1983).

Conclusion

In summary, the amount and types of family supports provided by the public school system to the families of handicapped children vary. This chapter has described the types of support available, and the factors that affect the level of support public schools provide. In order for parents to benefit most from the services available through the public school sytem, they need to have opportunities to participate in a variety of roles which may change over the course of their child's development and according to family needs. Parents need opportunities to exercise roles that reflect the ecological context in which they and their child are imbedded. And the schools need to bear in mind the unique contributions parents can make to the child's school programs. When all factors are favorable, the school system is capable of providing a comprehensive educational program that is uniquely tailored to meet the changing needs of each handicapped child as well as the needs of the child's family.

References

Aspy, D.N., & Roebuck, F.N. (1967, May). An investigation of the relationship between levels of cognitive functioning and the teacher's classroom behavior. *Journal of Educational Research.*

Barton, D.D. (1984). Uncharted course: Mothering the blind child. *Journal of Visual Impairment and Blindness, 78,* 66-68.

Bennett, J. (1978). Company halt. In A. Turnbull & H. R. Turnbull (Eds.), *Parents speak out: Views from the other side of the two-way mirror.* Columbus, OH: Charles E. Merrill.

Blackard, M.K., & Barsh, E.T. (1982). Parents' and professionals' perceptions of the handicapped child's impact on the family. *Journal of the Association for the Severely Handicapped, 7,* 62-69.

Bronfenbrenner, U. (1974). *Is early intervention effective? Report on longitudinal evaluations of preschool programs, Vol. 2.* Washington, DC: Office of Child Development, U.S. Department of Health, Education, and Welfare.

Cartwright, C.A. (1981). Effective programs for parents of young handicapped children. *Topics in Early Childhood Special Education, 1,* 1-9.

Craig, P. A. (1981). Provision of related services: A good idea gone awry. *Exceptional Education Quarterly, 2,* 11-15.

D'Arcy, E. (1968). Congenital defects: Mothers' reactions to first information. *British Medical Journal, 3,* 796-798.

Dunlap, W.R., & Hollingsworth, J.S. (1977). How does a handicapped child affect the family? Implications for practitioners. *Family Coordinator, 26,* 286-293.

Embry, L. H. (1980). Family support for handicapped preschool children at risk for abuse. *New Directions for Exceptional Children, 4,* 29-57.

Emde, R.N., & Brown, C. (1978). Adaptation to the birth of a Down syndrome infant. *Journal of the American Academy of Child Psychiatry, 18,* 299-323.

Fewell, R.R. (1984). *Sources of support for mothers of children with Down syndrome.* Paper presented at the Conference of Research on Mental Retardation and Developmental Disabilities, Gatlinburg, TN.

Fewell, R.R., & Gelb, S.A. (1983). Parenting moderately handicapped persons. In M. Seligman (Ed.), *The family with a handicapped child: Understanding and treatment* (pp. 175-202). New York: Grune & Stratton.

Fraiberg, S., Smith, M., & Adelson, E. (1969). An educational program for blind infants. *The Journal of Special Education, 3,* 121-139.

Gath, A. (1973). The school age siblings of mongol children. *British Journal of Psychiatry, 123,* 161-167.

Gearheart, B., & Wright, W. (1979). *Organization and administration of educational programs for exceptional children.* Springfield, IL: Charles C Thomas.

Goldstein, S., Strickland, B., Turnbull, A., & Curry, L. (1980). An observational analysis of the IEP conference. *Exceptional Children, 46,* 278-286.

Gorham, K.A., Des Jardinas, C., Page, R., Pettis, E., & Scheiber, B. (1975). Effects on parents. In N. Hobbs (Ed.), *Issues in the classifications of children* (Vol. 2, pp. 154-188). San Francisco: Jossey-Bass.

Halpern, R. (1982). Special education in rural America. *The Educational Forum, 46,* 491-501.

276 *Espinosa and Shearer*

Helge, D. (1984). The state of the art of rural special education. *Exceptional Children, 50,* 294-305.

Hocutt, A., & Wiegerink, R. (1983). Perspectives on parent involvement in preschool programs for handicapped children. In R. Haskins & D. Adams (Eds.), *Parent education and public policy* (pp. 211-229). Norwood, NJ: Ablex.

Hodge, D. (1980, Fall). Report on the national rural research project. *Counterpoint,* Falls Church, VA.

Karnes, M., & Teska, J. (1980). Toward successful parent involvement in programs for handicapped children. *New Directions for Exceptional Children, 4,* 85-111.

Kiernan, W.E. (1983). Planning for the future: Vocational and living alternatives. In J.A Mulick & S.M Pueschel (Eds.), *Parent-professional partnerships in developmental disability services* (pp. 173-193). Cambridge, MA: Ware Press.

Lavelle, N., & Keogh, B. (1980). Expectations and attributions of parents of handicapped children. *New Directions for Exceptional Children, 4,* 1-26.

Lillie, D., & Trohanis, P. (1976). *Teaching parents to teach.* New York: Walker.

Lynch, E., & Stein, R. (1982). Perspectives on parent participation in special education. *Exceptional Education Quarterly 3,* 56-63.

Marion, R. (1981). *Educators, parents and exceptional children.* Rockville, MD: Aspen Systems.

McKinney, J.D., & Hocutt, A. (1982). Public school involvement of parents of learning-disabled children and average achievers. *Exceptional Education Quarterly, 3,* 64-73.

Mopsik, S., & Agard, J. (Eds.). (1980). *An education handbook for parents of handicapped children.* Cambridge, MA: Abt Books.

Morgan, D. (1980). Parent participation in the IEP process: Does it enhance appropriate education? *Exceptional Education Quarterly, 3,* 33-40.

Price, M., & Goodman, L. (1980). Individualized education programs: A cost study. *Exceptional Children, 46,* 446-454.

Reynolds, M.C., & Birch, J.W. (1982). *Teaching exceptional children in all America's schools (2nd ed.).* Reston, VA: Council for Exceptional Children.

Roskies, E. (1972). *Abnormality and normality: The mothering of thalidomide children.* Ithaca, NY: Cornell University Press.

Schaefer, E.S. (1983). Parent-professional interaction: Research, parental, professional, and policy perspectives. In R. Haskins & D. Adams (Eds.), *Parent education and public policy* (pp. 283-303). Norwood, NJ: Ablex.

Schulz, J.B. (1982). A parent views parent participation. *Exceptional Education Quarterly, 3,* 17-24.

Seligman, M. (1983). Understanding and communicating with families of handicapped children. In S.G. Garwood (Ed.), *Educating young handicapped children: A developmental approach* (pp. 435-473). Rockville, MD: Aspen Systems.

Semmel, D., & Morrissey, P. (1981). Serving the unserved and underserved: Can the mandate be extended in an era of limitations? *Exceptional Education Quarterly, 2,* 17-25.

Stotland, J. (1984). Relationship of parents to professionals: A challenge to professionals. *Journal of Visual Impairment and Blindness, 78,* 69-74.

Sullivan, R. C. (1976). The role of the parent. In A. Thomas (Ed.), *Hey don't forget about me: Education's investment in the severely, profoundly, and multiply handicapped* (pp. 36-45). Reston, VA: Council for Exceptional Children.

Tudor, K. (1977). An exploratory study of teacher attitude and behavior toward parent education and involvement. *Education Research Quarterly, 2,* 22-28.

Turnbull, A.P. (1983). Parental participation in the IEP process. In J.A. Mulick & S.M. Pueschel (Eds.), *Parent-professional partnerships in developmental disability services* (pp. 107-122). Cambridge, MA: Ware Press.

Turnbull, A.P., & Turnbull, H.R. (1978). *Parents speak out: Views from the other side of the two-way mirror.* Columbus, OH: Charles E. Merrill.

Turnbull, A.P., & Turnbull, H.R. (Eds.). (1982). Parent participation in the education of exceptional children. *Exceptional Education Quarterly, 3*(2).

Walker, J.H., Thomas, M., & Russell, I.T. (1971). Spina bifida and the parents. *Developmental Medicine and Child Neurology, 13,* 456-461.

Winton, P.J., & Turnbull, A.P. (1981). Parent involvement as viewed by parents of preschool handicapped children. *Topics in Early Childhood Special Education, 1,* 11-19.

Wittmer, J., & Myrick, R. (1974). *Facilitating teaching: Theory and practice.* Pacific Palisades, CA: Goodyear.

11

Networks of Social Supports for Parents of Handicapped Children

Vaughan Stagg and Thomas Catron

John Donne's much quoted remark, "No man is an island, entire of itself," conveys the universal human need to form relationships with other human beings. Indeed, as life begins, most human neonates enter the world welcomed by a group of supportive adults. While it is a biological necessity that the mother be present at birth to support the newborn, fathers, in increasing numbers, are also present at birth. Also attending at this event is the medical staff, a secondary support group, but at this particular point in time, one very critical to the child's well-being. Literally "waiting in the wings" in many hospitals are members

This work was supported in part by the R. K. Mellon Foundation.

of the child's extended family who are etching in their memories the time, the place, and their feelings when they receive the news of the infant's birth. Although newborns are very new members of these human networks, they elicit immediate and often powerful responses from a wide variety of individuals as they begin interacting in their social environments.

The supportive persons who surround the new family member share similar hopes and dreams for the child: they want, first and foremost, a healthy, happy baby. Their immediate questions reveal their concerns: "Is the baby okay? What about the mother?" Even the child's sex is of secondary concern to family members next to the child's physical well-being. When the baby and mother are declared fit and fine, the extended family members begin to exercise their expected support roles.

What happens, though, when those first questions cannot be answered immediately, or when the answers suggest doubts or definite problems? Everyone in those networks is then affected and experiences shock, grief, and sadness. In addition to their deep feelings of concern for the baby's parents, support members begin to wonder about their own relationships to the new family member and to the child's immediate family. Schell (1981) expressed this so well in his description of his parents' reactions to the birth of his daughter with Down syndrome:

> Telling grandparents that their grandchild is handicapped is one of the first and most difficult emotional hurdles new parents face. The [child's] parents must try to steady their mercurially mixed feelings while anticipating the anger and frustration their own parents may feel when they learn that their grandchild is handicapped. We were relieved and surprised to find that both sets of grandparents were very supportive; they assured us of their concern and offered any help we might need. They did not immediately burden us with their own grief, which gave us time to get a more stable perspective on our own emotions. Only later did we find out how difficult their acceptance was. At the time, their supportive attitudes freed us to focus our immediate attention on our child's needs and to begin integrating our own feelings about Christina into a plan of action to optimize her progress. (p.24)

Each member of a support system that must integrate a new member who has very special needs is invariably affected. In this chapter we examine support systems, the roles of supporters, and their relationships to others in the network. We draw heavily on our own investigation of mothers of mentally retarded children; however, we feel the experiences of these mothers may be quite similar to those of mothers whose special children have other kinds of needs.

Defining the Social Network

Within and across disciplines, investigators have focused upon different units of analysis to explain human behavior. A unit that has come into focus in the 1980s is the "network." This term was first used to describe communication linkages in the media fields, and it has become a key descriptor for personal relationships. As often occurs when a term is borrowed from one field for use in others, multiple definitions have emerged. See Mitchell and Trickett (1980) for a complete list of definitions. The definition provided by Cobb (1976) is appropriate for the networks to be described in this chapter. Cobb defines a network as a set of individuals "who provide information leading the subject to believe he is cared for and loved, esteemed, and a member of a network of mutual obligations" (p. 300).

According to Cochran and Brassard (1979), networks have both a direct and indirect influence on parents and child, and the child's role in network interactions increases with the child's age.

> These processes interact with the developmental age of the child to stimulate the basic trust, empathy and mastery of the reciprocal exchange skills essential to network building. Movement through developmental time also brings with it the child's increasing capacity to influence the establishment and maintenance of network linkages and therefore to play an active part in the nature and extent of network ties. (p.607)

Schell's (1981) description of his sister-in-law's role in his family's life provides an excellent example of Cochran and Brassard's theory.

> My sister-in-law Cindy has played an extraordinary role in Christina's development. From the moment she heard about Christina, there was never any doubt that Cindy had a desire to take an active part in Christina's life. Cindy is a prime motivator for Christina when difficult things need to be done. Christina walked her first steps trying to stop Cindy from leaving. She will sit still for only one person when it is time to cut her hair. Her favorite times are when Cindy babysits.
>
> Cindy's involvement with Christina has provided us with practical and emotional benefits. . . .Cindy's remaining an energetic force in our lives, as she was before Christina's birth, has helped us to feel like any family with caring and sharing relatives. (pp. 24-25)

An effective social support network assists the parent to cope successfully with the stress of raising a handicapped child, and thereby preserves the parent's sense of well-being. The network has a direct effect on the parent and an indirect effect on the child by enhancing the parent's well-being and affecting, in turn, the child's well-being (Bowen, 1978).

Before turning to some of the specific dimensions of social support networks, we will take a broader perspective and examine the research on some of the more frequently examined attributes of families of mentally retarded children. An understanding of these family characteristics is helpful in our investigation of how and why social support networks develop, and why they might be different than expected when the family has a child with special needs.

Families of Mentally Retarded Children

Throughout this book are many indications that parents experience decreased social support when their child is handicapped. As McDowell and Gabel (1981) have noted, it is ironic that the parents of handicapped children, who are especially in need of a support system because of the additional stressors in their lives, frequently do not have one available because key members of the parental network (such as kin) are "often at a loss to know how to help the distraught parent" (p.2). Very few investigators have specifically examined the social support networks of parents of handicapped children. The current emphasis on family systems theory, as it relates to networks, including the handicapped member (Turnbull, Summers, & Brotherson, 1983), will no doubt lead to more studies focusing on the entire family system. Information about the characteristics of family support networks for parents of handicapped children is often imbedded in the literature concerning family stress, needs, isolation, and changes over the life-span.

Family Stresses and Needs

The impact of the handicapped child on the family has been documented by a number of authors of diverse orientation (Birenbaum, 1970, 1972; Farber, 1968, 1975; Gabel & Kotsch, 1981; Jacobson & Humphry, 1979; Olshansky, 1962). After examining the impact of a child with cerebral palsy on the family, Dodge (1976) labeled the resulting multiple stresses as the "stir crazy" syndrome. The birth and long-term responsibilities of raising a handicapped child result in a number of family problems. Those problems include: restricted social contacts (Gabel & Kotsch, 1981); additional expenses (Dunlap, 1979; Holt, 1958; Morrison, Beasley, & Williams, 1976; Schonell & Watts, 1956); and a need for greater instrumental assistance for activities such as babysitting, shopping, and household chores (Dunlap, 1979; Schonell & Watts, 1956). These needs are noted frequently when parents describe their experiences (Dunlap & Hollinsworth, 1977; Featherstone, 1980; Watson & Midlarsky, 1979). For example, the mothers of deaf-blind children and adolescents who were surveyed by Vadasy and Fewell (see Chapter 5) reported that their need for outside assistance in caring for their children increased with their children's age, whereas they indicated that family supports were very important when their children were young. Families' instrumental needs will vary according to the child's handicap and age, and according to the family's resources. In their study of the impact of the child's disability on maternal stress, Breslau, Staruch, and Mortimer (1982) found that the child's dependence on others in daily living activities was related to the mothers' depression and distress. When Moore, Hamerlynck, Barsh, Spieker, and Jones (1982) surveyed 448 families of young handicapped children, they found that the low and medium income groups had more problems and higher stress ratings than the high income group. Their study highlighted the predicament of middle income families who often fail to qualify for support services because of their income levels. As several study parents expressed:

> There is no financial help unless you are on welfare or give your child up. Otherwise, the rest of the family does without.

> We are making it but losing ground. There will come a time, I am sure, when our handicapped child will have to do without. (Moore et al., 1982, p. 69)

From these sources it is implied that families with a handicapped member have more needs which are likely to produce increased stress in the family. These characteristics will be felt in some way by those closest to the family. This could place more demands on the members of the support group and could limit the size of the support group.

Loneliness and Social Isolation

In addition to the problems noted above, one common finding is increased loneliness and social isolation of the parents of retarded children, particularly the mother (Birenbaum, 1970, 1972; Farber, 1968; Schonell & Watts, 1956). In writing about her own experiences as a mother of a disabled child and of the experiences of many other parents, Helen Featherstone (1980) notes that "a special loneliness is the most pervasive theme in the stories told by parents with disabled children. This loneliness is nourished from within and without. . . .The two most prominent ingredients of a parent's loneliness are difference— his own and the child's—and isolation" (p. 50). The isolation is felt in the delivery room or on the maternity ward: "She cannot share the happy inconsequential chatter about birth weights, labor, and nursing woes without a sense of heaviness and hypocrisy. Her heart simply is not in it" (p. 51).

Parents in the aforementioned studies (usually mothers) reported that visitation with others was curtailed after the birth of a mentally retarded child. Not only did parents make fewer visits outside the home, but also fewer people made visits to the parents' homes. Visiting patterns with kin were less affected than visiting patterns with friends (Birenbaum, 1970). Birenbaum (1970, 1972) interprets these changes in parents' visitation patterns as a means whereby parents can manage the "courtesy stigma," by which parents and family members are viewed by others as if they are part of the child's problem. Suelzle and Keenan's (1981) data suggest that social isolation of retarded children results more from the family's withdrawal of the child than from community avoidance of the family. One could also speculate that added strains on family resources leave the family less time and energy to engage in social activities. But regardless of the reason for the less frequent visits, the parents are more socially isolated and therefore they have less access to sources of instrumental and emotional support than other parents who have less need for those kinds of supports.

Furthermore, the quality of parents' social relationships appears to change after the birth of a handicapped child. Birenbaum (1970, 1972) reports that relationships with the mother's friends are maintained only so long as they extend "consideration" or do not intrude on the "polite fiction" that the mother is part of a normal family. For some parents, the strain has led to bitter loneliness. Featherstone (1980) quotes a letter from a parent:

> We have a twenty-six-year-old retarded daughter and for at least fifteen years my husband and I have not been able to "have a date." We really want to and have tried every source we know but we cannot find anyone to stay with our daughter, everyone has a million excuses, but it all boils down to the fact that they don't want to be bothered. I guess being an exceptional parent means really going through life alone with no caring or showing any human kindness. Our wish is that we could "have a date" just the two of us, but we can't find anyone at all to stay with our daughter. (Featherstone, 1980)

One would expect that common interests in their children would draw parents of handicapped children together. Yet Birenbaum's (1970, 1972) data suggest that relationships between mothers of mentally retarded children enrolled in the same program tend to be collegial rather than personal. That is to say, the mothers' relationships were limited to situations directly involving the children, and included little personal affective interchange. It may be that a mother's ability or need to form warm, close relationships with other mothers may depend upon the age of her child, or that these relationships need to be fostered by program staff. In Chapter 8, Roberts notes of one of the mothers she interviewed:

> Karen liked to talk to the other mothers. She particularly looked forward to getting to know and comparing notes with the mothers who had children with Down syndrome.

Another of the mothers confided:

The other moms filled a very real need. And I found I could talk about bad feelings like resentment and even a sort of dislike toward my disabled son, and they had had similar feelings. We helped each other and cried together and took our kids out together, so that we didn't feel like the only ones who had a disabled child. That really helped.

Featherstone's (1980) reflections on what a support group of mothers meant to her personal development, like the reflections of the mother Roberts interviewed, differ from Birenbaum's data:

We met for a morning every other week to discuss our children, our worries, and our lives. We continued to see one another even after our children moved on to other programs. These women became my friends; from them and with them I learned much of what I believe about families, and about people's response to tragedy, disappointment, and difference. I was very glad that they allowed me to share with others their struggles, their triumphs, and their insights. (p.9)

Another parent of a handicapped child provided insight into why support groups were important to her:

It doesn't comfort me that other parents have a similar misfortune. It does comfort me, however, to see that others have coped, have learned to live with their heartache, and go beyond it. Perhaps it was at this point that I turned the corner to full acceptance. (Murphy, 1981)

It appears from these sources that support groups differ and serve different purposes for mothers of handicapped children. Mothers come to these groups with different needs, and even within the same group, mothers may assume different roles and relationships.

Life-span Issues

Few of the studies related to mental retardation and the family discussed thus far have addressed the issue of changes in stresses over the parents' lives. Farber (1968, 1975) and Wolfensberger and Menolascino (1970), among others, have postulated stages of parental adjustment and adaptation to the diagnosis or labeling of mental retardation. Over the family's life cycle, the handicapped child poses chronic stressors that relate not only to the child's delayed development, but also to changing parental expectations and service needs (Wikler, 1981, 1983; Wikler, Wasow, & Hatfield, 1981).

Wikler (1983) examined family stress during two periods of transition in the life of a mentally retarded family member: the onset of puberty (ages 11-15) and the transition to adulthood (ages 20-21). Families ($n = 26$) whose members were in a transition period indicated significantly higher levels of stress ($p < .005$) on the *Questionnaire on*

Resources and Stress (Holroyd, 1973) than the families ($n = 28$) whose member was not undergoing a transition. Eight specific types of stress were significantly higher for those families who were experiencing a transition of their retarded child. In order of significance, these stressors were:

> 1) Excess time demands on the mother, 2) negative attitudes towards the handicapped child, 3) limits on family opportunity, 4) dependency needs of the child, 5) lack of activities for the child, 6) poor health of the mother, 7) low family integration, and 8) behavior problems of the child. (p. 9)

Jacobson and Humphry (1979) suggest that parental stress increases when the child begins school and during adolescence. Birenbaum (1972) contends that the mother of a retarded child must readjust her social role when the child reaches adolescence. Tavormina, Henggeler, and Gayton (1976) report age trends in parental assessments of their retarded child's problems. Concerns varied with the ages of the children. For children under the age of four, developmental problems predominated. In the four- to six-year grouping, specific behavior problems were of paramount concern to the parent. With older children (12 to 16 years), parents were concerned with the development of social interaction skills. Compliance behavior and toileting problems were concerns across all age groupings. As Vadasy and Fewell point out in Chapter 5, mothers of teenage handicapped children become increasingly concerned with the child's eventual work skills and residential placement.

More recently Blacher (1984) reviewed the literature on the stages of adjustment parents presumably experience and found little evidence of any scientific data to verify stages. Stages, as described in the literature, have been derived from clinical judgments based on parent interviews. According to Blacher, whether the stages do exist remains to be determined. Regardless of whether a specific stage exists, considerable data indicate that parents of handicapped children experience periods of increased stress as life events and changes are experienced by their children.

Life-span issues, while not unique to families of handicapped children, certainly add to their anxiety, worry, and fear. As parents face these difficult times, members of their support networks may share some of their concerns. Parents may seek new support networks, or they may need family members to take on new roles.

German and Maisto (1982) found that a number of support variables were associated with whether a retarded child remained in the home or was institutionalized, or whether parents used respite care. These variables included: perceived emotional support from the grandparents and parents' siblings, marital status of parent, degree of disruptive behavior of the retarded child, and the presence of an additional retarded child in the family.

Networks of Mothers
of Mentally Retarded Children

From the previous sections it is apparent that family members and those who are close to them are all affected by the presence of a child with special needs. In this section we will use the characteristics of social networks, based on Cochran and Brassard's (1979) theory of networks, to explore how networks of mothers of handicapped children might be similar to or different from the networks of mothers of nonhandicapped children. We draw almost entirely from our own recently completed study of the social networks of mothers of mentally retarded and nonretarded children (Catron, 1983; Stagg, 1983).

Participants of this study included 31 mothers of mentally retarded children. All of the children were moderately, severely, or profoundly retarded as defined by Grossman (1973). For purposes of this study, the mothers were divided into three groups based on the age of their handicapped children: those with young, preschool-age children (birth through six years); those with elementary-age children (7-12 years); and the mothers of older children (7-21 years). Children of these parents were living at home and attending public or private schools or programs. A contrast group of 29 mothers of nonretarded children was also recruited. Their data were divided into the same three groups. Both of these samples were recruited in the Birmingham, Alabama metropolitan area. These two groups of mothers were essentially equivalent in terms of such demographic variables as education, income, community stability (years at present address, number of moves in the last five years), religious preference, ethnic status, work status, living arrangement, and stressful life events (Stagg, 1983). Network characteristics were evaluated with the *Pattison Psychosocial Kinship Inventory* (Pattison, 1977) and the *Daily Interaction Rating Form* (Hirsch, 1980).

Location in Time and Space

Cochran and Brassard describe three dimensions of social networks. Location of the network members in time and space is the first dimension. This dimension permits us to examine how relationships form because of living arrangements or other personal characteristics that enable members to maintain ties over time and distances.

The network characteristics of the two groups of mothers in our study were very similar. This is seen in their responses indicating with whom they associated and the frequency of these contacts. Demographic variables indicated these groups were alike. Contacts to the mothers by letter, telephone, and visits were analyzed. Contact by letter proved to be so infrequent that its importance appeared negligible. Both telephone contacts and visits occurred with equal frequency across all participants.

Thus the mothers of mentally retarded children participating in this study had social support networks that did not differ in location in time and space characteristics from the mothers of nonhandicapped children.

Structural Characteristics

Cochran and Brassard's second dimension describes structural network characteristics. These are indicators of the size of the networks, the interconnectedness or density of its members, and the diversity of the members.

When we compared the structural characteristics of the networks of these two groups of mothers, we found no differences in terms of size or density. The average number of network members listed by all participants was 21.7. Roughly half of the network members listed by participants knew and associated with each other.

Few studies to date have attempted to investigate the size of social networks in the lives of families of retarded children. McDowell and Gabel (1981) contrasted the social support networks of mothers of mentally retarded and mothers of nonhandicapped infants. They found that mothers of mentally retarded infants had significantly smaller social networks than did mothers of nonhandicapped infants. The differences occurred in both the relative and friendship categories and were due to reduced extended kinship networks. It is important to note that this constriction of social networks was observed in a population of mothers enrolled in a successful parent-based preschool program. In addition, McDowell and Gabel (1981) found a negative correlation between the number of life stress events and network size. Fewell (1984) examined the relationship between network size and the amount of social support perceived by 80 mothers of children with Down syndrome. Mothers with medium amounts of social support received support from significantly more sources than did mothers with low total social support scores, while mothers with high amounts of social support had significantly more sources of support than mothers in both of the other two groups.

Given the finding of no differences in network size in our study, and the differences in network size in the McDowell and Gabel (1981) study, it is obvious that factors other than the presence of the index child must strongly influence network size. Fewell's (1984) finding that mothers who have greater amounts of family support also have support from more individual sources may indicate that number of supports or size of the support network alone is not the critical variable.

As with size and density or interconnectedness, we found no differences in the diversity of network members. From our data it did appear the mothers of retarded children were less likely to belong to community or group organizations. This finding may reflect a preference for one-to-one types of social activities resulting from fear of stigma, lack of free time, or some other factor. However, our research design was not suited to confirm any of these speculations.

Relational Characteristics

The third dimension of social networks described by Cochran and Brassard is that of relational characteristics. Relational characteristics focus on the directedness, intensity, and content of the networks. Again, no differences were found between the two groups of mothers. Both groups of mothers reported equal frequencies of socialization, technical assistance, emotional support, feedback and guidance, and advice and information. For both groups, socialization, such as going to a movie, dining out, or conversing was the most frequently reported type of support.

One might expect that the presence of a retarded child would produce a greater need for overall support, as well as an increased need for particular types of support. Although our study did not assess mothers' needs for supports, our data indicated these two groups of mothers do not differ in the actual frequency of overall contact with important people in their lives, nor do they differ in the types of contacts they report. These findings raise some questions when viewed in light of the reported literature. Previously reviewed studies of parents of handicapped children such as those by Birenbaum (1972), Dunlap (1979), Jacobson and Humphry (1979), and Morrison, Beasley and Williams (1976) have indicated increased parental need for certain kinds of support. We are unable to say, however, that the mothers in our study do not need extra supports, or that they have unmet needs.

We can conclude then that the social networks of the mothers of mentally retarded children did not differ from those of the mothers of nonretarded children on any of the three dimensions of networks described by Cochran and Brassard. Examination of other aspects of perceived support are needed.

Satisfaction with Available Supports

While there were few differences in the overall frequency and type of support received by these two groups of mothers, there were differences in mothers' perceptions of the quality of their support. Furthermore, these differences were related to the age of the child. For the categories of feedback and guidance, emotional support, tangible assistance, and advice and information, mothers of younger (birth through six years) retarded children were less satisfied than their counterparts who did not have retarded children. Ratings by mothers of preschool mentally retarded children fell toward the dissatisfied end of the continuum of ratings. On the other hand, mothers of teenage retarded children reported more satisfaction than their counterparts with all five types of support. With the exception of advice and information, both groups of mothers of elementary age children were equivalent in terms of their satisfaction with the quality of support they received.

The finding that mothers of younger retarded children experience less satisfaction with supports than mothers of teenage retarded children, despite the fact that both groups receive equal amounts and types of support, suggests variation in parents' experiences across the family's life cycle. The transition to parenthood for parents of normal children is stressful (Dyer, 1963; Hobbs, 1965), and the presence of a handicapped child may increase the degree to which these stresses are experienced. Wikler (1981) has suggested that the types or sources of stress may be different for parents of younger handicapped children than for parents of older handicapped children. Data collected from this sample indicated the total number of stressful life events did not differ across any combination of parent categories (presence or absence of a handicapped child) or age of child (preschool, elementary, teenage). However, the nature of these stressors may differ. Examples of unique stressors for parents of preschool mentally retarded children are: uncertainty about the child's education, unique medical complications often associated with the child's handicap, and the practical and emotional impact of these complications on family life. All of these are a part of having to adjust to the reality of having a handicapped child.

Mothers of preschool retarded and nonretarded children differed from one another in their perception of the quality of support; mothers of elementary-age children did not. That is to say, mothers of elementary-age mentally retarded children perceived the quality of their support no differently than mothers of nonretarded children. This finding may be attributable to several factors. By the time the retarded children reach elementary school age, their mothers may have developed efficient routines for daily family and community living. In addition, service delivery systems for youngsters in elementary school tend to be more developed than are those for preschool children. Public Law 94-142 and other legislation have provided this generation of parents with greater access to services than those the parents of the teenage retarded children had access to when their children were younger. From Birenbaum's (1972) perspective, these mandatory services may help families of school-age children maintain the "fiction of normality." With the child in school for much of the day, the mother has a more normal child-rearing routine. Concerns about the child's education may recede at this time. Medical care, if any, may have become routine, and parents may have knowledge of the medical and educational resources available within the community. These factors may account for their satisfaction with available supports.

In contrast to parents of the youngest mentally retarded children, mothers of teenage retarded children perceived greater satisfaction with supports than did their counterparts, mothers of nonretarded teenagers. This finding may be explained by the fact that parents of older retarded children may have developed realistic expectations regarding the development of their children, and their roles as parents of handicapped children. Mothers of older children may have come to terms with their child's potential, and may have developed a routine for caregiving, as well as for their participation in community activities. However, mothers' feelings may change as their children approach school-leaving age. Vadasy and Fewell, in Chapter 5, found that mothers of teenage deaf-blind children had quite negative expectations about their children's vocational potential. As parents approach the critical event of their child's transition from school- to community-based services, their satisfaction will vary with the level of local supports that are available.

It should be noted that this generation of older parents has seen marked changes in the legal and social status of the mentally retarded. Over the course of their children's lives, there has been a change in the availability and sophistication of services, as well as increased social awareness of the nature of retardation. Many of the older parents commented during the course of interviews on the fact that younger parents "have it easy" or "they don't know what it was like when our child was young." It may be that these older parents are more grateful for whatever types of support they receive, because they remember times when negative attitudes towards the retarded were more widespread, and education and related services were more difficult to obtain.

The ex post facto nature of our design did not provide the control available in a true experimental design. The cross-sectional analyses also pose a problem for interpretation. For example, differences between parents of different-aged children may reflect parents' generational differences rather than developmental trends in parents' life cycles related to their children. That is, parents of mentally retarded teenage children in our study may or may not have shared the views of the parents of preschool children when their teenagers were preschoolers. As Campbell and Stanley (1963) have noted, selection, mortality, and selection/maturation interactions may be sources of threats to validity.

Conclusion

As is evident in this book and throughout the literature, there are a variety of ways to approach the study of mentally retarded children and their families. Our research utilized the conceptual model of personal-social networks and child development developed by Cochran and Brassard (1979). We also chose to explore the nature of the social network per se because this is an area in which professionals can intervene to offer assistance.

In this study, as in most of the literature on social networks, the focus is on the network structure, particularly size, density, and types of supports provided. Very little is known about how individuals use their networks, particularly the strategies and skills that individuals employ to obtain the support they need from a network. Thus, there are two very important facets of network research: that of characterizing network composition and structural components, and that of identifying the processes by which individuals use their networks as a source of support. The study of network composition and structure is well documented in many areas of research, and a variety of methods have been developed. The study of the dynamic processes of accessing social support, however, has very little conceptual foundation or method, and future research in that area is warranted.

We feel that an understanding of the importance of social supports in the lives of parents of mentally retarded children requires the examination of the support structures as well as the processes of accessing supports. Future research needs to examine more intensively the interactions between parent chracteristics, parent behavior, and network members to see why and how parents contribute to, and likewise, are changed by network relations. Additionally, the impact of these interactions on the child's development will help us understand how all family members are affected by the ecology of the family's social networks. Through such knowledge, we will be able to better understand the stressors experienced by parents of handicapped children, and to determine whether they are a function of their life circumstances or their personal characteristics and skills. As well, such knowledge should facilitate identifying those parents who lack resources which we can help provide, and those parents who need assistance to access resources that are already available.

References

Birenbaum, A. (1970). On managing courtesy stigma. *Journal of Health and Social Behavior, 11*, 196-206.

Birenbaum, A. (1972). The mentally retarded child in the home and the family life cycle. *Journal of Health and Social Behavior, 12*, 55-65.

Blacher, J. (1984). Sequential stages of parental adjustment to the birth of a child with handicaps: Fact or artifact? *Mental Retardation, 22*, 55-68.

Bowen, M. (1978). *Family therapy and clinical practice*. New York: Jason Aaronson.

Breslau, N., Staruch, K.S., & Mortimer, E.A (1982). Psychological distress in mothers of disabled children. *American Journal of Diseases of Children, 136*, 682-686.

Campbell, D.T., & Stanley, J.C. (1963). Experimental and quasi-experimental design for research on teaching. In N.L. Gage (Ed.), *Handbook of research on teaching* (pp. 171-246). Chicago: Rand McNally.

Catron, T.F. (1983). *Personal social networks of mothers of mentally retarded children*. Unpublished master's thesis, George Peabody College for Teachers of Vanderbilt University, Nashville, TN.

Cobb, S. 1976. Social support as a moderator of life stress. *Psychosomatic Medicine, 38*, 300-314.

Cochran, M.M., & Brassard, J.A. (1979). Child development and personal social networks. *Child Development, 50*, 601-616.

Dodge, P. (1976). Neurological disorders of school aged children. *Journal of School Health, 46*, 338-343.

Dunlap, W.R. (1979). How do parents of handicapped children view their needs? *Journal of the Division for Early Childhood, 1*, 1-9.

Dunlap, W. R., & Hollinsworth, J. S. (1977). How does a handicapped child affect the family? Implications for practitioners. *The Family Coordinator, 26*, 286-293.

Dyer, E.D. (1963). Parenthood as crisis: A restudy. *Marriage and Family Living, 25*, 196-201.

Farber, B. (1968). *Mental retardation: Its social context and social consequences*. Boston: Houghton Mifflin.

Farber, B. (1975). Family adaptations to severely mentally retarded children. In M. Begab & S. Richardson (Eds.), *The mentally retarded and society: A social science perspective* (pp. 247-266). Baltimore: University Park Press.

Featherstone, H. (1980). *A difference in the family*. New York: Basic Books.

Fewell, R. R. (1984, March). *Sources of social support for mothers of children with Down Syndrome*. Paper presented at the 17th Annual Gatlinburg Conference on Research on Mental Retardation and Developmental Disabilities, Gatlinburg, TN.

Gabel, H., & Kotsch, L. S. (1981). Extended families and young handicapped children. *Topics in Early Childhood Special Education, 1*, 29-35.

German, M.L., & Maisto, A.A (1982). The relationship of a perceived family support system to the institutional placement of mentally retarded children. *Education and Training of the Mentally Retarded, 17*, 17-23.

Grossman, H.J. (1973). Manual on the terminology and classification in mental retardation. *American Journal of Mental Deficiency Special Publication* (Series No. 2).

Hirsch, B. J. (1980). Natural support systems and coping with major life changes. *American Journal of Community Psychology, 9,* 153-166.

Hobbs, D. F. (1965). Parenthood as crisis: A third study. *Journal of Marriage and the Family, 27,* 367-372.

Holroyd, J. C. (1973). *Manual for the questionnaire on resources and stress.* Los Angeles: U.C.L.A. Neuropsychiatric Institute.

Holt, K. S. (1958). The home care survey of retarded children. *Pediatrics, 22,* 746-755.

Jacobson, R. B., & Humphry, R. A. (1979). Families in crisis: Research and theory in child mental retardation. *Social Casework,* 597-601.

McDowell, J., & Gabel, H. (1981). *Social support among mothers of mentally retarded infants.* Unpublished manuscript, George Peabody College for Teachers of Vanderbilt University, Nashville, TN.

Mitchell, R.E., & Trickett, E.J. (1980). Task force report: Social workers as mediators of social support. *Community Mental Health Journal, 16,* 27-44.

Moore, J.A., Hamerlynck, L.A., Barsh, E.T., Spieker, S., & Jones, R.R. (1982). *Extending family resources.* (Available from Children's Clinic and Preschool, 1850 Boyer Avenue East, Seattle, WA 98112).

Morrison, A.A., Beasley, D.M., & Williams, K.I. (1976). *The intellectually handicapped and their families: A New Zealand study, 1962.* Wellington, New Zealand: Research Foundation for the New Zealand Society for the Intellectually Handicapped.

Olshansky, S. (1962). Chronic sorrow: A response to having a mentally defective child. *Social Casework, 43,* 190-193.

Pattison, E. M. (1977). A theoretical-empirical base for social systems therapy. In E. Folkes (Ed.), *Current perspectives in cultural psychiatry* (pp. 217-254). New York: Spectrum.

Schell, G. C. (1981). The young handicapped child: A family perspective. *Topics in Early Childhood Special Education, 1,* 21-27.

Schonell, F. J., & Watts, B.H. (1956). A first survey of the effects of a subnormal child on the family unit. *American Journal of Mental Deficiency, 61,* 210-219.

Stagg, V. (1983). *Personal-social networks of mothers of mentally retarded children.* Unpublished doctoral dissertation, George Peabody College for Teachers of Vanderbilt University, Nashville, TN.

Suelzle, M., & Keenan, V. (1981). Changes in family support networks over the life cycle of mentally retarded persons. *American Journal of Mental Deficiency, 86,* 267-274.

Tavormina, J. B., Henggeler, S. W., & Gayton, W. F. (1976). Age trends in parental assessment of behavior problems of their retarded children. *Mental Retardation, 14,* 38-39.

Turnbull, A. P., Summers, J. A., & Brotherson, M. J. (1983). *Working with families with disabled members: A family systems approach.* Unpublished manuscript.

Watson, R. L., & Midlarsky, E. (1979). Reactions of mothers with mentally retarded children: A social perspective. *Psychological Reports, 45,* 309-310.

Wikler, L. (1981). Chronic stresses of families of mentally retarded children. *Family Relations, 30,* 281-288.

Wikler, L. (1983, June). *Periodic stresses in families of children with mental retardation.* Paper presented to the American Association on Mental Deficiency, Annual Convention, Dallas, TX.

Wikler, L., Wasow, M., & Hatfield, E. (1981). Chronic sorrow revisited: Attitudes of parents and professionals about adjustment to mental retardation. *American Journal of Orthopsychiatry, 51,* 63-70.

Wolfensberger, W., & Menolascino, F. J. (1970). A theoretical framework for the management of parents of the mentally retarded. In F. S. Menolascino (Ed.), *Psychiatric approaches to mental retardation* (pp. 475-492). New York: Basic Books.

12

Supports from Religious Organizations and Personal Beliefs

Rebecca R. Fewell

When a person is born with an impairment, incurs a debilitating accident or illness, or in the course of development, fails to develop to a level where he or she can fully participate in society, many difficult questions and challenges arise. The person and his or her family must try to answer the question why this has happened, and the family must find a way to meet the increased needs of the impaired member. In some cases, family members will assume responsibilities that will last for the remainder of their lives. Family members who take on these roles are seldom prepared to do so. They, as well as the impaired person, will need various kinds of support, depending on the handicapped family member's needs, their own needs, the resources available, and many other factors. Support for immediate family members will often come from extended family members, such as maternal and paternal grandparents, other children, friends, and neighbors. Support may come from institutions such as the schools, churches, medical centers, national or community organizations such as the Lions Club or Easter Seal Society, and government agencies that provide special services for the handicapped. Some persons will derive important support from their inner resources, personal belief systems, and religious affiliation. Theorists and researchers have provided a rationale for examining how beliefs, particularly religious beliefs, are used by parents of handicapped children to help them cope with the added stresses they experience. Findings from several studies will be reviewed, and the two types of support families are found to derive from their religion will be discussed.

Support from Religious Beliefs

Theorists in family interactions, Folkman, Schaefer, and Lazarus (1979) proposed a model of how individuals cope with stressful situations. The theorists feel an individual's successful appraisal of a situation is based on the availability of five coping resources: utilitarian resources, health-energy-morale, social support, problem-solving abilities, and general and specific beliefs. The category of general and specific beliefs includes religious beliefs which help individuals face inexplicable questions.

In a study of mothers of retarded children, Friedrich, Cohen, and Wilturner (in press) examined locus of control and religiosity, two variables they considered to be included in Folkman et al.'s category of general and specific beliefs. The investigators used the term "religiosity" to describe the role religious beliefs play in one's adaptation to life experiences. The researchers found strong evidence that religiosity serves as a "buffer" to many of the stresses associated with raising a handicapped child, particularly for younger, less educated mothers. According to these researchers, a variety of beliefs are associated with religiosity. Two of these beliefs are that a supreme being has a reason for selecting the parents to raise a child with special needs, and that this being is aiding their coping. The researchers identified locus of control to be an important moderator variable, as mothers who had more internal locus of control felt more positive about themselves and had a wider range of coping resources available to them than mothers with less locus of control. Of particular interest to the researchers was the finding that religiosity and locus of control were not correlated ($r=.01$), yet both operate as buffers of stress. Parents and families, they concluded, use different resources and styles for coping with stressful events, and these may vary from one time in the life cycle to another.

Further information about the nature of religion and the role of beliefs in the lives of parents of retarded children comes from a study recently completed by the author. In an effort to investigate the types and amount of support available to parents of handicapped children, the author and her colleagues developed the *Questionnaire on Family Support Systems* (Fewell, Belmonte, & Ahlersmeyer, 1983). The 14-page questionnaire was composed on six subscales, including one on religious organizations and beliefs. An analysis of the responses of 80 mothers to the questions on this subscale is presented in this section.

The subjects were solicited from mothers of children with Down syndrome who had written to the Model Preschool Center at the Experimental Education Unit, University of Washington for information and resources on the education of young children with Down syndrome. The mothers had written in response to an article that appeared in *Family Circle* magazine (October 1982). Questionnaires were mailed to 135 mothers living in all areas of the United States, and responses were received from 80 mothers. This represented a return rate of 60%, a rate that exceeded the estimate of reasonable rates (10-50%) anticipated from mail surveys (Sellitz, Wrightsman, & Cook, 1981). The mean age of the mothers was 31.5 years. The mean age of the children with Down syndrome was 2.5 years.

The original Religion Scale (see Table 12.1) included 13 statements. Two subscales were subsequently formed. Six statements (1-6) were determined to be related to the church as a supportive organized body of persons, and six statements (7-12) were related to aspects of one's personal or spiritual beliefs. One additional question in the original scale was judged to be ambiguous for purposes of subscale classification; it was deleted when responses on the two subscales were considered. In the questionnaire, these 12 statements were ordered randomly, and there was no indication as to which aspects of religion the questions tapped. Mothers were asked to assign a number from 0 to 5 to each statement, indicating their agreement or disagreement based on their own experience.

The scores were as follows: 0-not applicable; 1-strongly disagree; 2-moderately disagree; 3-neither agree or disagree; 4-moderately agree; or 5-strongly agree. Table 12.1 includes the percentage of responses that were classified as not applicable, agree (strongly and moderately), neither agree nor disagree, or disagree (strongly and moderately).

When we compared mothers' responses to the first six questions on support mothers perceived from their church organization to their responses on the six questions on support from their spiritual beliefs, we found that mothers felt very different about the support they received from these two sources. Means, standard deviations, *t* values, and probabilities are seen in Table 12.2. Mothers reported significantly greater support from their personal or spiritual beliefs than from their religious organizations.

Table 12.1. Religion Scale

Items	Category	0	10	20	30	40	50	60	70	80	90	100
1. Our clergyman was helpful to us when our handicapped child was born.	N/A				34.2							
	Agreed					41.8						
	Neither		7.6									
	Disagree			16.5								
2. We are satisfied with availability of religious instruction for our handicapped child.	N/A				29.5							
	Agree				32.0							
	Neither			21.8								
	Disagree			16.7								
3. We are more active in our church since our handicapped child was born.	N/A			19.5								
	Agree		13.0									
	Neither				26.0							
	Disagree					41.6						
4. If we had problems associated with our handicapped child, we would seek help and guidance from members of our church or clergy.	N/A			18.2								
	Agree					37.7						
	Neither		13.0									
	Disagree				31.2							
5. The church has been more supportive to us than other agencies in our community by providing the help we need as parents of a handicapped child.	N/A			21.5								
	Agree		13.9									
	Neither				.25.3							
	Disagree					39.2						
6. Most of my social activities involve members of my church.	N/A			20.3								
	Agree				32.9							
	Neither		7.6									
	Disagree					39.2						
7. Our religion has helped us to understand and accept our handicapped child.	N/A			15.6								
	Agree								66.3			
	Neither		10.4									
	Disagree		7.8									
8. We are satisfied that our religion is fulfilling our family's spiritual needs	N/A		12.7									
	Agree							59.5				
	Neither			16.5								
	Disagree		11.4									
9. Having a handicapped child has brought us closer to God and our religion.	N/A		10.3									
	Agree							55.2				
	Neither			24.4								
	Disagree		10.2									
10. We seek comfort through prayer.	N/A		7.7									
	Agree									75.6		
	Neither		9.0									
	Disagree		7.7									
11. Our faith continues to be a source of help and support in coping with our handicapped child.	N/A		10.3									
	Agree								70.5			
	Neither		11.5									
	Disagree		7.6									
12. Our faith is a source of personal and family strength to us in everyday living.	N/A		8.9									
	Agree								69.6			
	Neither		11.4									
	Disagree		10.1									

**Table 12.2. Means, Standard Deviations, Differences and *t* Values
for Organized Religion and Personal Beliefs Scales (*n* = 78)**

Scales	*M*	*SD*	*t*	*p*
Organized Religion	13.22	7.75		
Personal Beliefs	21.85	8.44	-.1308	.000

Comparisons of mothers' responses within and across the two sets of
statements offer important information on the difference in support from
religious organizations and personal beliefs.

**Table 12.3. Percentage of Responses to Questions on
Support from Organized Religion and Personal Beliefs**

	Not Applicable	Neither Agree or Disagree	Agree	Disagree
	%	%	%	%
Statements Indicating Support From Organized Religion	24	17	29	31
Statements Indicating Support From Personal Beliefs	11	14	66	9

First, as seen in Table 12.3, the mean percentage of responses which
indicate agreement or disagreement with the statements on organized
religion as a support reveal only small differences. As many mothers
agree as disagree, and only a few less mothers indicate a religious
organization is not applicable as a source of support in their lives.

The mean percentages of mothers' responses to the statements
related to spiritual beliefs as supports reveal a very different pattern,
with the mean percentage of agreements being over seven times the
mean percentage of responses reflecting disagreement with the positive
statements, and six times the mean percentage of responses indicating
statements were not applicable to them. These differences indicate that
significantly more mothers find their spiritual or personal beliefs to be
sources of support and applicable to their daily lives than mothers who
do not perceive support from their own spiritual beliefs.

Comparisons across the two sets of statements provide further insight into sources of support. The mean percentages of mothers responding that support from their organized church was not applicable to them (24%) was twice the percentage of mothers who indicated that support from their belief systems was not applicable (11%). Thus, 89% of mothers were able to relate to the questions about personal beliefs and could indicate their feelings about these statements, whereas 24% of the mothers did not feel statements regarding support from religious organizations were relevant to them.

Comparisons of agreements between the two sets of items also yielded differences. Of the mothers responding, 66% responded positively about support emanating from their beliefs, whereas only 29% of the mothers responded positively about support they experienced from their organized religious group. These findings indicate the support these mothers derive from their belief system was extremely important to them as they understand and cope with the experience of having a child with Down syndrome.

Comparisons of disagreements also yielded very different results. While 31% of the mothers disagreed with the positive statements of support from the church organizations, only 9% disagreed with the positive statements of support from their beliefs.

Finally, when we examined the percentage of mothers who neither agreed nor disagreed with these positive statements of support, slightly more mothers were indecisive about organized religious support compared to mothers who were indecisive about the support they derived from personal beliefs.

The results of this study suggest a theme that will be further discussed in this chapter. It appears that a parent's formal religious affiliation and the parent's spiritual or personal beliefs are separate systems of support that can be considered independent of one another. The results indicate mothers of children with Down syndrome experience significant religious support in their parenting role, particularly from their personal or spiritual beliefs. These are beliefs that are closely aligned with faith, with belief in a spiritual being, and with the efficacy of prayer. For some mothers, religious organizations have been a source of strength, but fewer mothers indicated they derived support from this source. The findings of this study on the importance of personal beliefs in a spiritual being support the findings of Friedrich et al. (in press), and of Vadasy and Fewell (see Chapter 5) that religious beliefs are a source of support for parents of children with handicaps. Belief in a supreme being appears to buffer stress and enables mothers to cope on a daily basis. The distinct nature of these two types of religious support makes it important to examine each in more detail in an effort to understand how they benefit parents.

Support From Religious Organizations

Bronfenbrenner, Moen, and Garbarino (1984) suggest that "researchers concerned with the well-being of families would do well to attend to the part played by religious institutions within the community." (p. 30). The authors view religious organizations as extremely salient both as sources of support and as child rearing systems in their own right. They are one of the few social institutions according major importance and status to parenthood and child rearing.

Religious organizations offer many different benefits to their members, and individual members may take away quite different types of support from any one of these organizations. Membership in a religious organization may offer parents of handicapped children several different kinds of support, including: (a) instrumental support, (b) emotional or social support, (c) educational support, and (d) structural support.

Instrumental Support

In describing support individuals derive from social networks, Unger and Powell (1980) use the term instrumental support to refer to material goods and services provided to alleviate financial and economic crises. A major mission of many religious organizations is to provide instrumental support for their members and others in need. Members of religious organizations often believe that the provision of this instrumental support is more important for the giver than it is for the receiver. By providing food, medical supplies, money, and other forms of goods and services to those in need, both within and outside of their group, members of church organizations are able to put into action their beliefs.

Emotional or Social Support

Within many religious organizations, there exist strong bonds of support between members. These bonds develop through members' frequent associations, and their common embrace of church doctrines and causes. Members of some organizations view their fellow parishioners as members of an extended family or a caring community (Ball, 1983). Members support one another in their joys and sorrows. For example, a red rose may be included at a church service to signify the church community's celebration of the birth of a child for the child's family. Members who may not know a new family may nevertheless participate in vows to help the family nurture their child in the common faith of the organization. The social support that church members can provide for peers is captured so well by Rabbi Harold Kusher (1981) who relates a story told by Harry Golden.

> When he was young, he once asked his father, "If you don't believe in God, why do you go to synagogue so regularly?" His father answered, "Jews go to synagogue for all sorts of reasons. My friend Garfinkle, who is Orthodox, goes to talk to God. I go to talk to Garfinkle." (p.122)

Within other religious bodies, supportive relationships may be experienced quite differently. When queried about support provided by members of her urban parish, a mother of a child with a serious impairment said:

> I have never felt any support from the members. I really doubt that they know who we are. We worship in the same church, but we don't know each other.

This statement is from a mother who attends church regularly and who reports her religion to be an important source of support in her life. She experiences this support although she does not seem to obtain support of a social nature from her church. The notion of religious support and what that really means is clearly a complex issue.

Whether or not a family finds support from a religious organization appears to be greatly influenced by many variables. Certainly, the history of the particular congregation is one determinant of its present behavior. The doctrines of the religious organization may be another factor, some groups fostering a more active ministry among members than others. The members themselves also bring their personal histories, strengths, and needs to the organization. These attributes shape what happens to the group as a whole, and affect the lives of individual members. Church members are, in turn, influenced by each other and by their transactions. The church leader or pastor may set the example for the rest of the congregation. Ball (1983) describes five roles that a pastor should be prepared to play to foster effective church-community links: (1) an enabler, who helps families articulate their needs from their communities; (2) a broker, who helps identify and secure community services; (3) an expert, who has information and advice; (4) a planner, who gathers and helps analyze facts so that futures can be planned; (5) an advocate or paraclete, who supports the process of securing services (pp. 146-148). It is clear that not all church leaders are able to be as informed a resource or as effective an activist as Ball describes. Some families will encounter church leaders who assume an advocacy role, although other families may not derive this benefit from their church or may not even desire it if supports from other sources are adequate.

Other factors that could contribute to the emotional or social support a family might experience from a local religious group are the size and location of the group. In very large groups which meet infrequently, persons may have few opportunities to get to know each other. In small groups where members may have to contribute more to the ongoing functions, (i.e., teach in the church schools, usher at services, work as missionaries, visit the sick) there may be more opportunities to know and support one another. In some areas of the country, religious organizations appear to be more central to the life of the community than in other regions. For example, in the South, a very high percentage of families are members of religious organizations and participate actively in the functions of their institutions. Likewise, in rural areas churches serve as gathering places for persons in the area, thus supporting the social life of the community. In some of these organizations, large extended family networks may characterize the makeup of the church membership, thus reinforcing both church and family groups. Many religious organizations have established procedures for responding to crises in the lives of their members. Church leaders and often individual members visit one another to express their concern. Fellow members attend important services to participate in rituals of particular value to another member. One such crisis may be the birth of a child with a handicap into the church community, and members and clergy in some religious groups may offer valuable support to the new parents and family.

While members of a religious organization may provide the family with support at the time of a crisis, such as the birth of a child with severe impairments, the long-term support churches provide such families may be far from ideal. Turnbull (1983) describes her family's experiences:

> Rud and I have not yet found a church that had a systematic plan for including handicapped children in the church school program. . . .I longed to have the church school director approach Jay and invite him into a program or explain options to me on how he could be included. This, however, has never happened. (p. 14-15)

Educational Support

Religious organizations provide training for their members, regardless of age. This does not obviate the need for families within the organization to assume this responsibility; it simply supports their efforts. While the organization expects parents to provide religious training on a daily basis, the organization provides the more formal instruction, usually through a church school or through classes or training.

At times, religious education may provide very specific support in an attempt to provide children with a framework for understanding life's tragedies. Rabbi Kushner (1981) was asked to explain to neighborhood children and nursery school playmates why one of their friends had been killed in an accident. He provides a detailed account of the explanation he offered, and he reminds readers of the care with which such explanations must be given.

> Children are particularly susceptible to feelings of guilt. But even as adults, many of us never totally out-grow that tendency. A wrong word, even by someone trying to be helpful, will serve to reinforce the feeling that it was, in fact, our fault. (p.101)

Parents of children with handicaps seek two kinds of educational support from their religious bodies. First, they want their handicapped child to have appropriate opportunities to participate in the organization's services. Turnbull's previous quotes and remarks illustrate that desire, as do these further remarks from her:

> Whereas we could always make the assumption that there would be a program for Kate and Amy, we could not make the same assumption for Jay. It has not been that our churches have tried to exclude Jay; however, they have not responded with appropriate alternatives for him. (p. 14)

A second educational need families have is for guidance in how they might carry out some of their own responsibilities to their handicapped child. For example, they may seek help in how to explain to their child why he will not be able to participate in events his siblings experience. Or, parents may need help in explaining abstract religious concepts such as "God," the "Virgin Mary," or the "Holy Ghost" to a mildly mentally retarded child.

Structural Support

Religious organizations, like schools and other institutions, provide a framework for helping persons adapt to new roles and responsibilities as they mature. This framework parallels the different milestones, stages, or events in the lives of church members. Another form of structural support is that offered through the rituals and practices of the corporate community.

Developmental milestones in church life. Although religious organizations define these steps differently, these events share common meanings and have functional roles in the lives of religious communicants. Each of these steps has a special meaning for a child and for the family as they grow, both in their relationship as family members, and as members of the larger church family.

Baptism. Shortly after life begins, parents who want their newborn child to follow the religious traditions of their family will seek the blessings of the religious body for their child. This ceremony of initiation involves the clergyman, members of the extended family, and often members of the religious body. It is a time for parents and other family members to make a commitment to provide religious training for the child, and for the child to be welcomed into the care of the organization. In some religious bodies the rite of baptism incorporates organizational membership as well.

Membership. After a period of religious education, when parents, the child, and the religious organization's representatives feel the child is ready to make a personal decision to follow the creed of the organization, the child becomes a communicant or member of the church body with the full responsibilities of an adult member. This initiation usually occurs at a ceremony that includes certain rituals unique to the particular religious body. For many it is a time for the "first communion." It represents a full sharing of the organization's beliefs. Other ceremonies of full membership like bar mitzvah and confirmation acknowledge the ability of the young church members to fully comprehend, embrace, and defend the tenets of the religion.

Marriage. As children mature, they put more distance between themselves and their parents. They spend less time at home, they learn to enjoy the companionship of agemates, and they enjoy their own independence. The majority decide to make a new family with someone they have come to love. Many persons seek the blessings of their religious organization in this union. All religions have rituals to consecrate such unions and to provide for the entrances of new members into their denomination. Again, families turn to their religious organizations at this milestone, and together they help their children enter this new life stage.

Death. A goal of most religions is to prepare their members for death and an afterlife. Thus, it is natural that religious organizations have developed often elaborate ceremonies and rites of passage to support the dying person and the person's family and friends. Last rites mark the entrance of the dying person into this final stage, and these rites help family and friends cope with the death of their loved one, as well as contemplate their own mortality.

The major life stages marked by the church ceremonies of baptism, full membership, marriage, and death, are not unique to the experiences of persons who are members of religious organizations, but are stages that are closely aligned with the beliefs, doctrines and missions of these groups. Organizations and families use these ceremonies to observe these changes across the life-span, and religious organizations have developed ceremonies and rites of passage that enable members and their families to celebrate these joyous milestones, and to accept and understand the meaning of the sorrowful ones.

When a child is handicapped, he or she is often unable to participate fully in these ceremonies, or participation may be delayed. In this respect, these religious milestones may reinforce the parents' sadness and disappointment that their child cannot fully enjoy all of life's opportunities. Yet these ceremonies may also offer comfort, as when the child is baptized and welcomed into the congregation without regard for the child's disability.

Rituals and corporate worship. Religious organizations have predictable patterns to their formal meetings—the Catholic Mass, the prayer meeting, the church or temple service. Members often come to expect the rituals associated with church services to follow a certain form, and frequently are perturbed if church leaders deviate from the traditional forms. Many rituals take on symbolic functions and are perceived at times as the experience they represent. When the ritual is not a part of the worship service, the "experience" for some members did not occur. When asked about her attendance at church, one mother said: "I don't feel guilty when I miss, but I do miss it." When queried further, she explained "it" as "the rituals." She said, "It doesn't matter which parish church I attend, I will get the same feeling—I derive strength from the rituals."

Rituals and group worship experiences embody a form of supportive structure that some people find meaningful. For many it is a tie to the past, and through participating in events that were a part of their lives as children, they experience a comfort, aptly referred to in some circles as "mother church."

Support also comes from a religious organization's stated principles or beliefs that are central to the organization in the forms of written scriptures, creeds, and doctrines. As noted earlier, these principles are taught to members and are reflected through prayers and rituals. The beliefs provide the organization's interpretation of the nature of the universe, and offer explanations for what happens to people and why. This framework for understanding the world helps members answer questions that seem to many to be "unanswerable." Members can recall the scriptures, for example, to compare how another person responded to a difficult situation, and to find an example to follow. Members can derive comfort and forgiveness through acknowledging or confessing mistakes and violations of the rights of others. Likewise, members can feel thankful when good things happen to them, as their belief system has taught them how to interpret such experiences and how to make appropriate responses under such circumstances. For many, these creeds are accepted on faith and therefore they need not be questioned. Armed with the comfort of these answers, one may not have to seek other explanations or answers for life's happenings.

Beliefs: Their Sources and Support

Throughout the life-span, human beings strive to understand their existence. Age, mental prowess, environmental stimulants, cultural and physical conditions, and a host of other variables contribute to the questions and the answers that emerge in this continuing search for meaning, which is not restricted by culture, space, or time, but is influenced by these elements. The outcome of this search is the conviction that certain things are true or real. These beliefs may be unformulated assumptions about how and why things are as they appear to be, or they may be highly organized in creeds, doctrines, or tenets of faith that are set down in both written and verbal forms. As discussed earlier in the section on religious organizations, beliefs can be so highly personalized that an individual may not acknowledge that others share them, or beliefs can be widely held tenets that one holds in common with many others.

Beliefs, whether they are individual personal values or tenets one shares with others, play an important role in one's life. Beliefs provide individuals with a framework for living and for understanding life. Beliefs help persons determine how they will live, what they will do with their lives, how they will spend the hours of each day, what and when they will eat, how they will relate to other human beings, and in some cases, beliefs determine where one will live and die. Human beings, unlike other species, have the ability to think, to analyze, to experiment, and to learn from experiences. Human beings are not simply passive recipients of environmental experiences but they are dynamic beings, who contribute to their own development, to the development of others, and to the organization of the world around them. Because beliefs are so central to the formation of who and what human beings are, they serve as supports for the maintenance of life.

Many factors contribute to the beliefs a person espouses at a given point in time. Young individuals are likely to assume the beliefs of other family members. Certain beliefs about the world may be transmitted across generations both in word and in deed. Also influencing one's beliefs are the social institutions one experiences. The educational system, the religious organizations, the interactions between neighbors, the parents' attitudes toward systems, policies and people will have a definite impact on their children. As children move across the life-span and become independent, they take more responsibility for their own belief system. For some, this may mean a more clearly articulated profession of beliefs espoused during youth. Others may come to embrace a system of beliefs that is quite different from that they held when they were young. Education, experiences, and exposure to other persons, doctrines, and societies are likely to influence the beliefs or personal values that emerge during the adult years.

Another important source of beliefs is the specific doctrines and creeds of religious organizations. These institutions usually have written documents that are considered sacred, such as the Bible or Torah. Additionally, organizations have canons and other writings that embody beliefs specific to the particular organizations. Some members of religious organizations strictly adhere to all the organization's beliefs and use these beliefs to answer difficult questions about existence, and to help them cope with events in their daily lives.

Many persons are guided by beliefs that are not identified with an organized religious body, although these beliefs have to do with moral codes that are addressed in the doctrines of religious organizations. These spiritual or personal beliefs often are influenced by the religion an individual was exposed to at an earlier life stage. Individuals who leave a church group may continue to live by that religion's code of beliefs, which continues to represent the person's convictions about life and orderliness in the world. For example, an individual may continue to believe in a supreme being and to turn to that being for strength and comfort without acknowledging the relationship between that source of support and an organized religious body.

Thus, there are many ways in which personal beliefs function as extremely important sources of support for persons in their daily lives. When stressful events occur, beliefs, particularly those that are spiritual or religious in nature, seem to be especially valued. Some persons derive additional support from a religious organization that includes persons with similar beliefs. As Fewell's study indicates, these two types of support may not overlap, and each can stand alone as a coping support.

Beliefs as a Support for Parents of Handicapped Children

Beliefs, regardless of their origins, appear to be particularly important to persons who face stress due to events they did not expect, or cannot easily explain. As Fredrich et al. (in press) noted, the stress created by a mentally retarded child can be mediated through religious beliefs. This is so often seen by professionals as parents grapple with the personal question of "Why did this happen to me?" Given that almost all parents of handicapped children face this question, it is appropriate that we explore what it means and how some parents have answered it.

Invariably one of the earliest questions parents ask when they learn their child has a serious impairment is "Why?" If a natural cause-effect relationship exists between the handicap and some identifiable event, some parents may end their questioning. Many parents, however, will continue to ask "Why" even after they have found a cause. Sooner or later, the more general "Why" question becomes more personal: "Why did it happen to me?" This question represents a shift in the parent's perspective, as the parent moves from focusing solely upon the impact of a handicap on the child to questioning how that handicap reflects upon the parent, and the effect it will have over the parent's life.

Kushner (1981) reflected on what went on in his mind when the doctor told him and his wife that their child had progeria, a degenerative condition characterized by premature aging and death. What he was facing contradicted everything he had been taught about God. He said:

> I could only repeat over and over again in my mind, "This can't be happening. It is not how the world is supposed to work." Tragedies like this were supposed to happen to selfish, dishonest people whom I, as a rabbi, would then try to comfort by assuring them of God's forgiving love. How could it be happening to me, to my son, if what I believed about the world was true? (p. 3)

The parent who learns that his child is impaired will inevitably ask these questions, just as Rabbi Kushner did. If a parent believes in a creator of life, a God, or God-like spirit, then the question eventually becomes "Why did God give me this child?"

For many parents, the answer to this question is that the child's disability is a form of punishment for a parent's sin. This type of answer reflects a certain understanding or theory of the world and how it operates. If a parent believes that bad behavior results in bad consequences, the child's handicap may be seen as a punishment. The parent's reasoning is, "I have done something very bad." This conclusion can come from one's personal belief system, or from beliefs espoused by one's religious organization.

Whether a parent understands the world in this manner or not, this perspective is so widespread that a family member, friend, or stranger with well-meaning intentions, is likely to imply that the child's handicap must be somehow the fault of the parent. Oosterveen (1979), a chaplain and parent of a retarded son, notes, "I have heard it too frequently to be amazed any longer when parents tell me their friend or neighbor has urged them to 'repent, so God can forgive you and heal your child' " (p. 22).

This is one type of thoughtless response parents often experience from persons who regard the child's handicap as somehow the reflection of the parent's sins. Parents often encounter another response from individuals who attempt to comfort the hurting parent by explaining that "God only sends special children to special parents." One parent related such an experience to the author.

> The first words out of our parents' mouths when Philip was born was something to the effect "It's God's will you have been chosen, and we will pray for your strength."

Particularly distressful are poems that are circulated among parents of handicapped children that have as their theme the idea that the handicapped child and family were selected by God. Oosterveen and his wife, like so many parents of handicapped children, received the following poem from a well meaning person who probably believed the sentiments expressed in the poem would console the parents.

Heaven's Very Special Child

(by Mrs. John A. Massimilla, as cited in Oosterveen, 1979)

A meeting was held quite far from earth.
"It's time again for another birth"
The angels said to the Lord above.
"This dear little child will need much love;
His progress on earth may be quite slow;
Accomplishments great he may not show,
And he will require some extra care
From the folks he meets on earth down there.
He may never run or laugh or play;
His thoughts may seem odd and far away.
In various ways he won't adapt,
And he will be known as handicapped.
Please, Lord, find some parents for this child
Who'll do this work as unto You.
They'll not understand it right away,
The difficult role You have them play;
But with this dear child sent from above
Comes strength and new faith and richer love.
And soon they'll know the privilege given
To care for this gift that's straight from heaven.
This precious young charge so meek and mild
Will always remain Your Special Child."

Oosterveen, speaking from his background as a theologian, goes on to explain his deep concern with the sentiments expressed in the poem, no matter how well-intended:

> Besides violating biblical teachings under the guise of poetic license—nowhere is such a meeting described, nor does Scripture permit us to assume handicapped children come to us from a different place or through a different process than normal children—the poem abuses parents at the very time they suffer what may easily be the most traumatic experience of their life. (p. 22)

Another minister of the Mennonite Church, whose son Scott has Down syndrome, also received three copies of the poem. He has also spoken out on the stereotypes of handicapped children the poem contains, and on how little it helps parents understand why this has happened to them.

In dealing with our personal circumstances we have come to believe that God does not will the tragic birth of children like Scott. . .[whose] particular handicap is due to a genetic disorder which scientists cannot fully explain yet. We do not believe that God should be held responsible for this genetic "malfunctioning" beyond the natural laws of genetic development which he created but which were, in Scott's case, violated. We believe that God cried with us over the unexplainable mistake that occurred in Scott's prenatal development. In this respect, the idea expressed by the poet that God and his angels come together to pick us as Scott's parents is inconceivable to us and, with all due respect, slightly offensive. (Klassen, 1984, p. 50)

It should be noted that other parents have reported that they have found comfort in the sentiments expressed in these poems.

The idea that a parent has been especially chosen for this role permeates the reasoning of one mother interviewed for this chapter. This mother of a severely handicapped child expressed her family's perspective on the handicapped child in their family:

My parents feel that God has chosen me to have a handicapped child as a challenge to my religious beliefs and to remind our entire clan to stop and take stock of how very good God has been to each and every one of us.

She added later, "If I didn't have my religious base to keep me going, I'd be nuts by now." Two things are clear from her responses. First, the role of parents and extended family members in helping one "understand" or answer the "why" question is apparent. Many new parents from years of habit and experience continue to look to their parents for wisdom and answers. The idea is that "If one's parents say it, it must be true." Second, this mother has apparently accepted and incorporated that answer into her belief system, and that system is helping her cope.

If the framework of the chosen parent is not one that is acceptable to a family, then what might foster understanding and value clarification? Honest and cautious admission that "some questions have no answers" (p. 25) is suggested by Oosterveen (1979) to members of his own faith who wish to comfort parents and help them cope with their adversity and suffering: "Strong faith and deeply-rooted religious habits are great assets, but no guarantee that parents [of the handicapped] will escape the feelings of depreciation, failure, and shame" (p. 24). The experience always makes a difference in one's life—one is never again the same. The struggle and pain in Oosterveen's mind "lead to a challenged and changed view of God and his dealings with the world" (p. 24).

In grappling with the agony of understanding why a loving, all-powerful God allows bad things to happen to good people, Rabbi Kushner also came to a new understanding of God. First, he had to let go of an image of God as responsible for all things that happen. He says:

The conventional explanation, that God sends us the burden because He knows that we are strong enough to handle it, has it all wrong. Fate, not God, sends us the problem. (p. 129)

He goes on conclude:

God does not cause our misfortunes. Some are caused by bad luck, some are caused by bad people, and some are simply an inevitable consequence of our being human and being mortal, living in a world of inflexible natural laws. (p. 134)

By stopping to regard God as the cause of misfortunes, Kushner did not have to feel angry at God for having betrayed him; rather he could turn to God for help, strength, and perseverance in overcoming his hurt and anger. This enabled him to move on to a more relevant question:

Now that this has happened, what shall I do about it?. . . .Not "where does the tragedy come from?" but "Where does it lead?" (p. 137)

In addressing the "why" question, the answers that Oosterveen and Kushner give reflect strongly the support they experience from both their religious organizations and their personal beliefs. Of particular interest are the changes that both members and teachers of church organizations experienced in their belief systems. In both cases, it is apparent that their beliefs have provided valued support in coping with these stressful events.

Conclusion

In this chapter we have examined the support religious organizations and personal beliefs offer to parents as they carry out their parenting responsibilities for a child whose abilities and potential are quite different from what the parents had anticipated, resulting in greater stress for their family. The nature of religious organizations and of personal belief systems suggest why these supports are so highly valued: Both types of religious support help persons deal with the fundamental questions of life. By providing answers, regardless of their specificity or truth, these support sources help parents to get on with their lives, to attend to other things besides the stressful experience, and to discover new things about themselves and their world. For some parents, religion provides support directly related to the parent's role as a member of a religious group. For other parents, support comes from both the contributions of the group and the beliefs which group members share. Yet for other parents, support is provided by their personal belief systems alone. One thing, however, is clear: For far too long, professionals who work with families of handicapped children, including professionals associated with religious organizations, have failed to understand and realize the importance of these sources of religious support. Although neglected or rarely taken seriously by professionals, it has not been overlooked by parents, and from these sources they often derive much of the strength they need to nurture their child with special needs.

References

Ball, J.R. (1983). Pastoral help for families of handicapped children. In J.L. Paul (Ed.), *The exceptional child: A guidebook for churches and community agencies* (pp. 133-150). New York: Syracuse University Press.

Bronfenbrenner, U., Moen, P., & Garbarino, J. (1984). In R.D. Parke, R.N. Emde, H.P. McAdoo, & G.P. Sackett (Eds.), *The family*. Review of Child Development Research, Volume Seven (pp. 283-328). Chicago: University of Chicago Press.

Fewell, R.R. (1985). Sources of social support for mothers of children with Down syndrome (in preparation).

Fewell, R.R., Belmonte, J., & Ahlersmeyer, D. (1983). *Questionnaire on family support systems*. Unpublished manuscript, Experimental Education Unit, University of Washington, Seattle.

Folkman, S., Schaefer, C., & Lazarus, R.S. (1979). Cognitive processes as mediators of stress and coping. In V. Hamilton & D.W. Warburton (Eds.), *Human stress and cognition* (pp. 265-298). New York: Wiley.

Friedrich, W.N., Cohen, D.S., & Wilturner, L.T. (in press). Specific beliefs as moderator variables in maternal coping with mental retardation. *Journal of Pediatric Psychology*.

Klassen, M. (1984). Specially selected parents? *Down's Syndrome News, 8,* 49-50.

Kushner, H.S. (1981). *When bad things happen to good people*. New York: Avon Books.

Massimilla (Undated). *Your special child*. Unpublished poem.

Oosterveen, G. (1979). In support of parents with handicapped children. *Christianity Today, 23,* 22-25.

Sellitz, C., Wrightsman, L.S., & Cook, S. (1981). *Research methods in social relations*. New York: Holt, Rinehart & Winston.

Turnbull, A.P. (1983). Growing with a handicapped child in the family and community: A parent's perspective. In J.L. Paul (Ed.), *The exceptional child* (pp. 1-19). New York: Syracuse University Press.

Unger, D.G., & Powell, D.R. (1980). Supporting families under stress: The role of social networks. *Family Relations, 24,* 134-142.

13

Interactions Between Community Agencies and Families Over the Life Cycle

Bruce L. Mallory

The purpose of this chapter is to examine the interactions between various community agencies and families with handicapped children. The focus is on those supportive or direct service organizations that supplement the central role played by local education agencies and early intervention programs which primarily address the cognitive and behavioral needs of disabled children. These educational organizations and their roles have been described in Chapter 10 by Espinosa and Shearer. The informal support networks that are so critical to successful family functioning are discussed by Fewell in her chapter on religious supports (12), and in several of the other chapters on family members and their experiences. Specifically, those agencies which play a crucial role in initial diagnoses, referral, health care, parent education, respite care, and related services are described and analyzed. The analysis is based on a family life cycle perspective and proposes specific criteria which should guide the design and evaluation of community agencies.

Assumptions in Providing Services to Families

Before presenting a theoretical model and program criteria, it is necessary to articulate the underlying assumptions which provide the foundation for subsequent analyses. These assumptions are based on current state-of-the-art practices, the author's own experiences as a parent advocate and researcher, and an ideological framework that embraces the goals of normalization (Wolfensberger, 1972) and universal access to services without regard to categorical characteristics (Hobbs, 1975).

The first assumption is that families with handicapped members are more similar to other families than they are different. Although families with disabled children clearly experience stress related to the birth and subsequent development of a handicapped child, the patterns of stress and methods for ameliorating it are qualitatively similar to the experiences of all families in our culture. Marriage, conception, birth, infancy, school entry, adolescence, and the emancipation of the young adult mark difficult but exciting and potentially rewarding milestones. Adjustments in intrafamilial roles, the acquisition of new statuses, financial pressures, protection and advocacy for dependent members, attachment, separation, and individuation processes, and relations with external systems (formal and informal) are phenomena experienced by all families. The importance of a nonpathological, normative approach to families with a disabled member must be constantly reiterated (Crnic, Friedrich, & Greenberg, 1983). Professional training programs and the short-sightedness of helping professionals who view handicapped people and their families as "patients" have perpetuated the notion that our goals should only be to diagnose and prescribe rather than understand and support. To enter into a helping relationship with a family with a prior expectation of pathology or deviance will create a sense of unjustifiable power in the helper, and a sense of dependence and helplessness in the "recipient." Instead of searching for pathology, helpers must search for the existing coping resources, which all families possess to some degree, and must strive to change the ecological conditions in which the family is enmeshed in order to free up and bolster those existing strengths.

The second assumption is that not enough professionals have a longitudinal life-cycle perspective of children and families. Legal and historical factors seem to create a fragmented, static view of development that focuses too heavily on the accomplishment of short-term behavioral or academic goals, such as achieving the annual objectives on an individual service plan. Opportunities and means for modifying human development across the life-span have been well documented (Clarke & Clarke, 1976; Feuerstein, 1980). As well, modification of the ecosystem of the child and family at various points in the life cycle has been successfully attempted (Hobbs, 1982).

Policymakers and service providers must enlarge their perspectives and priorities to take into account historical changes in the structure and function of families. The ontogenetic character of family development, which has been proposed by sociologists in more recent analyses (Hill, 1981), must provide a basis for planning and evaluating intervention. In addition, service providers must not allow their visions of potential change to be dictated by legal requirements for periodic review and evaluation. Annual program planning in education or other human services can lead to discontinuous, short-term views of development that focus only on completion dates. Broader, long-term (more than 3 years) goals should be discussed between families and their helpers in order to develop plans that will lead to maximum achievement and independence for *all* family members. Financial and estate planning, alternative residential arrangements, vocational plans, sex education, and parenting skills are examples of areas that need to be anticipated and discussed well before a disabled person reaches adulthood.

This longitudinal perspective based on continuous care and planning is difficult to acquire and sustain if professionals only see children who are of a certain age, or who possess a specific disability. Despite the limitations of the medical model they commonly employ and their lack of adequate training in communicating with parents of handicapped children, health-care professionals are often the only group in a position to acquire a life cycle perspective of children and their families. The role of physicians and other health-care providers will be examined at length later in the chapter.

The third assumption is that family members, especially parents, can provide valid and well-informed assessment information. Several studies have demonstrated the validity of parents' assessments of their own children's abilities (Bagnato, Neisworth, & Eaves, 1978; Blacher-Dixon & Simeonsson, 1981; Frankel, 1979; Gradel, Thompson, & Sheehan, 1981). These findings suggest that families are capable of identifying and describing a variety of strengths and needs. Parents may feel that professionals perceive them as cognitively or emotionally limited because they have a retarded or disturbed child. This "guilt by association" attitude results in parents being talked down to or having their expressed opinions and desires ignored. In this light, parent participation in program planning and implementation becomes a cursory, superficial process to satisfy regulations rather than to develop an equal partnership among experts. Farber and Lewis (1975) have proposed that one reason professionals encourage parent involvement is to shift the burden of responsibility for program success from professionals to parents. If a child does not progress, it is because the parents were not conscientious enough or sufficiently committed. Professionals are thus exonerated for program failure. Yet professionals remain in control of the basic resources and information necessary for appropriate service delivery. This means that parents are held responsible for their child's development while the locus of control remains outside of the family — a situation that could lead to feelings of parental helplessness and dependence. Such feelings may result in family dysfunction, interfering with growth of the handicapped child (and other children). The child's failure to make progress may thus be falsely interpreted as confirmation that parents really are incapable and professionals always know best. Such paternalism clearly has no place in community agencies. Accepting parents as equal and competent partners will reduce such hierarchical relationships.

The fourth assumption is that the interactions between families and formal community systems are not always easy or successful. The role of mediating structures such as extended family, schools, churches, or voluntary agencies is critical in the successful utilization of bureaucratic systems (Berger & Neuhaus, 1977). These mediating social institutions can provide assistance to families in the form of advocacy, case management, counseling, crisis intervention, information and referral, and so on. Such nondirect services may reduce families' dependency on formal organizations and categorical programs. As well, informal organizations can respond more quickly to pressing needs without requiring lengthy application and eligibility-determination procedures. The utilization of mediating structures is critical to successful family adaptation. This is because families are small idiosyncratic systems, whose primary functions are to nurture, protect, and sustain their members. Public and private bureaucracies, on the other hand, are large, nomothetic organizations characterized by rigid role structures, hierarchical decision-making, and the delineation of well-defined rules and boundaries. Such systems are subject to external and internal policies that limit the scope and nature of the problems to which they can respond. Families, however, do not enjoy the luxury of rejecting some problems and addressing others. Families must respond to the unpredictable and highly variable needs of their members. The bureaucratic pattern of dealing with certain problems (or people or places) and not others is not an option for families (Mallory, 1981). The ecological systems in which families develop over time, whether they are proximal and informal, such as kin or neighborhood networks, or distant and formal, such as health clinics, determine the degree to which the family's own coping resources will be supported and enhanced.

The fifth assumption is that in many regions of the United States, necessary services are in place. Isolated, rural communities are the primary exception. Yet the presence of a service does not guarantee that families will use it, or that families' needs will be met. For example, Moore, Hamerlynck, Barsh, Spieker, and Jones (1982), after surveying 448 families with handicapped children in the state of Washington, concluded that families "did not need additional formal services. . .they needed help coping with and fully utilizing existing services, and they needed some relief from the daily burden of care" (p. 73). The underutilization of available services was due to a lack of information about where and how to obtain services, the expense of services, and income or other eligibility criteria that precluded utilization (Moore et al., 1982). Suelzle and Keenan's (1980) study of parental preference for services indicates that the greatest needs for service expansion are not in direct treatment areas, but in nondirect services necessary to make treatment services accessible, including babysitting, transportation, community referral services, crisis lines, and homemaker or home health aides. Certainly, there are many areas where direct services need to be created or expanded. However, such efforts will be futile if the support mechanisms which enable families to choose and use services are not in place. Thus, service coordination and refinement rather than the creation of new service delivery systems are more heavily emphasized in later sections of this chapter.

The final assumption is that the design of social policies that affect families with handicapped members is in itself often a barrier to effective service utilization (Mallory, 1981; Moroney, 1981). Social policies are often structured so they are responsive only to families experiencing acute stress. Rather than mandating preventive, supportive care, policies encourage intervention only *after* some demonstrable damage has occurred (e.g., child abuse, permanent and total disability, unemployment, or family dissolution). This pattern has been described as residual, substitutive, minimalist, and categorical. White (1973) provides a comprehensive review of this phenomenon and its rationales. Social policies are as much a part of the ecology of family development as are extended family members or transportation systems. Yet policies are usually invisible, complex, and fixed from the perspective of individual families, reinforcing the feeling that families are subject to external control by political systems or professional experts.

Theoretical Framework

With the above assumptions serving as a foundation, it is possible to suggest a theoretical model to understand the interactions of families and community agencies. We begin with a focus on family development over the life-span. The notion that families as systems have a life cycle similar to but distinct from the individual life cycles of their members has been proposed by sociologists such as Hill and Mattesich (1977). Family development theory, a blending of developmental psychology, the sociology of age stratification, and the sociology of participation in social and kinship networks is conceptualized as:

> The process of progressive structural differentiation and transformation over the family's history, . . .the active acquisition and selective discarding of roles by incumbents of family positions as they seek to meet the changing functional requisites for survival and as they adapt to recurring life stresses as a family system. (Hill & Mattesich, 1977, p. 9)

Network Participation Over the Life-span

As stresses occur, mediating variables such as participation in informal social networks enhance or hinder the family's coping abilities. If external network ties are underutilized during times of stress, the intensity and frequency of intrafamilial interactions increase. Over-reliance on family members due to lack of participation in extrafamilial activities may create "disenchantment" or "burnout" among family members (i.e., loss of attachment and commitment to each other). Psychological needs may no longer be met through family interactions, requiring individual members to turn away from each other and seek fulfillment through work or other outlets.

Farber (1959) has found significant decreases in social network participation in families with severely handicapped children, as well as marked role and status changes among family members. The family with a disabled child which reduces its extrafamilial contacts and roles risks internal disenchantment and possible dysfunction. Decreased social network participation may be caused by the daily care demands of the handicapped member, reallocation of scarce financial resources, or feelings of guilt or embarrassment related to the stigma of giving birth to an imperfect child. This decrease in network participation is accompanied by an *involuntary increase* in contacts with formal systems such as hospitals, welfare offices, schools, or advocacy organizations (involuntary in the sense that contacts with these formal agencies is caused by the unexpected and undesired birth of a handicapped child).

Voluntary participation in extrafamilial networks can aid families in seeking assistance, maintaining morale, managing tension, and meeting marital needs. The paradox, however, is that families who are experiencing extraordinary stress due to the presence of a handicapped child are at greatest risk for reducing social network participation, which in turn leads to family dysfunction and a less than optimal environment for the development of the disabled child. Dependence upon formal bureaucratic organizations rather than voluntarily chosen informal networks may only exacerbate the problem.

For most families, the peak in involvement with formal organizations occurs at the middle of the family life cycle when children draw their parents into school-related or recreation-related associations or networks. Families with handicapped children may experience an acceleration of this pattern by being compelled to interact with formal organizations much earlier in their life cycles. This, in turn, may lead to a desire on the part of families to *decrease* their participation as their children approach school age. Parents may view their child's entry into school as a time of relief from the constant arrangements and coordination needed to deal with multiple agencies in the child's early years of life. Social service providers working with school-age children must understand that lack of parent interest or participation in programs and support groups may be caused by these accelerated patterns of involvement. This would be most true for parents of severely handicapped children who have been intensely involved in formal external systems since the child's birth.

Interlocking Concepts of Time

A valuable perspective for this model of participation over the family life cycle is provided by Haraven's (1977) work on family time and historical time. Family historians, like other social analysts, have recently reconceptualized the roles of families, vis a vis social institutions, as more proactive and adaptive than was suggested by earlier views. Coupled with this view of the family as an "active agent," is a concern with the "synchronization of several concepts of time — individual time, family time, and historical time" (Haraven, 1977, p. 58). Individual time refers to the age of each family member, or the point each one has reached in his or her individual life cycle. Family time refers to the family's stage of development, and views the family as a system with its own life cycle, distinct from the individual ages of its members. Historical time refers to the larger social context of family development, and the political, economic, and cultural forces that affect family adaptation.

When this framework is applied to families with handicapped children, there are important implications for social services. The presence of a handicapped child often creates *asynchronicity* among the three levels of time proposed by Haraven. The handicapped child's *individual time* is by definition delayed. This is obvious for children with cognitive impairments, and also easily observable where physical or social-emotional impairments prolong dependency and reliance on both family members and formal extrafamilial systems. Moreover, the individual time of nonhandicapped family members, especially siblings, is altered. Siblings may find themselves taking on caregiving roles that require an acceleration of social development and a premature initiation into adult roles. This has been demonstrated by Farber's (1959) analysis of role changes and family reorganization in families with severely handicapped children. Adult members are also likely to experience a disruption in the course of their own life cycles if they are required to provide continued physical, emotional, and financial support as they enter the later stages of their careers and anticipate retirement and their own increased dependency on social service systems.

These changes in individual time correlate with changes in *family time*, leading to a deviant family life cycle. As mentioned earlier, handicapped children may draw their parents into formal associations with external systems earlier than usual. Families may be confronted with early separation of disabled offspring if out-of-home placement is chosen prior to adulthood, or the family life cycle may be arrested if the handicapped member remains at home after the normal age of launching into the adult world. Such deviations are a major source of stress for families and must be taken into account when planning support services for both individuals and the family systems in which they live.

Finally, changes in *historical time* can have a major impact on the abilities of families to be proactive in their dealings with social institutions. The increased reliance on formal services experienced by families with handicapped members makes them quite vulnerable to historical changes in social policies and program practices. The requirements for parent participation in decision-making, treatment, and program evaluation that characterize social services today place families in a much different position than was the case when parents first organized themselves after World War II. These changes have empowered families — a positive outcome — while making more rigid the nature, purpose, and patterns of their interactions with helping systems — a potentially negative outcome. The newer expectations and requirements that parents become therapists, policymakers, case managers, advocates, and quality assurance experts can create additional stress at a time when family members are adjusting to new roles and norms. Parent control over the type, intensity, and duration of their involvement in formal systems will be discussed later in the program criteria section.

Historical Changes in Family Roles

Beyond the obvious demands created by social-policy changes are more subtle changes in society's expectations for children and families. According to Haraven (1977), preindustrial society viewed children as playing both affective-emotional roles and instrumental-economic roles. For some societies, the individual's inability to perform instrumental roles was in itself justification for isolation or neglect of disabled people. Plato's suggestion that impaired children be abandoned because they could not contribute to social progress or national security is generally viewed as an unenlightened if not barbaric point of view, even while the occasional "Baby Doe" cases remind us that our ancient impulses are not fully suppressed. Although children in modern society are expected to fulfill fewer instrumental-economic roles, and this may lessen the stress of raising a handicapped child, the consequent exclusive reliance on affective roles can also be troublesome. Children who have difficulty expressing or engendering attachment behaviors due to cognitive, physical, or emotional impairments (e.g., children with severe retardation, cerebral palsy, behavior disorders, or sensory impairments) may find themselves with no meaningful role to play in a family system. And these children are unlikely to be able to substitute economic roles for their impaired affectional abilities.

At later points in the family life cycle, when most children become wage earners with increased financial responsibilities for their aging parents, the child's inability to make this shift may prolong reliance on affective roles, creating extended and intense attachment that can become very stressful when the reality of parental age and mortality must be confronted. Failure to adjust to these altered cycles of development and role expectations may be more difficult for middle-class families whose role structures, norms, and expectations are more rigid and narrow than is true of lower income families (see, for example, Farber's [1968] discussion of social mobility and class variables).

Society's expectations for family behavior relative to patterns of child-rearing is an additional historical time variable. The period of the 1950s and 1960s was unique in the United States in that most middle-class women were expected to assume only domestic roles that centered on raising children. Post-war prosperity and ample employment for males, as well as new "scientific" approaches to child-rearing, created this phenomenon. In spite of the consciousness-raising efforts of the women's liberation movement of the past decade, many middle-class families still strongly hold these values. The economic realities and career goals of women in the 1980s have resulted in sharply increased female labor force participation compared to the postwar era. Yet the return to prewar patterns of two-parent working families has not been accompanied by a return to shared sex roles in child-rearing and other domestic tasks. Women now must both work outside of the home and continue to be the primary nurturer, chauffeur, crisis manager, school or agency contact, record keeper, and so on. This is hard enough in families with normal children; it can be very difficult when a handicapped child is present (Poznanski, 1973; Zisserman, 1981). These historical changes also exacerbate confusion over male roles when a handicapped or chronically ill child must be raised (see, for example, Cummings, 1976). Thus, several historical factors are interacting with both the individual and family life cycles of families with handicapped children. Difficulty in adjusting to these historical patterns can increase the stress caused by asynchronicity in family and individual life cycles.

Model for Effective Family-Agency Interactions

This analysis is helpful for understanding the multiple, complex social forces that affect families. The theoretical model proposed here may be briefly summarized as follows:

1. Family-agency interactions are mediated by the availability of "buffer" systems, like extended kin networks, schools, churches, and voluntary associations.
2. Families are at risk for reduced participation in informal networks and accelerated participation in formal systems, leading to early burnout, disenchantment among family members, and a sense of helplessness due to external locus of control and unequal relationships with service providers.
3. Family development occurs within a stage-based or life cycle context. Consideration of only the individual life cycle of a handicapped child is insufficient. The life cycle of the family as a system and external historical factors also affect family adaptation and survival.
4. Families with handicapped children may experience asynchronicity of individual, family, and historical cycles, creating difficult role changes, unclear expectations about the future, prolonged attachment and dependency, and sex-related role stress.
5. Social service programs that focus only on remediating deficits in impaired children will not help families in the process of adapting and seeking equilibrium. A family-focused orientation that emphasizes internal locus of control, equity in responsibility and power between families and agencies, and consideration of long-term developmental goals must be the essential characteristics of helping systems.

In the next section, specific criteria for the design and evaluation of community agencies will be presented in light of the assumptions and theoretical model presented above. Then examples will be provided of health care and other family support systems whose practices are consistent with these criteria.

Program Criteria

In order to enhance the quality of interactions between families and formal community agencies, programs must ascribe to certain values and design principles consistent with the concepts presented above. Consideration is given here to a set of normative principles that is divided into socially normative criteria and therapeutically normative criteria. Then several suggestions are made for design elements that will provide the means toward attaining these normative goals. Finally, evaluation approaches consistent with these means and ends will be described.

Socially Normative Criteria

Community agencies should adhere to the basic principles of normalization proposed by Nirje (1976) and Wolfensberger (1972). The principle of normalization requires the utilization of culturally valued means in order to establish and maintain personal behaviors, experiences, and characteristics that are culturally normative or valued (Wolfensberger, 1972). Table 13.1 (adapted from Nirje, 1976) lists several examples of how the normalization principle can be realized in the everyday lives of handicapped children and adults. It is interesting to note the recurring emphasis on *time* in these examples. Given the earlier discussion of asynchronicity in individual time and family time, the principle of normalization is viewed as providing a basis for moving individuals and families closer to a healthy, normal pattern of growth and social participation.

Table 13.1. Application of the Normalization Principle

*Normalization means. . .*A normal rhythm of the day. You get out of bed in the morning, even if you are profoundly retarded and physically handicapped; you get dressed, and leave the house for school or work; you don't stay home; in the morning you anticipate events, in the evening you think back on what you have accomplished; the day is not a monotonous 24 hours with every minute endless.

*Normalization means. . .*You eat at normal times of the day and in a normal fashion, not just with a spoon, unless you are an infant; not in bed, but at a table; not early in the afternoon for the convenience of staff or family members.

*Normalization means. . .*A normal rhythm of the week. You live in one place, go to work in another, and participate in leisure activities in yet another. You anticipate leisure activities on weekends, and look forward to getting back to school or work on Monday.

*Normalization means. . .*A normal rhythm of the year. A vacation to break the routines of the year. Seasonal changes bring with them a variety of types of food, work, cultural events, sports, leisure activities. Just think. . .we thrive on these seasonal changes!

*Normalization means. . .*Normal developmental experience of the life cycle. In childhood, children, but not adults, go to summer camps. In adolescence, one is interested in grooming, hairstyles, music, boyfriends, and girlfriends. In adulthood, life is filled with work and responsibilities. In old age, one has memories to look back on, and can enjoy the wisdom of experience.

*Normalization means. . .*Having a range of choices, wishes, and desires respected and considered. Adults have the freedom to decide where they would like to live, what kind of job they would like to have and can best perform. Whether they would prefer to go bowling with a group, instead of staying home to watch television.

*Normalization means. . .*Living in a world made of two sexes. Children and adults both develop relationships with members of the opposite sex. Teenagers may become interested in having boyfriends and girlfriends, and adults may fall in love, and decide to marry.

*Normalization means. . .*The right to normal economic standards. All of us have basic financial privileges and responsibilities. All are able to take advantage of compensatory economic security means, such as child allowances, old age pensions and minimum wage regulations. We should have money to decide how to spend: on personal luxuries or necessities.

*Normalization means. . .*Living in normal housing in a normal neighborhood. Not in a large facility with 20, 50, or 100 other people because you are retarded, and not isolated from the rest of the community. Normal locations and normal-size homes will give residents better opportunities for successful integration with their communities.

Nirje's model also stresses the value of *choice*. Choice among a variety of service options, locations, and treatment approaches is critical in order to maintain the locus of control within the family and provide access to a socially pluralistic service system. This means that families should have access to both specialized and generic services that operate according to the values and expectations of the cultural group(s) served by such agencies. In addition to pluralistic services, the criteria and instruments used to assess individual progress or family adaptation must also respect divergent norms and patterns of life. Mercer's (1973) work continues to be the prototype of such an approach. Additional discussion of the need for a pluralistic approach is found in Jackson (1982).

Marmor (1971), in describing socially normative criteria which should be applied to policies aimed at reducing poverty, offers several guidelines applicable to service for families with handicapped children. These criteria are identified as adequacy, stigma, vertical and horizontal efficiency, work incentives, and political support. The application of each of these to services for families with disabled children will be described briefly.

Adequacy refers to the degree to which a service meets all or less than all of the specific needs of a family. Questions that may be posed to determine a program's level of adequacy include:

1. Is the program able to respond to most or all of a child's needs as described on an individual service plan?
2. For those need areas that are unmet, is there a referral mechanism in place to provide coordinated supplemental services?

3. Are the needs of other family members addressed, or does the program only respond to the needs of the disabled individual?
4. Do professionals bear in mind the characteristics and needs of the whole child, or only those deficit areas to be remediated by their particular discipline?
5. Does a program provide only enough support and intervention to reduce or eliminate pathology, or is there an effort to help the child and family achieve an optimal level of well-being and functioning?

Stigma refers to the concerns raised earlier in the discussion of normalization. Important sources of stigma include limiting services to low-income groups only; associating services with agencies perceived by the community as dealing only with deviant or ill people, such as a mental health center or residential institution; excluding children and families from participation in generic services, such as public transportation; and assuming that parents are incompetent or uncaring because they have a mentally or emotionally handicapped child. Questions relevant to an assessment of stigmatizing program characteristics include:

1. Does the program require proof of financial stress or poverty before providing services? If families are already receiving public assistance, do they have to reconfirm their devalued status every time they request a new kind of service?
2. Do programs exclude families unable to pay "up front" for a needed service, as is the case in many hospitals and health clinics?
3. Does the location of a program create an image of either deviance (e.g., on the grounds of a residential institution) or charity (e.g., in a church basement or goodwill center)?
4. Do program practices perpetuate a view that parents are incompetent or inferior (e.g., referring to parents by their first name while other professionals are addressed by formal titles, or attributing the cause of disability to a particular family rather than the ecological context in which the family lives)?

Vertical and horizontal efficiency refer to the impact of a program. Vertical efficiency measures the degree to which a program intended to benefit one group also benefits another. For example, Gray, Ramsey, and Klaus (1982) discovered unanticipated vertical efficiency, or diffusion, in the Early Training Program when benefits were observed for siblings as well as target children. Horizontal efficiency refers to "the ratio of the number of beneficiaries in the target group to the total number of persons in the target group" (Marmor, 1971, p. 40). Although recent government reports (GAO, 1981) indicate that most handicapped children are receiving services under P.L. 94-142, others argue that there remain significant target groups that are still unserved (Lakin, Hill, Hauber, & Bruininks, 1983). Questions useful for assessing efficiency include:

1. Are skills taught to parents which focus on caring for a handicapped child applicable to other family members, and to the handicapped child as he or she gets older?
2. Are existing support networks utilized to sustain and expand the impact of child-focused interventions?
3. Do program policies or practices exclude those families most in need of services (e.g., rural, isolated families, non- English speaking families, or families with single parents or with two working parents)?
4. Are children who live outside of their natural homes likely to be excluded from participation in community services?

Work incentives refers to the degree to which a program encourages participation in meaningful, income-generating employment. In this case, the concern is with both the work capacities and income of a disabled family member as well as the employment patterns of parents. Programs which use disabled adolescents or adults as employees but pay less than minimum wage under U.S. Department of Labor rules do not create work incentives. Similarly, public assistance programs such as SSI which prohibit the accumulation of assets above a minimum level create disincentives to full employment with appropriate remuneration. If parents are unable to work because of the daily care needs of handicapped children, or are not allowed leave time to attend clinic appointments or staffings, work incentives will not exist. Questions that might be raised relative to this criterion include:

1. Do educational and vocational training programs lead to gainful, normalized work opportunities?
2. Do disabled people lose access to some benefit or services if they are financially successful?
3. If a working parent chooses to stop work in order to care for a handicapped child at home, is there any job protection for that individual? Are such parents stigmatized by others who feel that a man's or woman's duty is to be a breadwinner?
4. If a parent seeks work to offset the expense of caring for a handicapped child, or continues to work after the birth of a disabled child, do employers provide flexible schedules and leave policies to allow the parent to attend to periodic needs without loss of job security?

Political support, the last of Marmor's criteria to be adapted here, refers to the nature and extent of approval for a particular program. Approval can entail either mass, public support or more narrow, legislative support. In either case, consideration must be given to such factors as public backlash against expenditures for handicapped people, demonstrating the social benefits of community services, and creating advocacy activities which are both informative and assertive. Questions which may be posed here include:

1. Does the public perceive community services for families and handicapped children as competing with other essential activities (e.g., general education programs or community recreation projects)?
2. Are nonhandicapped people excluded from participation in services or activities created for handicapped people?
3. Do key decision-makers fully understand the legal, developmental, and social rationales for services to handicapped children and their families?
4. Do generic community organizations such as the PTA or YMCA incorporate families with handicapped children, or are such families expected to "stick to their own kind"?

The five socially normative criteria proposed here are meant to alert program planners to the broader social consequences of their services. Administrators are often frustrated by the lack of public support or understanding of their efforts on behalf of families and children. This frustration may be due to a narrow conception of their role and a naive assumption that what they are doing will be viewed as laudable and beneficial by the community. The design of community services must consider these criteria if programs are to succeed and survive.

Therapeutically Normative Criteria

In addition to approaches which enhance a family member's personal image, respect families' cultural practices, and are socially acceptable, agencies must provide treatment and support services which are therapeutically normative. This means that individual service plans and treatment goals must be based on a developmental life cycle perspective. Behavior change and skill acquisition are only means toward the ultimate end of living independently and with dignity within mainstream society. Preparation for the transition to work in late adolescence, support in decision-making concerning sexual behavior and parenting, securing work that is economically rewarding, and living away from one's family of origin during adulthood are all long-term treatment goals that will assist an individual to approximate as closely as possible a normal life cycle. Age-appropriate materials should be utilized to help individuals attain these goals.

Therapeutic normalization applies to service plans for families as well as individuals. Just as individual service plans must prescribe the acquisition of normal patterns of living as well as the elimination of maladaptive behaviors, family service plans must work toward achieving a normal family life cycle in addition to reducing disorganization or pathology caused by extraordinary stress. This requires a search for strengths in family systems through the identification and enhancement of existing coping resources. Service providers must assess the availability and quality of proximal, mediating systems and modify them so they can better meet the needs of families with handicapped children. Since such systems may be less bound by the rigid bureaucratic rules of more distant, formal systems, intervention should begin with the family's immediate ecosystem. The Re-Ed model of Hobbs (1982), which focuses on ecological assessment and enablement, offers a concrete and successful example of how this can be accomplished.

Essential Design Elements

How can the values and criteria described above be translated into program practices? Given the relatively early stages of development that family-centered programs are in, the abstractness of the theoretical models that govern programs, the translation is neither easy nor obvious. However, some essential components can be described. These elements include: (a) ecologically-based services; (b) coordinated services supported by case management; (c) personalized, family-oriented services; and (d) centralized, comprehensive services. These elements will be detailed below.

Ecologically based services. The design and benefits of services based on ecological models of development have been well documented since Hobbs' (1966) benchmark description of Project Re-Ed. That literature will not be reiterated here. However, a concrete example of services to handicapped children which incorporates the family's ecosystem is presented. The illustration which follows is excerpted from the proceedings of the International Symposium on Services for Young Disabled Children and Their Families, sponsored by UNESCO and the National Institute of Handicapped Research in late 1981. The example comes from Cameroon, a Third World country with very underdeveloped education and social service systems (using modern Western standards as a basis for comparison). Although it may seem that the experience of a non-industrialized, tribal-oriented culture could not possibly offer guidance to the advanced governments of the West, it may be that our own culture has similar customs and values that determine our response to people with handicapping conditions. If the spiritual or social values expressed in the illustration seem primitive and "non-Western," we should examine our own culture's behavior relative to severely disabled newborns and adults.

Illustration of Ecologically Based Services

Kaele is located in the extreme northern portion of the Cameroon. This desert area is commonly referred to as the presahel belt. Cameroon is a developing country and, as in all Third World countries, the many vicissitudes of the world's economy have their effect on domestic life. While the middle class is rapidly emerging, the greater part of the population, peasants of the plains and mountains, have a subsistence living standard dependent upon the precarious rain season.

In the Cameroon, schooling is not obligatory. Programs in early childhood education do not exist. The sick and infirm persons who live in the villages are relegated to the back corners of the compound. There is superstitution that any handicapping condition would spread to all.

The family is very important in African life. Experience shows that the family unit is a component in the rehabilitation of handicapped people. The family has always had an empathy for the healthy as well as the unhealthy. For the normal child, inclusion into the family unit begins at the fetal stage. Most ethnic groups practice a Cult of the Ancestors Ceremony in which the expectant mother receives not only unctions other members of the family receive, but also an extra one on the abdomen, for the unborn child who is already considered part of the family. Tribal rites make a clear distinction between a biological birth and the official or social birth. The latter takes place when the child is taken from the mother's hut, which represents the womb, and is introduced into the father's courtyard. At this moment the child travels from the hands of women to the hands of men. The family is patriarchial, therefore the child will belong to the father's family. The acceptance of the newborn is celebrated by various initiation rites. The child is shown the different parts of the family compound and is brought into the bush area where he or she will later be expected to gather herbs for the sauce, wood for the heating and cooking, and straw for the roof. Tasks are assigned according to the child's sex.

An abnormal child cannot be integrated into this society. This problem begins at birth. Until a few years ago, the birth of twins or a disabled child was looked upon as an error. These children were not considered to be human, but rather to be water spirits who penetrated the body of a woman while bathing. Such a child therefore had to be returned to its own underworld. So the child would be placed on a rock on the edge of a water hole to enable it to rejoin its true parents. This explains why, until recent times, there appeared to be few, if any, children handicapped from birth. Today, pressures from both the mother's and father's families are exerted on the parents of a handicapped child. The entire family group reacts when a handicap manifests itself in the course of the child's growth.

Before the child is weaned, it is carried on the mother's back. During this period, the handicap poses few problems. After weaning, a child normally begins to discover the world, but for the disabled child the problem begins. It is by games or imitation of others that children initiate themselves into society. A little child who cannot stand alone or chase grasshoppers or mice like the others suffers enormously. The child's condition may restrict him to staying on all fours on the ground, and run the risk of being injured by playmates.

Parents of handicapped children try many methods or treatments to correct a handicapping condition. The parents and their handicapped child often come to the center at Kaele for treatment and additional help. The most urgent need is to provide primary care for the child and encourage parents to play an active role in the child's care. Once taboos are dispelled, parents are quick to understand what is expected of them. At Kaele, parents are taught the fundamentals of child care as well as special treatments they must know in order to cope with their children's particular disabilities. They not only tolerate but also encourage safe traditional treatments, such as therapeutic baths with leaves and roots, and warm mud baths.

The parents come to understand the normal functions of the bones and muscles by comparing their children's bodies with their own and those of the animals they hunt. They are taught how to make and adjust braces, calipers, and other aids from available materials. They are shown how these aids work. They are taught how to exercise outside in order to introduce their child to the natural elements: pebbles on mountain slopes, sands on the plain, cement at the schoolhouse. The children are taught how to fall so they can do so without getting hurt, so they can get up without help, and so that they can be independent. Once a child knows that he can progress, he is ready to return to the village. He can be part of the village.

Parent education is an essential part of this program. In the evening, the parents are gathered and the activities of the day are discussed: progress is pointed out, discoveries emphasized, methods used to encourage children are recognized, harshness and lack of patience are pointed out. This time is also used to teach methods for cleanliness, nutrition, prevention, and first aid. Special work is done with pregnant mothers, and attention is given to family education and social education. Private assistance is provided for the couple who is interested in spacing births or who may have problems in their sexual life.

The various stages of rehabilitation contribute to changes in attitudes among the parents. Parents' belief that their child can progress and be independent is the most essential ingredient to that child's independence. However, the main characters affecting the child's entry into the local society may be the child's peers and the villagers themselves. The parents must be prepared to help their child in this process, to help him maintain his dignity. The philosophy at Kaele is that of encouragement. The program does not rely upon specific skills, charts, or assessment tools. Progress is made by encouraging an awareness of handicapping conditions and developing a group approach toward helping the handicapped prepare for the future.

Coordinated services and case management. One source of stress for families is the need to interact with multiple professionals at any one time as well as over the life cycle of the child. This is particularly true in the preschool years when a child's medical, educational, therapy, and social service needs are often met by separate agencies. It is less true during school age when the public school has legal responsibility for assuring and coordinating education and related services. The need to integrate and coordinate services from diverse sources may increase at the point of school exit, when disabled adults are likely to use both specialized and generic community services.

During the preschool and early adult years, parents may be required to act as case managers. This responsibility comes at times of increased stress in the family's life cycle. Although public schools often do not have case managers per se, pupil placement team leaders often play such a role. Or school nurses may assume case management responsibilities.

In addition, the legal requirements for parent involvement are quite specific and tend to prescribe parent and professional roles in a way that assures some degree of coordination and monitoring.

Lack of case management in the preschool years can be ameliorated by use of a transdisciplinary team approach (Allen, Holm, & Schiefelbusch, 1978). In order to limit the number of different professionals parents must deal with, one individual is designated to deliver the bulk of developmental and therapeutic services. With the consultation and assistance of specialists, one specialist can implement service objectives and work with the family over several years. To assure continuity of support and coordination when a child enters the public school system (the age at which this occurs varies between 3 and 5 years in most states), the early intervention specialist should maintain contact during and after school entry. That individual can act as an advocate for the family to make sure school-based services are consistent with earlier approaches, and to monitor the delivery of noneducational services provided by health and welfare organizations. The transfer of all responsibility for services and case management from early intervention programs to schools at a legally predetermined chronological age can become an arbitrary decision that does not take into account the particular life cycle needs of families and children. Thus, there is a critical need for longitudinal case management that is constant during major transitions. The potential role of health-care providers as long-term service providers and case managers will be discussed later in the chapter.

At the time of school exit and entry into the world of work and independent living, case management needs again intensify. This is true because parents are anticipating the beginning of a new stage of their own lives when they are freed from the daily care of their children. To expect them to resume the role of case manager at this point may be unrealistic. Yet the use of multiple service providers housed in various locations recreates the earlier pattern families experience in the child's preschool years. Because health specialists usually do not play as prominent a role during the child's early adulthood, at this stage the family may lack access to a single provider who has ongoing contact with the disabled person and his or her family.

Suelzle and Keenan's (1981) study of changes in family support networks over the life cycle of mentally retarded persons documents these coordination and case management needs. They found that parents of preschool and elementary-age children relied primarily on physicians' advice concerning placement and treatment, while parents of teenagers and adults relied on school personnel for advice. Parents experienced decreased use of personal support networks as their children became adults, creating a greater need for formal case management. And, parents' needs for crisis lines, respite care, and counseling were highest among families with preschoolers and adults, and lowest for families with school-age children. These findings indicate the need for direct-service providers, such as health-care specialists in the early years and school personnel in late adolescence, to act as case managers. This can assure continuity of care and reduce stress on families during difficult life-cycle transitions.

Personalized family-oriented services. In order to modify the impersonal, externally regulated interactions between families and bureaucratic systems described earlier, service providers must seek intimate, trusting relationships with their clients (Gallagher, Beckman, & Cross, 1983). This concept has been advanced in the field of rural mental health care. Weller (1965) has called for the "personalization of services" to rural families in stress. Looff (1971) endorses this notion and suggests that the essential "capacity for relatedness" that characterized the Appalachian families he observed become a principle tool for intervention. This implies the use of locally controlled, accessible services; an emphasis on home-based or neighborhood service delivery; reliance on indigenous paraprofessionals and professionals; respect for the belief systems which affect families' reactions to the presence of a handicapped child; and inclusion of extended family members in treatment and support services (see for example, Gabel & Kotsch, 1981; Moore et al., 1982; Sonnek, Chapter 4).

The purposes of personalized, family-oriented services are to: (a) increase the likelihood that available services will be utilized; (b) enhance equity in the relationships between professionals and families; and (c) assure that the locus of control over the type, intensity, and duration of services rests with the family. If these goals can be achieved, the handicapped family member who is the focus of intervention will clearly benefit. Professionals whose ego needs prevent them from becoming intimate with families cannot be very effective except in providing short-term prescriptive interventions. The benefit of personalized services is expressed succinctly by a parent quoted in Winton and Turnbull (1981, p. 15):

> There's been this "We care about you as parents, and even though we're here to work with your child, you're involved and we want to work with you." So I never felt like I was shut out, or that they would do anything that I was not interested in having them do. In a way, they became a substitute family. I could tell them in the morning what had happened at home at night, and at the end of the day they would tell me what J _____ had done that day.

Centralized, comprehensive services. One way to increase the level of coordination is to integrate a variety of services together within a single organizational structure. This allows families to interact with one set of helping professionals who work in close proximity to each other over an extended period of time. Such an approach is *centralized* in the sense that most services are available from a common source. Within that central location, the range of services provided is *comprehensive*, so that the multiple needs of children and families can be addressed. This would help to reduce fragmentation of services and the resulting emphasis on remediating discrete deficits. A centralized and comprehensive service delivery system would be better able to take into account the interdependent, transdisciplinary developmental needs of children and the ecological changes necessary to support the family system.

It should be noted here that centralization of services does not mean regionalization. The service delivery system must be "decentralized" by being physically located as close to a handicapped child's community as possible, and the administration of those services must also be "decentralized" to allow local decision-making and congruence with local needs and priorities. The use here of the term "centralized" refers to the integration of multiple services in a single location.

There are several examples of centralized services outside of the United States (UNESCO, 1981). In 1975, India began a network of 200 Integrated Child Development Services. These programs provide nutritional supplements, immunization, health education, and preschool education for preventive and remedial purposes. Denmark has a similar array of integrated programs. Japan has integrated medical and educational services by making the Ministry of Education responsible for meeting the medical needs of handicapped children. The goals of the Japanese government are to:

1. Establish an integrated system of basic medical, health care, education, and social services for children and their families.
2. Encourage the interdisciplinary training of personnel.
3. Utilize the safe practices of traditional healers and other local customs.
4. Foster cooperation among professionals and traditional healers.
5. Establish preventive measures, especially immunization, sanitation, nutrition, and education.

The United States is unique in that our social policies seem to work against comprehensive, centralized approaches. This is due to the traditional separation of education from other direct services, especially health-care and family support services. Within P.L. 94-142, medical and family support service are very narrowly defined, and are limited to either initial diagnosis in the case of health care, or legally prescribed participation in decision-making. Although parent counseling is listed as a related service under P.L. 94-142, such counseling and support is often limited to that which enables the handicapped child to benefit from special education, rather than addressing more global family support needs.

The most recent amendments to P.L. 94-142, enacted in late 1983, show a greater sensitivity to the need for integrated, coordinated services for children from birth to six and for older adolescents moving from educational to work settings. These policy changes are consistent with the need to provide greater support at family life cycle transition stages. However, the separation of educational and health-related services continues to pose problems for families who must interact with multiple agencies and caregivers as they seek appropriate services for their children.

Finally, there have been proposals to expand the roles of public schools in coordinating comprehensive health and mental health services to children and families (Mallory & Cottom, 1978). The rationale for using schools for centralized service delivery has been summarized by Minzey and LeTarte (1973), who argue:

> The neighborhood school is the one unit that can be utilized as a basis of operations. It is the one facility that all neighborhoods have in common. No other agency or governmental system has a structural framework that approaches that available through the local elementary school, and it is the only governmental agency that exists in neighborhoods all over the country. (pp. 6-7)

Expanding the existing role of public schools might lead to services which are better integrated, coordinated, and centralized. As well, public schools are less restrictive, more normal environments than specialized and isolated agencies that serve only disabled people. However, expecting schools to play central coordinating roles when they are already overburdened and understaffed may be unrealistic. Public opinion, which recently has placed an increased value on basic skills and technical-scientific knowledge, may also prevent such an expanded role. In addition, schools in central urban areas are often preoccupied with major social issues such as racial balance and the control of behavior. Schools that must first clarify and defend their roles in society are not in a position to act as the locus of a comprehensive system of social and support services for families experiencing significant stress. The financial pressures faced by public schools will also be a constraint to the development of preventive, supportive activities. Yet in spite of the current realities which suggest that many schools are not ready to act as a central coordinating mechanism, it is an option that could be tested in those communities with a stable, respected school system where the necessary resources are made available.

Program Evaluation Principles

Any evaluation of social services for families with handicapped children must be designed so it is consistent with the normative and design criteria just described. First, the socially and therapeutically normative characteristics of a program may be assessed by using an instrument such as PASS (Program Analysis of Service Systems) (Wolfensberger & Glenn, 1975) or PASSING (Program Analysis of Service Systems' Implementation of Normalization Goals) (Wolfensberger & Thomas, 1983). These approaches to evaluation assess both the social image which a community program conveys and the degree to which its treatment methods enhance socially valued skills of disabled clients. The focus on age-appropriate treatment, use of generic, integrated services, and goals which enhance independence and economic self-sufficiency makes these tools very useful for understanding the impact of service design on individual and family life cycle patterns.

A second evaluation domain must be concerned with the ecology of implementation (Mallory & Glascoe, 1979). The historical, political, social, and cultural value contexts of programs will determine the degree to which they perpetuate narrow, static models of intervention or advance broader, family-wide, dynamic models. Variables such as unemployment rates, which influence the perception of the social value of disabled adolescents and adults (Farber, 1968), must be taken into account. Community-wide attitudes relative to: (a) educational achievement, (b) the scope of the public schools' roles, (c) external mandates prescribing the allocation of educational and social service dollars, and (d) the causes of handicapping conditions greatly affect the implementation and outcomes of services for children experiencing abnormal development. Programs designed at the state or federal level, as many are, risk being out of step with local priorities and values. The result can be either underutilization or modification of design to the point where those intended to receive the service and most in need are excluded (Mallory, in press; Meisels & Berkeley, 1980).

One comprehensive evaluation approach which considers both the ecology of implementation and individual outcomes is Stufflebeam's (1968) context, input, process, and products (CIPP) model. The CIPP design includes consideration of formative processes and the role of consumers and other key actors in the implementation phase. It is also comprehensive enough to measure both qualitative and quantitative change over time. A related area of evaluation focuses on community impact, or the degree to which the presence of a particular program affects the practices and values of related services within the same region. The Kirschner Report (1970) of Head Start's influence on other agencies serving low-income families is a good example of community-impact evaluation.

Whatever model is chosen, an evaluation design consistent with the criteria outlined earlier should focus on the following questions:

1. To what extent do services impede or advance the development of the family as a system?
2. Are services capable of meeting the critical needs that arise during

times of life cycle transitions, such as the birth of a new child, school entry, or launching young adults into the world of work and independent living?

3. To what extent do support services reduce family stress caused by interactions with multiple organizations which have varying eligibility criteria, catchment areas, and treatment approaches?

4. Do services complement and strengthen existing mediating structures and informal support systems?

5. Do services recognize and build on the traditional values and practices of subcultural groups?

6. Do services offer a range of options relative to such things as the location of treatment (home vs. out-of-home), the level of parent participation (passive recipient vs. active teacher or manager), times of operation (weekday vs. evenings and weekends), and the choice of treatment models (behavioral, developmental, biomedical, psychotherapeutic, etc.)?

7. Are professional helpers capable of developing intimate, personalized relationships with families while maintaining an objective understanding of their needs and priorities?

8. Do services advance the goals of normalization by making use of generic organizations and reducing stigmatizing characteristics as much as possible?

Interactions with Community Health-Care Systems

One of the most commonly used sources of help throughout a family's life cycle is the community health-care system. From the point of initial diagnosis (or even sooner during prenatal stages or during undiagnosed periods of delayed development), through treatment and follow-up care, physicians and nurses come into frequent and intense contact with families. The nature of those interactions and the use of various payment and treatment models will be discussed below. The design of health-care systems in light of the criteria presented earlier will also be considered.

Diagnosis and Referral

For obvious reasons, physicians play a central role in the initial diagnosis of a handicapping condition. Historical factors related to physicians' training have had a significant effect on how that diagnostic role is played. As well, decisions to refer to other specialists, recommendations concerning living arrangements, and the physician's role in multidisciplinary teams can either impede or enhance families' adaptation to having handicapped child.

The initial diagnosis may result in feelings of anger directed at the physician by the parents (Mori, 1983). Physicians need to be able to anticipate such a reaction in order to present diagnostic information in an objective but sympathetic manner. Important considerations in presenting an initial diagnosis include:

1. *Telling both parents together at the same time.* This is especially important in maternity wards where a new mother may be informed of her child's impairment without the father being present. Her responsibility to then inform the father and other family members immediately creates an unequal burden that can lead to an ongoing pattern of the father being a passive recipient of information while the mother acts as the primary contact with formal systems. This disparity can also create two separate cycles of adaptation and acceptance in the two spouses. Although we should not expect two parents always to be at similar emotional stages of reaction, professionals should try to avoid doing anything that would increase the psychological distance between the child's primary caregivers. Even if it means delaying telling the parents of a newborn's or older child's difficulties, every effort should be made to provide critical information or advice when both parents are present. For single-parent families, another family member such as an aunt, uncle, or grandparent of the disabled child could be invited.
2. *Using accurate, nonstigmatizing language when presenting diagnosis.* The use of outdated terms such as "mongoloid" or "cripple" can have a profound effect on the adaptation process, including the early bonding and attachment that is important to subsequent development. Parents' prior experiences and stereotypes, based on media images or the attitudes acquired from their own parents, partially determine their reaction to having a handicapped child. If they associate "mongoloids" with an evolutionarily inferior species, as Down implied when he first identified the syndrome 100 years ago, their very first attitudes toward their child will be negatively affected. Even more pejorative terms, such as "vegetable" or "life without meaning" have been used in the past and must be strenuously avoided. Early intervention and school personnel may find their interactions with some parents focus heavily on undoing earlier misconceptions or negative attitudes caused by careless diagnostic language.
3. *Being prepared to make necessary referrals to other specialists and experienced parents of handicapped children.* Parents, like any consumers of health-care services, have a right to additional information about their children's status. Obtaining second, third, or fourth opinions should not be viewed as a pathological symptom of unacceptance, as is denoted by the demeaning terms "doctor-

shopping" or"program-shopping." Rather, confirming or differing opinions and advice can empower parents to make their own judgments and support them in their roles as the ultimate decision-makers. Physicians should offer assistance in obtaining additional opinions or consulting with other experts.

Physicians play a key role in initiating referrals (Browder,1981; Mori, 1983). In one study, 97% of physicians surveyed refer parents to other specialists or agencies for further evaluation (McDonald, Carlson, Palmer, & Slay, 1983). Although this is an encouraging finding, one third of the same physicians were not aware of P.L. 94-142, and only one third had formal training in mental retardation, emotional distur-bance, or learning disabilities. Further, none of the physicians felt a need for additional training in any of these areas.

Once a referral is made, a family may not choose to follow through due to emotional stress, financial concerns, or a variety of other factors (Mori, 1983). The decision not to pursue a referral must be respected by the physician or other referring agent. Forcing parents to use services they do not want or are not ready for will only lead to even greater stress and discomfort, significantly reducing the potential value of specialized services. On the other hand, making information available and encouraging parents' use of available services are always part of the referral process.

In recent years, physicians have reduced their tendency to make referrals for out-of-home placement or other restrictive services. Physi-cians trained prior to the early 1970s are more likely to recommend institutional placement than physicians trained in the last decade, who refer children to local school programs and recommend caring for the child at home (Adams,1982). However, in small rural communities, physicians continue to recommend institutionalization, perhaps because older physicians often practice in rural towns or because lack of community-based support services creates unmanageable stress for families.

Physicians also must be prepared to refer parents to other parents with older handicapped children. Such a practice would be consistent with the need to use the informal mediating networks described earlier. Examples of peer support networks and their relation to formal systems will be provided at a later point in the chapter.

Sources of Treatment

Medical treatment of handicapped children may be provided through private physicians, community health clinics (including health maintenance organizations), or by school nurses. Obtaining either preventive or secondary treatment is a major task for families. Paying for treatment can be an even more critical issue.

Low-income families. One potential source of subsidized treatment for disabled children in low-income families is the federally mandated Early Periodic Screening, Diagnosis, and Treatment (EPSDT) program. The EPSDT experience is instructive in light of the socially normative criteria presented earlier.

A survey of 51 states and territories on the status of implementing EPSDT (Chang, Goldstein, Thomas, & Wallace, 1979) indicates it has been relatively unsuccessful in reaching those children most in need. This is partially due to its categorical eligibility standards. EPSDT services may only be used by Medicaid-eligible children. In 20 states, Medicaid eligibility is limited to recipients of Aid to Families with Dependent Children or Supplemental Security Income (Wallace, 1983). And most states limit AFDC eligibility to single-parent families. These narrow eligibility criteria obviously exclude many handicapped children whose families experience significant financial stress. Compounding the problem of limited eligibility is the finding that only one sixth of Medicaid-eligible children in the nation are participating (Wallace, 1983). Many health-care providers have chosen not to participate in EPSDT programs (Chang et al., 1979). Over one half of all mental retardation clinics are not providing services subsidized through the program. Only half of all school health services are participating, and the quality of their services is rated as fair to poor by 38% of the state health administrators surveyed. Health maintenance organizations (HMOs) are not being used for EPSDT services in over half of the states. On the brighter side, it should be noted that 34 states reported expanding existing hearing, vision, and dental screening services as a result of implementing EPSDT. This is an example of positive community impact similar to the Head Start effects documented by the Kirschner Report (1970). In sum, Chang et al. list the EPSDT implementation problems as: (a) insufficient primary-provider implementation, (b) under utilization of EPSDT services, (c) poor coordination among public agencies, (d) a high rate of broken appointments, and (e) insufficient outreach activities.

These problems may be due to those characteristics of EPSDT that violate socially normative criteria. For example, EPSDT is structured so participation in its subsidized services may be stigmatizing. Parents may not wish to present themselves as "welfare recipients" to health-care providers. The program is also clearly not horizontally efficient, given a 20% or less coverage level. The program is associated with public-assistance policies that are criticized by some for not providing a work incentive (AFDC). And the program enjoys little political support because it is aimed at such a narrow, politically powerless population. The program could be said to be "adequate," because it offers services from screening through treatment, but 46 states keep no information on the outcome of referrals following diagnosis, so actual treatment usage and outcomes are not known. As well, adequacy levels were reduced in 1983 when states were given the option of excluding 18- to 20-year-olds from Medicaid coverage, eliminating 661,000 young adults from coverage (Wallace, 1983). Recent efforts to reform EPSDT by replacing it with a less categorical Child Health Assurance Program (CHAP) have failed.

For low- and middle-income families, paying for medical treatment often means sacrificing other family needs. In a major study of over 4,000 developmentally disabled adults (Boaz,1978), lack of income did not appear to inhibit initial contact with a health-care provider. The availability of third-party insurance payments allowed disabled people to use outpatient services. However, the scope of insurance coverage varies directly with income. This means that out-of-pocket medical expenses as a percentage of total assets increase significantly for low-income disabled people. Thus, the effect of third-party coverage tied directly to income level is more and more regressive the lower one's income is. People who are disabled and poor are more likely to require and use health care than nondisabled poor people. The result is a greater tendency of low-income disabled people to sacrifice their limited economic assets for medical care. The stress of having a disability or caring for a disabled family member is exacerbated by being forced to choose between treatment and other necessities, such as food and shelter. Under such circumstances, it is understandable that some families feel powerless and behave passively when receiving medical services. It is difficult to be an assertive, confident consumer when faced with such financial stress.

Other sources. Recently, several states have begun small experiments to test the idea of cash subsidies or allowances to families with disabled children (Moore et al., 1982). Twelve states currently have such projects underway. Of these, only half are using any kind of means test for eligibility. The monthly or periodic allowances are aimed at families with severely handicapped children at risk for out-of-home or institutional placement. The amounts provided range from $30 to $350 per month. The services most commonly purchased with the allowances or reimbursements are respite care, therapy, transportation, adaptive equipment, and architectural remodeling. In the cash allowance experiment conducted by Moore and her colleagues in the state of Washington, no families actually used the maximum amount allowable ($200 per month), although some of the participants were described as experiencing real financial difficulties. But the additional out-of-pocket money reduced tension caused by decisions over the allocation of limited family finances. Because the payment of cash was made contingent upon accomplishing objectives on a family service plan, the money also acted as a short-term reinforcer for carrying out the recommendations of service providers. This kind of experiment has tremendous potential for future family-support policies. The Constant Care Allowance used for many years in England (Moroney, 1976) has been a successful means for helping families meet extraordinary medical and support expenses. The importation of the model into the U.S. is a welcome and long-awaited development.

Another alternative payment mechanism is found in the design of health maintenance organizations (HMOs). HMOs are potentially a means for reducing financial stress experienced by families with handicapped children. This is especially true for low-income families who may not have access to a long-term primary health-care provider. Because insurance policies generally do not cover preventive care, low-income families are not likely to use health care except in cases of significant illness or accidents. HMOs, however, place a primary emphasis on preventive health care due to their financing structure. HMO clients prepay a fixed amount either out of their own pockets or through third-party sources. This prepayment covers all preventive and secondary treatment services required by the client. Thus, HMOs have a vested interest in keeping their clients as healthy as possible, or else the HMO's expenses will increase (not the client's). This means that a client will be able to use health-care services at any point they are required, including preventive services, without sacrificing out-of-pocket cash or neglecting other family expenses (Wigley & Cook, 1975). The advantage of such an arrangement for families with handicapped children should be clear.

As of 1980, there were 236 HMOs in the U.S. Most of these are located in urban areas in the far west and mid-west. Although the federal government has promoted the expansion of HMOs into rural and medically underserved areas through the HMO Act of 1973 (P.L. 93-222), they are most often established close to existing medical facilities and teaching centers (Cromley & Shannon, 1983). It appears that the distribution of HMOs is not significantly changing the distribution of health-care resources. However, where they do exist, the quality of health care is at least as good as that provided by private physicans or public clinics. For example, compared to the general population, children born under HMO's auspices have higher birth weights, and improved outcomes for high-risk pregnancies have been documented (Quick, Greenlick, & Roghmann, 1981).

The design of HMOs meets several of the program criteria described earlier. Health-care services are centralized, coordinated, and comprehensive. On the other hand, HMOs have been criticized for providing impersonal care because patients often lack access to a single provider. However, nothing inherent in HMO design precludes the formation of long-term, individual relationships between patients and health-care providers. Further, public as well as private clinics have been accused of impersonal services (Wigley & Cook, 1975). The problem of personalization may be endemic to the health-care delivery system rather than unique to HMOs. In addition, HMOs, as generic providers, avoid the stigma attached to some public health clinics that serve primarily recipients of public assistance. From a life cycle perspective, HMOs offer the advantage of providing health care for infants, school-age children, and adults within the same organization. The type of medical care required by disabled people changes over the course of the life cycle, with greater reliance on family practitioners, neurologists, oral surgeons, and psychiatrists as the individual ages (Suelzle & Keenan, 1981). As medical needs change, families do not need to search for new specialists in diverse locations if comprehensive HMO services are utilized.

School nurses can also play a central role in meeting the needs of disabled children. Beginning in 1980, the American Nurses Association implemented a training program for school nurses to enable them to manage health evaluations and treatment for handicapped children in schools. The School Nurse Achievement Program (SNAP) is intended to increase the role of nurses in education and related services by incorporating an individualized health-care plan into the IEP. By 1982, SNAP training programs existed in 12 pilot states, with expansion to all 50 states projected by 1984 (Smith & Goodwin, 1982).

Interactions with Family Support Systems

The preceding section has focused on the interaction between health-care systems and families with handicapped children. Next, the information and support needs of families will be reviewed. These areas of service are not aimed directly at the disabled child, but rather are intended to help family members cope with the complex tasks related to raising a handicapped child. Information and support are viewed as necessary components of positive relations between families and direct service providers in health-care and education agencies.

There are a variety of ways in which the needs of family members can be addressed. Within the family-oriented perspective that is viewed as essential for working with handicapped children and youth, services may respond to the needs of parents, siblings, and extended family members. The most common forms of family support and involvement are: (a) parent participation in decision-making and treatment activities, (b) parent support groups, and (c) respite care.

Parent Participation in Services

Since the 1960s, parent participation has been a common characteristic in model programs for handicapped or economically disadvantaged children. Following the parent-led reform movement that began after World War II (such as the creation of the National Association for Retarded Children in 1950), federal policies began to mandate parent involvement and parent education through such programs as Head Start, the First Chance Network, and Title I programs. The Education for All Handicapped Children Act of 1975 broadened the mandate to include parents of all school-age handicapped children. The general thrust, then, for the past 20 years, has been to empower parents with certain rights and responsibilities that provide some control over the services received by their children.

Although these developments were initiated by parents, and they have received widespread acceptance by most professionals, there is recent evidence that not all parents want to play a central role in their children's services. Winton and Turnbull (1981) found that almost one fifth of the parents in a program for handicapped preschoolers wanted the option available to them of not participating in direct services. This does not imply that some parents never want to be involved, but the *option* of noninvolvement is one that parents will occasionally choose. In light of the earlier discussion about accelerated patterns of organizational involvement for parents of young children, it is clear that participation in decision-making or treatment can be a source of stress. To reduce this stress and help avoid early parent burnout, parents must be able to control their own levels of involvement.

Suelzle and Keenan (1980) discovered that parent involvement in services was ranked by parents as only the sixth most important feature of services for their children. The most important consideration for parents was that their children like the program. The parents' top five priorities focused on child-related variables rather than on opportunities for parent support and involvement. These findings illustrate the difficulty of applying uniform standards to all programs and all parents. The need for flexibility and variations in participation based on family life cycle needs is becoming known, but well-intended mandates meant to protect and empower parents may have a negative effect if individual differences are not recognized. The irony is that services for handicapped children have become highly individualized while roles for parents have become standardized and externally prescribed.

An additional irony is that mandates for participation often do *not* apply to parents of either infants or young adults who have left school. In the latter case, authority for parent involvement is tenuous because handicapped people 18 years old or older become their own guardians unless they are found to be legally incompetent. Yet parents of young disabled adults may not view their children as capable of independent decision-making (Daniels, 1982), thus prolonging their own roles as parents at a time when they might otherwise be entering into the stage of being a childless couple. Although these two periods of heightened stress, infancy and early adulthood, are not protected by requirements for parent control over services, parents are expected to be active participants in treatment during their child's infancy or to help launch their child into new work and living environments after secondary school. All this implies a lack of fit between broadly conceived legal mandates, the varying life cycle needs of families, and the individual needs of particular family systems. The solution to this problem will be of primary importance over the next several years. Vadasy and Fewell in Chapter 5 discuss the parties that must be included in early adulthood planning for the unique population of rubella adolescents.

Parent Support Groups

Participation in parent support groups also has certain life cycle characteristics. For example, parents of preschool children are more likely to have attended a parent group than parents of young adults, although the need exists for support groups at this later stage. Suelzle and Keenan (1980) quote one parent of a school-age child on this issue:

> I felt a great need for the support of such a group from birth to age six. Now, I'm more comfortable. I feel that with the problems of adolescence, I will need the group again. (p. 117)

Lately, this author has observed many school districts creating support groups for parents of elementary school children in what is apparently a direct replication of preschool parent support groups. Relying on a model appropriate for parents of younger children ignores changing life cycle needs, and such efforts are often not successful. Professionals who are miffed by the lack of parent participation must examine their own assumptions about the static common needs of all families vs. the dynamic, idiosyncratic characteristics of individual families.

One of the most ambitious and illustrative examples of parent support is the Pilot Parents program in Canada (Canadian Association for the Mentally Retarded, 1977). Pilot Parents began in 1974 when local chapters of the Canadian Association for the Mentally Retarded recognized a need to have parents share information and emotional support among each other. The basic purpose of Pilot Parents is to convey a sense of mutual support and care to parents of newly diagnosed children. The message conveyed is that:

> You are not alone; as Pilot Parents we understand what you're going through because we've been through it ourselves, and for this reason we are making ourselves available to you whenever you need us. (Canadian Association for the Mentally Retarded, 1977, p. 3)

Although the primary emphasis is on peer support for new parents, the program is also used frequently to support parents of older children facing transition points, and older parents whose children are returning from long-term institutionalization.

Using a role metaphor that could also be adopted by professional service providers, Pilot Parents describe themselves as:

> . . .like the harbor pilot who helps the captain guide his ship out of the harbor. He points out all danger spots in the harbor. When the ship moves into the open sea on course, the pilot leaves the ship. (p. 38)

And, the characteristics of good Pilot Parents are equally applicable to good professionals. These include (a) experience, (b) good adjustment to their own family situations, (c) compassion and understanding, (d) good listening skills, and (e) enthusiasm about helping others. Identifying these common qualities among good parents and good professionals is one step toward achieving the sense of equity and partnership so critical to positive interactions between families and community agencies.

Similar networks have recently emerged in the United States. Examples include: (a) the National Parent CHAIN: Coalition of Handicapped Americans Information Network, which acts both as a communications and advocacy organization; (b) Pilot Parents of Omaha, similar to the Canadian model; and (c) Parentele: An Alliance of Parents and Friends Networking for Those with Special Needs, with representatives in each state to link parents and others together.

Other examples of parent-operated networking activities include the Parent Hostel held in New Hampshire in 1983 (coordinated by the author). The Hostel was planned and implemented by parents of handicapped children and involved a two-day "learning vacation" with parent-led discussion groups, recreation activities, and a comprehensive resource center where books, films, magazines, and adaptive equipment were displayed. In addition, the Developmental Disabilities Planning councils in Maine, Maryland, and New Hampshire have published resource manuals written largely by parents which focus on obtaining services, legal rights, definitions of medical and educational terms, emotional needs, and self-advocacy techniques.

These networking and information-sharing activities are examples of the mediating roles played by informal systems necessary for successful family-agency interactions. The empowerment of families through peer support creates a greater degree of equity between service providers and consumers while helping to maintain a family-based locus of control.

An offshoot of parent support activities has been the recognition that the brothers and sisters of handicapped children also have unique emotional and social needs which must be addressed. Given the notion of altered individual life cycles for siblings, documented by Farber (1959; 1968), Featherstone (1980), Grossman (1972), and others, it is evident that programs need to attend to the stresses and adjustments which brothers and sisters experience. In the past few years, model programs designed to demonstrate approaches to sibling support have been implemented. These efforts and related issues have been described in Chapter 3 by Crnic and Leconte. However, it is worth noting here that there is now a national Sibling Information Network similar in purpose and function to the national parent networks mentioned above. The Sibling Information Network, located at the University of Connecticut, publishes a periodic newsletter and acts as a clearinghouse for literature, correspondence, and conference information. The needs and influence of extended family members also merit attention, and as Sonnek points out in Chapter 4, grandparents are often influential members of the extended family system. Efforts to address grandparents' concerns and needs are being made by the Helping Grandparent Program, conducted by the Advocates for Retarded Citizens in Seattle, Washington. The program is developing a model for grandparent workshops and support training, and publishes a quarterly newsletter, *Especially Grandparents*.

Respite Care

Another parent-initiated service that has proven to be a critical mediator in alleviating family stress is respite care. Respite care has emerged since the mid-1970s in response to the deinstitutionalization movement and the resulting reliance on family-based care for disabled children and adults. Two recent reports on families' respite needs are useful for understanding the role and function of this service.

Cohen (1982), in surveying families in New York, Maryland, and Maine, found that use of respite care leads to improved family functioning, more hopefulness about the future, a more positive attitude toward the handicapped family member, and an increased ability to cope with the daily demands caused by the handicapped person. One quarter of the families felt they could not have kept their children at home without respite services. All families reported a need for more respite care, a need also documented by Suelzle and Keenan (1980).

Upshur (1982), in a review of respite services available in Massachusetts, found that the primary reason for using respite care was to relieve chronic physical or emotional stress that often results from caring for a handicapped child. Upshur also identified a range of formal models of respite care being used.
These include:

1. Respite placement agencies which train community providers to work in a client's home or their own home.
2. Group day care or family day care outside of the handicapped person's home.

3. Community residences where a few beds are reserved for overnight respite.
4. Residential treatment facilities with a few beds reserved for respite.
5. Group respite facilities that only provide respite care.
6. Pediatric nursing homes or hospitals that provide emergency respite care during crises.
7. Private respite providers without any organizational affiliation who care for children in their own homes.
8. State institutions that provide a few respite beds for former residents.

Within the models examined, 60% of the respite services occurred in the child's own home, which matches parents' preferences for the location of care. The preference for in-home care is especially strong for parents of younger handicapped children (Cohen, 1982). Formal respite services are most often used for a few hours in the afternoon or evening. Upshur (1982) also found that families with autistic children, or children with severe behavioral or medical needs were often excluded from eligibility for formal respite services, a case of those most in need being least likely to receive help. Finally, although formal respite services are becoming available in many communities, almost one third of the families surveyed by Upshur did not know where to obtain such services, indicating a need for information and referral resources to make parents aware of where services are located and how they can be used.

At this stage in its evolution, respite care does not meet many of the criteria suggested earlier. As a specialized service available only for families with handicapped children, it is relatively segregated from generic community agencies. It is not available universally, and often has categorical limitations related to the child's age or handicapping condition. On the other hand, it is often a personalized service. It can be used to enable family members to work outside of the home, and it may have vertical efficiency characteristics if it benefits individuals other than the handicapped child and the immediate family. Although respite care is not yet a socially normative activity, its use can lead to a more normal pattern of life for nondisabled family members. Its use can also assist families to approximate more closely a normal family life cycle. Thus, it is a narrowly defined, often categorical means to normative ends. As it becomes more available and accessible, respite administrators will need to modify the existing designs to integrate the service into a comprehensive system of community care.

Summary

The model of interactions between families with handicapped children and community agencies described here is based on several assumptions about the nature and needs of such families. The model is nonpathological, longitudinal, and concerned with the enablement of families in order to assure equity between parents and professionals. Using a family life cycle perspective that considers individual time, family time, and historical time, a theoretical model of role adjustment and social participation is suggested as a framework for judging the normative characteristics of health-care and family support services. Design elements are proposed that incorporate ecologically valid approaches based on personal relationships with families. The need for coordinated, comprehensive services is emphasized as a way of reducing stress associated with family life cycle transitions.

In the health-care system, HMOs are proposed as one approach to meeting the suggested program criteria. As well, they are designed in a way that reduces financial stress related to caring for a handicapped family member. The use of HMOs, cash subsidies or allowances, and existing resources such as school health services are viewed as universal, socially acceptable means to treatment and support.

Indirect services such as parent information networks, peer support groups, and respite care are also viewed as essential for enhancing the interactions between formal community agencies and families. These mediating structures serve as means for assisting and empowering families as their needs change over time. Families could not survive without the direct treatment and services necessary for remediating their children's particular disabilities. But the effectiveness of those services, and their ultimate impact on families, depend upon the availability of caring, concerned helpers who view families from an individualized, normative, and personal perspective.

References

Adams, G.L. (1982). Referral advice given by physicians. *Mental Retardation, 20,* 16-20.

Allen, K.A., Holm, V.A., & Schiefelbusch, R.L. (1978). *Early intervention: A team approach.* Austin, TX: PRO-ED.

Bagnato, S.J., Neisworth, J.T., & Eaves, R.C. (1978). A profile of perceived capacities for the preschool child. *Child Care Quarterly, 7,* 326-335.

Berger, P.L., & Neuhaus, R.J. (1977). *To empower people: The role of mediating structures in public policy.* Washington, DC: American Enterprise Institute for Public Policy Research.

Blacher-Dixon, J., & Simeonsson, R.J. (1981). Consistency and correspondence of mother's and teacher's assessments of young handicapped children. *Journal of the Division for Early Childhood, 3,* 64-71.

Boaz, R.F. (1978). Paying for medical care: The burden on the disabled. *Medical Care, 16,* 705-722.

Browder, J.A. (1981). The pediatrician's orientation to infant stimulation programs. *Pediatrics, 67,* 42-44.

Canadian Association for the Mentally Retarded. (1977). *Pilot Parents: An organizer's handbook.* Toronto.

Chang, A., Goldstein, H., Thomas, K., & Wallace, H.M. (1979). The Early Periodic Screening, Diagnosis, and Treatment Program: Status of implementation in 51 state and territories. *Journal of School Health, 49,* 454-458.

Clarke, A.M., & Clarke, A.D. (Eds.) (1976). *Early experience: Myth and evidence.* New York: Free Press.

Cohen, S. (1982). Supporting families through respite care. *Rehabilitation Literature, 43,* 7-11.

Cromley, E.K., & Shannon, G.W. (1983). The establishment of health maintenance organizations: A geographical analysis. *American Journal of Public Health, 73,* 184-187.

Crnic, K.A., Friedrich, W.N., & Greenberg, M.T. (1983). Adaptation of families with mentally retarded children: A model of stress, coping, and family ecology. *American Journal of Mental Deficiency, 88,* 125-138.

Cummings, S.T. (1976). The impact of the child's deficiency on the father: A study of fathers of mentally retarded and of chronically ill children. *American Journal of Orthopsychiatry, 46,* 246-255.

Daniels, S.M. (1982). From parent-advocacy to self-advocacy: A problem of transition. *Exceptional Education Quarterly, 3,* 25-32.

Farber, B. (1959). Effects of a severely mentally retarded child on family integration. *Monographs of the Society for Research in Child Development, 24,* Series no. 71.

Farber, B. (1968). *Mental retardation: Its social context and social consequences.* Boston: Houghton Mifflin.

Farber, B., & Lewis, M. (1975). The symbolic use of parents: A sociological critique of educational practice. *Journal of Research and Development in Education, 8,* 34-43.

Featherstone, H. (1980). *A difference in the family: Life with a disabled child.* New York: Basic Books.

Feuerstein, R. (1980). *Instrument enrichment: An intervention program for cognitive modifiability.* Baltimore: University Park Press.

Frankel, R. (1979). Parents as evaluators of their retarded youngsters. *Mental Retardation, 17,* 40-42.

Gabel, H., & Kotsch, L.S. (1981). Extended families and young handicapped children. *Topics in Early Childhood Special Education, 1,* 29-36.

Gallagher, J.J., Beckman, P., & Cross, A.H. (1983). Families of handicapped children: Sources of stress and its amelioration. *Exceptional Children, 50,* 10-19.

General Accounting Office. (1981). *Disparities still exist in who gets special education.* Washington, DC: Government Printing Office.

Gradel, K., Thompson, M.S., & Sheehan, R. (1981). Parental and professional agreement in early childhood assessment. *Topics in Early Childhood Special Education, 1,* 31-39.

Gray, S., Ramsey, B.K., & Klaus, R.A. (1982). *From 3 to 20: The early training project.* Austin, TX: PRO-ED.

Grossman, F.K. (1972). *Brothers and sisters of retarded children: An exploratory study.* Syracuse: Syracuse University Press.

Haraven, T.K. (1977). Family time and historical time. *Daedalus, 106,* 57-70.

Hill, R. (1981). Theories and research designs linking family behavior and child development: A critical overview. *Journal of Comparative Family Studies, 12,* 1-18.

Hill, R., & Mattesich, P. (1977, October). *Reconstruction of family development theories: A progress report.* Paper presented at the National Council on Family Relations Annual Meeting, San Diego, CA.

Hobbs, N. (1966). Helping disturbed children: Psychological and ecological strategies. *American Psychologist, 21,* 1105-1115.

Hobbs, N. (1975). *The futures of children.* San Francisco: Jossey-Bass.

Hobbs, N. (1982). *The troubled and troubling child.* San Francisco: Jossey-Bass.

Jackson, E. (1982). Environments of high-risk and handicapped infants. In C.T. Ramey & P.L. Trohanis (Eds.). *Finding and educating high-risk and handicapped infants* (pp. 53-67). Baltimore: University Park Press.

Kirschner Associates, Inc. (1970). *A national survey of the impacts of Head Start centers on community institutions.* Washington, DC: Office of Child Development, Department of Health, Education, and Welfare.

Lakin, K.C., Hill, B.K., Hauber, F.A., & Bruininks, R.H. (1983). A response to the GAO report, "Disparities still exist in who gets special education." *Exceptional Children, 50,* 30-34.

Looff, D.H. (1971). *Appalachia's children: The challenge of mental health.* Lexington: University of Kentucky Press.

Mallory, B.L. (1981). Public policies and their impact on families with young handicapped children. *Topics in Early Childhood Special Education, 1,* 77-86.

Mallory, B.L. (In press). Implementation and evaluation of rural early intervention services: Discrepancies between policy making and local practice. *HCEEP Rural Network Monograph Series.* Macomb, IL: Western Illinois University.

Mallory, B.L., & Cottom, C. (1978). *An expanded role for public schools: Community-based delivery of comprehensive health and mental health services.* Prepared for President's Commission on Mental Health, Washington, DC.

Mallory, B.L., & Glascoe, D. (1979). *Evaluating the implementation of rural early intervention programs: A proposed methodology.* (Grant G 007-803-008, Bureau for Education of the Handicapped) George Peabody College, Nashville.

Marmor, T.R. (1971). *Poverty policy: A compendium of cash transfer proposals.* Chicago: Aldine-Atherton.

McDonald, A., Carlson, K., Palmer, D., & Slay, T. (1983). Special education and medicine: A survey of physicians. *Journal of Learning Disabilities, 16,* 93-94.

Meisels, S.J., & Berkeley, T.R. (1980). *Children in transition: A study of the provision of early intervention services in Massachusetts.* Belmont, MA: The Cambridge Workshop.

Mercer, J.R. (1973). *Labelling the mentally retarded.* Berkeley: University of California Press.

Minzey, J.D., & LeTarte, C. (1972). *Community education: From program to process.* Midland, MI: Pendell.

Moore, J.A., Hamerlynck, L.A., Barsh, E.T., Spieker, S., & Jones, R.R. (1982). *Extending family resources.* Seattle, WA: Children's Clinic and Preschool.

Mori, A. (1983). *Families of children with special needs.* Rockville, MD: Aspen Systems.

Moroney, R.M. (1976). *The family and the state: Considerations for social policy.* London: Longman.

Moroney, R.M. (1981). Public social policy: Impact on families with handicapped children. In J.L. Paul (Ed.), *Understanding and working with parents of children with special needs* (pp. 180-204). New York: Holt, Rinehart & Winston.

Nirje, B. (1976). The normalization principle. In R.B. Kugel & A. Shearer (Eds.), *Changing patterns in residential services for the mentally retarded.* Washington, DC: President's Commission on Mental Retardation.

Poznanski, E.O. (1973). Emotional issues in raising handicapped children. *Rehabilitation Literature, 34,* 322-326.

Quick, J.D., Greenlick, M.R., & Roghmann, K.J. (1981). Prenatal care and pregnancy outcome in an HMO and general population: A multivariate cohort analysis. *Public Health, 71,* 381-390.

Smith, A.N., & Goodwin, L.D. (1982). School nurse achievement program: Part I, program development in 12 states. *Journal of School Health, 52,* 535-538.

Stufflebeam, D. (1968). *Evaluation as enlightenment for decision-making.* Columbus: Ohio State University.

Suelzle, M., & Keenan, V. (1980). *Parents' choice of services for developmentally disabled children* (Final Report). Evanston, IL: Northwestern University.

Suelzle, M., & Keenan, V. (1981). Changes in family support networks over the life cycle of mentally retarded persons. *American Journal of Mental Deficiency, 86,* 267-274.

UNESCO. (1981). International Symposium on Services for Young Disabled Children and Their Families. Washington, DC: National Institute of Handicapped Research.

Upshur, C.C. (1982). Respite care for mentally retarded and other disabled populations: Program models and family needs. *Mental Retardation, 20,* 2-6.

Wallace, H.M. (1983). Policies regarding health and social care of mothers and children in the United States. *Clinical Pediatrician, 22,* 14-21.

Weller, J.E. (1965). *Yesterday's people: Life in contemporary Appalachia.* Lexington: University of Kentucky Press.

White, S.H. (1973). *Federal programs for young children: Review and recommendations.* Washington, DC: Government Printing Office.

Wigley, R., & Cook, J.R. (1975). Community health: Concepts and issues. New York: D. Van Nostrand.

Winton, P.J., & Turnbull, A.P. (1981). Parent involvement as viewed by parents of preschool handicapped children. *Topics in Early Childhood Special Education, 1,* 11-19.

Wolfensberger, W. (1972). *The principle of normalization in human services.* Toronto: National Institute on Mental Retardation.

Wolfensberger, W., & Glenn, L. (1975). *Program analysis of service systems (PASS): A method for the quantitative evaluation of human services* (3rd ed.). Handbook and Field Manual. Toronto: National Institute on Mental Retardation.

Wolfensberger, W., & Thomas, S. (1983). *PASSING: Program analysis of service systems' implementation of normalization goals, normalization criteria and ratings manual* (2nd ed.). Downsview, Ontario: National Institute on Mental Retardation.

Zisserman, L. (1981). The modern family and rehabilitation of the handicapped: A macrosociological view. *American Journal of Occupational Therapy, 35,* 13-20.

APPENDIX

Resources for Families of Children with Handicaps

National Organizations and Agencies

National organizations provide a wealth of information on specific handicapping conditions, from autism to visual impairments. Many of these groups publish information materials, pamphlets, and newsletters, and respond to individual inquiries from handicapped persons, their families, professionals, and the general public. The names and addresses of selected organizations follow. An excellent resource for more complete information on advocacy, consumer, voluntary health, professional, religious, and recreational organizations serving the handicapped and their families is the *Directory of National Information Sources on Handicapping Conditions and Related Services*, U.S. Department of Education No. E-82-22007; August, 1982. Much of the information included here was obtained from this guide.

Name, Address, Telephone	Services Available
Alexander Graham Bell Association for the Deaf 3417 Volta Place, N.W. Washington, DC 20007 (202) 337-5220 (Voice/TDD)	• Consultation for families on legal rights
American Brittle Bone Society 1256 Merrill Drive Marshallton West Chester, PA 19380 (215) 692-6248	• Consultations/referrals for families
American Cleft Palate Educational Foundation 331 Salk Hall University of Pittsburgh Pittsburgh, PA 15261 (412) 681-9620	• Series of pamphlets for parents • Parent newsletter • Referral service
American Coalition of Citizens with Disabilities (ACCD) 1012 14th Street, N.W. Suite 901 Washington, DC 20005 (202) 628-3470 (Voice and TDD)	• Job placement services • Local workshops in advocacy • Newsletters

Name, Address, Telephone	Services Available
American Council of the Blind (ACB) Suite 506 1211 Connecticut Avenue, N.W. Washington, DC 20036 (202) 833-1251	• Parents' organization • Legal assistance • Scholarships • Workshops on advocacy
American Foundation for the Blind (AFB) 15 West 16th Street New York, NY 10011 (212) 620-2000	• Public education materials and directories of services
Association for Children and Adults with Learning Disabilities (ACLD) 4156 Library Road Pittsburgh, PA 15234 (412) 341-1515 (412) 341-8077	• Pamphlets and scientific reprints • Lists of schools, summer camps serving learning disabled • Newsletter on clinical and legislative advances • Bibliography on lay publications
Association for Retarded Citizens of the United States National Headquarters 2501 Avenue J Arlington, TX 76011 (817) 640-0204	• Extensive in-house publications and file of references • Newsletters on local projects, research, and legislation
The Association for Persons with Severe Handicaps (TASH) 7010 Roosevelt Way, N.E. Seattle, WA 98115 (206) 523-8446	• Bibliography for parents on advocacy, recreation, self-help skills • Parent-to-parent network • Register of professional resources
Association of Birth Defect Children (ABDC) 3201 East Crystal Lake Avenue Orlando, FL 32806 (305) 898-5342	• Information service for parents
Children's Defense Fund 122 C Street, N.W., Suite 400 Washington, DC 20001 (202) 628-8787 (800) 424-9602	• Publications on health care, special education services • Newsletter
Cornelia de Lange Syndrome Foundation 60 Dyer Avenue Collinsville, CT 06022 (203) 693-0159	• Directory of parents and interested persons • Newsletter

Name, Address, Telephone	Services Available
Cystic Fibrosis Foundation (CFF) 6000 Executive Boulevard Suite 309 Rockville, MD 20852 (301) 881-9130	• Materials for parents • Newsletter
Disability Rights Center 1346 Connecticut Avenue, N.W. Suite 1124 Washington, DC 20036 (202) 223-3304	• Guide on rights under Section 501 (Rehabilitation Act of 1973)
Down's Syndrome Congress (DSC) Central Office 1640 West Roosevelt Road Chicago, IL 60608 (312) 226-0416	• Family support network • Information materials • Newsletters
Dysautonomia Foundation 370 Lexington Avenue New York, NY 10017 (212) 889-0300	• Printed materials and handbooks • Lists of local chapters and resources
Epilepsy Foundation of American (EFA) 4351 Garden City Drive, Suite 406 Landover, MD 20785 (301) 459-3700	• Information materials • Directory of clinics • Newsletter • Audiovisual materials
Foundation for Children with Learning Disabilities (FCLD) P.O. Box 2929 Grand Central Station New York, NY 10163 (212) 687-7211	• Annual periodical
Friedreich's Ataxia Group in America (FAGA) P.O. Box 1116 Oakland, CA 94611	• Newsletter, brochure
Human Growth Foundation (HGF) 4930 West 77th Street Minneapolis, MN 55435 (612) 831-2780	• Educational materials on growth disorders • Referrals to specialists
American Society for Deaf Children 814 Thayer Avenue Silver Spring, MD 20910 (301) 585-5400	• Parent referral network • Speaker list • Newsletter

Name, Address, Telephone	Services Available
Jewish Guild for the Blind (JGB) 15 West 65th Street New York, NY 10023 (212) 595-2000	• Free current literature recordings
Junior National Association of the Deaf (Jr. NAD) 814 Thayer Avenue Silver Spring, MD 20910 (301) 587-1788 (Voice and TDD)	• Summer camp programs • Local school chapters • Achievement awards • Quarterly magazine
March of Dimes Birth Defects Foundation 1275 Mamaroneck Avenue White Plains, NY 10605 (914) 428-7100	• Local parent programs • Educational materials
Mucopolysaccharidoses (MPS) Society 552 Central Avenue Bethpage, NY 11714 (516) 433-4410	• Brochure on rare hereditary enzyme deficiency diseases and management, living options for affected children
Muscular Dystrophy Association (MDA) 810 Seventh Avenue New York, NY 10019 (212) 586-0808	• Brochures • Audiovisual materials • Newsletter • Parent service publication
National Association for Hearing and Speech Action (NAHSA) 10801 Rockville Pike Rockville, MD 20852 (301) 897-8682 (Voice and TDD)	• Hotline for questions and referrals (call collect 0-301-897-8682) • Information materials
National Association for the Deaf- Blind (NADB) 2703 Forest Oak Circle Norman, OK 73071 (405) 360-2580 or 0431	• Newsletter • Regional directors provide information on services and resources
National Association for Visually Handicapped (NAVH) 305 East 24th Street, 17-C New York, NY 10010 (212) 889-3141	• Informational materials • Newsletters

Name, Address, Telephone	Services Available
National Association of the Deaf (NAD) 814 Thayer Avenue Silver Spring, MD 20910 (301) 587-1788 (Voice or TDD)	• Information on resources • Newsletters • Extensive library
National Committee, Arts for the Handicapped (NCAH) 1825 Connecticut Avenue, N.W. Suite 417 Washington, DC 20009 (202) 332-6960 (Voice and TDD)	• Lists of organizations with arts programs • Curriculum ideas for parents • Resource guides and bibliographies
National Down Syndrome Society 70 West 40th Street New York, NY 10018 (212) 764-3070 (800) 221-4602	• Information package for new parents
National Easter Seal Society 2023 West Ogden Avenue Chicago, IL 60612 (312) 243-8400 (312) 243-8880 (TDD)	• Bibliographies • Information materials (contact Program Services Dept. for list)
National Federation of the Blind (NFB) 1800 Johnson Street Baltimore, MD 21230 (301) 659-9314	• Information Center for mail or phone quetions • Monthly magazine
National Fraternal Society of the Deaf (NFSD) 1300 W. Northwest Highway Mt. Prospect, IL 60056 (312) 392-9282 (Voice) (312) 392-1409 (TDD)	• National library • Scholastic and athletic achievement awards
National Genetics Foundation, Inc. (NGF) 555 West 57th Street New York, NY 10019 (212) 586-5900	• Clearinghouse for inquiries • Referral services • Brochures
National Multiple Sclerosis Society 205 East 42nd Street New York, NY 10017 (212) 986-3240	• Parent information • Referrals and information on aids and equipment • Order lists for free publications

Name, Address, Telephone	Services Available
National Organization on Disability 2100 Pennsylvania Avenue, N.W. Washington, DC 20037 (202) 293-5960	• Newsletter • Bulletins on how to organize community programs
National Parkinson Foundation 1501 N.W. Ninth Avenue Miami, FL 33136 (305) 547-6666	• Research newsletter • Free publications
National Retinitis Pigmentosa Foundation (RP Foundation) Rolling Park Building 8331 Mindale Circle Baltimore, MD 21207 (301) 655-1011 (301) 655-1190 (TDD)	• Referral services • Fact sheets • Quarterly newsletter
The National Society for Children and Adults with Autism (NSAC) 1234 Massachusetts Avenue, N.W. Suite 1017 Washington, DC 20005-4599 (202) 783-0125	• Information and referral service • Newsletter
National Tay-Sachs and Allied Diseases Association, Inc. 92 Washington Avenue Cedarhurst, NY 11516 (516) 569-4300	• Brochures • List of screening centers • Bibliographies • Parent match program
Parents' Campaign for Handicapped Children and Youth 1201 16th Street, N.W. Washington, DC 20036	• Written materials
Prader-Willi Syndrome Association 5515 Malibu Drive Edina, MN 55436 (612) 933-0113	• Newsletter • Handbook • Referral service
Spina Bifida Association of America (SBAA) 343 South Dearborn Street Suite 319 Chicago, IL 60604 (312) 663-1562	• Newsletter • Manuals • Directory of local chapters • Price list of materials

Name, Address, Telephone	Services Available
Tourette Syndrome Association (TSA) Bell Plaza Building 41-02 Bell Boulevard Bayside, NY 11361 (212) 224-2999	• Referral service • Newsletter • Lists of local chapters, reprints
United Cerebral Palsy Associations (UCPA) 66 East 34th Street New York, NY 10016 (212) 481-6300	• Lay publications • Referral service

Resources Available at the State and Local Level

The Federal government and national offices of organizations for the handicapped are good resources for up-to-date written materials on handicaps and related topics of interest to family members. However, when families need information on specific services and programs available in their community, they will need to contact local public agencies or state groups serving children with disabilities and their families. For example, questions about special education programs available in a state would best be addressed to the office of the state's director of special education. A state's department of social and health services often administers vocational programs for handicapped students, services available for handicapped infants, and Early Periodic Screening, Diagnosis, and Treatment (EPSDT) services. Local chapters of the Association for Retarded Citizens, United Cerebral Palsy, and the Easter Seal Society are good sources of information on state resources, and they often offer support programs for handicapped children and their families. Universities that have a University Affiliated Facility (UAF) on their campus are another valuable resource. These centers, 48 of which are funded by the Federal government, provide interdisciplinary training and conduct applied research related to persons with developmental disabilities. UAFs provide comprehensive screening, evaluation, treatment, planning, and educational programming, and they offer technical assistance to a broad range of professionals who serve the developmentally disabled.

The National Information Center for Handicapped Children and Youth (P.O. Box 1492, Washington, DC, 20013) distributes resource sheets for each state which list the names and addresses of the key individuals and agencies serving the handicapped in each state.

General Written Resources

Directory of National Information Sources on Handicapping Conditions and Related Services. U.S. Department of Education, Office of Special Education and Rehabilitative Services, Clearinghouse on the Handicapped. August, 1982. (Publication No. E-82-22007).

This is the major reference on national level organizations which are information and direct service providers in the handicapped field. It includes information on Federal Government Organizations, advocacy, consumer, and voluntary health organizations, information and data banks, special facilities, schools and clinics, and religious and sports organizations that serve the handicapped. It is available for $7.50 from the U.S. Government Printing Office.

A Reader's Guide for Parents of Children with Mental, Physical, or Emotional Disabilities, by Cory Moore, Kathryn Gorham Morton, and Anne Southard. The Maryland State Planning Council on Developmental Disabilities, 201 West Preston Street, Baltimore, Maryland 21201. 1983.

This is an excellent resource which contains the names and addresses of agencies and organizations concerned with handicapped persons; titles of books about disabilities for parents and for young children; resources on training, genetic counseling, children's rights, sex education, and many other topics of concern to families.

National Information Center for Handicapped Children and Youth P.O. Box 1492, Washington, DC 20013.

The Center provides a wide selection of extremely useful up-to-date written information including the following: *state information sheets* including names and addresses of public and other state groups serving handicapped children and youth; *fact sheets on specific disabilities* with references and resources for additional information; *legal fact sheets* on children's rights, including rights to education; *parent information* on direct children's services and advocacy and support groups; *teacher-parent information* on educational concerns; *student information* on careers in special education and related services; *general information* on organizations and publications about handicapping conditions; *self-advocacy information*; *News Digest Newsletter*; and *Transition Summary Newsletter*.

Specific Resources

Access Guides

The International Directory of Access Guides
Rehabilitation International U.S.A.
1123 Broaway
New York, NY 10010

• Lists over 300 cities worldwide that publish guides to facilities accessible to handicapped persons.

Adult Day Care

Directory of Adult Day-Care Centers
Technical Services, Health Care Financing Administration
Area 1B1
Dogwood East Building
1849 Gwynn Oak Avenue
Baltimore, MD 21207

• Lists facilities by state, describes services.

Autism

Facilities and Programs for Persons with Autism
National Society for Children and Adults with Autism
1234 Massachusetts Avenue, N.W.
Suite 1017
Washington, DC 20005

• Lists and describes facilities by state.

Blind or Visually Impaired

Directory of Agencies Serving the Visually Handicapped in the United States
American Foundation for the Blind, Inc.
15 West 16th Street
New York, NY 10011

• Lists state education, rehabilitation, library services.

Children and Youth

Directory for Exceptional Children
Porter-Sargent Publishers, Inc.
11 Beacon Street
Boston, MA 02108

• Lists and describes state schools, societies, residential facilities and services.

Directory of Learning Resources for the Handicapped
Croft-Nei Publications
24 Rope Ferry Road
Waterford, CT 06386

• Lists information and professional training centers, federal and state agencies.

National Directory of Children and Youth Services
CPR Directory Services Company
1301 20th Street, N.W.
Washington, DC 20036

• Over 20,000 listings, by state of public and private agencies with descriptive information.

Cystic Fibrosis

The Cystic Fibrosis Foundation Directory
Cystic Fibrosis Foundation
6000 Executive Boulevard
Suite 309
Rockville, MD 20852

• Lists foundation chapters.

The Directory of Cystic Fibrosis Chapters and Centers.
Cystic Fibrosis Foundation
6000 Executive Boulevard
Suite 309
Rockville, MD 20852

• Lists foundation chapters and treatment centers.

Deaf

American Annals of the Deaf:
  Reference Issue
American Annals of the Deaf
814 Thayer Avenue
Silver Spring, MD 20910

- Annual updated reference on programs and services, listed by state.

Regional Directories of Services for
  Deaf Persons
Registry of Interpreters for the Deaf.
814 Thayer Avenue
Silver Spring, MD 20910

- Lists services available for deaf individuals by state. Separate directory available for each of the federal regions.

Deaf-Blind

Directory of Agencies Serving the
  Deaf-Blind
Helen Keller National Center for
  Deaf-Blind Youths and Adults
111 Middle Neck Road
Sands Point, NY 11050

- Lists agencies by state and describes services.

Dentistry

Academy of Dentistry for the
  Handicapped Membership
  Referral Roster
Academy of Dentistry for the
  Handicapped
1726 Champa
Suite 422
Denver, CO 80202

- State lists of dental professionals who serve handicapped patients.

Diabetes

Resource Directory of People with
  Diabetes
National Diabetes Information
  Clearinghouse
P.O. Box NDIC
Bethesda, MD 20205

- State lists of social services offices and ADA chapters, and list of federal information services

Genetic Disorders

Clinical Genetic Service Centers
National Clearinghouse for Human
  Genetic Diseases
805 15th Street, N.W.
Suite 500
Washington, DC 20005

- Locations of centers, including sickle cell and hemophilia treatment programs.

Learning Disabilities

Directory of Educational Facilities for the Learning Disabled
Association for Children and Adults with Learning Disabilities
4156 Library Road
Pittsburgh, PA 15234

- Lists and describes programs by state.

National Directory of Four-Year Colleges, Two-Year Colleges, and Post High School Training Programs for Young People with Learning Disabilities
Partners in Publishing Company
P.O. Box 50347
Tulsa, OK 74150

- Lists and describes programs by state.

Directory of Learning Resources for Learning Disabilities
Croft-Nei Publications
24 Rope Ferry Road
Waterford, CT 06386

- Lists centers and resources by state.

Mental Retardation

Directory of Members: National Association of Private Residential Facilities for the Mentally Retarded
National Association of Private Residential Facilities for the Mentally Retarded
6269 Leesburg Pike
Suite B5
Falls Church, VA 22044

- Lists and describes services by state.

Organizations of and for the Handicapped

Directory of Organizations Interested in the Handicapped
People to People Committee for the Handicapped
111 20th Street, N.W.
Suite 660
Washington, D.C. 20036

- Lists and describes over 200 national organizations.

Parent Training Programs

National Information Center for Handicapped Children and Youth
P.O. Box 1492
Washington, DC 20013

- Lists current parent training projects sponsored by the Department of Education's Division of Personnel Preparation, Special Education Programs.

Rehabilitation Facilities

*National Association of
Rehabilitation Facilities
Membership Directory*
National Association of
Rehabilitation Facilities
P.O. Box 17675
Washington, DC 20041

- Lists and describes facilities by state.

*National Resource Handbook: A
Guide to Vocational Rehabilitation
Services in the United States*
Vocational Rehabilitation Center
1123 Forbes Avenue
Pittsburgh, PA 15219

- Lists rehabilitation facilities by state.

Speech-Language-Audiology

*The Guide to Professional Services
in Speech-Language Pathology
and Audiology*
American Speech-Language-Hearing
Association (ASHA)
10801 Rockville Pike
Rockville, MD 20852

- Lists certified personnel and
describes accredited service
programs.

Sports Organizations Serving the Handicapped

American Athletic Association of the
Deaf
3916 Lantern Drive
Silver Spring, MD 20902

American Blind Bowling Association
15 N. Bellaire Avenue
Louisville, KY 40206

American Camping Association
Bradford Woods
Martinsville, IN 46151

American Wheelchair Bowling
Association
6718 Pinehurst Drive
Evansville, IN 47711

Blind Outdoor Leisure Development
(BOLD)
533 E. Main Street
Aspen, CO 81611

Health Sports, Inc.
1455 West Lake Street
Minneapolis, MN 55408

Indoor Sports Club
1145 Highland Street
Napoleon, OH 43545

International Committee of Silent
Sports
Gallaudet College
800 Florida Avenue, N.E.
Washington, DC 20002

Minnesota Outward Bound School
P.O. Box 250
Long Lake, MN 55356

National Archery Association
1750 E. Boulder Street
Colorado Springs, CO 80909

National Association of Sports for
Cerebral Palsied
c/o Craig Huber
66 East 34th Street
New York, NY 10016

National Foundation for Happy
Horsemanship for the
Handicapped
Box 462
Malvern, PA 19355

National Wheelchair Athletic
Association
Templeton Gap Road
Suite C
Colorado Springs, CO 80907

National Wheelchair Basketball
Association
110 Seaton Center
University of Kentucky
Lexington, KY 40506

National Wheelchair Softball
Association
P.O. Box 737
Sioux Falls, SD 57101

North American Riding for the
Handicapped Association, Inc.
P.O. Box 100
Ashburn, VA 22011

Special Olympics
1701 K Street, N.W.
Suite 203
Washington, DC 20006

U.S. Association of Blind Athletes
55 West California Avenue
Beach Haven, NJ 08008

United States Deaf Skiers
Association
Attention: Mr. Gutfran
Two Sunset Hill Road
Simsbury, CT 06070

United States Wheelchair Sports
Fund
c/o Nassau Community College
Garden City, NY 11530

Religious Organizations Serving the Handicapped

American Bible Society (ABS)
1865 Broadway
New York, NY 10023

Braille Circulating Library
2700 Stuart Avenue
Richmond, VA 23220

Christian Record Braille Foundation,
Inc. (CRBF)
444 South 52nd Street
Lincoln, NE 68506

Committee on Ministry to the
Developmentally Disabled
Attention: Marshall R. Nelson
3558 South Jefferson Avenue
St. Louis, MO 63118

Ephphatha Services with the Deaf
and Blind (ES)
P.O. Box 15167
Minneapolis, MN 55415

Episcopal Guild for the Blind
157 Montague Street
Brooklyn, NY 11201

Gospel Association for the Blind, Inc.
P.O. Box 62
Del Ray Beach, FL 33447

John Milton Society for the Blind
475 Riverside Drive, Room 832
New York, NY 10115

Lutheran Braille Evangelism
Association (LBEA)
660 East Montana Avenue
St. Paul, MN 55106

Lutheran Braille Workers, Inc. (LBW)
11735 Peach Tree Circle
Yucaipa, CA 92399

Lutheran Library for the Blind
3558 South Jefferson Avenue
St. Louis, MO 63118

Ministries to the Deaf and Blind
(MDB)
Division of Home Missions
General Council of Assemblies of
God
1445 Boonville Avenue
Springfield, MO 65802

Ministry to the Deaf
Lutheran Church-Missouri Synod
500 North Broadway
St. Louis, MO 63102

National Catholic Education
Association (NCEA)
Special Education Department
1077 30th Street, N.W.
Washington, DC 20007

National Catholic Office of the Deaf
814 Thayer Avenue
Silver Spring, MD 20910

National Congress of Jewish Deaf
(NCJD)
9102 Edmonston Court
Greenbelt, MD 20770

Xavier Society for the Blind
154 East 23rd Street
New York, NY 10010

Author Index

Abernethy, V., 168, 170, 189
Adams, B., 106, 118
Adams, G.L., 342, 353
Addison, S., 44-47, 49, 55, 60, 71, 86, 98
Adelberg, T., 243, 247
Adelson, E., 12, 29, 263, 275
Adler, B., 40, 69
Agard, J., 262, 267-269, 276
Ahlersmeyer, D., 7, 30, 299, 315
Albin, A.R., 80, 96
Albrecht, R., 103-106, 118
Allen, J.C., 20, 29
Allen, K.A., 335, 353
Allen, N.L., 20, 29
Antonucci, T.C., 168, 170, 192
Antrobus, J., 4, 32
Apley, J., 80, 96
Appell, M.A., 226, 245
Apple, D., 107, 118
Armstrong v Kline, 9, 29
Aspy, D.N., 263, 275
Atcheley, T., 100, 106, 118

Baer, N., 240, 245
Bagnato, S.J., 319, 353
Ball, J.R., 303-304, 315
Ball, N.J., 47, 72
Ballenski, C.B., 168-169, 189
Baltes, P.B., ix, xv, 167-168, 176, 189-190
Ban, P.L., 233, 245
Bane, M.J., 222, 224-226, 229, 238, 240, 243-246
Barbour, R.F., 80, 96
Barsh, E.T., 25, 29, 62, 71, 132, 147, 227, 247, 264, 275, 283, 294, 321, 355
Barton, D.D., 272, 275
Basham, R.B., 7, 29, 169, 172, 191, 234, 246
Baum, M.H., 216, 220
Bayley, M., 226, 245
Beasley, D.M., 282, 289, 294
Beckman, P., 15, 32, 52-53, 57, 70, 226, 245, 336, 354
Bell, C., 103-104, 118
Belmonte, J., 7, 30, 299, 315
Belsky, J., 4, 5, 29, 232, 234, 245
Bennett, J., 272, 275
Berger, M., 110, 118, 188, 190
Berger, P.L., 320, 353
Berkeley, T.R., 339, 355
Berman, W., 188, 192
Bianchi, S.M., 229, 239, 245

Billingsley, A., 170, 190
Binger, C.M., 80, 96
Birch, J.W., 263, 276
Birenbaum, A., 55, 57, 69, 109, 118, 282-284, 289-290, 293
Blacher, J., 52, 72, 237, 245, 286, 293, 319, 353
Blackard, M.K., 25, 29, 264, 275
Blumberg, B., 39-40, 69
Boaz, R.F., 344, 353
Bogdan, R., x, xv
Boggs, E.M., 144, 146
Borden, B., 103, 118
Bott, E., 170, 172, 189
Bowen, M, 281, 293
Bowen, G.L., 170, 189
Boyd, R.R., 103-104, 106, 118
Braginsky, B., 11 ,29
Braginsky, D., 11 ,29
Brandwein, R.A., 170, 189, 233, 245
Brassard, J., 171, 176, 189, 232, 234, 245, 281, 287, 289, 292-293
Brazelton, T.B., 38-39, 43, 69
Breslau, N., 21, 29, 79, 84, 96, 132, 146, 229, 245, 283, 293
Brewer, G.D., 123-124, 146
Brim, J.A., 171, 183, 189
Brim, O.G., ix, xv
Bristol, M.M., 60, 69
Brodie, F.H., 12, 32
Brody, G.H., 80, 98
Bronfenbrenner, U., 4, 20, 29, 96, 122, 146, 171, 176, 178, 188-189, 225, 245, 266, 275, 303, 315
Brotherson, M.J., 47, 72, 80-81, 92, 98, 282, 294
Brotman, H.B., 101 ,118
Browder, J.A., 342, 353
Brown, C., 262, 272, 275
Brown, C.A., 170, 189, 233, 245
Brown, N., 86, 97
Bruininks, R.H., 329, 354
Bruner, J.S., 6, 29
Burchinal, L., 8, 33
Bursk, B.J., 106, 119
Burton, L., 7, 29

Caldwell, B., 56, 69
Call, J., 46, 69
Callon, M.A., 234, 246
Campbell, D.T., 291, 293
Campeau, P.L., 130, 147

371

Canadian Association for the Mentally Retarded, 348, 353
Canning, C.D., 77, 96
Canning, J.P., 77, 96
Caplan, G., 8, 29, 171, 176, 189, 229, 245
Carlson, K., 342, 355
Cartwright, C.A., 272, 275
Cashion, B.G., 233, 245
Catron, T.F., 287, 293
Cauble, A.E., 191
Cerreto, M.C., 94, 96
Chandler, M.J., 4, 5, 11, 33
Chang, A., 343, 353
Chess, S., 4, 5, 33, 129, 133, 147
Christ-Sullivan, R., 25, 29
Cicirelli, V.C., 76, 96
Clarke, A.D., 319, 353
Clarke, A.M., 319, 353
Clarke-Stewart, K.A., 43, 66, 69
Cleveland, D.W., 78, 82-84, 96
Cobb, S., 281, 293
Cochran, M., 171, 176, 189, 232, 234, 245, 281, 287, 289, 292-293
Cohen, D.S., 298, 315
Cohen, J., 179, 189
Cohen, P., 179, 189
Cohen, S., 350-351, 353
Cohler, B.J., 8, 29, 101, 106, 118
Colletta, N.D., 229, 232, 242, 245-246
Collins, G., xi, 43, 69
Comeau, J., 191
Connally, K.J., 6, 29
Cook, A.S., 168-169, 189
Cook, J.R., 345, 356
Cook, S., 299, 315
Cottom, C., 338, 354
Cox, M., 172, 190, 233, 242, 246
Cox, R., 172, 190, 233, 242, 246
Craig, P.A., 259, 270, 275
Crnic, K.A., 7, 29, 76, 86, 90, 96, 169, 172, 189, 191, 234, 246, 318, 353
Crockenberg, S., 172, 189
Crocker, A.C., 79, 87, 96
Cromley, E.K., 345, 353
Cross, A., 7, 23, 30, 47-48, 52-53, 57, 62, 70, 169, 172, 175, 180, 189-190, 336, 354
Crowley, M., 51, 63, 65, 69
Cummings, S.T., 46, 53, 60, 62, 66, 69, 325, 353
Curry, L., 260, 275

Daniels, S.M., 347, 353
Dantona, R., 124, 146
D'Arcy, E., 7, 29, 262, 275

Darling, R.B., 15, 29
Darlington, R., 172, 191
David, H.P., 6, 19, 29
Davis, D.R., 108, 118
Dean, A., 177, 189
DeBoor, M., 56, 69
Delaney, S.W., 63-64, 69
Delk, M.T., 126, 129, 148
DesJardinas, C., 262, 275
Diamond, S., 162, 166
Dodge, D., 282, 293
Doris, J., 10-11, 33
Drotar, D., 90, 96
Duncan, G.J., 238, 246
Dunlap, W.R., 25, 29, 132, 146, 264, 275, 282, 289, 293
Dunn, J., 85, 96
Dunn, R.C., 47, 72
Dunst, C.J., 7, 30, 175, 177, 180, 185, 188-190, 192
Duvall, E., 169, 173, 190
Duvall, E.M., 36-38, 41-42, 48, 51, 54-55, 57-58, 69
Dyer, E. D., 290, 293
Dyson, L., 92, 96

Easp, J.A., 232, 248
Eaves, R.C., 319, 353
Edgerton, M., 169, 172, 174-175, 180-181, 183, 191
Edgerton, R.B., 10, 30
Egeland, B., 5, 34
Ehlers, W.H., 108, 118
Elder, G.H., 240, 244, 247
Elkind, D., 235, 246
Ellwood, D.T., 224-225, 243-246
Embry, L., 172, 190, 267, 275
Emde, R.N., 262, 272, 275
Erickson, M., 45, 69

Farber, B., 23-25, 30, 38, 46-47, 51, 60, 62, 69-70, 78-79, 82-83, 85, 91, 96, 108, 118, 132, 146, 226, 246, 282-283, 285, 293, 319, 322-325, 339, 349, 353
Featherstone, H., 17, 20-21, 30, 76, 88, 96, 216, 220, 282-285, 293, 349, 353
Fernandez, P., 5, 31, 129, 133, 147
Ferrara, S., 130, 147
Ferri, E., 225, 231, 233, 246
Ferris, C., 22, 30
Feuerstein, R., 80, 96, 319, 353
Fewell, R.R., 7, 11-14, 30, 33, 49, 51, 55, 64, 71-72, 86, 92, 94, 96-97, 111, 120, 136, 138, 146, 180, 190, 256, 260, 275,

288, 293, 299, 310, 315
Fishler, K., 21, 31, 84, 97
Folkman, S., 90, 96, 298, 315
Foster, M., 188, 190
Fotheringham, J.B., 57, 70
Fowle, C., 7, 30, 79, 96
Fowlkes, M.A., 110, 118
Fox, E.M., 170, 189, 233, 245
Fraiberg, S., 11-12, 29-30, 263, 275
Frankel, R., 319, 354
Fresco, N., 40, 72
Friedman, S., 81, 97
Friedrich, W.J., 86, 97, 173, 190
Friedrich, W.N., 7, 30, 76, 86, 96-97, 173,
    175, 190, 298, 302, 310, 315, 318, 353

Gabe, T., 100-101, 118
Gabel, H., 9, 21, 30, 109-110, 118-119, 138,
    146, 173-174, 190-191, 282-283, 288,
    293-294, 336, 354
Gallagher, J.J., 23, 30, 47, 50, 52-53, 57,
    62, 66, 70, 138, 146, 169, 172, 174, 177,
    181, 190, 336, 354
Garbarino, J., 303, 315
Gath, A., 7, 30, 38, 47, 70, 78, 81-83, 85,
    91, 132, 146, 264, 275
Gayton, W.F., 81, 97, 286, 294
Gearheart, B., 259, 275
Geismar, L., 6, 30
Gelb, S.A., 13-14, 30, 260, 275
General Accounting Office, 329, 354
German, M.L., 22, 30, 138, 146, 226, 246,
    286, 293
Ginsberg, N., 41, 71
Giovanoni, J., 172, 190
Glascoe, D., 339, 354
Glasser, P., 170, 190
Glenn, L., 339, 356
Glick, J., 4, 32
Glick, P.C., 224, 246
Gliedman, J., 10, 14, 27, 31
Goffman, E., 15, 27, 31, 92, 97
Golbus, H., 39-40, 69
Goldstein, H., 343, 353
Goldstein, S., 159, 166, 260, 275
Goodman, L., 258, 276
Goodwin, L.D., 346, 355
Gorham, K.A., 262, 275
Goulet, L.R., 168, 176, 190
Gourash, N., 174, 183, 190
Gradel, K., 319, 354
Graham, E.H., 172, 191
Graham, P., 11, 31
Graliker, B.V., 21, 31, 84, 86, 91, 94, 97,

226, 246
Grana, G., 49, 71
Granovetter, M., 174, 190
Gray, S., 329, 354
Greenberg, M., 43, 70
Greenberg, M.T., 7, 15, 32, 51, 55, 64, 72,
    76, 96, 169, 172, 189, 191, 234, 246, 318,
    353
Greene, B., xi
Greenfeld, J., 35, 45-46, 52, 56, 59-61, 70,
    193, 220
Greenlick, M.R., 345, 355
Grieve, B., 122, 129, 148
Grossman, F.K., 21, 24, 31, 60, 62, 70, 79,
    82, 84-86, 91, 97, 349, 354
Grossman, H.J., 287, 294
Grunebaum, H.U., 8, 29, 101, 106,
    118
Gubrium, J.F., 49, 70
Gumz, E.J., 49, 70
Guthrie, D., 178, 191
Guze, S., 56, 69

Halperin, D., 41, 71
Halpern, R., 256, 275
Hamerlynck, L.A., 62, 71, 132, 147, 227,
    247, 283, 294, 321, 355
Hamilton, M.E., 42, 73
Hampson, R., 67, 72
Hanson, K., 40, 69
Haraven, T.K., 323-324, 354
Hatfield, E., 36, 73, 285, 295
Hauber, F.A., 329, 354
Hawthorne, J.T., 234, 246
Healy, A., 12, 31
Helge, D., 256, 259, 275
Helsel, B., 24, 31, 58-59, 70
Helsel, E., 24, 31, 58-59, 70
Henderson, M., 226, 246
Henggeler, S.W., 286, 294
Hersch, A., 49, 54, 67, 70
Herzog, R., 232, 246
Herzog, J.M., 234, 246
Hetherington, E.M., 65, 101, 118, 172,
    190, 233, 242, 246
Hicks, W., 123, 126-127, 146-147
Higgins, L.C., 11, 31
Hill, B.K., 329, 354
Hill, M.S., 238, 246
Hill, R., 101, 109, 118, 322, 354
Hines, B., 234, 247
Hirsch, B.J., 287, 294
Hobbs, D.F., 290, 294
Hobbs, M.A., 226, 247

Hobbs, N., 19, 31, 171, 190, 318-319, 332, 354
Hocutt, A., 257, 260, 266, 271-272, 276
Hoddinot, B.A., 57, 70
Hodge, D., 256, 276
Hodges, B., 94, 97
Hofferth, S.L., 23, 31
Holahan, C.J., 171, 176, 190
Hollingshead, A.B., 177, 191
Hollinsworth, J.S., 25, 29, 132, 146, 264, 275, 282, 293
Holm, V.A., 335, 353
Holmes, T.H., 226, 247
Holroyd, J., 60, 70, 80, 86, 97, 177-178, 191, 226, 247, 285, 294
Holt, K.S., 82, 97, 282, 294
Horejsi, C.R., 25, 31
Humphry, R.A., 282, 286, 289, 294

Illingworth, R.S., 46, 51, 70

Jablow, M.M., 25, 28, 31
Jackson, E., 328, 354
Jacobson, R.B., 282, 286, 289, 294
Jauch, C., 233, 247
Jeffries, V., 232, 248
Jenkins, V. 94, 97, 177, 190
Jenne, W., 46, 70
Jensema, C.J., 125, 128, 133, 146
Jessner, L., 103, 119
Johnson, E.J., 106, 119
Johnson, P., 234, 248
Jones, R.R., 62, 71, 147, 227, 247, 283, 294, 321, 355
Joy, C., 191

Kagan, J., xv, 42, 67, 71
Kahana, B., 106-107, 119
Kahana, E., 106-107, 119
Kain, E.L., 240, 244, 247
Kakalik, J.S., 123-124, 146
Kamerman, S.B., 230, 239, 241-243, 247
Karchmer, M.A., 123, 147
Karnes, M., 258-259, 264, 267, 273, 276
Keane, K., 51, 63, 69
Keenan, V., 60, 67, 72, 284, 294, 321, 335, 346-348, 350, 355
Kendrick, C., 85, 96
Kennell, J.H., 20, 31, 216, 220
Kéogh, B., 258, 264, 276
Kershman, S.M., 139, 147
Kerstetter, P.P., 123, 147
Keshet, H.F., 224, 248
Kiernan, W.E., 261, 274, 276

Kirkpatrick, C., 44, 70
Kirschner Associates, Inc., 339, 343, 354
Kivnick, H.Q., 105, 119
Klassen, M., 312, 315
Klaus, M.H., 20, 31, 216, 220
Klaus, R.A., 329, 354
Klein, C., 24, 31, 231, 247
Koch, R., 21, 31, 84, 97, 226, 246
Koegel, R.L., 82, 98
Komarovsky, M., 107, 119
Korn, S.J., 5, 31, 129, 133, 147
Kotelchuck, M., 42, 67, 70-71
Kotsch, L.S., 9, 21, 30, 109-110, 118, 138, 146, 282, 293, 336, 354
Krauss, M.W., 139, 142, 147
Krugman, S., 122, 147
Kushner, H.S., 304-305, 310-311, 313-315
Kushnick, T., 40, 69

LaBarre, M.B., 103, 119
Lakin, K.C., 329, 354
Lamb, M.E., xi, 43, 70, 169, 191
Landau, B., 12, 31
Lavelle, N., 258, 264, 276
Lawrence, K.M., 47, 72, 80, 98, 132, 147
Lazar, I., 172, 191
Lazarus, R.S., 90, 96, 298, 315
Leichter, H.J., 101, 119
Lerner, R.M., ix, xv
LeTarte, C., 338, 355
Levine, E.S., 11, 31
Levine, J., xi
Lewis, M., 23-25, 30, 42, 71, 233, 245, 319, 353
Lidz, T., 6, 31
Lillie, D., 259, 263, 276
Lin, N., 172, 182
Lipman, A., 171, 183, 191
Litwak, E., 8, 31, 100, 119
Liversidge, E., 49, 71
Loda, F.A., 232, 248
Longino, C.R., 171, 183, 191
Looff, D.H., 336, 354
Lopata, H.Z., 105-106, 119
Love, H., 49, 67, 71, 132, 147
Lowenfeld, B., 26, 32
Luscomb, B., 47, 67, 72
Lynch, E., 259-261, 268, 276
Lyon, S., 24, 32

McAdoo, H.P., 9, 32
McAndrew, I., 108, 119, 173, 191
McArthur, D., 60, 70, 178, 191
McCubbin, H., 172, 191

McDonald, A., 342, 355
McDowell, J., 109, 119, 173, 191, 282, 288, 294
McEwan, P.J.M., 19, 32
McHale, S.M., 77, 81, 90, 97-98
McKinney, J.D., 260, 276
McLanahan, S., 233, 243, 247
McLean, M., 188, 190
Maisto, A.A., 21, 30, 138, 146, 226, 246, 286, 293
Mallory, B.L., 320, 338-339, 354
Manning, D., 234, 247
Marion, R., 254, 261, 273, 276
Markowitz, J., 50, 62, 64-65, 71
Marmor, T.R., 328-330, 355
Massimilla, 312, 315
Mattesich, P., 322, 354
Meisels, S.J., 339, 355
Menolascino, F.J., 36, 70, 285, 295
Mercer, J.R., 328, 355
Messenger, K., 21, 29, 79, 96
Meuwissen, H.J., 78, 97
Meyer, D., 15, 33, 49-51, 55, 63-65, 71-72, 86, 92, 94, 96-97, 111, 120
Meyerowitz, H.D., 53, 71
Meyers, C.E., 235, 247
Meyerson, R., 67, 72
Michaelis, C.T., 84, 97
Midlarsky, E., 282, 294
Miller, G., 27, 32
Miller, L.G., 36, 71
Miller, N.B., 77-78, 82-84, 96
Miller, S.G., 78, 82, 97
Mills, A.E., 12, 32
Minde, K.K., 234, 247
Mink, I.T., 235, 247
Mitchell, R.E., 171-172, 174, 176, 191, 281, 294
Mitchell, W.E., 101, 106, 119
Minzey, J.D., 338, 355
Moen, P., 303, 315
Moore, J.A., 62, 71, 132, 140, 144, 147, 227, 247, 283, 294, 321, 336, 344, 355
Moore, K.A., 23, 31
Moores, D.F., 11, 32
Mopsik, S., 262, 267-269, 276
Morgan, D., 261, 276
Morgan, J.N., 238, 246
Mori, A., 341-342, 355
Moroney, R.M., 25, 32, 141, 143, 147, 321, 345, 355
Morris, N., 43, 70
Morrison, A.A., 282, 289, 294
Morrissey, P., 259, 276

Mortimer, E.A., 132, 146, 283, 293
Morton, P., 234, 247
Moses, K., 94, 97
Mott, D.W., 94, 97
Murphy, A.T., 20, 32, 161, 166, 236, 247, 285
Myrick, R., 263, 277

Navarre, E., 170, 190
Needham, C., 51, 63, 69
Needle, R., 191
Neisworth, J.T., 319, 353
Nesselroade, J.R., 167, 189
Neugarten, B.L., 103-106, 119
Neuhaus, R.J., 320, 353
Newman, M.B., 79, 98
Nihira, K., 226, 235, 247-248
Nimkoff, M.F., 103, 119
Nirje, B., 327-328, 355
Norris, M., 12, 32
Norton, A.J., 224, 246

O'Connor, W., 86, 91, 98
Ogbu, J.U., 6, 32
Ogle, P.A., 83, 94, 98
Olshansky, S., 36, 71, 282, 294
O'Neill, B., 169-170, 181, 183, 191
O'Neill, J., 82, 98
O'Neill, R.E., 82, 98
Oosterveen, G., 311, 315
Osman, B.B., 13, 32

Page, R., 262, 275
Palmer, D., 342, 355
Palmer, P., 126, 128, 147
Parke, R.D., 43, 65, 71, 234, 248
Pascoe, J.M., 232, 248
Patterson, J., 191
Pattison, E.M., 287, 294
Paul, J.L., 15, 32
Payne, H., 47, 72
Pearlin, L.I., 169, 181, 191
Peck, J.R., 47, 61, 71, 86, 98
Pedersen, F.A., 43, 71
Pennsylvania Association for Retarded Children v. Commonwealth of Pennsylvania, 9, 32
Pergament, E., 41, 71
Pettis, E., 262, 275
Pfouts, J.H., 78, 98
Philliber, S., 172, 191
Pickarts, E., 10, 32
Pieper, E., 109, 119, 193, 220
Piers, E.P., 92, 98

Pleck, J.H., 233, 248
Polit, D.F., 226, 235, 238, 243-244, 248
Powell, D.R., 7, 33, 303, 315
Powell, T.H., xi, 83, 94, 98
Power, T.G., 43, 71
Poznanski, E.O., 325, 355
Preis, A., 24, 32
Price, M., 258, 276
Price-Bonham, S., 44-47, 49, 55, 60, 71, 86, 98

Quick, J.D., 345, 355

Radcliffe-Brown, A.R., 103, 119
Ragozin, A.S., 7, 29, 169, 172, 181, 189, 191, 234, 246
Rahe, R.H., 226, 247
Ramsey, B.K., 329, 354
Rawnsley, K., 47, 72
Reed, E.W., 47, 71
Reed, S.C., 47, 71
Reese, H.W., 167, 189
Reinhardt, H., 222, 248
Reis, R., 11, 32
Reynolds, M.C., 263, 276
Rhoades, E.A., 110, 119
Richards, M.P., 234, 246
Richmond, J.B., 216, 220
Riegel, K.F., ix, xv
Robertson, J.F., 103-107, 119
Robinson, H., 225, 231, 246
Robinson, H.B., 77, 98
Robinson, J.P., 233, 248
Robinson, N.M., 7, 29, 77, 98, 169, 172, 189, 191, 234, 246
Robson, K.S., 43, 71
Roebuck, F.N., 263, 275
Roghmann, K.J., 345, 355
Roos, P., 15, 32, 45, 71
Rosen, L., 15, 32
Rosenberg, S.A., 62, 71
Rosenthal, K.M., 224, 248
Roskies, E., 263, 276
Ross, G., 42, 67, 71
Ross, H.L., 222-223, 228, 232-233, 248
Rossi, A., 169, 191
Roth, W., 10, 14, 27, 31, 144, 147
Rude, H.A., 77, 81, 98
Russell, I.T., 263, 277
Rutter, M., 11, 31
Ryckman, D.B., 51, 70

Saenger, G., 226, 248
Salkever, D., 229, 245

Salzinger, S., 4, 32
Sameroff, A.J., 4-5, 10, 33
Sanik, M.M., 169-170, 181, 183, 191
San Martino, M., 79, 98
Sarason, S.B., 10-11, 33
Satir, V., 15, 33
Sawhill, I.V., 222-223, 228, 232-233, 248
Schaefer, C., 90, 96, 298, 315
Schaefer, E., 169, 172, 174-175, 180-181, 183, 191, 258, 265, 271, 276
Schaie, K.W., ix, xv
Scharfman, W., 23, 30, 47-48, 70, 169, 190
Scheiber, B., 262, 275
Schein, J.D., 126, 129, 148
Schell, G.C., 8, 15, 22, 33, 49, 55, 71-72, 109, 119, 280-281, 294
Schiefelbusch, R.L., 335, 353
Schonell, F.J., 51, 72, 282-283, 294
Schopler, E., 60, 69
Schorr, A., 104, 119
Schorr, A.L., 222-224, 248
Schreibman, L., 82, 84, 87, 98
Schufeit, L.J., 47, 72
Schulz, J.B., 258, 265, 276
Scott, A.C., 130-131, 142-143, 145, 157
Seelye, R.R., 122, 147
Seligman, M., 17, 24, 33, 67, 72, 85, 91, 98, 259, 263, 276
Sellitz, C., 299, 315
Seltzer, M.M., 139, 142, 147
Semmel, D., 259, 276
Shakespeare, W., 22. 33
Shanas, E., 101, 103-104, 109, 119
Shannon, G.W., 345, 353
Shaver, K., 122, 129, 148
Sheehan, R., 319, 354
Shellhaas, M.D., 226, 248
Shinn, M., 232, 248
Shulman, N., 169, 182, 191
Silvestre, D., 40, 72
Simeonsson, R.J., 77, 90, 97-98, 319, 353
Simmons, H., 86, 97
Skelton, M., 57, 70
Skrtic, T.M., 80, 92-93, 98
Slay, T., 342, 355
Sloan, J., 77, 97
Smith, A.N., 346, 355
Smith, M., 263, 275
Sonnek, I.M., 111, 115, 120
Spanier, G.B., ix, xv
Spaulding, P.J., 12, 32
Speer, D.C., 19-20, 33
Spieker, S., 62, 71, 132, 147, 227, 247, 283, 294, 321, 355

Sroufe, L., 5, 34
Stachowiak, J., 86, 91, 98
Stafford, F.P, 23, 33
Stagg, V., 287, 294
Stanley, J.C., 291, 293
Staruch, K.S., 132, 146, 229, 245, 283, 293
Stein, L.K., 126-128, 147
Stein, R., 259-261, 268, 276
Stephens, W.B., 47, 61, 71, 86, 98
Stoneman, Z., 80, 98
Stonequist, E.V., 14, 33
Stotland, J., 157, 166, 266, 268, 270, 276
Strauss, C.A., 103, 120
Strickland, B., 260, 275
Stryker, S., 106, 120
Stufflebeam, D., 339, 355
Sudia, C.E., 232, 246
Suelzle, M., 60, 67, 72, 284, 294, 321, 335, 346-348, 350, 355
Sullivan, R.C., 264, 276
Summers, J.A., 47, 72, 80-81, 92, 98, 282, 294
Susser, P., 109, 120
Sussman, M.B., 8, 33, 100, 103-104, 120
Sutton-Smith, B., xi
Szczypka, D., 234, 248

Tallman, I., 46, 72
Tamir, L.M., 168, 170, 192
Tapper, H., 144, 147
Tavormina, J.B., 47, 67, 72, 81, 97, 286, 294
Taylor, J.R., 47, 72
Taylor, S.J., x, xv
Teska, J., 258-259, 264, 267, 273, 276
Tew, B.J., 47, 72, 80, 98, 132, 147
Thomas, A., 4-5, 33
Thomas, K., 343, 353
Thomas, M., 263, 277
Thomas, S., 339, 356
Thomas, M.S., 319, 354
Tinsley, B.R., 234, 248
Tisdall, W.J., 226, 245
Toigo, R., 46, 70
Tolan, W.J., 4-5, 29
Townsend, P., 103-104, 120
Travis, G., 80, 98
Trickett, E.J., 717-172, 174, 176, 191, 281, 294
Trivette, C.M., 7, 30, 172, 175-176, 180, 190, 192
Trohanis, P., 259, 263, 276
Troll, L.E., 8, 33, 100, 106, 120
Trybus, R.J., 123, 125, 146-147

Tucker, F., 81, 97
Tudor, K., 268, 277
Turnbull, A., 81
Turnbull, A.P., 9, 14, 17, 20, 23, 33-34, 47, 52, 61, 64, 72, 80-81, 92, 98, 159, 166, 259-260, 265, 267-268, 272, 277, 282, 294, 305-306, 315, 336, 346, 356
Turnbull, H.R., 14, 17, 20, 23, 33, 47, 55, 72, 259, 265, 272, 277

UNESCO, 332, 337, 355
Unger, D.G., 7, 33, 303, 315
Upshur, C.C., 350-351, 355
Urwin, C., 12, 33
Ussery, L., 103, 119
Uzoka, A.F., 8, 33, 100, 120

Vadasy, P.F., 15, 23, 33, 49, 51, 55, 64, 71-72, 86, 94, 97, 111, 120
Vaughn, B., 5, 34
Verlinsky, Y., 41, 71
Vernon, M., 122-123, 125, 127-129, 133, 147-148
Vollmer, H., 103, 120

Walker, J.H., 263, 277
Walker, K., 233, 248
Wallace, H.M., 343-344, 353, 356
Ward, M.J., 63, 69
Warren, D., 12, 34
Warren, F., 60-61, 72
Wasow, M., 36, 73, 285, 295
Waters, E., 5, 34
Watson, R.L., 282, 294
Wattenberg, E., 222, 248
Watts, B.H., 51, 72, 282-283, 294
Wedemeyer, N.V., 243, 247
Weinberg, B., 126, 128, 147
Weigerink, R., 257, 266, 271-272, 276
Weinraub, M., 42-43, 71-72, 171-172, 183, 192, 227, 231-232, 235, 249
Weinstein, K.K., 103-106, 119
Weiss, R.S., 222, 226, 229-230, 235, 238, 245, 249
Weitzman, M., 21, 29, 79, 96
Weller, J.E., 336, 356
Westmacott, I., 80, 96
Wheeler, J.D., 130, 147
White, S.H., 321, 356
Wigley, R., 345, 356
Wikler, L., 36, 44, 46, 48-49, 52-56, 67, 72-73, 86, 97, 138, 148, 216, 220, 227, 242, 249, 285, 294-295
Will, M., 142, 148

Williams, K.I., 282, 289, 294
Willmott, P., 104, 120
Wilson, J.B., 240, 245
Wilturner, L.T., 298, 315
Winton, P.J., 23, 34, 154, 166, 336, 347, 356
Wittmer, J., 263, 277
Wohlwill, J., 5, 34
Wolf, B.M., 171-172, 183, 192, 227, 231-232, 235, 249
Wolf, E.G., 126-127, 129, 131, 133, 142, 145, 148
Wolfensberger, W., 285, 295, 318, 327, 339, 356
Woods, M., 233, 248
Wright, B.A., 27, 34
Wright, W., 259, 275
Wrightsman, L.S, 299, 315
Wurster, S.R., 47, 72

Yando, R., 142, 148
Young, J.C., 42, 73
Young, M., 101, 104, 109, 120

Zelazo, P., 42, 67, 71
Zigler, E., 142, 148, 188, 192
Zisserman, L., 325, 356

Subject Index

Abortion, 39-41

Acceptance, 53, 310-314, 333

Adolescents
concerns regarding, 17-18, 54-60, 207-216, 261, 290-291, 347-348
deaf-blind, 121-145
employment of, 330

Amniocentesis
decisions regarding, 39-41
and therapeutic abortion, 39

Anger, 46, 341

Assessment of children, 267-268
by parents, 319

Baby Doe, 325

Birth of child, 15, 41-45, 149-150, 195-196, 341

Brothers - See Siblings

Case management, 320, 334-336

Child care
needs of mothers, 230-231, 241-242

Child characteristics, 9-15
age, 53, 60
and educational needs, 260-261
handicap, 46, 53-54, 60-61
sex, 46, 53, 60

Chorionic villi sampling (CVS), 40-41

Chronic sorrow, 36, 198-199

Community agencies, 317-352
service, 320
religious, 303-305

Coping resources model, 90-91, 298-331

Coping strategies, 39, 60-62, 197-199
positive family, 19-20, 298-314, 318-322, 331

Crises in family, 15-19, 44-45, 49, 55, 67, 217
periodic, 44, 217, 273

Daily Interaction Rating Form, 287

Deaf-blind children, 121-148
adult placement of, 138-139
associated handicaps, 122-123, 125-127, 131-133
definition of, 124-125
regional centers for, 124-125, 130-131, 142-143
services for, 124-125, 130, 142-145
studies of, 128-129
training needs of, 137, 139-140
transition of, 139-145

Deinstitutionalization, 27, 56-57

Developmental milestones
crises related to, 15-16, 48-49, 52, 54-56
observed by religious groups, 306-308
stress from, 173, 201, 209-211, 217, 237-238, 285-286, 323, 325-326

Denial, 40, 45-46

Depression, 132, 217
in fathers, 46, 51, 53
in mothers, 51, 199

Developmental tasks
and family stages, 37-60

Diagnosis, 340-342
parent reactions to, 16, 20, 36, 44-47, 149-151, 195-199, 202-203, 209-214, 217, 341-342

Discrepancies in child's development, 15-16, 44, 48-49, 52, 173, 201, 209-12, 217, 237-238

Divorce
and desertion rates, 38, 47
economic impact of, 229, 238
remarriage rates, 227, 229
and single mothers, 224-225, 229, 238, 243

Down syndrome, 7-8, 38, 41, 45, 81, 138, 150, 152, 164, 194-201, 256, 280, 299, 341

Early intervention programs, 50-51, 152-163, 203-204, 335
and fathers, 65-66
scheduling of, 65
as social supports, 168, 172, 186-188

Ecological
based services, 321, 332-334, 339
conditions of families, 4-6, 20, 292, 318, 320-321, 329, 332-337
model, 20, 176, 188, 258

Economic stresses, 25-26, 49, 303, 342-346
in single-parent families, 232-233

Educational services, 253-274, 305-306

EPSDT program, 343-344

Engrossment
father's, 43-44

Evaluation services, 266-268

Extended family, 21-22, 138, 280, 350
and grandparents, 100-105, 108-109, 115-116, 280-282
impact of handicap on, 21-22
support from, 8, 138, 174, 181, 280-282

Families
assessment of child's abilities, 319
coping in, 298, 318, 322, 331

demographics of, 101
ecological conditions of, 318, 320-321, 329, 332-337
extended, See Extended family
father-headed, 222-224
female-headed, 222-224, 232-233, see also Single mothers
future needs of, 163-165, 319, 324-325
functions of, 92-93, 228-229, 319
life cycle stages in, 36-59
life span of, 298, 306-309, 318-319, 321-326, 331, 335, 338-340, 346, 348, 351-352
perceptions of, 318, 320, 329, 341
policies for, 321
roles of members, 22-24, 85, 181, 186-187, 228-229, 235, 297, 320, 322-325, 330 342, 347
rural, 138, 305
services for, 318-321, 344-346
SES, 62, 85, 90-91, 175, 259, 283
single parent, 101, 221-244, see also Single mothers
stress in, 322, 324-326, 329, 331, 334, 336, 338, 340, 342, 344-345, 347-348 350, 352
supports for, 6-9, 138-139, 169-188, 196-197, 286-292
    educational, 253-274, 305-306
    extrafamilial, 9, 143-145, 151-161, 174, 181, 186-187, 283-285, 297-314, 322-323, 348-350
    intrafamilial, 7-8, 103, 108, 112-117, 137-139, 151, 176, 181, 183, 186-187, 280-282
    instrumental, 303
    religious, 297-314
    social, 303-305
    structural, 306-308
theory of, 4-6, 298, 322, 326
time demands of, 184
Family, Infant, and Toddler Project, 9
Family life cycle, 36-58
Family Support Scale, 177, 190
Fathers, 35-68
and child attachment, 42-43
depression in, 46, 51, 53
involvement of 50-51, 62-68, 160-161
reactions, second-order effects of, 46-47, 61-62, 67, 234, 341
roles of, 42-50, 66, 173, 181, 232, 325
    adjustment to, 43-44
    breadwinner, 42, 66
    caregiver, 22-23, 42, 49-50, 66, 181-183
    play partner, 43, 48, 66
    self concept of, 46, 53, 64
Federal programs
    for deaf-blind, 124, 142-143
    mean-tested, 144
    for single mothers, 243-244
Future concerns, 58-60, 163-165, 200-201
    and fathers, 49, 54-59
    and mothers, 49, 133-137, 204, 206-207, 215-216, 133-145
    and siblings, 83, 88

Gallaudet College
    studies by, 125
Grandmothers
    roles of, 100-107, 111-117
    support from, 107-109, 136-137
    suspicions about handicap, 209
Grandparents, 21-22, 93, 99-116
    demographics on, 100-101
    grandmother's role, 111-117
    impact of handicap on, 21-22
    programs for, 109-111, 350
    relationship with grandchildren, 100-107
    roles of, 21-22, 100-107, 111-117
    supports from, 8, 21-22, 108-109, 286
Grief reactions, 21, 44-45, 151, 198-200, 207
Guilt, 306
    in parents, 57, 204, 319
    in siblings, 21, 78-79

Handicapped children
    hearing impaired, 11
    mentally retarded, 10-11
    mildly impaired, 13
    moderately impaired, 14-15
    physically impaired, 12
    severely impaired, 15, 121-145, 322-324, 332, 344
Health care systems, 335-338, 340-346
Helping Grandparent Program, 350
HMOs, 345-346, 352
Identification services, 266-268
IEPs, 159, 200, 205-206, 254, 260, 266, 268-270
Institutionalization
    of deaf-blind children, 133, 139
    decisions about, 56-57, 59, 262, 342
    and family structure, 226

Isolation
    in parents, 60, 67, 173, 196, 232, 235-236, 283-285

Life cycle needs of families, 290-291, 318-352
Life-span development, ix, 167-168, 176, 322
  and parent roles, 169, 173
  and social supports, 169, 173-174, 321-326
Locus of control, 298, 326

Marital relationship, 62
  effects of child upon, 7, 38, 46-47, 51
Mainstreaming, 205, 331
  effects on parents, 52
Medical concerns, 290, 342-346
Mothers
  of deaf-blind children, 121-148
  depression in, 51, 199
  divorced, 224-225, 229, 238, 243
  employment of, 42, 170-171, 175, 182-183, 186, 225, 227-230, 239-242, 325
  experiences of, 193-220
  isolation of, 283-285
  networks of, 167-188, 287-292
  roles of, 23, 161-163, 168-176, 179, 180-188, 242-243, 325
  single, 170-171, 221-244
  supports for, 7, 136-137, 167-186, 196-197, 290-291

Networks, 279-292
  family, 174, 281, 287, 320, 322-323, 335, 348-350
  of mothers, 167-188, 287-292
  neighborhood, 320
  social 322-323
Normalization, 318, 327-332, 351-352

P.L. 89-749, 124
P.L. 90-247, 124, 130
P.L. 91-230, 124
P.L. 93-380, 124
P.L. 94-142, 9, 13, 130, 143, 253-256, 258, 260, 266-268, 270-271, 290, 329, 337-338
P.L. 98-199, 111, 130
Parents
  as advocates, 260, 272
  aging, 58-60
  burnout in, 261, 326
  depression in, 46, 51, 53, 199
  expectations of, 38-39
  information needs of, 150, 213-214, 217-218, 348-350
  involvement in programs, 24-25, 50-51,

158-160, 255-258, 266-274, 318-319, 323, 346-350
  by fathers, 50-51, 62-68, 152, 160-161
  by mothers, 152, 197, 200, 205-206, 214
  peer support for, 151-152, 218, 236, 284-285, 348-350
  reactions to handicap, 36, 45-47, 202-203, 216-217
  roles of, 23-24, 161-163, 168-169, 172-175, 180-188, 228, 232-233, 243, 271-272, 324-326, 342, 347
  in rural areas, 256-257, 259
Parent-child interaction, 20-21, 64, 67, 185, 232
Parent-Child Interaction Rating Scale, 177-178, 189
Parent-professional relationship, 17, 65, 149-166, 218-219, 257-258, 262-274, 318-320, 329, 334-338
  with educational staff, 152-161, 203-204, 211-214, 219, 258-259, 262-266, 335-336, 346-350
  with physicians, 45, 150-152, 160-161, 195-196, 200, 202-203, 209-214, 335-336, 340-346
Parent Role Scale, 23, 174, 177-178, 190
Parent support groups, 152, 156, 197, 199, 204, 265, 271, 348-350
Parent-teacher interactions, 154-163, 262-266
Pattison Psychosocial Kinship Inventory, 287, 294
Placement of child
  in educational program, 53, 213-214, 269-271
Project Re-Ed, 332
Program Analysis of Service Systems (PASS), 339
Program Analysis of Service Systems' Implementation of Normalization Goals (PASSING), 339
Program evaluation, 338-340
Public school programs, 254-274

Questionnaire on Family Support Systems, 299
Questionnaire on Resources and Stress, 177-178, 191

Referrals by physicians, 340-342
Reframing (coping strategy), 61-62
Related services, 253, 256, 260, 269-271

Religious organizations, 65, 136-137, 297-314
  educational support from, 305-306
  instrumental support from, 303
  social/emotional support from, 136-137, 303-304
  structural support from, 306-308
Respite care, 52, 286, 317, 335, 344, 350-351
  and educational programs, 262
  needs of mothers for, 230, 236, 241-242
Rubella (maternal rubella syndrome), 122-127
  epidemic of 1963-1965, 122-124
Rural school districts, 256-257, 259

Second-order effects within family
  of father's participation, 51, 61-62, 67
  of father's reactions, 46-47, 53, 61, 234
  of parents on siblings, 85, 91
SEFAM Program, 22-23, 50-51, 63-68, 80, 94
Self esteem
  in fathers, 53, 64
  in mothers, 230, 233
Shock
  at diagnosis, 15, 36, 195
Siblings, 21, 75-98, 200, 323, 329, 349-350
  adjustment of, 82-86
  as caregivers, 24, 78, 80, 83-85, 323
  detrimental effects on, 21, 78-80
  future concerns of, 80, 83, 86, 88
  identification of, 80, 86, 92
  information needs of, 86-87
  peer interactions of, 88-92, 94
  as playmates, 80, 85
  programs for, 80, 94, 349-350
  relationship, 76-95
    effects of age on, 78, 83-84
    effects of handicap on, 21, 80
    effects of parents on, 85, 91
    effects of SES on, 85, 91
    effects of sex on, 78-83
  research on, 77-86
  responsibilities of, 24, 80, 87-88, 323-324
  roles of, 24
  self concept of, 86, 92
  studies of, 77-86, 90-94
  support from, 7-8
  as techers, 80, 82, 85, 87
Siegel Institute, 126
Single mothers, 101, 221-244
  children of, 235
  employment of, 229-230, 240

  of handicapped children, 226-228
  incomes of, 225, 229, 232-233, 238-240
  living arrangements of, 224-225, 231, 239, 243-244
  needs of, 227, 229
  numbers of families, 222-226
  physical needs of, 231-232
  policies for, 238-243
  roles of, 232-236, 239-243
  stress in, 227, 235-239
  studies of, 177, 182, 222-230, 235, 243-244
  supports for, 227-228, 234-236
Sisters - see Siblings
Social attitudes
  towards the handicapped, 14-15, 26-27
Social policies
  for deaf-blind children, 130, 141-145
  for families, 27-28, 321, 324-352
  for single mothers, 239-244
Social programs
  criteria for, 321, 327-338, 343
  for single mothers, 243-244
Stages of adjustment, 36, 286
Stages of family life cycle, 36-58
Stigma and handicap, 15, 17, 36, 48-49, 52, 85, 203, 283-284, 329
Stress
  in families, 14-15, 24-26, 138, 174, 282-283, 286, 326
  in fathers, 60-61, 64
  in mothers, 198-199, 226, 288
  recurring, 36, 52, 285
  and SES, 62, 344
  in single mothers, 237-238, 240
  and social supports, 175, 177, 310-314
Supports, 6-9, 136-138, 173-188, 229
  community, 317-352
  educational, 136
  for fathers, 65-66
  as intervention, 168, 172, 186-188
  for mothers, 136-137, 167-188, 287-292
  for parents, 7-9, 25-26, 168-169, 297-314
  religious, 136-137, 297-314
  from services, 26
  for single mothers, 227, 231-236, 243-244
  social, 279-292

Transactional model, 4-5, 19
Transitions, 16-19, 161, 173, 222, 233, 331, 334-335, 338
  and family stress, 285, 290-291
  of deaf-blind adolescents, 122, 130, 133, 138-139, 140-145

Twins, 201-207

Vocational training
  needs for, 131, 137, 139-145, 269, 273-274, 330

Young Adults, 18, 55-56, 207-216, 290, See also Adolescent